MW01114195

American Revolution

1745-1784

Volume 3 of the Original Source Series
by PowerThink Publishing

Edited by
Carlos L Packard
in cooperation with
Western Standard Publishing Company

Introduction by
James Michael Pratt
New York Times Bestselling Author

Cover by
Evan Frederickson

Published by PowerThink Publishing

ISBN 1-1-9364720-3-1
ISBN13 978-1-936472-03-1
PowerThink Publishing, L.L.C.
2020 Fieldstone Pkwy Ste. 900
Franklin, TN. 37069
Visit us at www.powerthink.com

Edited by Carlos L Packard
Introduction by James Michael Pratt
Cover Design by Evan Frederickson

Printed in the United States of America
10 9 8 7 6 5 4 3 2 1

HERE were held the town-meetings that ushered in the Revolution
HERE Samuel Adams, James Otis and Joseph Warren exhorted
HERE the men of Boston proved themselves independent
courageous freemen worthy to raise issues which were to concern
the liberty and happiness of millions yet unborn

(Sign at the main entrance of the Old South Meeting House Boston, Massachusetts)

Author unknown

Table of Contents

Dedicated to All Who Stand for Justice & Liberty

Preface: Why the Original Sources?

I am often asked how many books I've read. Those asking generally expect to hear some huge number. Yes, I have read a great deal of information in my life. Although, I have to confess that I have read very few books cover-to-cover. I'm not the type of person that enjoys sitting through a long story eagerly waiting to see how it ends. I guess my problem is that I simply don't have enough patience. This is probably the reason why I have read very few novels besides the fact that I'm not too much into fiction. Rather, I look for a subject that interests me and then I will look for the best snippets I can find that will best inform me on the topic. The two topics that I have spent the bulk of my life studying are faith and history. Personally, I believe they go hand-in-hand and generally speaking I believe them to be the basis of most writing. I have also found that I feel more enlightened and enriched when I study from the original sources than when I go to secondary accounts.

I believe that in this day and age way too many people study and research secondary accounts rather than from original sources. For example, many will read a commentary on the Bible rather than the Bible itself, or they may read an opinionated discourse on the United States Constitution rather than the Constitution itself.

I believe that most settle for the secondary accounts for three basic reasons:

1. They are generally much easier to find.
2. They give extra commentary that you believe will be more valuable than the original text.
3. We may feel we have a better connection with the more modern perspective.

In today's fast-paced society, many of us have adapted the attitude, 'I WANT IT AND I WANT IT NOW!' What we don't realize is that much of the information we are given is tainted in some way or another by someone else's opinion. And rather than take the time to research the original source and find the truth for ourselves, we blindly believe and follow the voices around us.

The reasons for going to secondary sources stated earlier can easily be turned around and you will find the importance of going to the original source. Taking the time to find and study the original source requires us to analyze with great thought the events we are researching. They require us to dig deeper into the lives of the individuals and events surrounding the accounts we are studying. And, we don't run the risk of the account being tainted by the opinion of somebody who wasn't involved in the event when it happened.

I believe there is no better source than that of the original. I owe everything I know to the original sources. No other document, speech, or commentary can replace the original.

I pray you will find as much joy in studying the original sources as I have.

—Carlos L. Packard

Introduction

Perhaps no other revolt against the mother country, giving birth to a land, parallels the American Revolution. For, from this revolution on a land separated by thousands of miles and an ocean, new ideas and identities were born. These ideas have sparked the call of freedom around the world as the American Revolution has inspired self-determination seekers for over two hundred years.

In this original source compilation you get the actual words of the founders, soldiers and statesmen, frontiersmen, enemy combatants, English, American, and French voices, as well as the common men and the women behind the scenes.

We hear their voices as we read their words, untainted by historical speculation of scholars and promoters of historical theories. Their words and actions set the stage for the making of the American government, and the creation of the single most important documents offering freedom to its citizens ever put by men into words on paper; the Declaration of Independence and Constitution of the United States of America.

Follow the American Revolution through the eyes of those who were there, in this PowerThink Publishing series of original source material, Volume 3, *The American Revolution*.

—James Michael Pratt

The Two Sieges of Louisbourg

Title: The Two Sieges of Louisbourg
Author: A. G. Bradley
Date: 1745 and 1758
Source: Great Epochs in American History, Vol.3, pp.3-14

At the northeast of Acadia, only severed from the mainland by the narrow gut of Canso, lay the island of Cape Breton, a name once as familiar to the world as the Cape of Good Hope, but now almost unknown. Its fame rested on the great fortress of Louisbourg, which with its considerable town and ample harbor dominated the North Atlantic, and was styled the "Dunkirk of America." All Acadia had been handed over to England at the Peace of Utrecht in 1713, with the exception of this little island of Cape Breton, or in other words Louisbourg. The latter, during the late war in the year 1745, had been stormed and captured in spirited fashion by a force of New England militia under Peperall, acting in conjunction with Admiral Warren and an English fleet.

It was restored to the French, however, three years later at the treaty of Aix-la-Chapelle, amid the loud protestations of the few in England who were conversant with the politics of the North Atlantic—protestations fully justified by the immense stress laid upon its restoration by the French.

The population of Nova Scotia consisted of a few thousand French-Canadian habitants, who chiefly occupied the more fertile spots on the western coast which looked across the Bay of Fundy to the even less populous mainland. There were also, as already indicated, two or three iso-

lated forts where small detachments of British regulars or Colonial militia under a British governor maintained an existence of appalling monotony and of almost unexampled seclusion from the outer world...

The great European war was chiefly marked in North America by the capture of Louisbourg at the hands of the New Englanders in 1745. This notable achievement sent a passing quiver of excitement through the dense forests of Acadia, even to the villages on the Bay of Fundy. The Canadian missionaries renewed their efforts, which were met with a fresh show of activity in enforcing the oath. But so far no very tangible evil had come of all this. The Acadians were not put to the test; they were far removed from all scenes of racial strife or discord, and among their diked-in meadows and orchards continued to propagate in peace and rude plenty the most reactionary and ignorant breed of white men on the North American continent.

When Louisbourg was given back to the French, however, and some vague claims to the northern shore of the province as the only winter route to Canada were put in by them to the commissioners appointed at the treaty of 1748, all was again agog. The founding of Halifax in the following year, and the advent in force of the dreaded British settler, tho on the further shore, seemed to demolish all hopes of French supremacy in the future. England might annex and rule, for their very great content and infinite happiness, the French American colonies, but she might get tired of such an unprofitable business. It was not likely, however, that Great Britain would ever allow a province, whither she had deliberately invited her own people, to pass again into the hands of a government who hounded even their own Protestants, like lepers, from their gates…

It was the 19th of February, 1758, when the Admiral sailed out of the Solent with Wolfe on board and a fraction of the army which was to operate against Louisbourg. The rest of the force was to be made up by troops from London's army of the previous year, which were waiting at Halifax. Amherst was to follow immediately. Buffeted by winds from the very outset, and forced for some days into Plymouth, it was nearly three months before the fleet appeared in Chebucto Bay and dropt anchor in Halifax harbor on May 10th. Quebec, of course, was in the mind of Pitt and of his generals, should Fortune favor them, and that quickly, at Louisbourg; but in the matter of weather she had so far been the reverse of kind, and they had already lost a month out of their quite reasonable calculations. Amherst arrived a fortnight later, and with a fleet of nearly two hundred ships of all kinds, and an army of 12,000 men, sailed out of Halifax harbor and bore away through heavy seas before a favoring wind to Louisbourg. On June 1st the soldiers had their first sight of "the Dunkirk of the North," lifting its formidable ramparts behind a white fringe of raging surf. Louisbourg was no town such as Boston or New York, or even Quebec and Montreal, the focus, that is to say, of a surrounding civilization; but, on the contrary, it stood like a lone oasis between a shaggy wilderness and a gray sea, the sport of storms and fogs. It counted a population of 4,000 souls, some of whom were fish-merchants and some priests, but many more were engaged in various pursuits connected with the trade of war. Louisbourg, indeed, scarcely profest to represent the interests of peace; it existed for war and for war alone. France, at the late treaty, had strained every diplomatic nerve to recover the town from the grip of the New Englanders, who in the last war, with the help of a British fleet, had seized her in a moment of comparative weakness. England, deaf to the cries of her colonial subjects, had then yielded, and was not paying the price of her blindness. With her fine harbor, her natural defenses, her commanding situation in the northern seas, Louisbourg only existed as a menace to the enemies of those who held her, a refuge to the hunted, a rallying-point for the hunters of the ocean; the scourge of Nova Scotia, the curse of the Newfoundland and New England coasts, and a name as familiar then in Europe as it is now forgotten.

Since its restoration to France, a million sterling had been spent on the fortifications. Franquet, the eminent engineer, assisted by skilled artificers, had done the work, and from behind its two-mile circle of stone bastions and massive curtains of well-mortared masonry nearly 400 cannon frowned defiance upon all comers. Drucour was now governor, while about 4,000 men, mostly French or Canadian regulars, in addition to the same number of inhabitants, with a year's provisions, awaited Amherst behind the walls. But this was by no means all, for the Sutherland, or sixty guns, met the British fleet in the offing with the news that seven line-of-battle ships and five frigates, carrying 550 guns and 3,000 sailors, were at anchor in the harbor to assist in the defense…

Boscawen had twenty-three ships of the line and seventeen frigates, and it was the 2d of June before his whole fleet arrived off the town. A heavy sea was running, and the rugged shore was white with an unbroken line of raging surf. Amherst, however, with Lawrence and Wolfe, the latter still suffering sorely from his dire enemy, sea-sickness, took boat, and rowing along the coast surveyed it through their glasses. There were only three places at which a landing was possible, even when the weather moderated, and these, it was seen, were all strongly entrenched. On the 5th the wind dropt a little, but gave way to a fog, which was even worse. On the 6th both wind and fog moderated, and the troops were placed in the boats; but the wind again increasing, they were ordered back to the ships. The sailors, with all the will in the world, thought gravely of any attempt to land. Boscawen sent for his captains one by one, and they were all inclined to shake their heads. A fine old sea-dog, however, one Ferguson, captain of a sixty-gun ship, the Prince, would have no halting, and by his vehemence turned the scale in favor of prompt action. On the evening of the 7th the wind fell slightly, the night proved clear, and soon after midnight the men were once more dropt into the boats. It had been arranged that the attack should be made in three divisions on three separate points. Lawrence and Whitmore were to threaten the two coves nearer the town, while Wolfe made the actual attack on Kennington Cove or Le Coromandiere, the farthest off, the most accessible, but also the most strongly defended, and some four miles distant from the city…

Wolfe, at once a disciplinarian and a creature of impulse, did not stand on ceremony. Feeling, no doubt, that he would himself have acted in precisely the same fashion as his gallant subalterns under like conditions, he signaled to the rest to follow their lead, setting the example himself with his own boat. The movement was successful, tho not without much loss both in boats and men. The surf was strong and the rocks were sharp; many boats were smashed to pieces, many men were drowned, but the loss was not comparable to the advantage gained. Wolfe himself, cane in hand, was one of the first to leap into the surf. These were not the men of Oswego, of Lake George, of the Monongahela, of the Virginia frontier…

Amherst's first move was to send Wolfe with his light infantry on a long, rough march of seven or eight miles around the harbor to erect somebatteries upon the farther shore, the necessary guns being dispatched by water. In this business, notwithstanding the scantiness of soil and the absence of suitable timber, he was so alert that by the 26th he had not only mounted his chief battery at Lighthouse Point, but had intrenched all his men in safety from the fire of the town and fleet, which had been fierce and continuous, and furthermore had effectually silenced the formidable French battery on Goat Island in the middle of the harbor entrance.

There was nothing now to prevent Boscawen, if he so chose, from sailing in with his whole fleet, so the French admiral, Desgouttes, rather than lose all his ships, prudently sunk four of them by night in the channel, to protect the rest. Wolfe, in the meantime, had been writing cheery letters to Amherst, telling him of his progress, and greatly jubilant that the French fleet were now "in a confounded scrape." This was precisely what the French admiral and his officers had been thinking for some time, and Desgouttes had urged on the Governor the desirability of getting his ships off while there was yet time. Drucour, however, thought differently, as he wanted the ships and the sailors to prolong the defense, and so prevent the besieging army from either proceeding to Quebec that season, or from helping Abercromby against Montcalm at Lake George. For a fortnight an artillery fire had been steadily proceeding upon the harbor side, while to the westward, where the serious attack was contemplated, Amherst's dispositions were not quite ready, the engineering difficulties being considerable. Wolfe, having done his work, now hurried back to the main lines, which were henceforward to be the chief scene of action…

On both the right and left the English batteries were now pushed forward to within half a mile of the town, and, with Wolfe on one side and Lawrence on the other, began their deadly work. Two hundred big guns and mortars, plied upon both sides by skilled gunners, shook that desolate coast with such an uproar as no part of North America since its first discovery had ever felt. Twenty thousand disciplined troops, soldiers and sailors, led by skilful and energetic commanders, made a warlike tableau, the like of which had never yet been seen, with all the blood that had been spilled between the Mississippi and the St. Lawrence, while infinite valor animated both sides. On July 6th, a sortie was made upon the advanced trenches on the British left, which was easily repulsed. Three days afterward a much more serious effort was prest by a thousand men, stimulated by brandy, the English accounts say, upon the right. The British Grenadiers were forced back out of the trenches, fighting desperately with the bayonet in the dark. Wolfe was here, reveling in the bloody melee, and the enemy was ultimately driven back into the town…

On both wings, indeed, the British advance was pushed so close that gun after gun was dismounted on the Louisbourg ramparts, and the masonry itself began to crack and crumble in all directions, while British soldiers were pressing forward to the very foot of the glacis, and firing upon the covered way. On the 21st one of the French ships in the harbor, the Celebre, was ignited by a bomb, and the flames spread to two others. The British batteries on the extreme left commanded the scene, and rained such a hail of balls upon the flaming decks that the ships could not be saved, and all three were burned to the water's edge. Shells, round shot and bombs were now falling in every part of the devoted town. Nearly all the sailors of the fleet were with the garrison, and all the townsmen who could bear arms helped to man the defenses.

On the 22d the chief house of the citadel, where the Governor and other officials were living, was almost wholly destroyed by fire. A thousand of the garrison were sick or wounded and were cowering in wretchedness and misery in the few sheltered spots and casements that remained. The soldiers had no refuge whatever from the shot and shell. Night and day—for there was a bright moon—the pitiless rain of iron fell upon the town, which, being built mostly of wood, was continually igniting and demanding the incessant labors of a garrison weakened and worn out by the necessity of sleepless vigilance. The gallantry of the defense equaled the vigor of the attack, and was all the more praiseworthy seeing how hopeless it had become. Only two ships of war were left in the harbor, and the British bluejackets, who had been spectators of the siege, now thought they saw a chance of earning some distinction for their branch of the service. So five hundred sailors, in boats, running the gantlet of the fire from the town upon the harbor side, dashed in upon Le Bienfaisant and Le Prudent, overpowered their feeble crews, burned the latter ship, and towed the other one into a corner of the harbor secured by British batteries. The harbor was now cleared of French shipping. Another great fire had just occurred in the town, destroying the barracks that had been an important point of shelter. The bastions on the land side were rapidly crumbling. On the 26th less than half a dozen guns were feebly replying to the uproar of 107 heavy pieces firing at close range from the British batteries, and more than one big breach in the walls warned the exhausted garrison of the imminence of an assault.

A council of war was now called, and the vote was unanimous that a white flag should be sent to Amherst with a request for terms. This was done, but when Amherst's answer came the opinion was equally unanimous against accepting what he offered, which was unconditional surrender within an hour. The officer was sent back again to urge a modification of such hard conditions, but Amherst, well knowing that he had Louisbourg at his mercy, refused even to see the envoy. With singular courage, seeing that no relief was possible, the French officers resolved to bear the brunt of the attack, and Franquet, the engineer who had constructed the fortifications with de la Houliere, the commander of the troops, proceeded to select the ground for a last stand.

But the townspeople had no mind to offer themselves up as victims to an infuriated soldiery, for they remembered Fort William Henry, and dreaded the result. The Commissary-General came to Drucour, and represented that whatever might be the feelings of the military with regard to their professional honor, it was not fair to subject 4,000 citizens, who had already suffered terribly, to the horrors of an assault upon that account alone. He pointed out, and with justice, that no stain, as it was, could rest on the garrison, who had acquitted themselves most bravely against a numerous and formidable foe, and his arguments had effect. The messenger, who for some cause or other had delayed in his mission, was overtaken and recalled, and Amherst's terms accepted. These last required that all the garrison should be delivered up as prisoners of war and transported to England. The non-combatants were at liberty to return to France, and the sick and wounded, numbering some 1,200, were to be looked after by Amherst. All Cape Breton and the adjacent island of Saint Jean (now the fertile province of Prince Edward), with any small garrisons or stores therein contained, were to be given up to the English.

On July the 27th the French troops were drawn up on parade before Whitmore, and, with gestures of rage and mortification, laid down their arms and filed gloomily off to the ships that were to take them to England. Five thousand six hundred and thirty-seven prisoners, soldiers and sailors, were included in the surrender. About two hundred and forty sound pieces of cannon and mortars, with a large amount of ammunition and stores, fell into the hands of the victors. The French fleet in attendance was totally destroyed, and French power upon the North Atlantic coast ceased to exist.

Washington's Expedition to the Ohio

Title: Washington's Expedition to the Ohio
Author: George Washington
Date: 1753
Source: America, Vol.3, p.11

The French and English were both claiming the Ohio country. In Virginia the Ohio Company was organized to settle and develop the new territory. About the same time the French began occupying it and erecting forts to safeguard their possessions. The Virginia Company decided to send a messenger to the French to order them out.

Their first messenger was an experienced frontiersman who lost courage and came home. It was then that Governor Dinwiddy decided to send George Washington on the perilous expedition. That he should have been selected for this hazardous journey when only 21 years of age is a lasting tribute to the high character of the youthful Washington.

Washington kept a journal of his expedition and Governor Dinwiddy was so favorably impressed with it that he decided to have it published at once, and gave Washington only 24 hours to put it in the hands of the printer, William Hunter, who published it at Williamsburg in January, 1754.

I WAS commissioned and appointed by the Honorable Robert Dinwiddy, Esq; Governor, &c., of Virginia, to visit and deliver a letter to the Commandant of the French forces on the Ohio, and set out on the intended journey the same day: The next, I arrived at Fredericksburg, and engaged Mr. Jacob Vanbraam (formerly Washington's fenc-ing-master) to be my French interpreter; and proceeded with him to Alexandria, where we provided necessaries. From thence we went to Winchester, and got baggage, horses, &c.; and from thence we pursued the new road to Wills-Creek (now Cumberland, Md.) where we arrived the 14th of November.

Here I engaged Mr. Gist to pilot us out, and also hired four others as servitors, Barnaby Currin and John Mac-Quire, Indian traders, Henry Steward, and William Jenkins; and in company with those persons, left the inhabitants the day following.

The excessive rains and vast quantity of snow which had fallen, prevented our reaching Mr Frazier's, an Indian trader, at the mouth of Turtle Creek, on Monongahela [river], till Thursday, the 22d. We were informed here, that expresses had been sent a few days before to the traders down the river, to acquaint them with the French General's death, and the return of the major part of the French army into winter quarters.

The waters were quite impassable, without swimming our horses; which obliged us to get the loan of a canoe from Frazier, and to send Barnaby Currin and Henry Steward down the Monongahela, with our baggage, to meet us at the forks of Ohio, about 10 miles, there to cross the Aligany.

As I got down before the canoe, I spent some time in viewing the rivers, and the land in the fork; which I think extremely well situated for a fort, as it has the absolute command of both rivers. The land at the point is 20 or 25 feet above the common surface of the water; and a considerable bottom of flat, well-timbered land all around it, very convenient for building: The rivers are each a quarter of a mile, or more, across, and run here very near at right angles: Aligany bearing N. E. and Monongahela S. E. The former of these two is a very rapid and swift running water; the other deep and still, without any percep-tible fall.

About two miles from this, on the south east side of the river, at the place where the Ohio Company intended to erect a fort, lives Shingiss, king of the Delawares: We called upon him, to invite him to council at the Loggs-town.

As I had taken a good deal of notice yesterday of the situation at the forks, my curiosity led me to examine this more particularly, and I think it greatly inferior, either for defense or advantages; especially the latter: For a fort at the forks would be equally well situated on the Ohio, and have the entire command of the Monongahela: which runs up to our settlements and is extremely well designed for water carriage, as it is of a deep still nature. Besides a fort at the fork might be built at a much less expense, than at the other place.

Nature has well contrived this lower place, for water defense; but the hill whereon it must stand being about a quarter of a mile in length, and then descending gradually on the land side, will render it difficult and very expensive, to make a sufficient fortification there.—The whole flat upon the hill must be taken-in, the side next the descent made extremely high, or else the hill itself cut away: Otherwise, the enemy may raise batteries within that distance without being exposed to a single shot from the fort.

Shingiss attended us to the Loggs-Town, where we arrived between sun-setting and dark, the 25th day after I left Williamsburg. We traveled over some extreme good and bad land, to get to this place.—

As soon as I came into town, I went to Monakatoocha (as the half-king was out at his hunting-cabin on little Beaver-Creek, about 15 miles off) and informed him by John Davison, my Indian interpreter, that I was sent a messenger to the French General; and was ordered to call upon the Sachems of the Six Nations, to acquaint them with it.—I gave him a string of wampum, and a twist of tobacco, and desired him to send for the half-king; which he promised to do by a runner in the morning, and for other sachems.—I invited him and the other great men present to my tent, where they stayed about an hour and returned.

According to the best observations I could make, Mr. Gist's new settlement (which we passed by) bears about W. N. W. 70 miles from Wills-Creek; Shanapins, or the forks N. by W. or N. N. W. about 50 miles from that; and from thence to the Loggs-Town, the course is nearly west about 18 or 20 miles: so that the whole distance, as we went and computed it, is at least 135 or 140 miles from our back inhabitants.

25th. Came to town four or ten Frenchmen who had deserted from a company at the Kuskuskas, which lies at the mouth of this river. I got the following account from them. They were sent from New Orleans with 100 men, and 8 canoe-loads of provisions to this place; where they expected to have met the same number of men, from the forts on this side Lake Erie, to convey them and the stores up, who were not arrived when they ran-off.

I enquired into the situation of the French, on the Mississippi, their number, and what forts they had built. They informed me, that there were four small forts between New Orleans and the Black-Islands, garrisoned with about 30 or 40 men, and a few small pieces in each. That at New Orleans, which is near the mouth of the Mississippi, there are 35 companies, of 40 men each, with a pretty strong fort mounting 8 carriage guns; and at the Black-Islands there are several companies, and a fort with 6 guns. The Black-Islands are about 130 leagues above the mouth of the Ohio, which is about 350 above New Orleans. They also acquainted me that there was a small palisadoed fort on the Ohio, at the mouth of the Obaish about 60 leagues from the Mississippi. The Obaish heads near the west end of Lake Erie, and affords the communication between the French on Mississippi and those on the Lakes. These deserters came up from the lower Shanoah Town with one Brown, an Indian Trader, and were going to Philadelphia.

About 3 o'clock this evening the half-king came to town. I went up and invited him with Davison, privately, to my tent; and desired him to relate some of the particulars of his journey to the French Commandant, and reception there: Also to give me an account of the ways and distance. He told me that the nearest and levelest way was now impassable, by reason of many large mirey savannas; that we must be obliged to go by Venango, and should not get to the near fort under 5 or 6 nights sleep, good traveling. When he went to the fort he said he was received in a very stern manner by the late Commander; who asked him very abruptly, what he had come about, and to declare his business: Which he said he did in the following speech:—

> FATHERS, I am come to tell you your own speeches; what your own mouths have declared. Fathers, you in former days, set a silver basin before us, wherein there was the leg of a beaver, and desired all the nations to come and eat of it; to eat in peace and plenty, and not to be churlish to one another: and that if any such person should be found to be a disturber, I here lay down by the edge of the dish a rod, which you must scourge them with; and if I your father, should get foolish, in my old days, I desire you may use it upon me as well as others.
>
> Now fathers, it is you who are the disturbers in this land, by coming and building your towns; and taking it away unknown to us, and by force.

Fathers, we kindled a fire a long time ago, at a place called Montreal, where we desired you to stay, and not to come and intrude upon our land. I now desire you may dispatch to that place; for be it known to you, fathers, that this is our land, and not yours.

Fathers, I desire you may hear me in civilness; if not, we must handle that rod which was laid down for the use of the obstreperous. If you had come in a peaceable manner, like our brothers the English, we should not have been against your trading with us, as they do; but to come, fathers, and build houses upon our land, and to take it by force, is what we cannot submit to.

Fathers, both you and the English are white, we live in a country between; therefore the land belongs to neither one nor t'other: But the great Being above allowed it to be a place of residence for us; so fathers, I desire you to withdraw, as I have done our brothers the English; for I will keep you at arm's length. I lay this down as a trial for both, to see which will have the greatest regard to it, and that side we will stand by and make equal shares with us. Our brothers, the English, have heard this, and I come now to tell it to you; for I am not afraid to discharge you off this land.

This he said was the substance of what he spoke to the General, who made this reply:

"Now my child, I have heard your speech: you spoke first, but it is my time to speak now. Where is my wampum that you took away, with the marks of towns in it? This wampum I do not know, which you have discharged me off the land with; but you need not put yourself to the trouble of speaking, for I will not hear you. I am not afraid of flies, or mosquitos, for Indians are such as those. I tell you, down that river I will go, and will build upon it, according to my command. If the river was blocked up, I have forces sufficient to burst it open and tread under my feet all that stand in opposition, together with their alliances; for my force is as the sand upon the sea shore: therefore, here is your wampum, I fling it at you. Child, you talk foolish; you say this land belongs to you, but there is not the black of my nail yours. I saw that land sooner than you did, before the Shannoahs and you were at war: Lead was the man who went down and took possession of that river: It is my land, and I will have it, let who will stand-up for, or say-

against it. I'll buy and sell with the English (mockingly).
If people will be ruled by me, they may expect kindness,
but not else."

The Half-King told me he inquired of the General after two Englishmen who were made prisoners, and received this answer:

"Child, you think it is a very great hardship that I made
prisoners of those two people at Venango. Don't you concern yourself with it: We took and carried them to Canada,
to get intelligence of what the English were doing in Virginia."

He informed me that they had built two forts, one on Lake Erie
(Fort Presque Isle, within the present limits of Erie), and another on
French-Creek (Fort le Boeuf. It stood near the present town of Water-
ford, Pa.) near a small lake about 15 miles asunder, and a large wagon
road between: They are both built after the same model, but different
in the size; that on the lake the largest. He gave me a plan of them, of
his own drawing.

The Indians inquired very particularly after their brothers in Carolina jail.

They also asked what sort of boy it was who was taken from the
south-branch; for they were told by some Indians, that a party of French
Indians had carried a white boy by the Kuskuska Town, towards the
lakes.

26th. We met in council at the Long-House, about 9 o'clock, where
I spoke to them as follows:

"Brothers, I have called you together in Council by order
of your brother, the Governor of Virginia, to acquaint you,
that I am sent, with all possible dispatch, to visit, and deliver a letter to the French Commandant, of very great importance to your brothers, the English; and I dare say, to
you their friends and allies.

"I was desired, brothers, by your brother the Governor, to
call upon you, the Sachems of the Nations, to inform you
of it, and to ask your advice and assistance to proceed the
nearest and best road to the French. You see, brothers, I
have gotten thus far on my journey.

"His Honor likewise desired me to apply to you for some
of your young men, to conduct and provide provisions for

All material contained herein was extracted from the
US Constitution Coach Kit at PowerThink.com
(Over 60,000 Works & Documents of American History)

us on our way; and be a safeguard against those French Indians who have taken up the hatchet against us. I have spoken this particularly to you brothers, because his Honor
our Governor treats you as good friends and allies; and
holds you in great esteem. To confirm what I have said, I
give you this string of wampum."

After they had considered for some time on the above discourse,
the half-king got up and spoke:

Now, my brothers, in regard to what my brother the Governor has desired me, I return you this answer.

I rely upon you as a brother ought to do, as you say we are
brothers and one people: We shall put heart in hand and
speak to our fathers and French concerning the speech they
made to me; and you may depend that we will endeavor to
be your guard.

Brother, as you have asked my advice, I hope you will be
ruled by it and stay till I can provide a company to go with
you. The French speech-belt is not here. I have it to go for
to my hunting cabin: Likewise the people whom I have ordered in, are not yet come, nor cannot till the third night
from this: till which time, brother, I must beg you to stay.

I intend to send a guard of Mingo's Shannoah's and
Delawares, that our brothers may see the love and loyalty
we bear them.

As I had orders to make all possible dispatch, and waiting here was
very contrary to my inclinations, I thanked him in the most suitable
manner I could; and told him, that my business required the greatest
expedition, and would not admit of that delay. He was not well pleased
that I should offer to go before the time he had appointed, and told me,
that he could not consent to our going without a guard, for fear some
accident should befall us and draw a reflection upon him. Besides, says
he, this is a matter of no small moment, and must not be entered into
without due consideration: For now I intend to deliver up the French
speech-belt, and make the Shannoahs and Delawares do the same. And
accordingly he gave orders to King Shingiss, who was present, to attend
on Wednesday night with the wampum; and two men of their nation to
be in readiness to set-out with us next morning. As I found it was impossible to get off without affronting them in the most egregious manner, I consented to stay.

I gave them back a string of wampum which I met with at Mr. Frazier's, and which they had sent with a speech to his Honor the Governor, to inform him, that three nations of French Indians, vis: Chippoways, Ottoways, and Orundaks had taken-up the hatchet against the English; and desired them to repeat it over again: But this they postponed doing till they met in full council with the Shannoahs and Delaware chiefs.

27th. Runners were now dispatched very early for the Shannoah chiefs. The half-king set out himself to fetch the French speech-belt from his hunting cabin.

28th. He returned this evening, and came with Monokatoocha, and two other Sachems to my tent, and begged (as they had complied with his Honor the Governor's request, in providing men, &c.) to know on what business we were going to the French? this was a question I all along expected, and had provided as satisfactory answers to, as I could; which allayed their curiosity a little.

Monokatoocha informed me, that an Indian from Venango brought news, a few days ago, that the French had called all the Mingo's, Delawares, &c., together at that place; and told them, that they intended to have been down the river this fall, but the waters were growing cold, and the winter advancing, which obliged them to go into quarters: But that they might assuredly expect them in the spring, with a far greater number; and desired that they might be quite passive, and not to intermeddle, unless they had a mind to draw all their force upon them: For that they expected to fight the English three years (as they supposed there would be some attempts made to stop them), in which time they should conquer: But that if they should prove equally strong, they and the English would join to cut them all off, and divide the land between them: That though they had lost their general, and some few of their soldiers, yet there were men enough to reinforce them, and make them masters of the Ohio.

This speech, he said, was delivered to them by one Captain Joncaire, their interpreter in chief, living at Venango, and a man of note in the army.

29th. The half-king and Monokatoocha came very early, and begged me to stay one day more: For notwithstanding they had used all the diligence in their power, the Shannoah chiefs had not brought the wampum they ordered, but would certainly be in to-night; if not, they would delay me no longer, but would send it after us as soon as they arrived.—When I found them so pressing in their request, and knew that returning of wampum was the abolishing of agreements; and giving this up, was shaking-off all dependence upon the French, I consented to stay, as I believed an offense offered at this crisis, might be attended with greater ill consequence, than another day's delay. They also informed me, that Shingiss could not get in his men; and was prevented from coming himself by his wife's sickness (I believe, by fear of the French); but that the wampum of that nation was lodged with Kustaloga one of their chiefs at Venango.

In the evening late they came again and acquainted me that the Shannoahs were not yet arrived, but that it should not retard the prosecution of our journey. He delivered in my hearing, the speeches that were to be made to the French by Jeskakake, one of their old chiefs, which was giving up the belt the late Commandant had asked for, and repeating near the same speech he himself had done before.

He also delivered a string of wampum to this chief, which was sent by King Shingiss, to be given to Kustaloga, with orders to repair to the French, and deliver up the wampum.

He likewise gave a very large string of black and white wampum, which was to be sent up immediately to the six nations, if the French refused to quit the land at this warning; which was the third and last time, and was the right of this Jeskakake to deliver.

30th. Last night the great men assembled to their council-house, to consult further about this journey, and who were to go: The result of which was, that only three of their chiefs, with one of their best hunters, should be our convoy. The reason they gave for not sending more, after what had been proposed at council the 26th, was, that a greater number might give the French suspicions of some bad design, and cause them to be treated rudely: But I rather think they could not get their hunters in.

We set out about 9 o'clock with the half-king Jeskakake, White Thunder, and the Hunter; and traveled on the road to Venango, where we arrived the 4th of December, without any thing remarkable happening but a continued series of bad weather.

This is an old Indian town, situated at the mouth of French Creek on Ohio: and lies near N. about 60 miles from the Loggs-Town, but more than 70 the way we were obliged to go.

We found the French colors hoisted at a house from which they had driven Mr. John Frasier, an English subject. I immediately repaired to it, to know where the Commander resided. There were three officers, one of whom, Capt. Joncaire, informed me, that he had the command of the Ohio: But that there was a general officer at the near fort, where he advised me to apply for an answer. He invited us to sup with them; and treated us with the greatest complaisance.

The wine, as they dosed themselves pretty plentifully with it, soon banished the restraint which at first appeared in their conversation; and gave a license to their tongues to reveal their sentiments more freely.

They told me, that it was their absolute design to take possession of the Ohio, and by G—— they would do it: For that although they were sensible the English could raise two men for their one; yet they knew their motions were too slow and dilatory to prevent any undertaking of theirs. They pretend to have an undoubted right to the river, from a discovery made by one La Salle 60 years ago; and the rise of this expedition is, to prevent our settling on the river or waters of it, as they had heard of some families moving out in order thereto. From the best intelligence I could get, there have been 1,500 men on their side Ontario Lake: But upon the death of the general all were recalled to about 6 or 700, who were left to garrison four forts, 150 or there abouts in each. The first of them is on French Creek near a small lake, about 60 miles from Venango, near N. N. W. the next lies on Lake Erie, where the greater part of their stores are kept, about 15 miles from the other. From this it is 120 miles to the carrying place at the falls of Lake Erie where there is a small fort; which they lodge their goods at, in bringing them from Montreal, the place whence all their stores come from. The next fort lies about 20 miles from this, on Ontario Lake. Between this fort and Montreal there are three others, the first of which is near opposite to the English Fort Oswego. From the fort on Lake Erie to Montreal is about 600 miles, which they say requires no more, if good weather, than Tour weeks' voyage, if they go in barks or large vessels, so that they may cross the lake: But if they come in canoes it will require 5 or 6 weeks, for they are obliged to keep under the shore.

5th. Rained excessively all day, which prevented our traveling. Capt. Joncaire sent for the half-king, as he had but just heard that he came with me: He affected to be much concerned that I did not make free to bring them in before. I excused it in the best manner I was capable, and told him, I did not think their company agreeable, as I had heard him say a good deal in dispraise of Indians in general. But another motive prevented me from bringing them into his company: I knew he was interpreter, and a person of very great influence among the Indians, and had lately used all possible means to draw them over to their interest; therefore I was desirous of giving no opportunity that could be avoided.

When they came in, there was great pleasure expressed at seeing them. He wondered how they could he so near without coming to visit him; made several trifling presents; and applied liquor so fast, that they were soon rendered incapable of the business they came about, notwithstanding the caution which was given.

6th. The half-king came to my tent, quite sober, and insisted very much that I should stay and hear what he had to say to the French. I fain would have prevented his speaking anything till he came to the Commandant, but could not prevail. He told me that at this place a council fire was kindled, where all their business with these people was to be transacted; and that the management of the Indian affairs was left solely to Monsieur Joncaire. As I was desirous of knowing the issue of this, I agreed to stay, but sent our horses a little way up French Creek to raft over and encamp; which I knew would make it near night.

About 10 o'clock they met in council. The King spoke much the same as he had before done to the General, and offered the French speech-belt which had before been demanded, with the marks of four towns on it, which Monsieur Joncaire refused to receive; but desired him to carry it to the fort to the Commander.

7th. Monsieur La Force, commissary of the French stores, and three other soldiers came over to accompany us up. We found it extremely difficult to get the Indians off to-day, as every stratagem had been used to prevent their going-up with me. I had last night, left John Davison (the Indian interpreter whom I brought with me from town), and strictly charged him not to be out of their company, as I could not get them over to my tent; for they had some business with Kustaloga, and chiefly to know the reason why he did not deliver up the French belt which he had in keeping: But I was obliged to send Mr. Gist over to-day to fetch them; which he did with great persuasion.

At 11 o'clock we set out for the fort, and were prevented from arriving there till the 11th by excessive rains, snows, and bad traveling, through many mires and swamps. These we were obliged to pass, to avoid crossing the creek, which was impossible, either by fording or rafting, the water was so high and rapid.

We passed over much good land since we left Venango, and through several extensive and very rich meadows; one of which I believe was near four miles in length, and considerably wide in some places.

12th. I prepared early to wait upon the Commander, and was received and conducted to him by the second officer in command. I acquainted him with my business, and offered my commission and letter, both of which he desired me to keep till the arrival of Monsieur Riparti, Captain at the next fort, who was sent for and expected every hour.

This Commander is a knight of the military order of St. Lewis, and named Legardeur de St. Pierre. He is an elderly gentleman, and has much the air of a soldier. He was sent over to take the command immediately upon the death of the late General, and arrived here about seven days before me.

At 2 o'clock the gentleman who was sent for arrived, when I offered the letter, &c, again; which they received, and adjourned into a private apartment for the captain to translate, who understood a little English. After he had done it, the Commander desired I would walk in, and bring my interpreter to peruse and correct it; which I did.

13th. The chief officers retired, to hold a council of war; which gave me an opportunity of taking the dimensions of the fort, and making what observations I could.

It is situated on the south or west fork of French Creek, near the water; and is almost surrounded by the creek, and a small branch of it which forms a kind of island. Four houses compose the sides. The bastions are made of piles driven into the ground, standing more than 12 feet above it, and sharp at top: With port-holes cut for cannon, and loopholes for the small arms to fire through. There are eight 6 lb. pieces mounted, in each bastion; and one piece of four pound before the gate. In the bastions are a guard-house, chapel, doctor's lodging, and the Commander's private store, around which are laid platforms for the cannon and men to stand on. There are several barracks without the fort, for the soldiers' dwelling; covered, some with bark and some with boards, made chiefly of logs. There are also several other houses, such as stables, smiths shop, &c.

I could get no certain account of the number of men here: But according to the best judgment I could form, there are an hundred exclusive of officers, of which there are many. I also gave orders to the people who were with me, to take an exact account of the canoes which were hauled-up to convey their forces down in the spring. This they

All material contained herein was extracted from the
US Constitution Coach Kit at PowerThink.com
(Over 60,000 Works & Documents of American History)

did, and told 50 of birch bark, and 170 of pine; besides many others which were blocked-out, in readiness to make.

14th. As the snow increased very fast, and our horses daily became weaker, I sent them off unloaded; under the care of Barnaby Currin, and two others, to make all convenient dispatch to Venango, and there wait our arrival, if there was a prospect of the rivers freezing, if not, then to continue down to Shanapin's Town, at the forks of Ohio, and there to wait till we came to cross Aliganey; intending myself to go down by water, as I had the offer of a canoe or two.

As I found many plots concerted to retard the Indians' business, and prevent their returning with me; I endeavored all that lay in my power to frustrate their schemes, and hurry them on to execute their intended design. They accordingly pressed for admittance this evening, which at length was granted them, privately, with the Commander and one or two other officers. The half-king told me, that he offered the wampum to the Commander, who evaded taking it, and made many fair promises of love and friendship; said he wanted to live in peace, and trade amicably with them, as a proof of which he would send some goods immediately down to the Loggs-Town for them. But I rather think the design of that is, to bring away all our straggling traders they meet with, as I privately understood they intended to carry an officer, &c, with them. And what rather confirms this opinion, I was inquiring of the Commander, by what authority he had made prisoners of several of our English subjects. He told me that the country belonged to them; that no Englishman had a right to trade upon those waters; and that he had orders to make every person prisoner who attempted it on the Ohio, or the waters of it.

I inquired of Capt. Riparti about the boy who was carried by this place, as it was done while the command devolved on him, between the death of the late General, and the arrival of the present. He acknowledged, that a boy had been carried past; and that the Indians had two or three white men's scalps (I was told by some of the Indians at Venango eight) but pretended to have forgotten the name of the place which the boy came from, and all the particular facts, though he had questioned him for some hours, as they were carrying him past. I likewise inquired what they had done with John Trotter and James MacClocklan, two Pennsylvania traders, whom they had taken, with all their goods. They told me, that they had been sent to Canada, but were now returned home.

This evening I received an answer to his Honor the Governor's letter from the Commandant.

15th. The Commandant ordered a plentiful store of liquor, provision, &c, to be put on board our canoe; and appeared to be extremely complaisant, though he was exerting every artifice which he could invent to set our own Indians at variance with us, to prevent their going 'till after our departure. Presents, rewards, and everything which could be suggested by him or his officers.—I can't say that ever in my life I suffered so much anxiety as I did in this affair: I saw that every stratagem which the most fruitful brain could invent, was practiced, to win the half-king to their interest; and that leaving him here was giving them the opportunity they aimed at.—I went to the half-king and pressed him in the strongest terms to go: He told me the Commandant would not discharge him till the morning. I then went to the Commandant, and desired him to do their business; and complained of ill treatment: For keeping them, as they were part of my company, was detaining me. This he promised not to do, but to forward my journey as much as he could. He protested he did not keep them, but was ignorant of the cause of their stay; though I soon found it out:—He had promised them a present of guns, &c, if they would wait 'till the morning.

As I was very much pressed, by the Indians, to wait this day for them, I consented, on a promise, that nothing should hinder them in the morning.

16th. The French were not slack in their inventions to keep the Indians this day also: But as they were obligated, according to promise, to give the present, they then endeavored to try the power of liquor; which I doubt not would have prevailed at any other time than this. But I urged and insisted with the King so closely upon his word, that he refrained, and set off with us as he had engaged.

We had a tedious and very fatiguing passage down the creek. Several times we had like to have been staved against rocks; and many times were obliged all hands to get out and remain in the water half an hour or more, getting over the shoals. At one place the ice had lodged and made it impassable by water; therefore we were obliged to carry our canoe across a neck of land, a quarter of a mile over. We did not reach Venango, till the 22d, where we met with our horses.

This creek is extremely crooked, I dare say the distance between the fort and Venango can't be less than 130 miles, to follow the meanders.

23d. When I got things ready to set off, I sent for the half-king, to know whether he intended to go with us, or by water. He told me that White Thunder had hurt himself much, and was sick and unable to walk; therefore he was obliged to carry him down in a canoe. As I found he intended to stay here a day or two, and knew that Monsieur Joncaire would employ every scheme to set him against the English as he had before done; I told him I hoped he would guard against his flattery, and let no fine speeches influence him in their favor. He desired I might not be concerned, for he knew the French too well, for anything to engage him in their behalf; and that though he could not go down with us, he yet would endeavor to meet at the forks with Joseph Campbell, to deliver a speech for me to carry to his Honor the Governor. He told me he would order the young hunter to attend us, and get provision, &c. if wanted.

Our horses were now so weak and feeble, and the baggage so heavy (as we were obliged to provide all the necessaries which the journey would require) that we doubted much their performing it; therefore myself and others (except the drivers, who were obliged to ride) gave up our horses for packs, to assist along with the baggage. I put myself in an Indian walking dress, and continued with them three days, till I found there was no probability of their getting home in any reasonable time. The horses grew less able to travel every day; the cold increased very fast; and the roads were becoming much worse by a deep snow, continually freezing: Therefore as I was uneasy to get back, to make report of my proceedings to his Honor, the Governor, I determined to prosecute my journey the nearest way through the woods, on foot.

Accordingly I left Mr. Vanbraam in charge of our baggage: with money and directions to provide necessaries from place to place for themselves and horses, and to make the most convenient dispatch in traveling.

I took my necessary papers; pulled off my clothes; and tied myself up in a match coat. Then with gun in hand and pack at my back, in which were my papers and provisions, I set out with Mr. Gist, fitted in the same manner, on Wednesday the 26th.

The day following, just after we had passed a place called the Murdering-Town (where we intended to quit the path, and steer across the country for Shannapins Town) we fell in with a party of French Indians, who had lain in wait for us. One of them fired at Mr. Gist or me, not 15 steps off, but fortunately missed. We took this fellow into custody, and kept him till about 9 o'clock at night; Then let him go, and walked all the remaining part of the night without making any stop; that we might get the start, so far, as to be out of the reach of their pursuit the next day, since we were well assured they would follow our tract as soon as it was light. The next day we continued traveling till quite dark, and got to the river about two miles above Shannapins. We expected to have found the river frozen, but it was not, only about 50 yards from each shore; The ice suppose had broken up above, for it was driving in vast quantities.

There was no way for getting over but on a raft; Which we set about with but one poor hatchet, and finished just after sun-setting. This was a whole day's work. Then set off; But before we were half way over, we were jammed in the ice, in such a manner that we expected every moment our raft to sink, and ourselves to perish. I put out my setting pole to try to stop the raft, that the ice might pass by; when the rapidity of the stream threw it with so much violence against the pole, that it jerked me out into ten feet of water: but I fortunately saved myself by catching hold of one of the raft logs. Notwithstanding all our efforts we could not get the raft to either shore; but were obliged, as we were near an island, to quit our raft and make to it.

The cold was so extremely severe, that Mr. Gist had all his fingers, and some of his toes frozen; but the water was shut up so hard, that we found no difficulty in getting off the island, on the ice, in the morning, and went to Mr. Frazier's. We met here with 20 warriors who were going to the southward to war, but coming to a place upon the head of the great Kunnaway, where they found seven people killed and scalped (all but one woman with very light hair) they turned about and ran back for fear the inhabitants should rise and take them as the authors of the murder. They report that the bodies were lying about the house, and some of them much torn and eaten by hogs. By the marks which were left, they say they were French Indians of the Ottaway nation, &c., who did it.

As we intended to take horses here, and it required some time to find them, I went-up about three miles to the mouth of Yaughyaughane to visit Queen Aliquippa, who had expressed great concern that we passed her in going to the fort. I made her a present of a matchcoat and a bottle of rum; which latter was thought much the best present of the two.

Tuesday the 1st Day of January, we left Mr. Frazier's house, and arrived at Mr. Gist's at Monongahela the 2d, where I bought a horse, saddle, etc: the 6th we met 17 horses loaded with materials and stores, for a fort at the forks of Ohio, and the day after some families going out to settle: This day we arrived at Wills Creek, after as fatiguing a journey as it is possible to conceive, rendered so by excessive bad weather. From the first day of December to the 15th, there was but one day on which it did not rain or snow incessantly: and throughout the whole journey we met with nothing but one continued series of cold wet weather, which occasioned very uncomfortable lodgings: especially after we had quitted our tent, which was some screen from the inclemency of it.

On the 11th I got to Belvoir: where I stopped one day to take necessary, rest; and then set out and arrived in Williamsburgh the 16th; when I waited upon his Honor the Governor with the letter I had brought from the French Commandant; and to give an account of the success of my proceedings. This I beg leave to do by offering the foregoing narrative as it contains the most remarkable occurrences which happened in my journey.

I hope what has been said will be sufficient to make your Honor satisfied with my conduct; for that was my aim in undertaking the journey, and chief study throughout the prosecution of it.

Washington's Expedition to the Ohio and the Battle of Great Meadows

Title: Washington's Expedition to the Ohio and the Battle of Great Meadows
Author: A. G. Bradley
Date: 1753-1754
Source: Great Epochs in American History, Vol.3, pp.25-30

Dinwiddie, the shrewd Scotch Governor of Virginia, was the first to move, and this he could only do by way of protest, since he had no forces worth mentioning and no money to pay the handful that he had. It is a strange coincidence that the agent he selected for the business—the first British soldier, in fact, who went out formally to proclaim King George's title to the West—should have been George

Washington. The young Virginian was at this time only twenty-one, a major in the colonial service and adjutant-general of the Virginia militia. In the opinion of Dinwiddie, an opinion which did him credit, there was no one in the colony so well qualified to perform a mission of danger, delicacy, and hardship...

The mission was to march through the woods from the Potomac River to the new French fort of Le Boeuf, only twenty miles south of Lake-Erie, no mean performance in the year 1753! The chill rains of late autumn fell ceaselessly upon the small party as they pushed their way through the dripping forests, and it was December before they reached the nearer station of the French at Venango. Here an officer named Joncaire commanded, having seized an English trading-house and hoisted above it the French flag. Washington kept a journal of the whole expedition, and tells us how he dined here with the French officers, who, when flushed with wine, declared that, tho the English were in a great majority, their movements were too slow, and for their own part they intended to take the Ohio Valley and "by G—d to keep it."...

It was now the early spring of 1754. Forty backwoodsmen under an Ensign Ward were sent across the Alleghanies to erect a fort at a place previously selected by Washington, where the two large streams of the Alleghany and Monongahela meet to form the Ohio—a spot to become famous enough in the succeeding years, and in another sense still more famous now.

Washington struck out into the wilderness, the ultimate object of the British attack being the fort which the French were said to be building at the beforementioned forks of the Ohio, and had already named after their Governor, Duquesne.

Washington and his 150 men slowly pushed their way northwestward, cutting roads over the lofty forest-clad ridges of the Alleghanies for their guns and pack-trains. They had covered sixty miles, nearly half the march, and had arrived at an oasis in the mountain wilderness, where stood a trading station, known as "The Great Meadows," when word was brought that a French detachment was advancing from the new fort Duquesne to clear the English out of the country. Taking forty of his men with him, Washington groped his way through the whole of a pitch-dark and soaking night to the quarters of the "Half King," a friendly Indian chief, who had formed one of his party in the diplomatic mission of the previous year. The Indian had some news to give of an advanced scouting party of the French, supposed to be lurking in the neighborhood, and with some of his people joined Washington at daylight in an attempt to track them. In this they succeeded, and surprized the French lying in a ravine, who, on being discovered, all sprang to their feet, rifle in hand. Washington promptly gave the order to fire. A volley was given and returned. Coulon de Jumonville, the ensign who commanded the French, was shot dead, and a few of his men killed and wounded, while the remaining twenty-one were taken prisoners. The killing of Jumonville raised a great commotion, not only in the colonies, but in Europe. "It was the volley fired by a young Virginian in the back-woods of America," says Horace Walpole, "that set the world on fire." It was pretended by the French that Jumonville was on a quasi-diplomatic errand, ordering the English to retire…

Jumonville and his men, it transpired, had been lying concealed for two days in the neighborhood of Washington's superior force—scarcely the natural method of procedure for a peaceful convoy! De Contrecoeur, commanding the main force of some 500 men, was advancing in the rear, and his scouting subaltern, who, as a matter of fact, had sent messengers to hurry him up, was simply waiting for his arrival to overwhelm the small British detachment.

Washington after this retired to the Great Meadows, where his second battalion, tho without their colonel, who had died, now arrived, together with the South Carolina company, consisting of fifty so-called regulars, raised in the colony but paid by the Crown. The young Virginian was now in command of 350 men, but the Carolina captain, being in some sort a king's officer, refused to take orders from his as a provincial, admirably illustrating one of the many difficulties which then hampered military action in the colonies. His men assumed similar airs, and would lend no hand in road-making, carrying packs, or hauling guns. So Washington labored on with his Virginians, seeking for some good defensive point at which to receive the attack of the large force he heard was advancing against him. After much labor it was decided to return again to the Great Meadows, and there entrench themselves as best they could…

He drew up his force outside the poor entrenchments, which he had aptly called Fort Necessity, and seems to have had some vague idea of encountering the French in the open. But when at eleven o'clock some eight or nine hundred of the enemy, including Indians, emerged from the woods, it soon became evident that, with such excellent cover as nature afforded in the overhanging hills, they were not going to take the superfluous risks of a frontal attack.

The British thereupon withdrew inside their works and the French riflemen scattered among the wooded ridges that so fatally commanded them. A musketry duel then commenced and continued for nine hours, while a heavy rain fell incessantly. Washington's guns were almost useless, for they were so exposed that the loss of life in serving them was far greater than any damage they could inflict on the enemy. The men were up to their knees in water and mud; their bread had been long exhausted, and they were reduced to a meat diet, and a very poor one at that. This ragged regiment, in homespun and hunting-shirts, half-starved, soaked to the skin, and with ammunition failing, not from expenditure only, but from wet, fought stubbornly throughout the day. From time to time the very force of the rain caused a lull in the combat, the opposing forces being hidden from one another by sheets of falling water.

The French, as the day waned, proposed a capitulation, which Washington refused. But his ammunition at length gave out entirely, and as the gloomy light of the June evening began to fade, a fresh proposal to send an envoy to discuss terms was accepted. The indispensable Van Braam, as the only one of the British force who could speak French, was sent to negotiate. Nearly a hundred men of the defending force lay killed or wounded, while the French loss, tho not so great, turned out to be considerable. The terms offered, after a little discussion, were at length accepted, and were honorable enough; namely, that the garrison were to march out with honors of war, carrying their effects and one gun with them. The French were indeed in no position to take or maintain prisoners...

The fifty-mile march return over the mountains to Wills Creek was a pitiful business. The wounded had to be carried on the backs of their weakened, travel-worn comrades, for the Indians, threatening and noisy, were with difficulty prevented from a general onslaught, and, as it was, killed all the horses and destroyed the medicine chests. It was a sorry band that struggled back with Washington across the Alleghanies, by the rough track that a year hence was to be beaten wider by the tramp of British infantry marching to a fate far more calamitous...

The fight at the Great Meadows was in itself a small affair, but its effect was prodigious. Judged by modern ethics, it seems incredible that formal peace between France and England should remain undisturbed by such proceedings; but we shall see that the peace outlasted events far more critical, owing to the desire of France to get more forward in her preparations before the coming struggle actually opened, and to the apathy reigning in the councils of England. But, peace or war, the great conflict had begun, and the incapacity of the colonies to help themselves had been so fully demonstrated as to turn men's minds across the sea, as to the only quarter from which efficient help could be expected.

Benjamin Franklin's Plan of Union

Title: Benjamin Franklin's Plan of Union
Author: Benjamin Franklin
Date: 1754
Source: America, Vol.3, p.38

Although the Plan of Union adopted by the Albany Convention, representing seven of the colonies, in 1754, failed, it was the most important federal measure in the colonies before the Revolution. It did not entirely satisfy Franklin himself. "It is not altogether to my mind," he said afterwards, "but it is [as good] as I could get it." And curiously it proved acceptable in almost no quarter, being rejected by the Colonial Assemblies, because, as Franklin records, "there was too much prerogative in it," and rejected by the Board of Trade in England because "it was thought to have too much of the democratic."

But the plan familiarized the colonists with the union idea, doing much to prepare them for the Revolutionary struggle twenty years later; and it constitutes a notable landmark in the development of the national principle.

I T IS proposed, that humble application be made for an act of Parliament of Great Britain, by virtue of which one general government may be formed in America, including all the said colonies, within and under which government each colony may retain its present constitution, except in the particulars wherein a change may be directed by the said act, as hereafter follows.

PRESIDENT-GENERAL AND GRAND COUNCIL

"That the said general government be administered by a President-General, to be appointed and supported by the crown; and a Grand Council, to be chosen by the representatives of the people of the several Colonies met in their respective assemblies."

It was thought that it would be best the President-General should be supported as well as appointed by the crown, that so all disputes between him and the Grand Council concerning his salary might be prevented; as such disputes have been frequently of mischievous consequence in particular colonies, especially in time of public danger. The quit-rents of crown lands in America might in a short time be sufficient for this purpose. The choice of members for the Grand Council is placed in the House of Representatives of each government, in order to give the people a share in this new general government, as the crown has its share by the appointment of the President-General.

But it being proposed by the gentlemen of the Council of New York, and some other counsellors among the commissioners, to alter the plan in this particular, and to give the governors and councils of the several provinces a share in the choice of the Grand Council, or at least a power of approving and confirming, or of disallowing, the choice made by the House of Representatives, it was said:

"That the government or constitution, proposed to be formed by the plan, consists of two branches; a President-General appointed by the crown, and a council chosen by the people, or by the people's representatives, which is the same thing.

"That, by a subsequent article, the council chosen by the people can effect nothing without the consent of the President-General appointed by the crown; the crown possesses, therefore, full one-half of the power of this constitution.

"That in the British constitution, the crown is supposed to possess but one-third, the lords having their share.

"That this constitution seemed rather more favorable for the crown.

"That it is essential to English liberty, that the subject should not be taxed but by his own consent, or the consent of his elected representatives.

"That taxes to be laid and levied by this proposed constitution will be proposed and agreed to by the representatives of the people, if the plan in this particular be preserved;

"But if the proposed alteration should take place, it seemed as if matters may be so managed, as that the crown shall finally have the appointment, not only of the President-General, but of a majority of the Grand Council; for seven out of eleven governors and councils are appointed by the crown;

"And so the people in all the colonies would in effect be taxed by their governors.

"It was therefore apprehended, that such alterations of the plan would give great dissatisfaction, and that the colonies could not be easy under such a power in governors, and such an infringement of what they take to be English liberty.

"Besides, the giving a share in the choice of the Grand Council would not be equal with respect to all the colonies, as their constitutions differ. In some, both governor and council are appointed by the crown; in others, they are both appointed by the proprietors. In some, the people have a share in the choice of the council; in others, both government and council are wholly chosen by the people. But the House of Representatives is everywhere chosen by the people; and, therefore, placing the right of choosing the Grand Council in the representatives is equal with respect to all.

"That the Grand Council is intended to represent all the several Houses of Representatives of the colonies, as a House of Representatives doth the several towns or counties of a colony. Could all the people of a colony be consulted and unite in public measures, a House of Representatives would be needless, and could all the assemblies conveniently consult and unite in general measures, the Grand Council would be unnecessary.

"That a House of Commons or the House of Representatives, and the Grand Council, are thus alike in their nature and intention. And, as it would seem improper that the King or House of Lords should have a power of disallowing or appointing members of the House of Commons; so, likewise, that a governor and council appointed by the crown should have a power of disallowing or appointing members of the Grand Council, who, in this constitution, are to be the representatives of the people.

"If the governors and councils therefore were to have a share in the choice of any that are to conduct this general government, it should seem more proper that they choose the President-General. But, this being an office of great trust and importance to the nation, it was thought better to be filled by the immediate appointment of the crown...

ELECTION OF MEMBERS

"Within—months after the passing such act, the House of
Representatives that happen to be sitting within that time,
or that shall be especially for that purpose convened, may
and shall choose members for the Grand Council, in the
following proportion: that is to say, Massachusetts Bay, 7;
New Hampshire, 2; Connecticut, 5; Rhode Island, 2; New
York, 4; New Jersey, 3; Pennsylvania, 6; Maryland, 4; Virginia, 7; North Carolina, 4; South Carolina, 4. Total, 48."

It was thought, that if the least colony was allowed two, and the
others in proportion, the number would be very great, and the expense
heavy; and that less than two would not be convenient, as, a single person being by any accident prevented appearing at the meeting, the
colony he ought to appear for would not be represented. That, as the
choice was not immediately popular, they would be generally men of
good abilities for business, and men of reputation for integrity; and that
forty-eight such men might be a number sufficient. But, though it was
thought reasonable that each colony should have a share in the representative body in some degree according to the proportion it contributed
to the general treasury, yet the proportion of wealth or power of the
colonies is not to be judged by the proportion here fixed; because it
was at first agreed, that the greatest colony should not have more than
seven members, nor the least less than two; and the setting these proportions between these two extremes was not nicely attended to, as it
would find itself, after the first election, from the sums brought into
the treasury, as by a subsequent article.

PLACE OF FIRST MEETING

"The Grand Council shall meet for the first time at the city
of Philadelphia in Pennsylvania, being called by the President-General as soon as conveniently may be after his appointment."

Philadelphia was named as being nearer the center of the colonies,
where the commissioners would be well and cheaply accommodated.
The high roads, through the whole extent, are for the most part very
good, in which forty or fifty miles a day may very well be, and frequently are, traveled. Great part of the way may likewise be gone by
water. In summer time, the passages are frequently performed in a week
from Charleston to Philadelphia and New York; and from Rhode Island
to New York through the Sound, in two or three days; and from New
York to Philadelphia, by water and land, in two days, by stage, boats,

and wheel-carriages that set out every other day. The journey from Charleston to Philadelphia may likewise be facilitated by boats running up Chesapeake Bay three hundred miles. But if the whole journey be performed on horseback, the most distant members, viz., the two from New Hampshire and from South Carolina, may probably render themselves at Philadelphia in fifteen or twenty days; the majority may be there in much less time…

MEETINGS OF THE GRAND COUNCIL, AND CALL

"The Grand Council shall meet once in every year, and oftener if occasion require, at such time and place as they shall adjourn to at the last preceding meeting, or as they shall be called to meet at by the President-General on any emergency; he having first obtained in writing the consent of seven of the members to such call, and sent due and timely notice to the whole."

It was thought, in establishing and governing new colonies or settlements, regulating Indian trade, Indian treaties, &c., there would every year sufficient business arise to require at least one meeting, and at such meeting many things might be suggested for the benefit of all the colonies. This annual meeting may either be at a time or place certain, to be fixed by the President-General and Grand Council at their first meeting; or left at liberty, to be at such time and place as they shall adjourn to, or be called to meet at by the President-General.

In time of war, it seems convenient that the meeting should be in that colony which is nearest the seat of action.

The power of calling them on any emergency seemed necessary to be vested in the President-General; but, that such power might not be wantonly used to harass the members, and oblige them to make frequent long journeys to little purpose, the consent of seven at least to such call was supposed a convenient guard…

MEMBERS' ALLOWANCE

"The members of the Grand Council shall be allowed for their service ten shillings sterling per diem, during their session and journey to and from the place of meeting; twenty miles to be reckoned a day's journey.

It was thought proper to allow some wages, lest the expense might deter some suitable persons from the service; and not to allow too great wages, lest unsuitable persons should be tempted to cabal for the employment, for the sake of gain. Twenty miles were set down as a day's journey, to allow for accidental hindrances on the road, and the greater expenses of traveling than residing at the place of meeting.

ASSENT OF PRESIDENT-GENERAL AND HIS DUTY

"The assent of the President-General be requisite to all acts of the Grand Council, and that it be his office and duty to cause them to be carried into execution."

The assent of the President-General to all acts of the Grand Council was made necessary, in order to give the crown its due share of influence in this government, and connect it with that of Great Britain. The President-General, besides one-half of the legislative power, hath in his hands the whole executive power.

POWER OF PRESIDENT-GENERAL AND GRAND COUNCIL; TREATIES OF PEACE AND WAR

"The President-General, with the advice of the Grand Council, hold or direct all Indian treaties, in which the general interest of the Colonies may be concerned; and make peace or declare war with Indian nations."

The power of making peace or war with Indian nations is at present supposed to be in every colony, and is expressly granted to some by charter, so that no new power is hereby intended to be granted to the colonies. But as, in consequence of this power, one colony might make peace with a nation that another was justly engaged in war with; or make war on slight occasions without the concurrence or approbation of neighboring colonies, greatly endangered by it; or make particular treaties of neutrality in case of a general war, to their own private advantage in trade, by supplying the common enemy; of all which there have been instances; it was thought better to have all treaties of a general nature under a general direction, that so the good of the whole may be consulted and provided for…

NEW SETTLEMENTS

"They make new settlements on such purchases, by granting lands in the King's name, reserving a quit-rent to the crown for the use of the general treasury."

… A particular colony has scarce strength enough to extend itself by new settlements, at so great a distance from the old; but the joint force of the Union might suddenly establish a new colony or two in those parts, or extend an old colony to particular passes, greatly to the security of our present frontiers, increase of trade and people, breaking off the French communication between Canada and Louisiana, and speedy settlement of the intermediate lands.

The power of settling new colonies is therefore thought a valuable part of the plan, and what cannot so well be executed by two unions as by one.

RAISE SOLDIERS, AND EQUIP VESSELS

"They raise and pay soldiers and build forts for the defense of any of the colonies, and equip vessels of force to guard the coasts and protect the trade on the oceans, lakes, or great rivers; but they shall not impress men in any colony, without the consent of the legislature.

It was thought that quotas of men, to be raised and paid by the several colonies, and joined for any public service, could not always be got together with the necessary expedition. For instance, suppose one thousand men should be wanted in New Hampshire on any emergency. To fetch them by fifties and hundreds out of every colony, as far as South Carolina, would be inconvenient, the transportation chargeable, and the occasion perhaps passed before they could be assembled; and therefore it would be best to raise them (by offering bounty-money and pay) near the place where they would be wanted, to be discharged again when the service should be over.

Particular colonies are at present backward to build forts at their own expense, which they say will be equally useful to their neighboring colonies; who refuse to join, on a presumption that such forts will be built and kept up, though they contribute nothing. This unjust conduct weakens the whole; but the forts being for the good of the whole, it was thought best they should be built and maintained by the whole, out of the common treasury.

In the time of war, small vessels of force are sometimes necessary in the colonies to scour the coasts of small privateers. These being provided by the Union will be an advantage in turn to the colonies which are situated on the sea, and whose frontiers on the landside, being covered by other colonies, reap but little immediate benefit from the advanced forts.

POWER TO MAKE LAWS, LAY DUTIES, &C.

"For these purposes they have power to make laws, and lay and levy such general duties, imposts, or taxes, as to them shall appear most equal and just (considering the ability and other circumstances of the inhabitants in the several colonies), and such as may be collected with the least inconvenience to the people; rather discouraging luxury, than loading industry with unnecessary burdens."

The laws which the President-General and Grand Council are empowered to make are such only as shall be necessary for the government of the settlements; the raising, regulating, and paying soldiers for the general service; the regulating of Indian trade; and laying and collecting the general duties and taxes. They should also have a power to restrain the exportation of provisions to the enemy from any of the colonies, on particular occasions, in time of war. But it is not intended that they may interfere with the constitution and government of the particular colonies; who are to be left to their own laws, and to lay, levy, and apply their own taxes, as before…

EACH COLONY MAY DEFEND ITSELF IN EMERGENCY

"The particular military as well as civil establishments in each colony remain in their present state, the general constitution notwithstanding; and that on sudden emergencies any colony may defend itself, and lay the accounts of expense thence arising before the President-General and General Council, who may allow and order payment of the same, as far as they judge such accounts just and reasonable."

Otherwise the union of the whole would weaken the parts, contrary to the design of the union. The accounts are to be judged of by the President-General and the Grand Council, and allowed if found reasonable. This was thought necessary to encourage colonies to defend themselves, as the expense would be light when borne by the whole; and also to check imprudent and lavish expense in such defenses.

The Defeat of Braddock

Title: The Defeat of Braddock
Author: A. G. Bradley
Date: 1755
Source: Great Epochs in American History, Vol.3, pp.39-48

On the 20th of February the small British armament cast anchor in Hampton Roads, Virginia, when General Braddock, who was in command, proceeded at once to Williamsburg, the capital of the colony, to confer with its eager and expectant Governor, Dinwiddie. The fleet then sailed up the Potomac and deposited the troops where the Virginia town of Alexandria, then in its infancy, now looks across the broad river toward the noble buildings of the city of Washington. These two regiments were the first substantial force of British regulars that had ever landed on American soil, unless, indeed, we go back to that curious revolt against Governor Berkeley in 1676, and the brief civil war in Virginia, which was finally extinguished by the landing of a mixed battalion of Guards.

Concerning Braddock, seeing that his name has been immortalized by the tragedy for which some hold him, in part, accountable, a word or two must be said. He was now over sixty years of age, and was the choice of the Duke of Cumberland, then commander-in-chief. As he had neither wealth nor influence, American warfare not being in request by fortune's favorites, we may fairly suppose that he was selected on his merits. No name has been more irresponsibly played upon and few reputations perhaps more hardly used than Braddock's by most writers of history and nearly all writers of fiction. His personality, from its very contrast to the wild woods in which he died, has caught the fancy of innumerable pens, and justice has been sadly sacrificed to picturesque effect. One is almost inclined to think that the mere fact of his name beginning with a letter which encourages a multiplication of strenuous epithets, has been against him. He is regarded as the typical redcoat of the Hanoverian period by all American writers—burly, brutal, blundering, blasphemous, but happily always, and without a dissentient note, brave—brave indeed as a lion. This familiar picture of our poor general, as a corpulent, red-faced, blaspheming bulldog, riding roughshod over colonial susceptibilities, tones down amazingly when one comes to hard facts. Legends of his former life are, with peculiar lack of generosity, quoted for what they are worth, and when examined they seem to be worth nothing. Walpole airs his wit in one or two doubtful aspersions, and a play of Fielding's is with little reason supposed to satirize the general's earlier years.

What is really known about Braddock is in his favor. Vanquished in a duel, he had been too proud to ask his life. In command at Gibraltar he was "adored by his men," and this tho he was notorious as a strict disciplinarian, a quality which Wolfe at this very time declares to be themost badly needed one in the British army. He had been in the Guards, had enjoyed a private income of some þ300 a year, which it may be noted, since spendthrift is one of the epithets hurled at him, he slightly increased during his lifetime. The night before Braddock sailed, he went with his two aides, Burton and Orme, to see Mrs. Bellamy, and left her his will, drawn up in favor of her husband. He also produced a map, and remarked, with a touch of melancholy, that he was "going forth to conquer whole worlds with a handful of men, and to do so must cut his way through unknown woods." He was, in fact, the first British general to conduct a considerable campaign in a remote wilderness. He had neither precedents nor the experience of others to guide him, and he found little help in the colonies where he had been taught to look for much…

The two British regiments in the meantime were being raised from 500 men to a strength of 700 by provincial enlistment. The 44th was commanded by Sir Peter Halkett, a good officer, who, ten years previously, had been captured by the Pretender, and released on parole. The 48th were under Dunbar, who acquitted himself but poorly as we shall see. The camp of exercise on the Potomac was a strange and inspiring sight to the colonists, who had now begun in some sort to realize the French danger. With all their seeming apathy, the Virginians and Marylanders were stanchly loyal. The echoes from far-off European fields, won or fiercely disputed by the intrepidity of British soldiers, were still ringing in their ears. Stories of Dettingen and Fontenoy were yet told by cabin fires and on the planters' shady porches by new-comers from England and sometimes, no doubt, by men who had assisted in those glorious victories, and scarcely less glorious defeats. Here now were these redoubtable redcoats, gay in all the glitter and panoply of war, actually marching and maneuvering on the warm soil of the Old Dominion. If there had been anything in this French scare, there was now at any rate no further cause for alarm. It was a great opportunity, too, for the gentry of the Potomac shore to indulge at the same time their loyal and their social instincts. Tradition says that the ladies appreciated the situation more than the gentlemen of the colony, who were not over-pleased at the supercilious bearing of the British officers. Washington, whose estate at Mount Vernon lay within a few miles of the Alexandria camp, was a frequent visitor…

Benjamin Franklin, then postmaster at Philadelphia, was at the general's right hand, dining daily at his table—"the first capable and sensible man I have met in the country," wrote poor Braddock to his Government. Franklin undertook the wagon business, and with great effect he turned to Pennsylvania, a colony of prosperous small farmers, apathetic as to the war, but possest of abundant agricultural requisites. Franklin appealed not to their pockets, or rather to their fears, telling them roundly that it would be better to hire their wagons and teams to His Majesty's Government than wait till they were dragooned, as with a fine touch of ready audacity he assured them they certainly would be. He, moreover, pledged his personal credit, and both the required wagons and several hundred horses were collected in a few days. With the food contractors in Virginia, too, there was infinite difficulty; the meat was rancid, the flour was short, while many of the horses were afterward stolen by the very men who had sold them. Whatever were Braddock's faults, and one of them no doubt was cursing both the country and the Government which sent him there, he at least spared neither himself nor his private purse, which last he drew upon freely, Orme tells us, in his struggle for ways and means…

The route followed to the Great Meadows was much the same as that used by Washington and his small force in the preceding year, but now a road twelve feet wide had to be opened over the rugged, tree-encumbered ground. Its course lay neither over veldt, nor plain, nor prairie, nor sandy desert, nor Russian steppe; but over two high ranges of mountains and several lesser ridges, clad in the gloom of mighty forests, littered with the wreckage of unnumbered years, riven this way and that by turbulent streams, and swarming hostile Indians…

On the 7th of July, after a month's march, the column arrived within a dozen miles of its destination, and its difficulties seemed almost over. Whatever reenforcements might have reached Fort Duquesne, the French and their allies could hardly be in great strength, or some sort of demonstration would surely have been made, particularly as the Indians had small liking for open spaces and artillery. "Men and officers," says Orme, "had now become so skilful in the woods that they were no longer in fear of an ambuscade." Nor did Brad-dock for that matter, as is often loosely stated, eventually run into one. The army was now within a few miles of the Monongahela, which rolled with broad and shallow current on the left, and in a northwesterly direction to its junction with the Alleghany. These two rivers unite to form the Ohio, and in the angle of their junction, on a site now buried amid the smoke and din of Pittsburgh, then stood the lonely fortress.

In this order the troops had proceeded the better part of a mile, and had reached a spot where the underbrush grew thicker than usual beneath the trees. The vanguard under Gage had just crossed a shallow ravine, when the scouts and horsemen came rapidly in, and at the same moment Gordon, the engineer who was marking out the road, caught sight of a man, drest as an Indian, but wearing the gorget of an officer, running toward him. The latter, as soon as he saw the English, pulled up short and waved his hat over his head, when the woods in front became of a sudden alive with warriors, and the Indian war-whoop ringing from nearly a thousand throats shook the arches of the forest with its novel and appalling clamor. Forms innumerable, some in white uniforms, some in blue, still more in the weird feathered headdress and garish pigments of the Indian, could be seen speeding to right and left among the trees. In a few moments a musketry fire, at first desultory but as each fresh enemy found cover quickening rapidly into a formidable fusillade, poured in upon Gage's men. For a short time many of the foe were visible, and the small British vanguard wheeled into line and delivered two or three volleys with steadiness and precision. But the enemy, with a far greater superiority of aim than the modern Boer has over the modern redcoat, and with a bright-colored exposed target such as was rarely offered to him in forest warfare, was already playing deadly havoc. The British bullets did little more than sliver the bark from trees and cut the saplings…

Braddock, when the firing grew hot enough to show that his vanguard was seriously engaged, prest rapidly up with the main column, leaving Sir Peter Halkett with 400 men, including most of the provincials, to guard the baggage. As the supports reached Gage's company, the latter seem even in so short a time to have received heavy punishment and fell back in some confusion on the new-comers, shaking their steadiness and mixing the men of the two regiments together. Never perhaps was a battle fought more difficult in one sense and in another more painfully simple to describe.

The doubtful moment with the Indians seems to have passed when the main body and the vanguard of the British melted into one. Henceforth it was an almost purely Indian fight and of a nature more astoundingly one-sided than had ever occurred in the annals of backwoods warfare. From right and left and front, and from an enemy that was practically invisible, a deadly fire that scarcely tested the well-known accuracy of the men behind the rifles, was poured for two hours into bewildered, huddling groups of redcoats. It was a butchery rather than a battle. Anglo-Saxon writers have followed one another in monotonous abuse of these two hapless battalions. The French victor, Dumas, is more generous when he tells us they re-mained to be shot at for two hours with obstinate firmness. Braddock was a helpless amateur at such work, and his men still more so. Hopelessly disorganized, they crowded together in groups firing wildly into the trees or into the air, or some-times even into their own comrades.

Braddock proved himself a very lion in combat, but his reckless courage was of no avail. His officers exposed their lives with splendid valor, but the sacrifice was useless. To fight enemies they could not see, and who mowed them down like corn, was something terribly novel to the routine British soldier of that day, brave and stanch tho he was amid more familiar dangers. In vain it was endeavored, by planting the regimental standards in the ground, to disentangle the medley. It was in vain that officer after officer gathered together small groups of men and led them into the teeth of the storm. They were picked off with deadly accuracy, and their followers, bereft of leadership, thrown back upon the slaughter pen…

British officers as well as colonials who were there have declared that no pen could describe the scene. One actor in it wrote that the dreadful clangor of the Indian war-whoop would ring in his ears till his dying day. One can imagine the pack-horses, stung to madness by bul-let-wounds and fright, stumbling about among the dead and wounded, adding their dying shrieks to the general uproar, and the cattle, smitten by the fire of both sides, rushing terror-stricken through the woods. At the tail of the column toward the ford and in rear of the baggage Halkett's 400 men, prest by the advanced points of the Indian flank fire, were faring somewhat better, tho Sir Peter himself was killed, and his son, while trying to raise him, fell dead by his side. Most of the hundred or so Virginia riflemen, about whose action in this fight a good deal of fable has gathered, were here. They did their duty, and fought gallantly behind trees according to backwoods custom. But the con-temporary plan of the battle shows the attack on the rear guard to have been far weaker than where the mass of the demoralized redcoats drew the bulk of the fire.

The pandemonium had lasted over two hours. Only the wagoners and axmen so far had fled. Washington, in the thick of the fight, had nobly seconded his chief's endeavors. He was still unhurt, though several bullets had passed through his clothes and two horses had been killed under him. Braddock, hoarse, hot, smoke-grimed, and stung with the bitterness of defeat, at last gave the signal for retreat. He was riding his fifth horse, and at this moment fell from it with a ball in his lungs.

Everything was abandoned to the enemy—wagons, guns, cattle, horses, baggage, and þ25,000 in specie, while scores of helpless wounded were left victims to the tomahawk and scalping-knife. The long strain once loosened, it became a race for life by every man who could drag his legs behind him. Regulars and provincials splashed in panic and in dire confusion through the ford they had crossed in such pomp but three hours before. Arms and accouterments were flung away in the terror with which men fled from those ghastly shambles. A few Indians followed the fugitives into the water, but none crossed it. There was nopursuit; with such a wealth of spoil and scalps on the battle-field, it would not have been Indian tactics.

Braddock, tho suffering from a mortal wound, made an effort with his surviving officers to gather some men together and make a stand beyond the first ford. It was useless, however, and they soon found themselves alone. Beyond the second ford another attempt was made with no more success. From here Washington, Braddock's only uninjured aide-de-camp, was sent forward to Dunbar's camp, over sixty miles away, to hurry on help and provisions for the wounded.

At the Great Meadows, a stage beyond, Braddock died. He was buried there beneath the forest leaves, Washington reading the funeral service over his grave, while wagons were rolled over the fresh mould lest his remains should be found and desecrated. Twenty years later, when the wilderness had given away to civilization, his bones, recognized by the articles buried with him, were accidentally unearthed by a farmer's spade, and found a strange and discreditable resting-place in a glass case at a local museum.

Braddock's Defeat

Title: Braddock's Defeat
Author: George Washington
Date: 1755
Source: America, Vol.3, p.51

In this letter to his mother, Mary, written at Fort Cumberland on July 18, 1755, after the battle in which the English Colonial forces under General Braddock were defeated and routed by the French and Indians, George Washington describes the historic action in which Braddock was mortally wounded. Everything was abandoned to the enemy—wagons, guns, cattle, horses, baggage and £25,000 in specie, while scores of helpless wounded were left victims of the tomahawk and scalping-knife.

Washington, then twenty-three years old, had accompanied Braddock into what is now western Pennsylvania as a volunteer aide-de-camp, and was the only staff officer who escaped uninjured. He read the funeral service over Braddock's grave in the wilderness, while wagons were rolled over the fresh mound lest the General's body be found and desecrated. It still rests there; and until recently no monument, only a clump of trees, marked the grave of this luckless British commander.

HONORED MADAM: As I doubt not but you have heard of our defeat, and, perhaps, had it represented in a worse light, if possible, than it deserves, I have taken this earliest opportunity to give you some account of the engagement as it happened, within ten miles of the French fort, on Wednesday the 9th instant.

We marched to that place, without any considerable loss, having only now and then a straggler picked up by the French and scouting Indians. When we came there, we were attacked by a party of French and Indians, whose number, I am persuaded, did not exceed three hundred men; while ours consisted of about one thousand three hundred well-armed troops, chiefly regular soldiers, who were struck with such a panic that they behaved with more cowardice than it is possible to conceive. The officers behaved gallantly, in order to encourage their men, for which they suffered greatly, there being near sixty killed and wounded; a large proportion of the number we had.

The Virginia troops showed a good deal of bravery, and were nearly all killed; for I believe, out of three companies that were there, scarcely thirty men are left alive. Captain Peyrouny, and all his officers down to a corporal, were killed. Captain Polson had nearly as hard a fate, for only one of his was left. In short, the dastardly behavior of those they call regulars exposed all others, that were inclined to do their duty, to almost certain death; and, at last, in despite of all the efforts of the officers to the contrary, they ran, as sheep pursued by dogs, and it was impossible to rally them.

The General was wounded, of which he died three days after. Sir Peter Halket was killed in the field, where died many other brave officers. I luckily escaped without a wound, though I had four bullets through my coat, and two horses shot under me. Captains Orme and Morris, two of the aids-de-camp, were wounded early in the engagement, which rendered the duty harder upon me, as I was the only person then left to distribute the General's orders, which I was scarcely able to do, as I was not half recovered from a violent illness, that had confined me to my bed and a wagon for above ten days. I am still in a weak and feeble condition, which induces me to halt here two or three days in the hope of recovering a little strength, to enable me to proceed homewards; from whence, I fear, I shall not be able to stir till toward September; so that I shall not have the pleasure of seeing you till then, unless it be in Fairfax… I am, honored Madam, your most dutiful son.

The Deportation of the Acadians of Nova Scotia

Title: The Deportation of the Acadians of Nova Scotia
Author: A. G. Bradley
Date: 1755
Source: Great Epochs in American History, Vol.3, pp.51-57

I have already spoken somewhat fully of the troubles with the Acadians, and made brief allusion to the crowning scene of their forcible removal, which ocurred this year. The unquenchable yearning of the French to recover their long-lost province was by no means lessened by their successes elsewhere. The strong fort of Beausejour, that they had erected on the neck of the isthmus, in doubtful territory, but commanding the most troubled part of the English dominion of Nova Scotia, became a busy scene of intrigue and action. Nearly 2,000 men, French regulars and insurgent or outlawed Acadians, besides large bands of Indians, were gathered either inside or within hail of it; while at the far end of the province the great naval and military post of Louisbourg boded mischief no less dangerous. The recent English settlement of Halifax, now the capital of the province, and a few isolated forts containing each their handful of men, represented all the power available for resisting a French attack, and protecting the scanty English settlers from the constant raiding of Acadians and Micmacs.

Nova Scotia, so far as military occupation went, was now wholly in British hands. But tho rid of pressing danger from French forts and soldiers, it remained a seething hotbed of misery, treachery, and disorder. Its security was of vital importance to the British at this most crucial moment. For similar reasons its recovery was no less an object with the French. The small handful of British regulars, with the raw and scant militia of the infant Halifax, would be ridiculously inadequate as a protecting force; while the two Massachusetts regiments, in accordance with custom and necessity, were only enlisted for a season. A small force of French invaders, in the present temper of the Acadians, could count on their almost unanimous assistance. Hitherto any of these latter people who had abandoned their farms could return and make their peace without difficulty. Those who had remained at home could at any time insure the continued favor of the British Government by taking an unqualified oath of allegiance to King George, who had treated them with unbroken indulgence, and under whose rule most of them had been actually born. Yet never had these strange people been more generally hostile than now, and at no time, thanks to magnified reports of French successes, had they been so insolent. It is not surprising that the patience of the British authorities at last gave out; and Lawrence, tho eminently a just man, was not quite so soft-hearted as some of his predecessors... A certain number of exiles had petitioned for reinstatement, and received it on taking the full oath, but the mass yet awaited the test. Time prest, and none was lost. Shirley amid his own troubles on the far-off Mohawk was as strong as Lawrence for an ultimatum. The latter, after submitting the matter to his Council at Halifax, communicated his intentions to Monckton, Winslow and the other British officers. In every district it was then proclaimed that an unqualified oath of allegiance would be required from every inhabitant who had not already taken it. The appeal was responded to by deputations from the several districts, all making objections to the terms of the oath, chief among these being the liability to bear arms. Others made stipulations that the priests should be free from all supervision. Lawrence went so far as to promise them that, for the present at any rate, they should not be liable to military service. It was in vain that firmly and kindly he reminded them of the consistent indulgence shown them by the King of England, and explained how impossible it was that he should tolerate such a grudging return. But it was neither the King of England, nor the King of France, nor any question of race or patriotism, that these infatuated people had in their minds, but the fear of eternal damnation, which the Bishop of Quebec, through his all too zealous missionaries, had struck deep into their unsophisticated souls, and the dread of Le Loutre's Micmac Indians.

"Then," at last said Lawrence, "you are no longer subjects of the King of England, but of the King of France. You will be treated as such, and removed from the country." At this they werestaggered, and most of them relenting, profest a willingness to take the oath. "No," said Lawrence; "you have had your opportunity and rejected it. Such an oath as you would now take, and such loyalty as mere fear extorts from you, is worthless. We shall now have regard solely to the king's inter-ests, and the consequences must rest on your own heads." I have here endeavored to condense what extended in fact over many interviews, much tedious going to and fro of deputations, and much consultation in the Acadian villages.

It was the middle of July when Lawrence and Winslow commenced that final step which made such a harrowing picture for the somewhat ill-instructed sympathies of half a dozen generations of Britons and Americans. The troops were divided into four or five bodies, and marched through the province to the chief centers of population, which were mostly on the western shore. The object in hand was kept a dead secret from all but the leading British officers. Winslow had command at Grandpre, and has kept a useful journal of the whole business. Sep-tember the 5th was the day decided upon for action, when the officer of each district was to summon all its able-bodied men to come and hear the intentions of the king toward them. Accustomed to regard the rare bark of the British Government as infinitely worse than its still rarer bite, they came in a large proportion of their strength, and without a thought of the trap that was being laid for them, to hear what sugges-tions that benign shadow, the King of England, had to make for their future.

The parish church in most cases was the appointed rendezvous, and there the king's orders were read aloud to them by the officer in com-mand. These were to the effect that all such Acadians as had not already taken the oath were to be shipt out of the country with their families; that their lands and stock, which at any time till now they could have saved by an oath of allegiance to a king "who had treated them with greater indulgence than any of his subjects in any part of his domin-ions," were forfeited to the Crown. Their money only, and such household goods as there might be room for in the ships, they were to be allowed to take.

The wretched Acadians were dumfounded at the nature of this announcement. Many refused to believe it. They were, however, prisoners, with only too much time before them for the terrible truth to sink into their minds. There was no escape, for outside the churches stood the New England soldiery, in their blue uniforms, with loaded muskets. The number of Acadians secured on this 5th of September varied in the several districts. Everywhere, however, it was supplemented by forays of the British troops, which became no easy matter when the direful news spread abroad. The transports for removing the emigrants were dilatory in their arrivals. Winslow and his brother officers chafed at the delay, for their small divided force was none too strong, and, moreover, as humane men, they heartily detested the job. No hint, however, comes down from any of them that, under the circumstances, there was any alternative, which is significant. There seems, indeed, to have been but one opinion as to its necessity. It is not for us to dwell here on the details of this mel-ancholy deportation. All the women and children who so desired could go, and every care was made to keep together not only families, but so far as possible neighbors. Many did not believe the sentence would be actually carried out till the first detachments were marched on board ship at the bayonet's point. The whole wretched business occupied over two months. About six thousand in all were deported, while more than half that number were left behind in Acadia, to say nothing of as many more who had fled into French territory. Some of these became practically outlaws, and harassed the British till the close of the war. But their sting was drawn: the province rapidly became in the main British by race as well as by territory, as hastened to this end by the fall of Louisbourg.

The hapless emigrants were distributed throughout the English colonies. That people so profoundly ignorant and bigoted as the Acadians did not flourish when pitchforked thus on to alien soil, is not surprizing. Nor is it more so by the same token that the British colonists upon whom they were unceremoniously precipitated, showed no alacrity to receive them. Their after wanderings, which were wide, and subsequent groupings, are of interest to the American ethnologist, but do not concern us here. It will be sufficient to say that, of all the communities upon whom they were cast, the uncompromising heretics of Massachusetts exhibited most practical charity, while it was the exiles who found their way to Quebec, to their coreligionists and their own countrymen, whose tools they had been, that fared the worst. It would be unprofitable to examine here to whatextent this radical operation was justifiable. The reader must pass his own judgment on it. It will be well, however, to remember that the year was not 1900, but 1755; that the perpetrators of it, colonists and British officials, were confronted with what proved one of the most pregnant struggles in modern history, and were ill equipped for it; that they had treated these people with a consistent indulgence that had then no parallel under such circumstances; that the lives and fortunes of 4,000 peaceful English settlers on the Halifax side of the province were in daily jeopardy; and lastly, that a considerable number of the exiles themselves had their hands red with the blood of Englishmen, not killed in fair fight, but murdered in Indian fashion while peacefully pursuing their daily avocations on British soil.

The Deportation of the Acadians

Title: The Deportation of the Acadians
Author: Colonel John Winslow
Date: 1755
Source: America, Vol.3, p.54

Acadia was originally a French colony which was acquired by the English under the Treaty of Utrecht, and renamed Nova Scotia. In order to destroy the French influence, which continued to predominate, the English Government in 1755 commissioned Colonel Winslow, a Massachusetts officer, to manage the deportation of some 6000 Acadians (probably about half of the total population of French descent) and scatter them among the English colonies to the south.

That Winslow, from whose journal, in the Nova Scotia Historical Society, this article is taken, found the task exceedingly disagreeable, indeed painful, is evidenced by his written statement that "The affair is more grievous to me than any service I was ever employed in." The question of the necessity of the removal and dispersion of the Acadians has been much disputed; the historian Parkman thinks it was inevitable. This dramatic event forms the theme of Longfellow's "Evangeline."

L AST evening [August 30, 1755] Captain Murray arrived and brought with him the afore resights commissions and instructions and letters and with whom I consulted methods for removing the whole inhabitants of the villages of Grand Pr,, Mines, Rivers Cannard, Habbertong and Gaspereau, and agreed that it would be most convenient to cite all the male inhabitants of said villages to assemble at the church in this place on the 5th of September next to hear the King's orders, and that at the same time Captain Murray to collect the inhabitants of Piziquid, and villages adjacent to Fort Edward for the same purpose, and wrote Colonel Lawrence this day our determination, and after Captain Murray's departure convened the Captains, viz: Adams, Hobbs and Osgood together and after taking an oath of secrecy from them, laid before them my instructions and papers and also of the proposed agreement made between Captain Murray and myself, of which they unanimously approved...

1755, August 31. Sunday. In the afternoon took a tour with Doctor Whitworth and Mr. Gay and 50 men two third parts round Grand Pr,. Find abundance of wheat &c on the ground. Returned in the evening...

September 2nd. Set out early in the morning in a whale boat for Fort Edward having with me Doctor Whitworth and adjutant Kennedy to consult with Captain Murray in this critical conjuncture. Confirmed our proposed plan and determined three of the clock in the afternoon to be the time. Made out a citation to the inhabitants to convene them, viz: those in my district at the church in Grand Pre, those of Captain Murray at Fort Edward at Piziquid. Got it put into French by Mr. Beauchamp, a merchant...

September 3rd. This morning Captain Adams and party returned from their march to the River Cannard &c and reported it was a fine country and full of inhabitants, a beautiful church and abundance of the goods of the world. Provisions of all kinds in great plenty...

This day had a consultation with the Captains, the result of which was that I should give out my citation to the inhabitants to-morrow morning...

1755, September the 4th. This morning sent for Doctor Rodion and delivered him a citation to the inhabitants with a strict charge to see it executed. Which he promised should be faithfully done.

A fine day and the inhabitants very busy about their harvest, &c.

September 5th. This morning had returns of the horns of the several companies and ordered such as had them to deliver up what cartridges they had to complete those who had no horns, which near about did it and then gave out to those who had horns powder at half a pound each to the amount of half a barrel and twelve balls to each half pound of powder. Ordered the whole camp to lie upon their arms this day.

At three in the afternoon the French inhabitants appeared agreeable to their citation at the church in Grand Pre amounting to 418 of their best men upon which I ordered a table to be set in the center of the church and being attended with those of my officers who were off guard delivered them by interpreters the King's orders in the following words:

Gentlemen,—I have received from his Excellency Governor Lawrence the King's commission which I have in my hand and by whose orders you are convened together to manifest to you his Majesty's final resolution to the French inhabitants of this his province of Nova Scotia. Who for almost half a century have had more indulgence granted them, than any of his subjects in any part of his dominions. What use you have made of them you yourself best know.

The part of duty I am now upon is what though necessary, is very disagreeable to my natural make and temper as I know it must be grievous to you who are of the same species.

But it is not my business to animadvert, but to obey such orders as I receive and therefore without hesitation shall deliver you his majesty's orders and instructions, viz:

That your lands and tenements, cattle of all kinds and live stock of all sorts are forfeited to the crown with all other your effects saving your money and household goods and you yourselves to be removed from this his province.

Thus it is peremptorily his Majesty's orders that the whole French inhabitants of these districts, be removed, and I am through his Majesty's goodness directed to allow you liberty to carry of your money and household goods as many as you can without discommoding the vessels you go in. I shall do everything in my power that all those goods be secured to you and that you are not molested in carrying them off and also that whole families shall go in the same vessel. And make this remove which I am sensible must give you a great deal of trouble as easy as his Majesty's service will admit and hope that in whatever part of the world you may fall you may be faithful subjects, a peaceable and happy people.

I must also inform you that it is his Majesty's pleasure that you remain in security under the inspection and direction of the troops that I have the honor to command. And then declared them the King's prisoners…

After delivering these things I returned to my quarters and they the French inhabitants soon moved by their elders that it was a great grief to them, that they had incurred his Majesty's displeasure and that they were fearful that the surprise of their detention here would quite overcome their families whom they had no means to apprise of these their melancholy circumstances and prayed that part of them might be returned as hostages for the appearance of the rest and the bigger number admitted to go home to their families, and that as some of their men were absent they would be obliged to bring them in. I informed them I would consider of their motion, and report.

And immediately convened my officers, to advise, who with me all agreed that it would be well that they themselves should choose twenty of their number for whom they would be answerable viz: ten of the inhabitants of Grand Pre and village and other ten of the river Cannard inhabitants and they to acquaint the families of their districts how matters were and to assure them that the women and children should be in safety in their absence in their habitations and that it was expected the party indulged should take care to bring in an exact account of their absent brethren and their circumstances on the morrow…

September 5th. The French people not having any provisions with them and pleading hunger begged for bread on which I gave them. And ordered that for the future they be supplied from their respective families. Thus ended the memorable fifth of September, a day of great fatigue and trouble…

1755, September 7. Proved a very busy day, advice arrived from every quarter which I answered as well as I could in the foregoing letters. The French remained in quiet. We mounted guard with half our party, Captain Adams and Osgood doing duty by turns. Captain Hobbs sick. We all lay on our arms since detaining the French here. Kept a good look out and I not wanting in turning out at all times when I awoke so that I was on both watches…

September 10. The French this morning discovered some uncommon motions among themselves which I did not like. Called my officers together and communicated to them what I had observed, and after debating matters it was determined, nemo contra dissente, that it would be best to divide the prisoners, and that as there were five transports idle which came from Boston, it would be for the good of his Majesty's service and that it tended to the better security of the whole, that fifty men of the French inhabitants be embarked on board each of the five vessels, taking first all their young men, and that Captain Adams in the

Warren be desired and directed as he was a vessel of force and in his Majesty's service to take the transports under his directions and when the prisoners were embarked to give such orders to the masters of the transports as would be best for his Majesty's service, and also determined that six non-commissioned officers or private men be put on board each transport as a guard and that Captain Adams and the masters be immediately ordered to get things in readiness for that service after which I sent for Father Landrey their principal speaker who talks English and told him the time was come for part of the inhabitants to embark and that the number concluded for this day was 250 and that we should begin with the young men and desired he would inform his brethren of it.

He was greatly surprised. I told him it must be done and that I should order the whole prisoners to be drawn up six deep, their young men on the left, and as the tide in a very little time favored, my design could not give them above an hour to prepare for going on board, and ordered our whole party to be under arms and post themselves between the two gates and the church in the rear of my quarters, which was obeyed, and agreeable to my directions. The whole of the French inhabitants were drawn together in one body, their young men as directed on the left. I then ordered Captain Adams with a Lieutenant 80 non-commissioned officers and private men to draw off from the main body to guard the young men of the French amounting to 141 men to the transports and order the prisoners to march. They all answered they would not go without their fathers. I told them that was a word I did not understand for that the King's command was to me absolute and should be absolutely obeyed and that I did not love to use harsh means but that time did not admit of parleys or delays and then ordered the whole troop to fix their bayonets and advance towards the French, and bid the 4 right-hand files of the prisoners, consisting of 24 men which I told off myself to divide from the rest, one of whom I took hold on (who opposed the marching) and bid march. He obeyed and the rest followed though slowly, and went off praying, singing and crying, being met by the women and children all the way (which is 1 1/2 mile) with great lamentations upon their knees praying &c.

I then ordered the remaining French to choose out 109 of their married men to follow their young people (the ice being broken) they readily complied and drew up in a body as said the number, who, upon Captain Adams' return, I ordered off under a guard commanded by Captain Osgood: one subaltern 80 noncommissioned officers and private men who marched them off, but when he came to put them on board the vessels found them but 89 instead of 109. So that the number embarked was but 230, and thus ended this troublesome job, which was a scene of sorrow. After this Captain Adams with the transports fell down from Gaspereau and anchored in the mouth of that river and Piziquid…

Wolfe Defeats Montcalm at Quebec

Title: Wolfe Defeats Montcalm at Quebec
Author: Captain John Knox
Date: 1759
Source: America, Vol.3, p.62

The victory of the Anglo-American forces under General James Wolfe and the capture of Quebec from the French under Montcalm, in 1759, was one of the most important events in modern history. John Fiske asserts that "it marks the greatest turning point yet discovered in modern history." This importance came from the fact that the battle decided for North America that its civilization should be English rather than French.

Captain Knox, from whose "journal" this account is taken, was an English naval officer who accompanied the expedition against the French in Canada and was an eye-witness of the events recorded.

The night before the battle General Wolfe read aloud to some of his officers Gray's "Elegy Written in a Country Churchyard," and announced in conclusion: "Gentlemen, I would rather have written those lines than to capture Quebec tomorrow."

GREAT preparations are making throughout the fleet and army to surprise the enemy, and compel them to decide the fate of Quebec by a battle. All the long-boats below the town are to be filled with seamen, marines, and such detachments as can be spared from Points Levi and Orleans, in order to make a feint off Beauport and the Point de Lest, and endeavor to engross the attention of the Sieur de Montcalm, while the army are to force a descent on this side of the town. The Officer of our regiment who commanded the escort yesterday on the reconnoitring party, being asked in the General's hearing, after the health of one of the gentlemen who was reported to be ill, replied "he was in a very low indifferent state, which the other lamented, saying, "He has but a puny, delicate constitution." This struck his Excellency, it being his own case, who interrupted, "Don't tell me of constitution; that officer has good spirits, and good spirits will carry a man through everything."

A soldier of the Royal Americans deserted this day [September 12, 1759] from the south shore, and one came over to us from the enemy, who informed the General "that he belonged to a detachment composed of two officers and fifty men who had been sent across the river to take a prisoner; that the French generals suspect we are going higher up to lay waste the country and destroy such ships and craft as they have got above; and that Monsieur Montcalm will not be prevailed on to quit his situation, insisting that the flower of our army are still below the town; that the reduction of Niagara has caused great discontent in the French army, that the wretched Canadians are much dissatisfied, and that Monsieur de Levis is certainly marched, with a detachment of the army, to Montreal, in order to reenforce Bourlemacque and stop General Amherst's progress." This fellow added "that, if we were fairly landed on the north side of the river, an incredible number of the French regulars would actually desert to us."...

Before daybreak this morning [September 13] we made a descent upon the north shore, about half a quarter of a mile to the eastward of Sillery; and the light troops were fortunately by the rapidity of the current carried lower down between us and Cape Diamond. We had in this debarkation thirty flat-bottomed boats, containing about sixteen hundred men. This was a great surprise on the enemy, who from the natural strength of the place did not suspect, and consequently were not prepared against so bold an attempt. The chain of sentries which they had posted along the summit of the heights galled us a little, and picked off several men and some officers before our light infantry got up to dislodge them. This grand enterprise was conducted and executed with great good order and discretion.

As fast as we landed, the boats put off for reenforcements, and the troops formed with much regularity. The General, with Brigadiers Monckton and Murray, was ashore with the first division. We lost no time here, but clambered up one of the steepest precipices that can be conceived, being almost a perpendicular, and of an incredible height. As soon as we gained the summit, all was quiet, and not a shot was heard, owing to the excellent conduct of the light infantry under Colonel Howe. It was by this time clear daylight. Here we formed again, the river and the south country in our rear, our right extending to the town, our left to Sillery, and halted a few minutes. The general then detached the light troops to our left to rout the enemy from their battery, and to disable their guns, except they could be rendered serviceable to the party who were to remain there; and this service was soon performed. We then faced to the right, and marched toward the town by files till

All material contained herein was extracted from the
US Constitution Coach Kit at PowerThink.com
(Over 60,000 Works & Documents of American History)

we came to the Plains of Abraham, an even piece of ground which General Wolfe had made choice of, while we stood forming upon the hill. Weather showery. About six o'clock the enemy first made their appearance upon the heights between us and the town, whereupon we halted and wheeled to the right, thereby forming the line of battle...

The enemy had now likewise formed the line of battle, and got some cannon to play on us, with round and canister shot; but what galled us most was a body of Indians and other marksmen they had concealed in the corn opposite to the front of our right wing, and a coppice that stood opposite to our center inclining toward our left. But Colonel Hale, by Brigadier Monckton's orders, advanced some platoons alternately from the forty-seventh regiment, which after a few rounds obliged these skulkers to retire. We were now ordered to lie down, and remained some time in this position. About eight o'clock we had two pieces of short brass six-pounders playing on the enemy, which threw them into some confusion, and obliged them to alter their disposition; and Montcalm formed them into three large columns. About nine the two armies moved a little nearer each other. The light cavalry made a faint attempt upon our parties at the battery of Sillery, but were soon beat off; and Monsieur de Bougainville, with his troops from Cape Rouge, came down to attack the flank of our second line, hoping to penetrate there. But, by a masterly disposition of Brigadier Townshend, they were forced to desist; and the third battalion of Royal Americans was then detached to the first ground we had formed on after we gained the heights, to preserve the communication with the beach and our boats.

About ten o'clock the enemy began to advance briskly in three columns, with loud shouts and recovered arms, two of them inclining to the left of our army, and the third toward our right, firing obliquely at the two extremities of our line, from the distance of one hundred and thirty, until they came within forty yards, which our troops withstood with the greatest intrepidity and firmness, still reserving their fire and paying the strictest obedience to their officers. This uncommon steadiness, together with the havoc which the grape-shot from our field-pieces made among them, threw them into some disorder, and was most critically maintained by a well-timed, regular, and heavy discharge of our small arms, such as they could no longer oppose. Hereupon they gave way, and fled with precipitation, so that by the time the cloud of smoke was vanished our men were again loaded, and, profiting by the advantage we had over them, pursued them almost to the gates of the town and the bridge over the little river, redoubling our fire with great eagerness, making many officers and men prisoners.

The weather cleared up, with a comfortably warm sunshine. The Highlanders chased them vigorously toward Charles River, and the fifty-eighth to the suburb close to John's gate, until they were checked by the cannon from the two ships. At the same time a gun which the town had brought to bear upon us with grape-shot galled the progress of the regiments to the right, who were likewise pursuing with equal ardor, while Colonel Hunt Walsh, by a very judicious movement, wheeled the battalions of Bragg and Kennedy to the left, and flanked the coppice where a body of the enemy made a stand as if willing to renew the action; but a few platoons from these corps completed our victory. Then it was that Brigadier Townshend came up, called off the pursuers, ordered the whole line to dress and recover their former ground.

Our joy at this success is inexpressibly damped by the loss we sustained of one of the greatest heroes which this or any other age can boast of,—General James Wolfe,—who received his mortal wound as he was exerting himself at the head of the grenadiers of Louisburg; and Brigadier Monckton was unfortunately wounded upon the left of the Forty-third and right of the Forty-seventh Regiment at much the same time, whereby the command devolved on Brigadier Townshend, who, with Brigadier Murray, went to the head of every regiment and returned thanks for their extraordinary good behavior, congratulating the officers on our success. There is one incident very remarkable, and which I can affirm from my own personal knowledge,—that the enemy were extremely apprehensive of being rigorously treated; for, conscious of their inhuman behavior to our troops upon a former occasion, the officers who fell into our hands most piteously (with hats off) sued for quarter, repeatedly declaring they were not at Fort William Henry (called by them Fort George) in the year 1757. A soldier of the Royal Americans who deserted from us this campaign, and fought against us to-day, was found wounded on the field of battle. He was immediately tried by a general court-martial, and was shot to death pursuant to his sentence.

While the two armies were engaged this morning, there was an incessant firing between the town and our south batteries. By the time our troops had taken a little refreshment, a quantity of intrenching tools were brought ashore, and the regiments were employed in redoubting our ground and landing some cannon and ammunition. The officers who are prisoners say that Quebec will surrender in a few days. Some

All material contained herein was extracted from the
US Constitution Coach Kit at PowerThink.com
(Over 60,000 Works & Documents of American History)

deserters who came out to us in the evening agree in that opinion, and inform us that the Sieur de Montcalm is dying, in great agony, of a wound he received to-day in their retreat.

Thus has our late renowned commander by his superior eminence in the art of war, and a most judicious coup d'etat, made a conquest of this fertile, healthy, and hitherto formidable country, with a handful of troops only, in spite of the political schemes and most vigorous efforts of the famous Montcalm, and many other officers of rank and experience at the head of an army considerably more numerous. My pen is too feeble to draw the character of this British Achilles; but the same may, with justice, be said of him as was said of Henry IV. of France: he was possessed of courage, humanity, clemency, generosity, affability, and politeness…

Last night Brigadier Townshend went with a detachment of two hundred men to the French general hospital, situated on the river Charles, and about a mile from the town. This is a convent of nuns of the Augustine Order, who—from principles of charity and piety—take care of all sick and wounded men and officers. Lands are appropriated for the support of this institution, besides which the French king endows it with a yearly salary; and a table is kept there at his expense for convalescent officers, directors, surgeons, apothecaries, etc. The Brigadier found an officer's guard at the convent, but he immediately took possession of the place by posting a captain's command there. The unfortunate Marquis de Montcalm was then in the house, dying of his wound, attended by the bishop and his chaplains. A transport, a schooner, and a parcel of boats, with ordnance and stores, passed the town last night. The enemy fired briskly on them, but without any effect. The garrison appear to be at work upon their ramparts, as if resolved to prolong the siege. Some deserters who came out to us this day inform us that Monsieur de Levis, who has rejoined and collected their shattered forces, had intended to surprise the rear of our camp at daybreak this morning, but upon reconnoitring our situation and finding we had made such excellent use of our time in erecting redoubts and other works, prudently declined the undertaking.

The Sieur de Montcalm died late last night. When his wound was dressed and he settled in bed, the surgeons who attended him were desired to acquaint him ingenuously with their sentiments of him; and, being answered that his wound was mortal, he calmly replied, "he was glad of it." His Excellency then demanded "whether he could survive it long, and how long." He was told, "About a dozen hours, perhaps more, peradventure less." "So much the better," rejoined the eminent warrior. "I am happy I shall not live to see the surrender of Quebec." He then ordered his secretary into the room to adjust his private affairs, which, as soon as they were dispatched, he was visited by Monsieur de Ramsey, the French King's lieutenant, and by other principal officers who desired to receive his Excellency's commands, with the farther measures to be pursued for the defense of Quebec, the capital of Canada. To this the Marquis made the following answer: "I'll neither give orders nor interfere any farther. I have much business that must be attended to, of greater moment than your ruined garrison and this wretched country. My time is very short, therefore pray leave me. I wish you all comfort, and to be happily extricated from your present perplexities." He then called for his chaplain, who, with the bishop of the colony, remained with him till he expired. Some time before this great man departed, we are assured he paid us this compliment: "Since it was my misfortune to be discomfited, and mortally wounded, it is a great consolation to me to be vanquished by so brave and generous an enemy. If I could survive this wound, I would engage to beat three times the number of such forces as I commanded this morning with a third of their number of British troops."...

After our late worthy General of renowned memory was carried off wounded to the rear of the front line, he desired those who were about him to lay him down. Being asked if he would have a surgeon, he replied, "It is needless: it is all over with me." One of them then cried out, "They run, see how they run!" "Who runs?" demanded our hero with great earnestness, like a person roused from sleep. The officers answered: "The enemy, sir. Egad, they give way everywhere." Thereupon the General rejoined: "Go, one of you, my lads, to Colonel Burton—; tell him to march Webb's regiment with all speed down to Charles River, to cut off the retreat of the fugitives from the bridge." Then, turning on his side, he added, "Now, God be praised, I will die in peace!" and thus expired.

In Opposition to Writs of Assistance

Title: In Opposition to Writs of Assistance
Author: James Otis
Date: 1761
Source: The World's Famous Orations, Vol.8, pp.27-36

Delivered before the Superior Court in Boston in February, 1761, and the earliest important word publicly uttered in the controversies which precipitated the Revolution. John Adams declared that in this oration "American independence was born." Abridged.

Born in 1725, died in 1783; a Law Officer under the Crown; Member of the Massachusetts House of Representatives; Delegate to the Stamp Act Congress in 1765; wrote a pamphlet entitled, "Rights of the British Colonies Asserted," in 1764, and others that attracted wide attention in England as well as here; owing to illness, not active during the war; killed by lightning in 1783.

MAY it please your honors, I was desired by one of the court to look into the books, and consider the question now before them concerning writs of assistance. I have, accordingly, considered it, and now appear not only in obedience to your order, but likewise in behalf of the inhabitants of this town, who have presented another petition, and out of regard to the liberties of the subject. And I take this opportunity to declare that, whether under a fee or not (for in such a cause as this I despise a fee), I will to my dying day oppose with all the powers and faculties God has given me all such instruments of slavery on the one hand, and villainy on the other, as this writ of assistance is.

It appears to me the worst instrument of arbitrary power, the most destructive of English liberty and the fundamental principles of law, that ever was found in an English law book. I must, therefore, beg your honors' patience and attention to the whole range of argument that may, perhaps, appear uncommon in many things, as well as to points of learning that are more remote and unusual; that the whole tendency of my design may the more easily be perceived, the conclusions better descend, and the force of them be better felt.

I shall not think much of my pains in this cause, as I engaged in it from principle. I was solicited to argue this cause as advocate-general; and because I would not, I have been charged with desertion from my office. To this charge I can give a very sufficient answer. I renounced that office, and I argue this cause from the same principle; and I argue it with the greater pleasure, as it is in favor of British liberty, at a time when we hear the greatest monarch upon earth declaring from his throne that he glories in the name of Briton, and that the privileges of his people are dearer to him than the most valuable prerogatives of his crown; and as it is in opposition to a kind of power, the exercise of which, in former periods of history, cost one king of England his head and another his throne. I have taken more pains in this cause than I ever will take again, altho my engaging in this and another popular cause has raised much resentment. But I think I can sincerely declare that I cheerfully submit myself to every odious name for conscience' sake; and from my soul I despise all those whose guilt, malice, or folly has made them my foes. Let the consequences by what they will, I am determined to proceed. The only principles of public conduct that are worthy of a gentleman or a man are to sacrifice estate, ease, health, and applause, and even life, to the sacred calls of his country.

These manly sentiments, in private life, make the good citizen; in public life, the patriot and the hero. I do not say that when brought to the test, I shall be invincible. I pray God I may never be brought to the melancholy trial; but if ever I should, it will be then known how far I can reduce to practise principles which I know to be founded in truth. In the meantime I will proceed to the subject of this writ.

Your honors will find in the old books concerning the office of a justice of the peace precedents of general warrants to search suspected houses. But in more modern books, you will find only special warrants to search such and such houses, specially named, in which the complainant has before sworn that he suspects his goods are concealed; and will find it adjudged that special warrants only are legal. In the same manner I rely on it, that the writ prayed for in this petition, being general, is illegal. It is a power that places the liberty of every man in the hands of every petty officer. I say I admit that special writs of assistance, to search special places, may be granted to certain persons on oath; but I deny that the writ now prayed for can be granted, for I beg leave to make some observations on the writ itself, before I proceed to other Acts of Parliament.

In the first place, the writ is universal, being directed "to all and singular justices, sheriffs, so that, in short, it is directed to every subject writ may be a tyrant; if this commission be legal, a tyrant in a legal manner, also, may control, imprison, or murder any one within the realm.

In the next place, it is perpetual; there is no return. A man is accountable to no person for his doings. Every man may reign secure in his petty tyranny, and spread terror and desolation around him, until the trump of the archangel shall excite different emotions in his soul.

In the third place, a person with this writ, in the daytime, may enter all houses, shops, etc., at will, and command all to assist him.

Fourthly, by this writ, not only deputies, etc., but even their menial servants, are allowed to lord it over us. What is this but to have the curse of Canaan with a witness on us; to be the servant of servants, the most despicable of God's creation?

Now one of the most essential branches of English liberty is the freedom of one's house. A man's house is his castle; and while he is quiet, he is as well guarded as a prince in his castle. This writ, if it should be declared legal, would totally annihilate this privilege. Custom-house officers may enter our houses when they please; we are commanded to permit their entry. Their menial servants may enter, may break locks, bars, and everything in their way; and whether they break through malice or revenge, no man, no court can inquire. Bare suspicion without oath is sufficient. This wanton exercise of this power is not a chimerical suggestion of a heated brain.

I will mention some facts. Mr. Pew had one of these writs, and when Mr. Ware succeeded him, he indorsed this writ over to Mr. Ware; so that these writs are negotiable from one officer to another, and so your honors have no opportunity of judging the persons to whom this vast power is delegated. Another instance is this: Mr. Justice Walley had called this same Mr. Ware before him, by a constable, to answer for a breach of the Sabbath Day Acts, or that of profane swearing. As soon as he had finished, Mr. Ware asked him if he had done. He replied: "Yes." "Well, then," said Mr. Ware, "I will show you a little of my power. I command you to permit me to search your house for uncustomed goods"; and went on to search the house from the garret to the cellar, and then served the constable in the same manner! But to show another absurdity in this writ, if it should be established, I insist upon it that every person, by the 14th of Charles II., has this power as well as the custom-house officers. The words are: "It shall be lawful for any person or persons authorized," etc. What a scene does this open! Every man prompted by revenge, ill humor, or wantonness, to inspect the inside of his neighbor's house, may get a writ of assistance. Others will ask it from self-defense; one arbitrary exertion will provoke another, until society be involved in tumult and in blood.

2. "He asserted that every man, merely natural, was an independent sovereign, subject to no law but the law written on his heart and revealed to him by his Maker, in the constitution of his nature, and the inspiration of his understanding and his conscience. His right to his life, his liberty, no created being could rightfully contest. Nor was his right to his property less incontestible. The club that he had snapped from a tree, for a staff or for defense, was his own. His bow and arrow were his own; if by a pebble he had killed a partridge or a squirrel, it was his own. No creature, man or beats, had a right to take it from him. If he had taken an eel, or a smelt, or a sculpin, it was his property. In short, he sported upon this topic with so much wit and humor, and at the same time with so much indisputable truth and reason, that he was not less entertaining than instructive. He asserted that these rights were inherent and inalienable; that they never could be surrendered or alienated, but by idiots or madmen, and all the acts of idiots and lunatics were void, and not obligatory, by all the laws of God and man. Nor were the poor negroes forgotten. Not a Quaker in Philadelphia, or Mr. Jefferson in Virginia, ever asserted the rights of negroes in stronger terms. Young as I was, and ignorant as I was, I shuddered at the doctrine he taught; and I have all my life shuddered, and still shudder, at the consequences that may be drawn from such premises. Shall we say that the rights of masters and servants clash, and can be decided only by force? I adore the idea of gradual abolitions! but who shall decide how fast or how slowly these abolitions shall be made?

3. "From individual independence he proceeded to association. If it was inconsistent with the dignity of human nature to say that men were gregarious animals, like wild geese, it surely could offend no delicacy to say they were social animals by nature; that there were natural sympathies, and, above all, the sweet attraction of the sexes, which must soon draw them together in little groups, and by degrees in larger congregations, for mutual assistance and defense. And this must have happened before any formal covenant, by express words or signs, was concluded. When general councils and deliberations commenced, the objects could be no other than the mutual defense and security of every individual for his life, his liberty, and his property. To suppose them to have surrendered these in any other way than by equal rules and general consent was to suppose them idiots or madmen, whose acts were never binding. To suppose them surprised by fraud, or compelled by force into any other compact, such fraud and such force could confer no obligation. Every man had a right to trample it under foot whenever he derived only from nature and the Author of nature; that they were in-

herent, inalienable, and indefeasible by any laws, pacts, contracts, covenants, or stipulations which man could devise.

4. "These principles and these rights were wrought into the English Constitution as fundamental laws. And under this head he went back to the old Saxon laws, and to Magna Charta, and the fifty confirmations of it in Parliament, and the executions ordained against the violators of it, and the national vengeance which had been taken on them from time to time, down to the Jameses and Charleses, and to the Petition of Right and the Bill of Rights and the Revolution. He asserted that the security of these rights to life, liberty, and property had been the object of all those struggles against arbitrary power, temporal and spiritual, civil and political, military and ecclesiastical, in every age. He asserted that our ancestors, as British subjects, and we, their descendants, as British subjects, were entitled to all those rights, by the British Constitution, as well as by the law of nature and our provincial charter, as much as any inhabitant of London or Bristol, or any part of England; and were not to be cheated out of them by any phantom of 'virtual representation,' or any other fiction of law or politics, or any monkish trick of deceit and hypocrisy.

5. "He then examined the Acts of Trade, one by one, and demonstrated that if they were considered as revenue laws, they destroyed all our security of property, liberty, and life, every right of nature, and the English Constitution, and the charter of the province. Here he considered the distinction between 'external and internal taxes,' at that time a popular and commonplace distinction. But he asserted that there was no such distinction in theory, or upon any principle but 'necessity.' The necessity that the commerce of the Empire should be under one direction was obvious. The Americans had been so sensible of this necessity that they had connived at the distinction between external and internal taxes, and had submitted to the Acts of Trade as regulations of commerce, but never as taxations or revenue laws. Nor had the British government till now ever dared to attempt to enforce them as taxations or revenue laws. They had lain dormant in that character for a century almost. The Navigation Act he allowed to be binding upon us, because we had consented to it by our own legislature. Here he gave a history of the Navigation Act of the 1st of Charles II., a plagiarism from Oliver Cromwell. This act had lain dormant for fifteen years. In 1675, after repeated letters and orders from the king, Governor Leverett very candidly informs his majesty that the law had not been executed, because it was thought unconstitutional, Parliament not having authority over us."

The Stamp Act and its Repeal

Title: The Stamp Act and its Repeal
Author: William E. H. Lechy
Date: 1765
Source: Great Epochs in American History, Vol.3, pp.66-77

The Stamp Act, when its ultimate consequences are considered, must be deemed one of the most momentous legislative Acts in the history of mankind; but in England it passed almost completely unnoticed. The Wilkes excitement absorbed public attention, and no English politician appears to have realized the importance of the measure. It is scarcely mentioned in the contemporary correspondence of Horace Walpole, of Grenville, or of Pitt. Burke, who was not yet a member of the House of Commons, afterward declared that he had followed the debate from the gallery, and that he had never heard a more languid one in the House; that not more than two or three gentlemen spoke against the bill; that there was but one division in the whole course of the discussion, and that the minority in that division was not more than thirty-nine or forty. In the House of Lords he could not remember that there had been either a debate or division, and he was certain that there was no protest...

In truth, the measure, altho it was by no means as unjust or as unreasonable as has been alleged, and altho it might perhaps in some periods of colonial history have passed almost unperceived, did unquestionably infringe upon a principle which the English race both at home and abroad have always regarded with a peculiar jealousy. The doctrine that taxation and representation are in free nations inseparably connected, that constitutional government is closely connected with the rights of property, and that no people can be legitimately taxed except by themselves or their representatives, lay at the very root of the English conception of political liberty. The same principle that had led the English people to provide so carefully in the Great Charter, in a well-known statute of Edward I, and in the Bill of Rights, that no taxation should be drawn from them except by the English Parliament; the same principle which had gradually invested the representative branch of the Legislature with the special and peculiar function of granting supplies, led the colonists to maintain that their liberty would be destroyed if they were taxed by a Legislature in which they had no representatives, and which sat 3,000 miles from their shore.

It was a principle which had been respected by Henry VIII and Elizabeth in the most arbitrary moments of their reigns, and its violation by Charles I was one of the chief causes of the rebellion. The principle which led Hampden to refuse to pay 20s. of ship money was substantially the same as that which inspired the resistance to the Stamp Act...

It is quite true that this theory, like that of the social contract, which has also borne a great part in the history of political liberty, will not bear a severe and philosophical examination. The opponents of the American claims were able to reply, with undoubted truth, that at least nine-tenths of the English people had no votes; that the great manufacturing towns, which contributed so largely to the public burdens, were for the most part wholly unrepresented; that the minority in Parliament voted only in order to be systematically overruled; and that, in a country where the constituencies were as unequal as in England, that minority often represented the large majority of the voters...

It was a first principle of the Constitution that a member of Parliament was the representative not merely of his own constituency, but also of the whole Empire. Men connected with, or at least specially interested in the colonies, always found their way into Parliament; and the very fact that the colonial arguments were maintained with transcendent power within its walls was sufficient to show that the colonies were virtually represented.

A Parliament elected by a considerable part of the English people, drawn from the English people, sitting in the midst of them, and exposed to their social and intellectual influence, was assumed to represent the whole nation, and the decision of its majority was assumed to be the decision of the whole. If it be asked how these assumptions could be defended, it can only be answered that they had rendered possible a form of government which had arrested the incursions of the royal prerogative, had given England a longer period and a larger measure of self-government than was enjoyed by any other great European nation, and had created a public spirit sufficiently powerful to defend the liberties that had been won.

Such arguments, however worthless they might appear to a lawyer or a theorist, ought to be very sufficient to a statesman. Manchester and Sheffield had no more direct representation in Parliament than Boston or Philadelphia; but the relations of unrepresented Englishmen and of colonists to the English Parliament were very different. Parliament could never long neglect the fierce beatings of the waves of popular discontent around its walls. It might long continue perfectly indifferent to the wishes of a population 3,000 miles from the English shore. When parliament taxed the English people, the taxing body itself felt the weight of the burden it imposed; but Parliament felt no part of the weight of colonial taxation, and had therefore a direct interest in increasing it...

The Stamp Act received the royal assent on March 22, 1765, and it was to come into operation on the first of November following. The long delay, which had been granted in the hope that it might lead to some proposal of compromise from America, had been sedulously employed by skilful agitators in stimulating the excitement; and when the news arrived that the Stamp Act had been carried, the train was fully laid, and the indignation of the colonies rose at once into a flame.

A congress of representatives of nine States was held at New York, and in an extremely able State paper they drew up the case of the colonies. They acknowledged that they owed allegiance to the Crown, and "all due subordination to that august body, the Parliament of Great Britain"; but they maintained that they were entitled to all the inherent rights and liberties of natural-born subjects; "that it is inseparably essential to the freedom of a people, and the undoubted right of Englishmen, that no taxes be imposed on them but with their own consent, given personally or by their representatives"; that the colonists "are not, and from their local circumstances cannot be, represented in the House of Commons of Great Britain"; that the only representatives of the colonies, and therefore the only persons constitutionally competent to tax them were the members chosen in the colonies by themselves; and "that all supplies of the Crown being free gifts from the people, it is unreasonable and inconsistent with the principles and spirit of the British Constitution for the people of Great Britain to grant to his Majesty the property of the colonies." A petition to the King and memorials to both Houses of Parliament were drawn up embodying these views.

It was not, however, only by such legal measures that the opposition was shown. A furious outburst of popular violence speedily showed that it would be impossible to enforce the Act. In Boston, Oliver, the secretary of the province, who had accepted the office of stamp distributer, was hung in effigy on a tree in the main street of the town. The building which had been erected as a stamp office was leveled with the dust; the house of Oliver was attacked, plundered, and wrecked, and he was compelled by the mob to resign his office and to swear beneath the tree on which his effigy had been so ignominiously hung, that he never would resume it. A few nights later the riots recommenced with redoubled fury. The houses of two of the leading officials connected with the Admiralty Court and with the Custom-house were attacked and rifled, and the files and records of the Admiralty Court were burned. The mob, intoxicated with the liquors which they had found in one of the cellars they had plundered, next turned to the house of Hutchinson, the Lieutenant-Governor and Chief Justice of the province. Hutchinson was not only the second person in rank in the colony, he was a man who had personal claims of the highest kind upon his countrymen…

Altho Hutchinson was opposed to the policy of the Stamp Act, the determination with which he acted as Chief Justice in supporting the law soon made him obnoxious to the mob. He had barely time to escape with his family, when his house, which was the finest in Boston, was attacked and destroyed. His plate, his furniture, his pictures, the public documents in his possession, and a noble library which he had spent thirty years in collecting, were plundered and burned.

The flame rapidly spread. In the newly annexed provinces, indeed, and in most of West India islands, the Act was received without difficulty, but in nearly every American colony those who had consented to be stamp distributers were hung and burned in effigy, and compelled by mob violence to resign their posts. The houses of many who were known to be supporters of the Act or sympathizers with the government were attacked and plundered. Some were compelled to fly from the colonies, and the authority of the Home Government was exposed to every kind of insult. In New York the effigy of the Governor was paraded with that of the devil round the town and then publicly burned, and threatening letters were circulated menacing the lives of those who distributed stamps…

When the 1st of November arrived, the bells were tolled as for the funeral of a nation. The flags were hung half-mast high. The shops were shut, and the Stamp Act was hawked about with the inscription, "The folly of England and the ruin of America." The newspapers were obliged by the new law to bear the stamp, which probably contributed much to the extreme virulence of their opposition, and many of them now appeared with a death's head in the place where the stamp, which probably contributed much to the extreme virulence of their opposition, and many of them now appeared with a death's head in the place where the stamp should have been. It was found not only impossible to distribute stamps, but even impossible to keep them in the colonies, for the mob seized on every box which was brought from England and committed it to the flames. Stamps were required for the validity of every legal document, yet in most of the colonies not a single sheet of stamped paper could be found. The law courts were for a time closed, and almost all business was suspended. At last the governors, considering the impossibility of carrying on public business or protecting prop-erty under these conditions, took the law into their own hands, and issued letters authorizing noncompliance with the Act on the ground that it was absolutely impossible to procure the requisite stamps in the colony...

Parliament met on December 17, 1765, and the attitude of the different parties was speedily disclosed. A powerful opposition, led by Grenville and Bedford, strenuously urged that no relaxation or indulgence should be granted to the colonists. In two successive sessions the policy of taxing America had been deliberately affirmed, and if Parliament now suffered itself to be defied or intimidated its authority would be forever at an end. The method of reasoning by which the Americans maintained that they could not be taxed by a Parliament in which they were not represented, might be applied with equal plausibility to the Navigation Act and to every other branch of imperial legislation for the colonies, and it led directly to the disintegration of the Empire. The supreme authority of Parliament chiefly held the different parts of that Empire together. The right of taxation was an essential part of the sovereign power. The colonial constitutions were created by royal charter, and it could not be admitted that the King, while retaining his own sovereignty over certain portions of his dominions, could be a mere exercise of his prerogative withdraw them wholly or in part from the authority of the British Parliament.

It was the right and the duty of the Imperial Legislature to determine in what proportions the different parts of the Empire should contribute to the defense of the whole, and to see that noone part evaded its obligations and unjustly transferred its share to the others. The conduct of the colonies, in the eyes of these politicians, admitted of no excuse or palliation. The disputed right of taxation was established by a long series of legal authorities, and there was no real distinction between internal and external taxation. It now suited the Americans to describe themselves as apostles of liberty, and to denounce England as an oppressor. It was a simple truth that England governed her colonies more liberally than any other country in the world. They were the only existing colonies which enjoyed real political liberty. Their commercial system was more liberal than that of any other colonies. They had attained, under British rule, to a degree of prosperity which was surpassed in no quarter of the globe. England had loaded herself with debt in order to remove the one great danger to their future; she cheerfully bore the whole burden of their protection by sea. At the Peace of Paris she had made their interests the very first object of her policy, and she only asked them in return to bear a portion of the cost of their own defense.

Somewhat more than eight millions of Englishmen were burdened with a national debt of þ140,000,000. The united debt of about two millions of Americans was now less than þ800,000. The annual sum the colonists were asked to contribute in the form of stamp duties was less than þ100,000, with an express provision that no part of that sum should be devoted to any other purpose than the defense and protection of the colonies. And the country which refused to bear this small tax was so rich that in the space of three years it had paid off þ1,755,000 of its debt. No demand could be more moderate and equitable than that of England; and amid all the high-sounding declarations that were wafted across the Atlantic, it was not difficult to perceive that the true motive of the resistance was of the vulgarest kind. It was a desire to pay as little as possible; to throw as much as possible upon the mother country.

Nor was the mode of resistance more respectable—the plunder of private houses and custom-houses; mob violence connived at by all classes and perfectly unpunished; agreements of merchants to refuse to pay their private debts in order to attain political ends. If this was the attitude of America within two years of the Peace of Paris, if these were the first fruits of the new sense of security which British triumphs in Canada had given, could it be doubted that concessions would only be the prelude to new demands? Already the Custom-house officers were attacked by the mobs almost as fiercely as the stamp distributers...

These were the chief arguments on the side of the late ministers. Pitt, on the other hand, rose from his sick-bed, and in speeches of extraordinary eloquence, which produced an amazing effect on both sides of the Atlantic, he justified the resistance of the colonists. He stood apart from all parties, and, while he declared that "every capital measure" of the late ministry was wrong, he ostentatiously refused to give his confidence to their successors. He maintained in the strongest terms the doctrine that self-taxation is the essential and discriminating circumstance of political freedom.

The task of the ministers in dealing with this question was extremely difficult. The great ma-jority of them desired ardently the repeal of the Stamp Act; but the wishes of the King, the abstention of

Pitt, and the divided condition of parties had compelled Rockingham to include in his Government Charles Townshend, Barrington, and Northington, who were all strong advocates of the taxation of America, and Northington took an early opportunity of delivering an invective against the colonies which seemed specially intended to prolong the exasperation…

The Stamp Act had already produced evils far outweighing any benefits that could flow from it. To enforce it over a vast and thinly populated country, and in the face of the universal and vehement opposition of the people, had proved hitherto impossible, and would always be difficult, dangerous, and disastrous. It might produce rebellion. It would certainly produce permanent and general disaffection, great derangement of commercial relations, a smothered resistance which could only be overcome by a costly and extensive system of coercion. It could not be wise to convert the Americans into a nation of rebels who were only waiting for a European war to throw off their allegiance. Yet this would be the natural and almost inevitable consequence of persisting in the policy of Grenville…

The debates on this theme were among the fiercest and longest ever known in Parliament. The former ministers opposed the repeal at every stage, and most of those who were under the direct influence of the King plotted busily against it. Nearly a dozen members of the King's household, nearly all the bishops, nearly all the Scotch, nearly all the Tories voted against the ministry, and inthe very agony of the contest Lord Strange spread abroad the report that he had heard from the King's own lips that the King was opposed to the repeal. Rockingham acted with great decision. He insisted on accompanying Lord Strange into the King's presence, and in obtaining from the King a written paper stating that he was in favor of the repeal rather than the enforcement of the Act, tho he would have preferred its modification to either course. The great and manifest desire of the commercial classes throughout England had much weight; the repeal was carried through the House of Commons, brought up by no less than 200 members to the Lords, and finally carried amid the strongest expressions of public joy. Burke described it as "an event that caused more universal joy throughout the British dominions than perhaps any other that can be remembered."

Pitt's Protest Against the Stamp Act

Title: Pitt's Protest Against the Stamp Act
Author: William Pitt
Date: 1765
Source: America, Vol.3, p.77

This address, one of the last made by William Pitt in the House of Commons before he was raised to the peerage, echoed the strong opposition of many Englishmen to taxing the American colonies oppressively, and shows how far the whole question involved the relative rights of the Crown and Parliament in England. Pitt was nothing if not patriotic; indeed, it was his intense love of country that inspired his condemnation of the Stamp Act, in which he foresaw disaster to Britain.

When France came to the aid of the colonies, causing such alarm in England as to raise a popular outcry against continuing the war, Pitt, then Earl of Chatham, in a powerful address in the House of Lords protested against the disruption of the Empire and the implied subjugation of Britain by France. It was his last effort; at its conclusion he sank to the floor exhausted, and died a few days later.

GENTLEMEN, Sir (to the Speaker), I have been charged with giving birth to sedition in America. They have spoken their sentiments with freedom against this unhappy act, and that freedom has become their crime. Sorry I am to hear the liberty of speech in this House imputed as a crime. But the imputation shall not discourage me. It is a liberty I mean to exercise. No gentleman ought to be afraid to exercise it. It is a liberty by which the gentleman who calumniates it might have profited. He ought to have desisted from his project. The gentleman tells us, America is obstinate; America is almost in open rebellion. I rejoice that America has resisted. Three millions of people so dead to all the feelings of liberty, as voluntarily to submit to be slaves, would have been fit instruments to make slaves of the rest. I come not here armed at all points, with law cases and acts of Parliament, with the statute-book doubled down in dog's ears, to defend the cause of liberty: if I had, I myself would have cited the two cases of Chester and Durham. I would have cited them, to have shown that, even under former arbitrary reigns, Parliaments were ashamed of taxing a people without their consent, and allowed them representatives... The gentleman tells us of many who are taxed, and are not represented.—The India Company, merchants, stockholders, manufacturers. Surely many of these are represented in other capacities, as owners of land, or as freemen of boroughs. It is a misfortune that more are not equally represented. But they are all inhabitants, and as such, are they not virtually represented? Many have it in their option to be actually represented. They have connections with those that elect, and they have influence over them...

The gentleman boasts of his bounties to America! Are not these bounties intended finally for the benefit of this kingdom? If they are not, he has misapplied the national treasures. I am no courtier of America—I stand up for this kingdom. I maintain, that the Parliament has a right to bind, to restrain America. Our legislative power over the colonies is sovereign and supreme. When it ceases to be sovereign and supreme, I would advise every gentleman to sell his lands, if he can, and embark for that country. When two countries are connected together, like England and her colonies, without being incorporated, the one must necessarily govern; the greater must rule the less; but so rule it, as not to contradict the fundamental principles that are common to both.

If the gentleman does not understand the difference between external and internal taxes, I cannot help it; but there is a plain distinction between taxes levied for the purposes of raising a revenue, and duties imposed for the regulation of trade, for the accommodation of the subject; although, in the consequences, some revenue might incidentally arise from the latter.

The gentleman asks, when were the colonies emancipated? But I desire to know, when they were made slaves? But I dwell not upon words. When I had the honor of serving his Majesty, I availed myself of the means of information, which I derived from my office: I speak, therefore, from knowledge. My materials were good, I was at pains to collect, to digest, to consider them; and I will be bold to affirm, that the profits to Great Britain from the trade of the colonies, through all its branches, is two millions a year. This is the fund that carried you triumphantly through the last war. The estates that were rented at two thousand pounds a year, threescore years ago, are at three thousand pounds at present. Those estates sold then from fifteen to eighteen years purchase; the same may now be sold for thirty. You owe this to America. This is the price America pays for her protection. And shall a miserable financier come with a boast, that he can bring a pepper-corn into the exchequer, to the loss of millions to the nation! I dare not say, how much higher these profits may be augmented. Omitting the immense increase of people by natural population, in the northern colonies, and the emigration from every part of Europe, I am convinced the commercial system of America may be altered to advantage. You have prohibited where you ought to have encouraged, and encouraged where you ought to have prohibited...

A great deal has been said without doors, of the power, of the strength of America. It is a topic that ought to be cautiously meddled with. In a good cause, on a sound bottom, the force of this country can crush America to atoms. I know the valor of your troops. I know the skill of your officers. There is not a company of foot that has served in America, out of which you may not pick a man of sufficient knowledge and experience to make a governor of a colony there. But on this ground, on the Stamp Act, when so many here will think it a crying injustice, I am one who will lift up my hands against it.

In such a cause, your success would be hazardous. America, if she fell, would fall like the strong man. She would embrace the pillars of the state, and pull down the constitution along with her. Is this your boasted peace? Not to sheath the sword in its scabbard, but to sheath it in the bowels of your countrymen? Will you quarrel with yourselves, now the whole House of Bourbon is united against you? . . The Americans have not acted in all things with prudence and temper. The Americans have been wronged. They have been driven to madness by injustice. Will you punish them for the madness you have occasioned? Rather let prudence and temper come first from this side. I will undertake for America, that she will follow the example. There are two lines in a ballad of Prior's, of a man's behavior to his wife, so applicable to you, and your colonies, that I cannot help repeating them:

Be to her faults a little blind:
Be to her virtues very kind.

Upon the whole, I will beg leave to tell the House what is really my opinion. It is, that the Stamp Act be repealed absolutely, totally, and immediately. That the reason for the repeal be assigned, because it was founded on an erroneous principle. At the same time, let the sovereign authority of this country over the colonies be asserted in as strong terms as can be devised, and be made to extend to every point of legislation whatsoever. That we may bind their trade, confine their manufactures, and exercise every power whatsoever, except that of taking their money out of their pockets without their consent.

Declaration of Rights

Title: Declaration of Rights
Author: Delegates from Nine Colonies
Date: 1765
Source: Harvard Classics, Vol.43, p.157

On the passage of the Stamp Act by the British Parliament in March, 1765, requiring that all legal instruments used in the American colonies should bear a government stamp in order to be valid, delegates from nine colonies met in New York on October 7 of the same year, to protest against this and other encroachments upon their rights, and drew up this Declaration. The Stamp Act was repealed in March, 1766.

THE members of this congress, sincerely devoted, with the warmest sentiments of affection and duty to his majesty's person and government, inviolably attached to the present happy establishment of the protestant succession, and with minds deeply impressed by a sense of the present and impending misfortunes of the British colonies on this continent; having considered as maturely as time will permit, the circumstances of the said colonies, esteem it our indispensable duty to make the following declarations of our humble Opinion, respecting the most essential rights and liberties of the colonists, and of the grievances under which they labour, by reason of several late acts of parliament.

1. That his majesty's subjects in these colonies, owe the same allegiance to the crown of Great Britain, that is owing from his subjects born within the realm, and all due subordination to that august body the parliament of Great Britain.

2. That his majesty's liege subjects in these colonies, are entitled to all the inherent rights and liberties of his natural born subjects, within the kingdom of Great Britain.

3. That it is inseparably essential to the freedom of a people, and the undoubted right of Englishmen, that no taxes be imposed on them but with their own consent, given personally, or by their representatives.

4. That the people of these colonies are not, and, from their local circumstances, cannot be, represented in the House of Commons in Great Britain.

5. That the only representatives of the people of these colonies, are persons chosen therein by themselves; and that no taxes ever have been,

All material contained herein was extracted from the
US Constitution Coach Kit at PowerThink.com
(Over 60,000 Works & Documents of American History)

or can be constitutionally imposed on them, but by their respective legislatures.

6. That all supplies to the crown being free gifts of the people, it is unreasonable and inconsistent with the principles and spirit of the British constitution, for the people of Great Britain to grant to his majesty the property of the colonists.

7. That trial by jury, is the inherent and invaluable right of every British subject in these colonies.

8. That the late act of parliament, entitled, an act for granting and applying certain stamp duties, and other duties, in the British colonies and plantations in America, &c., by imposing taxes on the inhabitants of these colonies, and the said act, and several other acts, by extending the jurisdiction of the courts of admiralty beyond its ancient limits, have a manifest tendency to subvert the rights and liberties of the colonists.

9. That the duties imposed by several late acts of parliament, from the peculiar circumstances of these colonies, will be extremely burdensome and grievous; and from the scarcity of specie, the payment of them absolutely impracticable.

10. That as the profits of the trade of these colonies ultimately center in Great Britain, to pay for the manufactures which they are obliged to take from thence, they eventually contribute very largely to all supplies granted there to the crown.

11. That the restrictions imposed by several late acts of parliament on the trade of these colonies, will render them unable to purchase the manufactures of Great Britain.

12. That the increase, prosperity and happiness of these colonies, depend on the full and free enjoyments of their rights and liberties, and an intercourse with Great Britain mutually affectionate and advantageous.

13. That it is the right of the British subjects in these colonies, to petition the king, or either house of parliament.

Lastly, That it is the indispensable duty of these colonies, to the best of sovereigns, to the mother country, and to themselves, to endeavour by a loyal and dutiful address to his majesty, and humble applications to both houses of parliament, to procure the repeal of the act for granting and applying certain stamp duties, of all clauses of any other acts of parliament, whereby the jurisdiction of the admiralty is extended as aforesaid, and of the other late acts for the restriction of American commerce.

The Repeal of the Stamp Act

Title: The Repeal of the Stamp Act
Author: Secretary Henry Seymour Conway
Date: 1766
Source: America, Vol.3, p.82

Conway was one of the English Secretaries of State in 1766 when he wrote this official communication to the governors of the American colonies. Incidentally, he persistently opposed the war with America, and in 1782, in an address to Parliament, urged the advisability of discontinuing the struggle. This is particularly interesting in view of the fact that, during the same year, he succeeded Lord North as Commander-in-Chief of the British army.

Receipt of this communication from the mother country was the signal for great rejoicing throughout the colonies, though dissatisfaction was soon expressed with regard to the Declaratory Act asserting a right to "bind the colonies and people of America...in all cases whatsoever." The whole affair has been regarded as one of the chief causes of the Revolution.

HEREWITH I have the pleasure of transmitting to you copied of two acts of Parliament just passed. The first for securing the dependency of the colonies on the mother country; the second for the repeal of the act of [the] last session, granting certain stamp duties in America; and I expect shortly to send you a third, for the indemnity of such persons, as have incurred the penalties imposed by the act just repealed, as such a bill is now depending, and has made a considerable progress in the House of Commons.

The moderation, the forbearance, the unexampled lenity and tenderness of Parliament towards the colonies, which are so signally displayed in those acts, cannot but dispose the province, committed to your care, to that return of cheerful obedience to the laws and legislative authority of Great Britain and to those sentiments of respectful gratitude to the mother country, which are the natural, and I trust, will be the certain effects of so much grace and condescension, so remarkably manifested on the part of his Majesty' and of the Parliament; and the future happiness and prosperity of the colonies will very much depend on the testimonies they shall now give of these dispositions.

For, as a dutiful and affectionate return to such peculiar proofs of indulgence and affection, may, now at this great crisis, be a means of fixing the mutual interests and inclinations of Great Britain and her colonies on the most firm and solid foundations, so it cannot but appear visible that the least coldness or unthankfulness, the least murmuring or dissatisfaction on any ground whatever, of former heat, or too much prevailing prejudice, may fatally endanger that union, and give the most severe and affecting blow to the future interests of both countries.

You will think it scarcely possible, I imagine, that the paternal care of His Majesty for his colonies, or the lenity or indulgence of the Parliament should go further than I have already mentioned: yet, so full of true magnanimity are the sentiments of both, and so free from the smallest color of passion or prejudice that they seem disposed not only to forgive, but to forget those most unjustifiable marks of an undutiful disposition too frequent in the late transactions of the colonies, and which, for the honor of those colonies, it were to be wished had been more discountenanced and discouraged by those, who had knowledge to conduct themselves otherwise.

A revision of the late American Trade Laws is going to be the immediate object of Parliament; nor will the late transactions there, however provoking, prevent, I dare say, the full operation of that kind and indulgent disposition prevailing both in His Majesty and his Parliament to give to the trade and interests of America every relief which the true state of their circumstances demands or admits. Nothing will tend more effectually to every conciliating purpose, and there is nothing therefore I have it in command more earnestly to require of you, than that you should exert yourself in recommending it strongly to the assembly, that full and ample compensation be made to those, who, from the madness of the people, have suffered for their deference to acts of the British legislature; and you will be particularly attentive that such persons be effectually secured from any further insults; and that as far as in you lies, you will take care, by your example and influence, that they may be treated with that respect to their persons, and that justice in regard to all their pretensions, which their merit and their sufferings undoubtedly claim. The resolutions of the House of Commons, which, by His Majesty's commands I transmit to you, to be laid before the assembly, will show you the sense of that house on those points; and I am persuaded it will, as it certainly ought, be, the glory of that assembly to adopt and imitate those sentiments of the British Parliament, founded on the clearest principles of humanity and justice…

Benjamin Franklin's Examination Before the House of Commons, 1766

Title: Benjamin Franklin's Examination Before the House of Commons
Author: Benjamin Franklin
Date: 1766
Source: The World's Famous Orations, Vol.8, pp.37-52

First published in London in 1766 as "The Examination of Doctor Franklin." Owing to the secrecy of the session of Parliament no clue was given in the pamphlet as to the place where the examination had been held, nor as to where or by whom the pamphlet was printed. J. Almon, who caused it to be printed, feared prosecution, but none having been begun, he next year printed the examination as having taken place "before an honorable assembly relative to the repeal of the American Stamp Act in 1766." A still later edition described the examination as having taken place "before an august assembly." The pamphlet was reprinted in 1766 in several American cities, including Philadelphia, New York, Boston, and New London. In Pennsylvania it was said that the demand for it "from all parts of the province was beyond conception."

It has been often stated that many of the questions propounded to Franklin had already been skilfully arranged for between Franklin and the enemies of the Stamp Act. But John T. Morse, one of Franklin's biographers, says: "It does not appear that such prearrangements went further than that certain friendly interrogators had discussed the topics with him, so as to be familiar with his views. Every lawyer does this with his witnesses. Nor can it be supposed that the admirable replies which he made to the enemies of America were otherwise than strictly impromptu." Burke likened the proceedings to "an examination of a master, by a parcel of schoolboys." Franklin afterward said that the friends of the repeal "were ready to hug me for the assistance that I afforded them." Among those that asked questions were Grenville, Townshend, North, Thurlow, and Burke. The examination closed on February 15, 1766. Abridged.

Born in Boston in 1706, died in 1790; settled in Philadelphia in 1729; Postmaster of Philadelphia in 1737; discovered the identity of lightning with electricity in 1753; proposed a "Plan of Union" at Albany in 1754; Colonial Agent for Pennsylvania in England, 1757-62 and 1764-75; Member of the Second Continental Congress in 1775; Member of the Committee which drew up the Declaration of Independence in 1776; Ambassador to France in 1776; helped to negotiate the treaty of peace

All material contained herein was extracted from the
US Constitution Coach Kit at PowerThink.com
(Over 60,000 Works & Documents of American History)

with France in 1778; helped to negotiate the treaty of peace with England in 1783; President of Pennsylvania 1785-88; Member of the Constitutional Convention in 1787.

Q. ARE not the Colonies, from their circumstances, very able to pay the stamp duty?

A. In my opinion there is not gold and silver enough in the Colonies to pay the stamp duty for one year.

Q. Do you not know that the money arising from the stamps was all to be laid out in America?

A. I know it is appropriated by the Act to the American service; but it will be spent in the conquered Colonies, where the soldiers are; not in the Colonies that pay it.

Q. Do you think it right that America should be protected by this country and pay no part of the expense?

A. That is not the case. The Colonies raised, clothed, and paid, during the last war, near twenty-five thousand men, and spent many millions.

Q. Were you not reimbursed by Parliament?

A. We were only reimbursed what, in your opinion, we had advanced beyond our proportion, or beyond what might reasonably be expected from us; and it was a very small part of what we spent. Pennsylvania, in particular, disbursed about þ500,000, and the reimbursements, in the whole, did not exceed þ60,000.

Q. Do you not think the people of America would submit to pay the stamp duty if it was moderated?

A. No, never, unless compelled by force of arms.

Q. What was the temper of America toward Great Britain before the year 1763?

A. The best in the world. They submitted willingly to the government of the Crown, and paid, in their courts, obedience to acts of Parliament. Numerous as the people are in the several old provinces they cost you nothing in forts, citadels, garrisons, or armies, to keep them in subjection. They were governed by this country at the expense only of a little pen, ink, and paper; they were led by a thread. They had not only a respect but an affection for Great Britain; for its laws, its customs, and manners, and even a fondness for its fashions, that greatly increased the commerce. Natives of Britain were always treated with particular regard; to be an Old England-man was of itself a character of some respect, and gave a kind of rank among us.

Q. And what is their temper now?

A. Oh, very much altered!

Q. Did you ever hear the authority of Parliament to make laws for America questioned till lately?

A. The authority of Parliament was allowed to be valid in all laws, except such as should lay internal taxes. It was never disputed in laying duties to regulate commerce.

Q. In what light did the people of America use to consider the Parliament of Great Britain?

A. They considered the Parliament as the great bulwark and security of their liberties and privileges, and always spoke of it with the utmost respect and veneration. Arbitrary ministers, they thought, might possibly, at times, attempt to oppress them; but their relied on it, that the Parliament, on application, would always give redress. They remembered, with gratitude, a strong instance of this, when a bill was brought into Parliament with a clause to make royal instructions laws in the Colonies which the House of Commons would not pass, and it was thrown out.

Q. And have they not still the same respect for Parliament?

A. No; it is greatly lessened.

Q. To what causes is that owing?

A. To a concurrence of causes: the restraints lately laid on their trade, by which the bringing of foreign gold and silver into the Colonies was prevented; the prohibition of making paper money among themselves, and then demanding a new and heavy tax by stamps; taking away, at the same time, trials by juries, and refusing to receive and hear their humble petitions.

Q. Do you not think they would submit to the Stamp Act if it was modified, the obnoxious parts taken out, and the duty reduced to some particulars of small moment?

A. No; they will never submit to it.

Q. Was it an opinion in America before 1763 that the Parliament had no right to lay taxes and duties there?

A. I never heard an objection to the right of laying duties to regulate commerce; but a right to lay internal taxes was never supposed to be in Parliament, as we are not represented there.

Q. On what do you found your opinion that the people in America made any distinction?

A. I know that whenever the subject has occurred in conversation where I have been present, it has appeared to be the opinion of every one that we were not represented. But the payment of duties laid by an act of Parliament as regulations of commerce was never disputed.

Q. But can you name any act of assembly or public act of any of your governments that made such distinction?

A. I do not know that there was any. I think there was never an occasion to make any such act till now that you have attempted to tax us; that has occasioned resolutions of assembly declaring the distinction, in which I think every assembly on the continent and every member in every assembly have been unanimous.

Q. You say the Colonies have always submitted to external taxes, and object to the right of Parliament only in laying internal taxes; now can you show that there is any kind of difference between the two taxes to the Colony on which they may be laid?

A. I think the difference is very great. An external tax is a duty laid on commodities imported; that duty is added to the first cost and other charges on the commodity, and, when it is offered for sale, makes a part of the price. If the people do not like it at that price, they refuse it; they are not obliged to pay it. But an internal tax is forced from the people without their consent if not laid by their own representatives. The Stamp Act says we shall have no commerce, make no exchange of property with each other, neither purchase nor grant, nor recover debts; we shall neither marry nor make our wills, unless we pay such and such sums; and thus it is intended to extort our money from us or ruin us by the consequence of refusing to pay it.

Q. But supposing the external tax or duty to be laid on the necessities of life imported into your Colony; will not that be the same thing in its effects as an internal tax?

A. I do not know a single article imported into the northern Colonies but what they can either do without or make themselves.

Q. Do you not think cloth from England absolutely necessary to them?

A. No, by no means absolutely necessary; with industry and good management, they may very well supply themselves with all they want.

Q. Will it not take a long time to establish that manufacture among them; and must they not, in the meanwhile, suffer greatly?

A. I think not. They have made a surprising progress already. And I am of the opinion that before their old clothes are worn out they will have new ones of their own making.

Q. Can they possibly find wool enough in North America?

A. They have taken steps to increase the wool. They entered into general combinations to eat no more lamb, and very few lambs were killed last year. This course persisted in will soon make a prodigious difference in the quantity of wool. And the establishment of great manufactories, like those in the clothing towns here, is not necessary as it is where the business is to be carried on for the purpose of trade. The people will all spin and work for themselves in their own houses.

Q. Considering the resolutions of Parliament, as to the right; do you think if the Stamp Act is repealed that the North Americans will be satisfied?

A. I believe they will.

Q. Why do you think so?

A. I think the resolutions of right will give them very little concern if they are never attempted to be carried into practise. The Colonies will probably consider themselves in the same situation in that respect with Ireland; they know you claim the same right with regard to Ireland, but you never exercise it. And they may believe you never will exercise it in the Colonies any more than in Ireland, unless on some very extraordinary occasion.

Q. But who are to be the judges of that extraordinary occasion? Is it not the Parliament!

A. Tho the Parliament may judge of the occasion, the people will think it can never exercise such right till representatives from the

Colonies are admitted into Parliament; and that, whenever the occasion arises, representatives will be ordered.

Q. Can anything less than a military force carry the Stamp Act into execution?

A. I do not see how a military force can be applied to that purpose.

Q. Why may it not?

A. Suppose a military force sent into America: they will find nobody in arms; what are they then to do? They can not force a man to take stamps who chooses to do without them. They will not find a rebellion; they may, indeed, make one.

Q. If the Act is not repealed, what do you think will be the consequences?

A. A total loss of the respect and affection the people of America bear to this country, and of all the commerce that depends on that respect and affection.

Q. How can the commerce be affected?

A. You will find that if the Act is not repealed they will take very little of your manufactures in a short time.

Q. Is it in their power to do without them?

A. I think they may very well do without them.

Q. Is it to their interest not to take them?

A. The goods they take from Britain are either necessaries, mere conveniences, or superfluities. The first, as cloth, etc., with a little industry, they can make at home; the second they can do without till they are able to provide them among themselves; and the last, which are much the greatest part, they will strike off immediately. They are mere articles of fashion in a respected country, but will now be detested and rejected. The people have already struck off, by general agreement, the use of all goods fashionable in mourning, and many thousand pounds' worth are sent back as unsalable.

Q. Then no regulation with a tax would be submitted to?

A. Their opinion is that when aids to the Crown are wanted they are to be asked of the several assemblies according to the old-established usage, who will, as they always have done, grant them freely, and that their money ought not to be given away without their consent, by persons at a distance, unacquainted with their circumstances and abilities. The granting aids to the Crown is the only means they have of recommending themselves to their sovereign, and they think it extremely hard and unjust that a body of men in which they have no representatives should make a merit to itself of giving and granting what is not its own but theirs, and deprive them of a right they esteem of the utmost value and importance, as it is the security of all their other rights.

Q. Supposing the Stamp Act continued and enforced, do you imagine that ill humor will induce the Americans to give as much for worse manufactures of their own, and use them, preferable to better of ours?

A. Yes, I think so. People will pay as freely to gratify one passion as another—their resentment as their pride.

Q. If the Stamp Act should be repealed, would not the Americans think they could oblige the Parliament to repeal every external tax-law now in force?

A. It is hard to answer questions of what people at such a distance will think.

Q. But what do you imagine they will think were the motives of repealing the Act?

A. I suppose they will think that it was repealed from a conviction of its inexpediency; and they will rely upon it that while the same inexpediency subsists you will never attempt to make such another.

Q. What do you mean by its inexpediency?

A. I mean its inexpediency on several accounts: the poverty and inability of those who were to pay the tax, the general discontent it has occasioned, and the impracticability of enforcing it.

Q. But if the legislature should think fit to ascertain its right to lay taxes by any act laying a small tax, contrary to their opinion, would they submit to pay the tax?

A. The proceedings of the people in America have been considered too much together. The proceedings of the assemblies have been very different from those of the mobs, and should be distinguished as having no connection with each other. The assemblies have only peaceably resolved what they take to be their rights; they have taken no measures for opposition by force, they have not built a fort, raised a man, or provided a grain of ammunition, in order to such opposition. The ringleaders of riots, they think, ought to be punished; they would punish them themselves if they could. Every sober, sensible man would wish to see rioters punished, as otherwise peaceable people have no security of person or estate; but as to an internal tax, how small soever, laid by the legislature here on the people there, while they have no representatives in this legislature, I think it will never be submitted to; they will oppose it to the last; they do not consider it as at all necessary for you to raise money on them by your taxes, because they are, and always have been, ready to raise money by taxes among themselves and to grant large sums, equal to their abilities, upon requisition from the Crown. They have not only granted equal to their abilities, but during all the last war they granted far beyond their proportion with this country (you yourselves being judges) to the amount of many hundred thousand pounds; and this they did freely and readily, only on a sort of promise from the secretary of state that it should be recommended to Parliament to make them compensation. It was accordingly recommended to Parliament in the most honorable manner for them. America has been greatly misrepresented and abused here, in papers and pamphlets and speeches,... as ungrateful and unreasonable and unjust; in having put this nation to immense expense for their defense, and refusing to bear any part of that expense. The Colonies raised, paid, and clothed near twenty-five thousand men during the last war—a number equal to those sent from Britain, and far beyond their proportion; they went deeply into debt in doing this, and all their taxes and estates are mortgaged for many years to come for discharging that debt.

Q. But suppose Great Britain should be engaged in a war in Europe, would North America contribute to the support of it?

A. I do think they would, as far as their circumstances would permit. They consider themselves as a part of the British Empire, and as having one common interest with it; they may be looked on her as foreigners, but they do not consider themselves as such. They are zealous for the honor and prosperity of this nation, and while they are well used will always be ready to support it as far as their little power goes. In 1739 they were called upon to assist in the expedition against Cartagena, and they sent three thousand men to join your army. It is true Cartagena is in America, but as remote from the northern Colonies as if it had been in Europe. They make no distinction of wars as to their duty of assisting in them. I know the last war is commonly spoken of here as entered into for the defense or for the sake of the people of America. I think it is quite misunderstood. It began about the limits between Canada and Nova Scotia, about territories to which the Crown indeed laid claim, but which were not claimed by any British Colony; none of the lands had been granted to any colonist; we had, therefore, no particular interest or concern in that dispute. As to the Ohio, the contest there began about your right of trading in the Indian country, a right you had by the treaty of Utrecht, which the French infringed; they seized the traders and their goods, which were your manufactures; they took a fort which a company of your merchants and their factors and correspondents had erected there to secure that trade. Braddock was sent with an army to retake that fort (which was looked on here as another encroachment on the king's territory) and to protect your trade. It was not till after his defeat that the Colonies were attacked. They were before in perfect peace with both French and Indians; the troops were not, therefore, sent for their defense. The trade with the Indians, tho carried on in America, is not an American interest. The people of America are chiefly farmers and planters; scarce anything that they raise or produce is an article of commerce with the Indians. The Indian trade is a British interest; it is carried on with British manufactures, for the profit of British merchants and manufacturers; therefore, the war, as it commenced for the defense of territories of the Crown (the property of no American) and for the defense of a trade purely British, was really a British war—and yet the people of America made no scruple of contributing their utmost toward carrying it on, and bringing it to a happy conclusion.

Q. Do you think the assemblies have a right to levy money on the subject there to grant to the Crown?

A. I certainly think so; they have always done it.

Q. Are they acquainted with the Declaration of Rights? And do they know that, by that Statute, money is not to be raised on the subject but by consent of Parliament?

A. They are very well acquainted with it.

Q. How, then, can they think they have a right to levy money for the Crown or for any other than local purposes?

A. They understand that clause to relate to subjects only within the realm; that no money can be levied on them for the Crown but by consent of Parliament. The Colonies are not supposed to be within the realm; they have assemblies of their own, which are their parliaments, and they are, in that respect, in the same situation with Ireland. When money is to be raised for the Crown upon the subject in Ireland, or in the Colonies, the consent is given in the Parliament of Ireland or in the assemblies of the Colonies. They think the Parliament of Great Britain can not properly give that consent till it has representatives from America, for the Petition of Right expressly says it is to be by common consent in Parliament, and the people of America have no representatives in Parliament to make a part of that common consent.

Q. If the Stamp Act should be repealed, and the Crown should make a requisition to the Colonies for a sum of money, would they grant it?

A. I believe they would.

Q. Why do you think so?

A. I can speak for the Colony I live in. I had it in instruction from the Assembly to assure the ministry that as they always had done, so they should always think it their duty to grant such aids to the Crown as were suitable to their circumstances and abilities, whenever called upon for that purpose, in the usual constitutional manner; and I had the honor of communicating this instruction to that honorable gentleman then minister.

Q. Would they do this for a British concern, as suppose a war in some part of Europe, that did not affect them?

A. Yes; for anything that concerned the general interest. They consider themselves as part of the whole.

Q. If the Stamp Act should be repealed, would it induce the assemblies of America to acknowledge the rights of Parliament to tax them, and would they erase their resolutions?

A. No, never!

Q. Are there no means of obliging them to erase those resolutions?

A. None that I know of; they will never do it, unless compelled by force of arms.

Q. Is there a power on earth that can force them to erase them?

A. No power, how great soever, can force men to change their opinions.

Q. What used to be the pride of the Americans?

A. To indulge in the fashions and manufactures of Great Britain.

Q. What is now their pride?

A. To wear their old clothes over again till they can make new ones.

Daniel Boone Migrates to Kentucky

Title: Daniel Boone Migrates to Kentucky
Author: Daniel Boone
Date: 1769
Source: America, Vol.3, p.89

Boone wrote this account, which appears in Hart's "Source Book of American History," many years after his migration. As his schooling was extremely limited, the article was put into literary form by a friend. His life, from the time of his first trip to Kentucky in 1769 to his death in Missouri in 1820, was a constant duel with hardships and Indians.

On the site of Boonesboro, Kentucky, he built a fort and settled his family a year before the Declaration of Independence was signed. Not long afterwards he was captured by the redskins, who took him to Detroit, finally adopted him and allowed him such freedom that he escaped and made his way back to Kentucky on foot, reaching his fort in time to help defend it against a savage attack. Losing his Kentucky lands through defective titles, he settled in Missouri and again became landless through Government litigation.

IT WAS on the first of May, in the year 1769, that I resigned my domestic happiness for a time, and left my family and peaceable habitation on the Yadkin River, in North Carolina, to wander through the wilderness of America, in quest of the country of Kentucky, in company with John Finley, John Stewart, Joseph Holden, James Monay, and William Cool.

We proceeded successfully, and after a long and tiresome journey through a mountainous wilderness, in a westward direction, on the seventh day of June following, we found ourselves on Red River, where John Finley had formerly gone trading with the Indians; and, from the top of an eminence, saw with pleasure the beautiful level of Kentucky.

We found everywhere abundance of wild beasts of all sorts, through this vast forest. The buffalo were more frequent than I have seen cattle in the settlements, browsing on the leaves of the cane, or cropping the herbage on those extensive plains, fearless, because ignorant of the violence of man. Sometimes we saw hundreds in a drove, and the numbers about the salt springs were amazing.

As we ascended the brow of a small hill, near Kentucky River, a number of Indians rushed out of a thick cane-brake upon us, and made us prisoners. The time of our sorrow was now arrived, and the scene fully opened. They plundered us of what we had, and kept us in confinement seven days, treating us with common savage usage. During this time we showed no uneasiness or desire to escape, which made them less suspicious of us. But in the dead of night, as we lay in a thick cane-brake by a large fire, when sleep had locked up their senses, my situation not disposing me for rest, I touched my companion and gently woke him.

We improved this favorable opportunity, and departed, leaving them to take their rest, and speedily directed our course toward our old camp, but found it plundered, and the company dispersed and gone home.

Soon after this my companion in captivity, John Stewart, was killed by the savages, and the man that came with my brother returned home by himself. We were then in a dangerous, helpless situation, exposed daily to perils and death among savages and wild beasts, not a white man in the country but ourselves.

One day I undertook a tour through the country, and the diversity and beauties of nature I met with in this charming season expelled every gloomy and vexatious thought. I laid me down to sleep, and I awoke not until the sun had chased away the night. I continued this tour, and in a few days explored a considerable part of the country, each day equally pleased as the first.

I returned again to my old camp, which was not disturbed in my absence. I did not confine my lodging to it, but often reposed in thick cane-brakes to avoid the savages, who, I believe, often visited my camp, but fortunately for me, in my absence. In this situation I was constantly exposed to danger and death. How unhappy such a situation for a man! Tormented with fear, which is vain if no danger comes. The prowling wolves diverted my nocturnal hours with perpetual howlings.

In 1772 I returned safe to my old home, and found my family in happy circumstances. I sold my farm on the Yadkin, and what goods we could not carry with us; and on the twenty-fifth day of September, 1773, bade a farewell to our friends and proceeded on our journey to Kentucky, in company with five families more, and forty men that joined us in Powel's Valley, which is one hundred and fifty miles from the now settled parts of Kentucky.

This promising beginning was soon overcast with a cloud of adversity; for upon the tenth day of October the rear of our company was attacked by a number of Indians, who killed six and wounded one man. Of these my eldest son was one that fell in the action.

Though we defended ourselves, and repulsed the enemy, yet this unhappy affair scattered our cattle, brought us into extreme difficulty, and so discouraged the whole company that we retreated forty miles to the settlement on Clench River.

Within fifteen miles of where Boonsborough now stands we were fired upon by a party of Indians that killed two and wounded two of our number; yet although surprised and taken at a disadvantage, we stood our ground. This was on the twentieth of March, 1775.

Three days after we were fired upon again, and had two men killed and three wounded. Afterward we proceeded on to Kentucky River without opposition; and on the first day of April began to erect the fort of Boonsborough at a salt lick, about sixty yards from the river, on the south side. On the fourth day the Indians killed one man.

In a short time I proceeded to remove my family from Clench to this garrison, where we arrived safe without any other difficulties than such as are common to this passage, my wife and daughter being the first white women that ever stood on the banks of Kentucky River. On the twenty-fourth day of December following we had one man killed and one wounded by the Indians, who seemed determined to persecute us for erecting this fortification.

On the fourteenth day of July, 1776, two of Colonel Calaway's daughters and one of mine were taken prisoners near the fort. I immediately pursued the Indians, with only eight men, and on the sixteenth overtook them, killed two of the party and recovered the girls. The same day on which this attempt was made the Indians divided themselves into different parties and attacked several forts, which were shortly before this time erected, doing a great deal of mischief. This was extremely distressing to the new settlers. The innocent husbandman was shot down while busy in cultivating the soil for his family's supply. Most of the cattle around the stations were destroyed. They continued their hostilities in this manner until the fifteenth of April, 1777, when they attacked Boonsborough with a party of above one hundred in number, killed one man and wounded four. Their loss in this attack was not certainly known to us.

On the fourth day of July following a party of about two hundred Indians attacked Boonsborough, killed one man and wounded two. They besieged us forty-eight hours; during which time seven of them were killed, and finding themselves not likely to prevail, they raised the siege and departed.

The Indians had disposed their warriors in different parties at this time and attacked the different garrisons to prevent their assisting each other, and did much injury to the inhabitants.

On the nineteenth day of this month Colonel Logan's fort was besieged by a party of about two hundred Indians. During this dreadful siege they did a great deal of mischief, distressed the garrison, in which were only fifteen men, killed two and wounded one.

This campaign in some measure damped the spirits of the Indians, and made them sensible of our superiority. Their connections were dissolved, their armies scattered, and a future invasion put entirely out of their power; yet they continued to practise mischief secretly upon the inhabitants, in the exposed parts of the country.

In October following a party made an excursion into that district called the Crab Orchard, and one of them, who was advanced some distance before the others, boldly entered the house of a poor defenseless family, in which was only a negro man, a woman and her children, terrified with the apprehensions of immediate death. The savage, perceiving their defenseless situation, without offering violence to the family, attempted to captivate the negro, who happily proved an overmatch for him, threw him on the ground, and, in the struggle, the mother of the children drew an ax from a corner of the cottage and cut his head off, while her little daughter shut the door. The savages instantly appeared, and applied their tomahawks to the door. An old rusty gun-barrel, without a lock, lay in a corner, which the mother put through a small crevice, and the savages, perceiving it, fled. In the mean time the alarm spread through the neighborhood; the armed men collected immediately, and pursued the ravagers into the wilderness. Thus Providence, by the means of this negro, saved the whole of the poor family from destruction. From that time until the happy return of peace between the United States and Great Britain the Indians did us no mischief.

To conclude, I can now say that I have verified the saying of an old Indian who signed Colonel Henderson's deed. Taking me by the hand, at the delivery thereof, "Brother," says he, "we have given you a fine land, but I believe you will have much trouble in settling it." My footsteps have often been marked with blood, and therefore I can truly subscribe to its original name. Two darling sons, and a brother, have I lost by savage hands, which have also taken from me forty valuable horses and abundance of cattle. Many dark and sleepless night have I been a companion for owls, separated from the cheerful society of men, scorched by the summer's sun, and pinched by the winter's cold, an instrument ordained to settle the wilderness. But now the scene is changed: peace crowns the sylvan shade.

Daniel Boone's Migration to Kentucky

Title: Daniel Boone's Migration to Kentucky
Author: Theodore Roosevelt
Date: 1769-1775
Source: Great Epochs in American History, Vol.3, p.78-86

The American backwoodsmen had surged up, wave upon wave, till their mass trembled in the troughs of the Alleghanies, ready to flood the continent beyond. The people threatened by them were dimly conscious of the danger which as yet only loomed in the distance. Far off, among their quiet adobe villages, in the sun-scorched lands by the Rio Grande, the slow Indo-Iberian peons and their monkish masters still walked in the tranquil steps of their fathers, ignorant of the growth of the power that was to overwhelm their children and successors; but nearer by, Spaniard and Creole Frenchman, Algonquin and Appalachian, were all uneasy as they began to feel the first faint pressure of the American advance.

As yet they had been shielded by the forest which lay over the land like an unrent mantle. All through the mountains, and far beyond, it stretched without a break; but toward the mouth of the Kentucky and Cumberland rivers the landscape became varied with open groves of woodland, with flower-strewn glades and great barrens or prairies of long grass. This region, one of the fairest in the world, was the debatable ground between the northern and the southern Indians. Neither dared dwell therein, but both used it as their hunting-grounds; and it was traversed from end to end by the well-marked war traces which they followed when they invaded each other's territory. The whites, on trying to break through the barrier which hemmed them in from the western lands, naturally succeeded best when pressing along the line of least resistance; and so their first great advance was made in this debatable land, where the uncertainly defined hunting-grounds of the Cherokee, Creek, and Chickasaw marched upon those of Northern Algonquin and Wyandot.

Unknown and unnamed hunters and Indian traders had from time to time pushed some little way into the wilderness; and they had been followed by others of whom we do indeed know the names, but little more. One explorer had found and named the Cumberland River and mountains, and the great pass called Cumberland Gap. Others had gone far beyond the utmost limits this man had reached, and had hunted in the great bend of the Cumberland and in the woodland region of Kentucky, famed among the Indians for the abundance of the game. But their accounts excited no more than a passing interest; they came and went without comment, as lonely stragglers had come and gone for nearly a century. The backwoods civilization crept slowly westward without being influenced in its movements by their explorations.

Finally, however, among these hunters one arose whose wanderings were to bear fruit; whowas destined to lead through the wilderness the first body of settlers that ever established a community in the Far West, completely cut off from the seaboard colonies. This was Daniel Boone. He was born in Pennsylvania in 1734, but when only a boy had been brought with the rest of his family to the banks of the Yadkin in North Carolina. Here he grew up, and as soon as he came of age he married, built a log hut, and made a clearing, whereon to farm like the rest of his backwoods neighbors. They all tilled their own clearings, guiding the plow among the charred stumps left when the trees were chopped down and the land burned over, and they were all, as a matter of course, hunters. With Boone hunting and exploration were passions, and the lonely life of the wilderness, with its bold, wild freedom, the only existence for which he really cared. He was a tall, spare, sinewy man, with eyes like an eagle's, and muscles that never tired; the toil and hardship of his life made no impress on his iron frame, unhurt by intemperance of any kind, and he lived for eighty-six years, a backwoods hunter to the end of his days. His thoughtful, quiet, pleasant face, so often portrayed, is familiar to every one; it was the face of a man who never blustered or bullied, who would neither inflict nor suffer any wrong, and who had a limitless fund of fortitude, endurance, and indomitable resolution upon which to draw when fortune proved adverse. His self-command and patience, his daring, restless love of adventure, and, in time of danger, his absolute trust in his own powers and resources, all combined to render him peculiarly fitted to follow the career of which he was so fond.

Boone hunted on the western waters at an early date. In the valley of Boone's Creek, a tributary of the Watauga, there is a beech-tree still standing, on which can be faintly traced an inscription setting forth that "D. Boone cilled a bar on (this) tree in the year 1760." On the expeditions of which this is the earliest record he was partly hunting on his own account, and partly exploring on behalf of another, Richard Henderson. Henderson was a prominent citizen of North Carolina, a speculative man of great ambition and energy. He stood high in the colony, was extravagant and fond of display, and his fortune being jeopardized he hoped to more than retrieve it by going into speculations in western lands on an unheard-of scale; for he intended to try to establish on his own account a great proprietary colony beyond the mountains. He had great confidence in Boone; and it was his backing which enabled the latter to turn his discoveries to such good account.

Boone's claim to distinction rests not so much on his wide wanderings in unknown lands, for in this respect he did little more than was done by a hundred other backwoods hunters of his generation, but on the fact that he was able to turn his daring woodcraft to the advantage of his fellows. As he himself said, he was an instrument "ordained of God to settle the wilderness." He inspired confidence in all who met him, so that the men of means and influence were willing to trust adventurous enterprises to his care; and his success as an explorer, his skill as a hunter, and his prowess as an Indian fighter, enabled him to bring these enterprises to a successful conclusion, andin some degree to control the wild spirits associated with him.

Boone's expeditions into the edges of the wilderness whetted his appetite for the unknown. He had heard of great hunting-grounds in the far interior from a stray hunter and Indian trader, who had himself seen them, and on May 1, 1769, he left his home on the Yadkin "to wander through the wilderness of America in quest of the country of Kentucky." He was accompanied by five other men, including his informant, and struck out toward the northwest, through the tangled mass of rugged mountains and gloomy forests. During five weeks of severe toil the little band journeyed through vast solitudes, whose utter loneliness can with difficulty be understood by those who have not themselves dwelt and hunted in primeval mountain forests. Then, early in June, the adventurers broke through the interminable wastes of dim woodland, and stood on the threshold of the beautiful blue-grass region of Kentucky; a land of running waters, of groves and glades, of prairies, cane-brakes, and stretches of lofty forests. It was teeming with game. The shaggy-maned herds of unwieldly buffalo—the bison as they should be called—had beaten out broad roads through the forest, and had furrowed the prairies with trails along which they had traveled for countless generations. The round-horned elk, with spreading, massive antlers, the lordliest of the deer tribe throughout the world, abounded, and like the buffalo traveled in bands not only through the woods but also across the reaches of waving grass land. The deer were extraordinarily numerous, and so were bears, while wolves and panthers were plentiful. Wherever there was a salt spring the country was fairly thronged with wild beasts of many kinds. For six months Boone and his companions enjoyed such hunting as had hardly fallen to men of their race since the Germans came out of the Hercynian forest.

In December, however, they were attacked by Indians. Boone and a companion were captured; and when they escaped they found their camp broken up, and the rest of the party scattered and gone home. About this time they were joined by Squire Boone, the brother of the great hunter, and himself a woodsman of but little less skill, together with another adventurer; the two had traveled through the immense wilderness, partly to explore it and partly with the hope of finding the original adventurers, which they finally succeeded in doing more by good luck than design. Soon afterward Boone's companion in his first short captivity was again surprised by the Indians, and this time was slain—the first of the thousands of human beings with whose life-blood Kentucky was bought. The attack was entirely unprovoked. The Indians had wantonly shed the first blood. The land belonged to no one tribe, but was hunted over by all, each feeling jealous of every other intruder; they attacked the whites, not because the whites had wronged them, but because their invariable policy was to kill any strangers on any grounds over which they themselves ever hunted, no matter what man had the best right thereto. The Kentucky hunters were promptly taught that in this no-man's land, teeming with game and lacking even a solitary human habitation, every Indian must be regarded as a foe.

The man who had accompanied Squire Boone was terrified by the presence of the Indians, and now returned to the settlements. The two brothers remained alone on their hunting-grounds throughout the winter, living in a little cabin. About the first of May Squire set off alone to the settlements to procure horses and ammunition. For three months Daniel Boone remained absolutely alone in the wilderness, without salt, sugar, or flour, and without the companionship of so much as a horse or a dog. But the solitude-loving hunter, dauntless and self-reliant, enjoyed to the full his wild, lonely life; he passed his days hunting and exploring, wandering hither and thither over the country, while at night he lay off in the canebrakes or thickets, without a fire, so as not to attract the Indians. Of the latter he saw many signs, and they sometimes came to his camp, but his sleepless wariness enabled him to avoid capture.

Late in July his brother returned, and met him according to appointment at the old camp. Other hunters also no came into the Kentucky wilderness, and Boone joined a small party of them for a short time. Such a party of hunters is always glad to have anything wherewith to break the irksome monotony of the long evenings passed round the camp fire; and a book or a greasy pack of cards was as welcome in a camp of Kentucky riflemen in 1770 as it is to a party of Rocky Mountain hunters in 1888. Boone has recorded in his own quaint phraseology an incident of his life during this summer, which shows how eagerly such a little band of frontiersmen read a book, and how real its characters became to their minds. He was encamped with five other men on Red River, and they had with them for their "amusement the history of Samuel Gulliver's travels, wherein he gave an account of his young master, Glumdelick, careing [sic] him on a market day for a show to a town called Lulbegrud." In the party who, amid such strange surroundings, read and listened to Dean Swift's writings was a young man named Alexander Neely. One night he came into camp with two Indian scalps, taken from a Shawnese village he had found on a creek running into the river; and he announced to the circle of grim wilderness veterans that "he had been that day to Lulbegrud, and had killed two Brobdignags in their capital." To this day the creek by which the two luckless Shawnees lost their lives is known as Lulbegrud Creek.

Soon after this encounter the increasing danger from the Indians drove Boone back to the valley of the Cumberland River, and in the spring of 1771 he returned to his home on the Yadkin.

A couple of years before Boone went to Kentucky, Steiner, or Stoner, and Harrod, two hunters from Pittsburgh, who had passed through the Illinois, came down to hunt in the bend of the Cumberland, where Nashville now stands; they found vast numbers of buffalo, and killed a great many, especially around the licks, where the huge clumsy beasts had fairly destroyed most of the forest, treading down the young trees and bushes till the ground was left bare or covered with a rich growth of clover. The bottoms and the hollows between the hills were thickset with cane. Sycamore grew in the low ground, and toward the Mississippi were to be found the persimmon and cottonwood. Sometimes the forest was openand composed of huge trees; elsewhere it was of thicker, smaller growth. Everywhere game abounded, and it was nowhere very wary.

Other hunters of whom we know even the names of only a few, had been through many parts of the wilderness before Boone, and earlier still Frenchmen had built forts and smelting furnaces on the Cumberland, the Tennessee, and the head tributaries of the Kentucky. Boone is interesting as a leader and explorer; but he is still more interesting as a type. The west was neither discovered, won, nor settled by any single man. No keen-eyed statesman planned the movement, nor was it carried out by any great military leader; it was the work of a whole people, of whom each man was impelled mainly by sheer love of adventure; it was the outcome of the ceaseless strivings of all the dauntless, restless backwoods folk to win homes for their descendants and to each penetrate deeper than his neighbors into the remote forest hunting-grounds where the perilous pleasures of the chase and of war could be best enjoyed. We owe the conquest of the west to all the backwoodsmen, not to any solitary individual among them; where all alike were strong and daring there was no chance for any single man to rise to unquestioned preeminence.

The Spanish Settle in California

Title: The Spanish Settle in California
Author: Josiah Royce
Date: 1769
Source: America, Vol.2, p.314

In addition to being a recognized authority on the early history of California, and the author of "California from the Conquest in 1846 to the Second Vigilance Committee in San Francisco," the fame of Professor Royce is world-wide as a metaphysician and philosopher. As an historian he was prominent in what is known as the Cabrillo National Movement, which some years ago established as a memorial to the pioneer Spanish explorer, Juan Roderiguez Cabrillo, at Point Loma, California, a tract of land containing 21,910 square feet within the Fort Rosecrans reservation, of historic interest as the spot where Cabrillo first landed on our Pacific Coast.

That was in 1542. In the subsequent mission period of sixty-five years it is significant that over 80,000 Indians were converted, at least $1,000,000 worth of buildings were erected in the wilderness, and that stock and wheat raising was developed on an astonishing scale.

THE settlements of the Spanish missionaries within the present limits of the State of California date from the first foundation of San Diego in 1769. The missions that were later founded north of San Diego were, with the original establishment itself, for a time known merely by some collective name, such as the Northern Missions. But later the name California, already long since applied to the country of the peninsular missions to the southward, was extended to the new land, with various prefixes or qualifying phrases; and out of these the definitive name Alta (Upper) California at last came, being applied to the territory during the whole period of the Mexican Republican ownership.

As to the origin of the name California, no serious question remains but that this name, as first applied, between 1535 and 1539 to a portion of Lower California, was derived from an old printed romance, the one which Edward Everett Hale rediscovered in 1862, and from which he drew this now accepted conclusion. In this romance the name California was already before 1520 applied to a fabulous island, described as near the Indies and also very near the Terrestrial Paradise." Colonists whom Cortez brought to the newly discovered peninsula in 1535, and who returned the next year, may have been the first to apply the name to this supposed island, on which they had been for a time resident.

The coast of Upper California was first visited during the voyage of the explorer Juan Cabrillo in 1542-43. Several landings were then made on the coast and on the islands, in the Santa Barbara region. Cabrillo himself died during the expedition (on January 3, 1543) and the voyage was continued by his successor, Ferralo, who sailed as far north as 420. The whole undertaking resulted in some examination of the coast line as far as Cape Mendocino, and in a glimpse of the native population that lived along the southern shores of the present State.

In 1579 Drake's famous visit took place. During the latter half of June and nearly the whole of July of that year he remained in what "The World Encompassed" calls a "convenient and fit harbor" (about 380 30'), where the ship was grounded for repairs, and where the expedition had considerable intercourse with the natives.

One of the accounts complains, in extravagant fashion, of the chilly air and of the fogs of the region, and, in general, we get information from the accounts about the "white banks and cliffs, which lie toward the sea," and hear about what we now know as the Farallones, the rocky islets that lie just outside what we call the Golden Gate. While the other details of the stories, as given, are obviously in large part imaginary, there can be no doubt that Drake did land near this point on the coast, and did find a passable harbor, where he stayed some time.

It is, however, almost perfectly sure that he did not enter or observe the Golden Gate, and that he got no sort of idea of the existence of the great Bay; while for the rest, it is and must remain quite uncertain what anchorage he discovered, although the chances are in favor of what is now called Drake's Bay, under Point Reyes. This result of the examination of the evidence about Drake's voyage is now fairly well accepted although some people will always try to insist that Drake discovered the Bay of San Francisco.

The name San Francisco was probably applied to a port on this coast for the first time by Cermenon, who, in a voyage from the Philippines in 1595, ran ashore while exploring the coast near Point Reyes. It is now perfectly sure that neither he nor any other Spanish navigator before 1769 applied this name to our present bay, which remained utterly unknown to Europeans during all this period.

The name Port of San Francisco was given by Vizcaino, and by later navigators and geographers, to the bay under Point Reyes, characterized by the whitish cliffs and by the rocky islets in the ocean in front of it. The coincidence of the name San Francisco with the name of Sir Francis Drake is remarkable, but doubtless means nothing. Christian names are, after all, limited in number; and those who applied this name to the new port were Spaniards and Catholics, while Drake was a free-booter and an Englishman.

In 1602-3, Sebastian Vizcaino conducted a Spanish expedition along the California coast. He visited San Diego and Monterey bays, saw during his various visits on shore a good deal of the natives, and in January 1603, anchored in the old Port of San Francisco under Point Reyes. From this voyage a little more knowledge of the character of the coast was gained; and thenceforth geographical researches in the region of California ceased for over a century and a half.

With only this meager result we reach the era of the first settlement of Upper California. The missions of the peninsula of Lower California passed, in 1767, by the expulsion of the Jesuits, into the hands of the Franciscans; and the Spanish Government, whose attention was attracted in this direction by the changed conditions, ordered the immediate prosecution of a long-cherished plan to provide the Manilla ships, on their return voyage, with good ports of supply and repairs, and to occupy the northwest land as a safeguard against Russian or other aggressions.

For the accomplishment of this end the occupation of the still but vaguely known harbors of San Diego and Monterey was planned. The zeal of the Franciscans for the conversion of the gentiles of the north seconded the official purposes, and in 1768 the Visitador General of New Spain, Jose de Galvez, took personal charge at La Paz of the preparation of an expedition intended to begin the new settlement in the north. The official purpose here, as in older mission undertakings, was a union of physical and spiritual conquest, soldiers under a military governor cooperating to this end with missionaries and mission establishments. The natives were to be overcome by arms in so far as they might resist the conquerors, were to be attracted to the missions by peaceable measures in so far as might prove possible, were to be instructed in the faith, and were to be kept for the present under the paternal rule of the clergy, until such time as they might be ready for a free life as Christian subjects.

Meanwhile, Spanish colonists were to be brought to the new land as circumstances might determine, and, to these, allotments of land were in some fashion to be made. No grants of land in a legal sense were made or promised to the mission establishments, whose position was to be merely that of spiritual institutions, intrusted temporarily with the education of neophytes, and with the care of the property that should be given or hereafter produced for this purpose. On the other hand, government tended to regard the missions as purely subsidiary to its purposes, the outgoing missionaries to this strange land were so much the more certain to be quite uncorrupted by worldly ambitions, by a hope of acquiring wealth, or by any intention to found a powerful ecclesiastical government in the new colony. They went to save souls and their motive was as single as it was worthy of reverence.

In the sequel the more successful missions in Upper California became, for a time, very wealthy; but this was only by virtue of the gifts of nature and of the devoted labors of the padres...

Thus began the career of Spanish discovery and settlement in California. The early years show a generally rapid progress, only one great disaster occurring,—the destruction of San Diego Missions in 1775, by assailing Indians. But this loss was quickly repaired. In 1770 the Mission of San Carlos was founded at Monterey. In 1772, a land expedition, under Fages and Crespi, first explored the eastern shore of our San Francisco Bay, in an effort to reach by land the old Port of San Francisco. This expedition discovered the San Joaquin River, and, unable to cross it, returned without attaining the object of the exploration.

After 1775 the old name began to be generally applied to the new bay, and so, thenceforth, the name Port of San Francisco means what we now mean thereby. In 1775, Lieutenant Ayala entered the new harbor by water. In the following year the Mission at San Francisco was founded, and in October its church was dedicated. Not only missions, however, but pueblos, inhabited by Spanish colonists, lay in the official plan of the new undertakings. The first of these to be established was San Jose' founded in November 1777. The next was Los Angeles, founded in September 1781.

An Eye-witness Describes the Boston Massacre

Title: An Eye-witness Describes the Boston Massacre
Author: John Tudor
Date: [Not given]
Source: America, Vol.3, p.85

The author of this document was a Boston merchant who was in the midst of the stirring events in the New England metropolis from 1732 to 1793. The soldiers involved in the so-called massacre were indicted for murder, were defended by John Adams, and were acquitted, though two of them were declared guilty of manslaughter and received light punishments.

There is much difference of opinion about the event, some writers regarding it as a lawless affair discreditable to the people and soldiers alike and without any great historical significance; others, including John Adams, look upon it as the "first act in the drama of the Revolution."

O N Monday evening the 5th current, a few minutes after 9 o'-clock a most horrid murder was committed in King Street before the Customhouse door by 8 or 9 soldiers under the command of Captain Thomas Preston, drawn off from the main guard on the south side of the Townhouse.

This unhappy affair began by some boys and young fellows throwing snow balls at the sentry placed at the Customhouse door. On which 8 or 9 soldiers came to his assistance. Soon after a number of people collected, when the Captain commanded the soldiers to fire, which they did and 3 men were killed on the spot and several mortally wounded, one of whom died the next morning. The Captain soon drew off his soldiers up to the main guard, or the consequences might have been terrible, for on the guns firing the people were alarmed and set the bells a-ringing as if for fire, which drew multitudes to the place of action. Lieutenant Governor Hutchinson, who was commander-in-chief, was sent for and came to the council chamber, where some of the magistrates attended. The Governor desired the multitude about 10 o'clock to separate and go home peaceably and he would do all in his power that justice should be done, etc. The 29th regiment being then under arms on the south side of the Townhouse, but the people insisted that the soldiers should be ordered to their barracks first before they would separate, which being done the people separated about one o'clock. Captain Preston was taken up by a warrant given to the high Sheriff by Justice Dania and Tudor and came under examination about 2 o'clock and we sent him to jail soon after 3, having evidence sufficient to commit him on his ordering the soldiers to fire. So about 4 o'clock the town became quiet. The next forenoon the 8 soldiers that fired on the inhabitants were also sent to jail. Tuesday A.M. the inhabitants met at Faneuil Hall and after some pertinent speeches, chose a committee of 15 gentlemen to wait on the Lieutenant Governor in council to request the immediate removal of the troops. The message was in these words: That it is the unanimous opinion of this meeting, that the inhabitants and soldiery can no longer live together in safety; that nothing can rationally be expected to restore the peace of the town and prevent blood and carnage but the removal of the troops; and that we most fervently pray his honor that his power and influence may be exerted for their instant removal. His honor's reply was, "Gentlemen I am extremely sorry for the unhappy difference and especially of the last evening," and signifying that it was not in his power to remove the troops, &c., &c.

The above reply was not satisfactory to the inhabitants, as but one regiment should be removed to the castle barracks. In the afternoon the town adjourned to Dr. Sewill's meetinghouse, for Faneuil Hall was not large enough to hold the people, there being at least 3,000, some supposed near 4,000, when they chose a committee to wait on the Lieutenant Governor to let him and the council know that nothing less will satisfy the people, than a total and immediate removal of the troops out of the town. His honor laid before the council the vote of the town. The council thereon expressed themselves to be unanimously of opinion that it was absolutely necessary for his Majesty's service, the good order of the town, &c., that the troops should be immediately removed out of the town. His honor communicated this advice of the council to Colonel Dalrymple and desired he would order the troops down to castle William. After the Colonel had seen the vote of the council he gave his word and honor to the town's committee that both the regiments should be removed without delay. The committee returned to the town meeting and Mr. Hancock, chairman of the committee, read their report as above, which was received with a shout and clap of hands, which made the meetinghouse ring. So the meeting was dissolved and a great number of gentlemen appeared to watch the center of the town and the prison, which continued for 11 nights and all was quiet again, as the soldiers were moved off to the castle.

(Thursday) Agreeable to a general request of the inhabitants, were followed to the grave (for they were all buried in one) in succession the 4 bodies of Messrs. Samuel Gray, Samuel Maverick, James Caldwell and Crispus Attucks, the unhappy victims who fell in the bloody massacre. On this sorrowful occasion most of the shops and stores in town were shut, all the bells were ordered to toll a solemn peal in Boston, Charleston, Cambridge and Roxbury. The several hearses forming a junction in King Street, the theatre of that inhuman tragedy, proceeded from thence through the main street, lengthened by an immense concourse of people, so numerous as to be obliged to follow in ranks of 4 and 6 abreast and brought up by a long train of carriages. The sorrow visible in the countenances, together with the peculiar solemnity, surpasses description, it was supposed that the spectators and those that followed the corpses amounted to 5,000, some supposed 20,000. Note Captain Preston was tried for his life on the affair of the above October 24, 1770. The trial lasted 5 days, but the jury brought him in not guilty.

Indentured "White Slaves" in the Colonies

Title: Indentured "White Slaves" in the Colonies
Author: William Eddis
Date: 1770
Source: America, Vol.2, p.309

Indentured white servants—virtually slaves—existed in large numbers in the colonies. This writer, William Eddis, who was surveyor of customs at Annapolis, Maryland, and remained loyal to England during the Revolutionary War, paints a dark picture of the barbarous custom. The time of which he writes was six years before the signing of the Declaration of Independence.

It was a common English practice to "transport" criminals instead of hanging them, and it is estimated that 50,000 convicts came over. As examples, a Scotchman was sold to life—slavery in America for burning

All material contained herein was extracted from the
US Constitution Coach Kit at PowerThink.com
(Over 60,000 Works & Documents of American History)

a Bible; and in 1736 a London barrister stole books and was sentenced to seven years of servitude in Virginia. The notorious Judge Jeffreys assigned over 800 persons to be thus indentured; and after the battle of Worcester, in 1650, about 1000 prisoners met the same fate.

PERSONS in a state of servitude are under four distinct denominations: negroes, who are the entire property of their respective owners: convicts, who are transported from the mother country for a limited term: indented servants, who are engaged for five years previous to their leaving England; and free-willers, who are supposed, from their situation, to possess superior advantages…

Persons convicted of felony, and in consequence transported to this continent, if they are able to pay the expense of passage; are free to pursue their fortune agreeably to their inclinations or abilities. Few, however, have means to avail themselves of this advantage. These unhappy beings are, generally, consigned to an agent, who classes them suitably to their real or supposed qualifications; advertises them for sale, and disposes of them, for seven years, to planters, to mechanics, and to such as choose to retain them for domestic service. Those who survive the term of servitude, seldom establish their residence in this country: the stamp of infamy is too strong upon them to be easily erased: they either return to Europe, and renew their former practices; or, if they have fortunately imbibed habits of honesty and industry, they remove to a distant situation, where they may hope to remain unknown, and be enabled to pursue with credit every possible method of becoming useful members of society…

The generality of the inhabitants in this province are very little acquainted with those fallacious pretenses, by which numbers are continually induced to embark for this continent. On the contrary, they too generally conceive an opinion that the difference is merely nominal between the indented servant and the convicted felon: nor will they readily believe that people, who had the least experience in life, and whose characters were unexceptionable, would abandon their friends and families, and their ancient connections, for a servile situation, in a remote appendage to the British Empire. From this persuasion they rather consider the convict as the more profitable servant, his term being for seven, the latter, only for five years; and, I am sorry to observe, that there are but few instances wherein they experience different treatment. Negroes being a property for life, the death of slaves, in the prime of youth or strength, is a material loss to the proprietor; they are, therefore, almost in every instance, under more comfortable circumstances than the miserable European, over whom the rigid planter exercises an inflexible severity. They are strained to the utmost to perform their allotted labor; and, from a prepossession in many cases too justly founded, they are supposed to be receiving only the just reward which is due to repeated offenses.

There are doubtless many exceptions to this observation. Yet, generally speaking, they groan beneath a worse than Egyptian bondage. By attempting to enlighten the intolerable burden, they often render it more insupportable. For real or imaginary causes, these frequently attempt to escape, but very few are successful; the country being intersected with rivers, and the utmost vigilance observed in detecting persons under suspicious circumstances, who, when apprehended, are committed to close confinement, advertised, and delivered to their respective masters; the party who detects the vagrant being entitled to a reward. Other incidental charges arise. The unhappy culprit is doomed to a fevered chastisement; and a prolongation of servitude is decreed in full proportion to expenses incurred, and supposed inconveniences resulting from a desertion of duty.

The situation of the free-willer is, in almost every instance, more to be lamented than either that of the convict or the indented servant; the deception which is practiced on those of this description being attended with circumstances of greater duplicity and cruelty. Persons under this denomination are received under express conditions that, on their arrival in America, they are to be allowed a stipulated number of days to dispose of themselves to the greatest advantage. They are told, that their services will be eagerly solicited, in proportion to their abilities; that their reward will be adequate to the hazard they encounter by courting fortune in a distant region; and that the parties with whom they engage will readily advance the sum agreed on for their passage; which, being averaged at about nine pounds sterling, they will speedily be enabled to repay, and to enjoy, in a state of liberty, a comparative situation of ease and affluence.

With these pleasing ideas they support with cheerfulness, the hardships to which they are subjected during the voyage; and with the most anxious sensations of delight, approach the land which they consider as the scene of future prosperity. But scarce have they contemplated the diversified objects which naturally attract attention; scarce have they yielded to pleasing reflection, that every danger, every difficulty, is happily surmounted, before their fond hopes are cruelly blasted, and they find themselves involved in all the complicated miseries of a tedious, laborious and unprofitable servitude.

Persons resident in America being accustomed to procure servants for a very trifling consideration, under absolute terms, for a limited period, are not often disposed to hire adventurers, who expect to be gratified in full proportion to their acknowledged qualifications; but, as they support authority with a rigid hand, they little regard the former situation of their unhappy dependants.

This disposition, which is almost universally prevalent, is well known to the parties, who on your side of the Atlantic engage in this iniquitous and cruel commerce.

It is, therefore, an article of agreement with these deluded victims, that if they are not successful in obtaining situations, on their own terms, within a certain number of days after their arrival in the country, they are then to be sold, in order to defray the charges of passage, at the discretion of the master of the vessel, or the agent to whom he is consigned in the province.

The Boston Tea Party

Title: The Boston Tea Party
Author: Thomas Hutchinson
Date: 1773
Source: America, Vol.3, p.96

Governor Hutchinson, from whose history of Massachusetts Bay this account of the Boston Tea Party exploit is taken, has been criticized for not ordering the tea-laden ships back to England, as was done in Philadelphia and New York, but there was a shortage of tea that winter of 1773 in New England and, we are assured, "the merchants would never have submitted to the disappointment and loss." The tea in question was consigned, among others, to two sons of the Governor and to Benjamin Faneuil, whose name is commemorated in Faneuil Hall.

It is noteworthy that Hutchinson's biographer, James K. Hosmer, is also the most popular biographer of Samuel Adams. "It was while writing the life of that sturdy Son of Liberty." says Professor Hosmer, "that the worth and greatness of his opponent became plain to me. Hutchinson's estate was confiscated, and later in life he was forced through poverty to decline an English baronetcy.

THE assembly being prorogued, there was again room to hope for a few months of freedom from civil contention. The complaint against the Governor was gone to England; the salaries of the judges were suspended for the consideration of the next session: these were the two subjects of controversy peculiar to Massachusetts colony. Not more than two or three months had passed before a new subject was brought on, which had its effect in all the colonies, but greater in Massachusetts than in any other.

When the affairs of the East India Company were under the consideration of Parliament, to facilitate the consumption of tea, a vast quantity whereof then lay in the warehouses, it was determined to export a part of it, on account of the company, to the colonies, there to be sold by factors at a much lower price than it could be afforded by particular merchants who purchased it in England. When the intelligence first came to Boston, it caused no alarm. The threepenny duty had been paid the last two years without any stir, and some of the great friends to liberty had been importers of tea. The body of the people were pleased with the prospect of drinking tea at less expense than ever. The only apparent discontent was among the importers of tea, as well those who had been legal importers from England, as others who had illegally imported from Holland; and the complaint was against the East India Company for monopolizing a branch of commerce which had been beneficial to a great number of particular merchants. And the first suggestion of a design in the ministry to enlarge the revenue, and to habituate the colonies to parliamentary taxes, was made from England; and opposition to the measure was recommended, with an intimation that it was expected that the tea would not be suffered to be landed. The committees of correspondence in the several colonies soon availed themselves of so favorable an opportunity for promoting their great purpose. It soon appeared to be their general determination that, at all events, the tea should be sent back to England in the ships which brought it. The first motions were at Philadelphia where, at a meeting of the people, every man who should be concerned in unlading, receiving, or vending the tea was pronounced an enemy to his country.

The example was soon followed at Boston. The people were summoned, by notifications posted in different quarters, to meet at the tree of liberty, to hear the resignation of the consignees of the tea, which was then daily expected. The consignees also, by a letter left at one of their houses, were required to attend at the same time at their peril. The people met, but, the consignees not appearing, a committee was appointed to acquaint them at one of their warehouses where they had met that, as they had neglected to attend, the people thought themselves warranted to consider them as their enemies...

Three vessels were expected every hour with the teas. The consignees were afraid of exposing themselves and their bondsmen to damages, which might arise from a refusal or neglect to execute their trust; on the other hand, they were anxiously concerned for their personal safety, and made their application to the Governor. He foresaw that this would prove a more difficult affair than any which had preceded it since he had been in the chair. The controversies with the council and house had a tendency to deprive him of the esteem and favor of the people; but he had not been apprehensive of injury to his person. He was now to encounter with bodies of the people collected together, and a great proportion of them the lowest part of the people, from whom, when there is no power to restrain them, acts of violence are to be expected. He knew that the council would give him no aid... He considered that, if the ships came into the harbor above the castle, they could not pass by it again without a permit under his hand, and that his granting such permit would be more than he should be able to justify. He therefore advised to their anchoring without the castle, and their waiting for orders; and this advice was approved of by the consignees, and by the owner of the ship first expected, if not by the owners of the other ships; and orders were given to the pilots accordingly...

On Sunday one of the ships with the tea arrived, and anchored below the castle. Notification in a form proper to inflame the people was posted up, calling upon them to assemble; and while the Governor and council were sitting on the Monday in the council chamber, and known to be consulting upon means for preserving the peace of the town, several thousands, inhabitants of Boston and other towns, were assembled in a public meeting-house at a small distance, in direct opposition and defiance...

The people assembled in Boston took the name of "the body" instead of a "legal town meeting," and began with that spirit with which all established powers ought to act in the exercise of their legal constitutional authority. They resolved that, "at all events," the tea arrived in [in the ship commanded by] Captain Hall should be returned to the place from whence it came, and that no duty should be paid upon it. They then adjourned to the afternoon, to give time for the consignees to deliberate. As soon as they reassembled, they resolved that the tea should be sent back in the same bottom in which it came. To this resolve the owner of the vessel, who was present in the meeting, said he must enter a protest. It was thereupon resolved that Mr. Rotch, the owner, be directed not to enter the tea, and Captain Hall, the master, not to suffer any of it to be landed, at their peril. They did not stop at mere declaratory acts or naked resolves. This, they knew, would render future acts and resolves contemptible. They established a watch of twenty-five inhabitants for securing the ship and cargo, and appointed a captain for the night…

The consignees, in a letter to the selectmen of Boston, which was read to the meeting, signified that it was utterly out of their power to send the tea back to England, but they would engage to keep it in a store until they could receive further directions from England, to which they afterwards added that they would be content to have it under the constant inspection of a committee, to be appointed by the town. But all was declared not in the least degree satisfactory, and that nothing short of sending back the tea would be so. The owner and master of the ship were directed to attend the "body"; and a vote passed, while they were present, without a negative, "that it is the firm resolution of the body that the owner shall return the tea in the same vessel in which it came, and that they now require it of him." The owner promised to comply, but intimated that it was by compulsion, and that he should be obliged to protest, to save himself from damage. The master also promised to carry it back…

As a permit or pass was always required at the castle, for all vessels except small coasters, and there were several men of war in the harbor, which it was supposed would stop the ship from proceeding any other way, the destruction of the tea was considered as necessary to prevent payment of the duty. A demand was made from the collector, in form, of a clearance for the ship, which he could not grant until the goods which were imported, and regularly entered, were landed, and the duties paid, or secured; and the like demand of a permit was made of the naval officer, with whom blank permits were intrusted by the Governor, to be filled up, and delivered to such vessels only as had been cleared at the custom-house, and, therefore, in this case was refused. It was expected that in twenty days after the arrival of the tea a demand of the duty would be made by the collector, and the ship or goods be seized; which would occasion additional difficulties. Another meeting of the body was, therefore, called, in order to inquire the reason of the delay in sending the ship back to England. The people came into Boston from the adjacent towns within twenty miles, from some, more, from others, less, as they were affected; and, as soon as they were assembled, enjoined the owner of the ship, at his peril, to demand of the collector of the customs a clearance for the ship, and appointed ten of their number a committee to accompany him; and adjourned for two days to receive the report. Being reassembled and informed by the owner that a clearance was refused, he was then enjoined immediately to apply to the Governor for a pass by the castle. He made an apology to the Governor for coming upon such an errand, having been compelled to it; and received an answer that no pass ever had been, or lawfully could be, given to any vessel which had not first been cleared at the custom house, and that, upon his producing a clearance, such pass would immediately be given by the naval officer. The Governor inquired of him whether he did not apprehend his ship in danger from the people, and offered him a letter to Admiral Montagu, desiring him to afford all necessary protection. He said he had been advised to remove his vessel under the stern of the admiral's ship, but, among other reasons for not doing it, mentioned his fears of the rage of the people; that his concern was not for his ship, which he did not believe was in danger, but he could not tell what would be the fate of the tea on board. He declined taking any letter to the admiral, and returned to the people. The Governor was unable to judge what would be the next step. The secretary had informed him that a principal leader of the people had declared, in the hearing of the deputy secretary, that, if the Governor should refuse a pass, he would demand it himself, at the head of one hundred and fifty men, &c.; and he was not without apprehensions of a further application. But he was relieved from his suspense, the same evening, by intelligence from town of the total destruction of the tea.

It was not expected that the Governor would comply with the demand; and, before it was possible for the owner of the ship to return from the country with an answer, about fifty men had prepared themselves, and passed by the house where the people were assembled to the wharf where the vessels lay, being covered with blankets, and making the appearance of Indians. The body of the people remained until they had received the Governor's answer; and then, after it had been observed to them that, every thing else in their power having been done, it now remained to proceed in the only way left, and that, the owner of the ship having behaved like a man of honor, no injury ought to be offered to his person or property, the meeting was declared to be dissolved, and the body of the people repaired to the wharf, and surrounded the immediate actors, as a guard and security, until they had finished their work. In two or three hours they hoisted out of the holds of the ships three hundred and forty-two chests of tea, and emptied them into the sea…

The Governor was unjustly censured by many people in the province, and much abused by the pamphlet and newspaper writers in England for refusing his pass, which, it was said, would have saved the property thus destroyed; but he would have been justly censured if he had granted it…

Even the declarations of the Governor against the unlawful invasions of the people upon the authority of government were charged against him as officious, unnecessary acts, and were made to serve to inflame the people and increase disorders…

Notwithstanding the forlorn state he was in, he thought it necessary to keep up some show of authority, and caused a council to be summoned to meet at Boston the day after the destruction of the tea, and went to town himself to be present at it; but a quorum did not attend. The people had not fully recovered from the state of mind which they were in the preceding night. Great pains had been taken to persuade them that the obstructions they had met with, which finally brought on the loss of the tea, were owing to his influence; and, being urged to it by his friends, he left the town, and lodged that night at the castle, under pretence of a visit to his sons, who were confined there with the other consignees of the tea. Failing in an attempt for a council the next day at Milton, he met them, three days after, at Cambridge, where they were much divided in their opinion. One of them declared against any step whatever. The people, he said, had taken the powers of government into their hands,—any attempt to restrain them would only enrage them, and render them more desperate; while another observed that, having done everything else in their power to prevent the tea from being landed, and all to no purpose, they had been driven to the necessity of destroying it, as a less evil than submission to the duty. So many of the actors and abettors were universally known that a proclamation, with a reward for discovery, would have been ridiculed. The attorney-general, therefore, was ordered to lay the matter before the grand jury, who, there was no room to expect, would ever find a bill for what they did not consider as an offence.

This was the boldest stroke which had yet been struck in America. The people in all parts of the province showed more or less concern at the expected consequences. They were, however, at a distance; something might intervene to divert them. Besides, the thing was done: there was no way of nullifying it. Their leaders feared no consequences. To engage the people in some desperate measure had long been their plan. They never discovered more concern than when the people were quiet upon the repeal of an act of Parliament, or upon concessions made, or assurances given; and never more satisfaction than when government had taken any new measures, or appeared to be inclined to them, tending, or which might be improved, to irritate and disturb the people. They had nothing to fear for themselves. They had gone too far to recede. If the colonies were subject to the supreme authority and laws of Great Britain, their offences, long since, had been of the highest nature. Their all depended upon attaining to the object which first engaged them. There was no way of attaining to it but by involving the body of the people in the same circumstances they were in themselves. And it is certain that ever after this time an opinion was easily instilled, and was continually increasing, that the body of the people had also gone too far to recede, and that an open and general revolt must be the consequence; and it was not long before actual preparations were visibly making for it in most parts of the province.

The First Continental Congress

Title: The First Continental Congress
Author: John Adams
Date: 1774
Source: America, Vol.3, p.106

That John Adams, school-master, lawyer, public man, member of the Continental Congress, diplomat and later Vice-President and President of the United States, was one of the keenest observers of his time is evidenced by this informal report of the sessions of the 1774 Continental Congress in Philadelphia, to which he was one of the five Massachusetts delegates. He modestly refrains from dwelling upon his own activities in the historic body, but his energy was devoted to the adoption of a comprehensive program having three distinct elements—the organization of commonwealth governments on an independent basis, the formation of a national confederate government, and the establishment of diplomatic relations with foreign powers.

His success in finally getting the Congress of 1776 to adopt resolutions recommending the formation of permanently independent state governments made the Declaration of Independence natural, if not inevitable. Adams was on the committee which drafted that document.

A T ten the delegates all met at the City Tavern, and walked to the Carpenters' Hall, where they took a view of the room, and of the chamber where is an excellent library; there is also a long entry where gentlemen may walk, and a convenient chamber opposite to the

All material contained herein was extracted from the
US Constitution Coach Kit at PowerThink.com
(Over 60,000 Works & Documents of American History)

library. The general cry was that this was a good room, and the question was put, whether we were satisfied with this room? It passed in the affirmative. A very few were for the negative, and they were chiefly from Pennsylvania and New York. Then Mr. Lynch arose, and said there was a gentleman present who had presided with great dignity over a very respectable society, greatly to the advantage of America, and he therefore proposed that the Honorable Peyton Randolph, Esquire, one of the delegates from Virginia, and the late Speaker of their House of Burgesses, should be appointed Chairman, and he doubted not it would be unanimous.

The question was put, and he was unanimously chosen.

Mr. Randolph then took the chair, and the commission of the delegates were all produced and read.

Then Mr. Lynch proposed that Mr. Charles Thomson, a gentleman of family, fortune and character in this city, should be appointed Secretary, which was accordingly done without opposition, though Mr. Duane and Mr. Jay discovered at first an inclination to seek further.

Mr. Duane then moved that a committee should be appointed to prepare regulations for this Congress. Several gentlemen objected.

I then arose and asked leave of the President to request of the gentleman from New York an explanation, and that he would point out some particular regulations which he had in mind. He mentioned particularly the method of voting, whether it should be by colonies, or by the poll, or by interests.

Mr. Henry then arose, and said this was the first general Congress which had ever happened; that no former Congress could be a precedent; that we should have occasion for more general Congresses, and therefore that a precedent ought to be established now; that it would be great injustice if a little colony should have the same weight in the councils of America as a great one, and therefore he was for a committee.

Major Sullivan observed that a little colony had its all at stake as well as a great one...

Mr. Henry. Government is dissolved. Fleets and armies and the present state of things show that government is dissolved. Where are your landmarks, your boundaries of colonies? We are in a state of nature, sir. I did propose that a scale should be laid down; that part of North America which was once Massachusetts Bay, and that part which was once Virginia, ought to be considered as having a weight. Will not people complain? Ten thousand Virginians have not outweighed one thousand others. I will submit, however; I am determined to submit, if I am overruled. A worthy gentleman (ego) near me seemed to admit the necessity of obtaining a more adequate representation. I hope future ages will quote our proceedings with applause. It is one of the great duties of the democratical part of the constitution to keep itself pure. It is known in my province that some other colonies are not so numerous or rich as they are. I am for giving all the satisfaction in my power. The distinctions between Virginians, Pennsylvanians, New Yorkers, and New Englanders, are no more. I am not a Virginian, but an American. Slaves are to be thrown out of the question, and if the freemen can be represented according to their numbers, I am satisfied.

Mr. Lynch. I differ in one point from the gentleman from Virginia, that is, in thinking that numbers only ought to determine the weight of colonies. I think that property ought to be considered, and that it ought to be a compound of numbers and property that should determine the weight of the colonies. I think it cannot be now settled.

Mr. Rutledge. We have no legal authority; and obedience to our determinations will only follow the reasonableness, the apparent utility and necessity of the measures we adopt. We have no coercive or legislative authority. Our constituents are bound only in honor to observe our determinations.

Governor Ward. There are a great number of counties, in Virginia, very unequal in point of wealth and numbers, yet each has a right to send two members.

Mr. Lee. But one reason, which prevails with me, and that is, that we are not at this time provided with proper materials. I am afraid we are not.

Mr. Gadsden. I can't see any way of voting but by colonies.

Colonel Bland. I agree with the gentleman (ego) who spoke near me, that we are not at present provided with materials to ascertain the importance of each colony. The question is, whether the rights and liberties of America shall be contended for, or given up to arbitrary powers.

Mr. Pendleton. If the committee should find themselves unable to ascertain the weight of the colonies, by their numbers and property, they will report this, and this will lay the foundation for the Congress to take some other steps to procure evidence of numbers and property at some future time.

Mr. Henry. I agree that authentic accounts cannot be had, if by authenticity is meant attestations of officers of the Crown. I go upon the supposition that government is at an end. All distinctions are thrown down. All America is thrown into one mass. We must aim at the minutiae of rectitude.

Mr. Jay. Could I suppose that we came to frame an American Constitution, instead of endeavoring to correct the faults in an old one—I can't yet think that all government is at an end. The measure of arbitrary power is not full, and I think it must run over, before we undertake to frame a new Constitution. To the virtue, spirit, and abilities of Virginia, we owe much. I should always, therefore, from inclination as well as justice, be for giving Virginia its full weight. I am not clear that we ought not to be bound by a majority, though ever so small, but I only mentioned it as a matter of danger, worthy of consideration...

7. Wednesday. Went to Congress again, heard Mr. Duche read prayers; the collect for the day, the 7th of the month, was most admirably adapted, though this was accidental, or rather providential. A prayer which he gave us of his own composition was as pertinent, as affectionate, as sublime, as devout, as I ever heard offered up to Heaven. He filled every bosom present...

10. Saturday. Attended my duty upon the subcommittee. Dined at home. Dr. Morgan, Dr. Cox, Mr. Spence, and several other gentlemen, Major Sullivan and Colonel Folsom, dined with us upon salt fish. Rambled in the evening with Jo Reed, and fell into Mr. Sprout's meeting, where we heard Mr. Spence preach. Mr. Reed returned with Mr. Adams and me to our lodgings, and a very sociable, agreeable, and communicative evening we had. He says we never were guilty of a more masterly stroke of policy, than in moving that Mr. Duche might read prayers; it has had a very good effect, &c. He says the sentiments of people here are growing more and more favorable every day.

11. Sunday. There is such a quick and constant succession of new scenes, characters, persons, and events, turning up before me, that I can't keep any regular account...

12. Monday... dined with Mr. Dickinson at his seat at Fair Hill... Mr. Dickinson has a fine seat, a beautiful prospect of the city, the river, and the country, fine gardens, and a very grand library.

Mr. Dickinson is a very modest man, and very ingenious as well as agreeable; he has an excellent heart, and the cause of his country lies near it. He is full and clear for allowing to Parliament the regulation of trade, upon principles of necessity, and the mutual interest of both countries.

13. Tuesday. Attended my duty all day on the sub-committee. Agreed on a report.

14. Wednesday. Visited Mr. Gadsden, Mr. Deane, Colonel Dyer, &c., at their lodgings. Gadsden is violent against allowing to Parliament any power of regulating trade, or allowing that they have anything to do with us. "Power of regulating trade," he says, "is power of ruining us; as bad as acknowledging them a supreme legislative in all cases whatsoever; a right of regulating trade is a right of legislation, and a right of legislation in one case is a right in all; this I deny." Attended the Congress and committee all the fore-noon; dined with Dr. Cox... A mighty feast again; nothing less than the very best of Claret, Madeira, and Burgundy; melons, fine beyond description, and pears and peaches as excellent. This day Mr. Chase introduced to us a Mr. Carroll, of Annapolis, a very sensible gentleman, a Roman Catholic, and of the first fortune in America. His income is ten thousand pounds sterling a year now, will be fourteen in two or three years, they say; besides, his father has a vast estate which will be his after his father...

17. Saturday. This was one of the happiest days of my life. In Congress we had generous, noble sentiments, and manly eloquence. This day convinced me that America will support the Massachusetts or perish with her.

28. Wednesday. Dined with Mr. R. Penn; a magnificent house, and a most splendid feast, and a very large company. Mr. Dickinson and General Lee were there, and Mr. Moylan, besides a great number of the delegates. Spent the evening at home, with Colonel Lee, Colonel Washington, and Dr. Shippen, who came in to consult with us...

[Oct] 10. Monday. The deliberations of the Congress are spun out to an immeasurable length. There is so much wit, sense, learning, acuteness, subtlety, eloquence, &c. among fifty gentlemen, each of whom has been habituated to lead and guide in his own province, that an immensity of time is spent unnecessarily. Johnson of Maryland has a clear and a cool head, an extensive knowledge of trade as well as law. He is a deliberating man, but not a shining orator; his passions and imagination don't appear enough for an orator; his reason and penetration appear, but not his rhetoric. Galloway, Duane, and Johnson are sensible and learned, but cold speakers. Lee, Henry, and Hooper, are the orators; Paca is a deliberator too; Chase speaks warmly; Mifflin is a sprightly and spirited speaker; John Rutledge don't exceed in learning or oratory, though he is a rapid speaker; young Edward Rutledge is young and zealous, a little unsteady and injudicious, but very unnatural and affected as a speaker; Dyer and Sherman speak often and long, but very heavily and clumsily…

20. Thursday. Dined with the whole Congress, at the city tavern, at the invitation of the House of Representatives of the province of Pennsylvania. The whole House dined with us, making near one hundred guests in the whole; a most elegant entertainment. A sentiment was given: "May the sword of the parent never be stained with the blood of her children." Two or three broad-brims over against me at table; one of them said, this is not a toast, but a prayer; come, let us join in it. And they took their glasses accordingly… .

24. Monday. In Congress, nibbling and quibbling as usual. There is no greater mortification than to sit with half a dozen wits, deliberating upon a petition, address, or memorial. These great wits, these subtle critics, these refined geniuses, these learned lawyers, these wise statesmen, are so fond of showing their parts and powers, as to make their consultations very tedious. Young Ned Rutledge is a perfect Bob-o-Lincoln,—a swallow, a sparrow, a peacock; excessively vain, excessively weak, and excessively variable and unsteady; jejune, inane, and puerile. Mr. Dickinson is very modest, delicate, and timid. Spent the evening at home. Colonel Dyer, Judge Sherman, and Colonel Floyd came in, and spent the evening with Mr. Adams and me. Mr. Mifflin and General Lee came in. Lee's head is running upon his new plan of a battalion…

26. Wednesday. Dined at home. This day the Congress finished. Spent the evening together at the city tavern; all the Congress, and several gentleman of the town. .

28. Friday. Took our departure, in a very great rain, from the happy, the peaceful, the elegant, the hospitable, and polite city of Philadelphia. It is not very likely that I shall ever see this part of the world again, but I shall ever retain a most grateful, pleasing sense of the many civilities I have received in it, and shall think myself happy to have an opportunity of returning them.

Logan to Lord Dunmore

Title: Logan to Lord Dunmore
Author: Logan
Date: 1774
Source: The World's Famous Orations, Vol.8, pp.3-4

Lord Dunmore at this time was governor of Virginia. Logan's speech was really a message sent to Dunmore by Logan through John Gibson, an Indian trader. There was war at that time between the Indians and whites on the western frontier of Virginia. Trouble had long existed in that region, but the killing of Logan's family had now become the immediate cause of a general outbreak. The war was brought to a close on October 10 by the Battle of Point Pleasant, in which Logan is said personally to have taken thirty scalps.

Born about 1725, died in 1780; his real name, Tahgahjute; by birth a Cayuga, but made a Chief of the Mingoes; lived for many years in western Pennsylvania; his family murdered by the whites in 1774; killed near Detroit in a skirmish with Indians.

I APPEAL to any white man to say if ever he entered Logan's cabin hungry, and he gave him not meat; if ever he came cold and naked, and he clothed him not. During the course of the last long and bloody war Logan remained idle in his cabin, an advocate for peace. Such was my love for the whites that my countrymen pointed at me as they passed, and said: "Logan is the friend of white men."

I had even thought to have lived with you, but for the injuries of one man. Colonel Cresap, the last spring, in cold blood and unprovoked, murdered all the relations of Logan, not sparing even my women and children. There runs not a drop of my blood in the veins of any living creature.

This called on me for revenge. I have sought it. I have killed many. I have glutted my vengeance. For my country, I rejoice at the beams of peace. But do not think that mine is the joy of fear. Logan never felt fear. Logan will not turn on his heel to save his life. Who is there to mourn for Logan? Not one!

Patrick Henry's Call to Arms

Title: Patrick Henry's Call to Arms
Author: William Wirt
Date: 1775
Source: Great Epochs in American History, Vol.3, p.103-109

On Monday, the 20th of March, 1775, the convention of delegates, from the several counties and corporations of Virginia, met for the second time. This assembly was held in the old church in the town of Richmond. Mr. Henry was a member of that body also. The reader will bear in mind the tone of the instructions given by the convention of the preceding year to their deputies in Congress. He will remember that, while they recite with great feeling the series of grievances under which the colonies had labored, and insist with firmness on their constitutional rights, they give, nevertheless, the most explicit and solemn pledge of their faith and true allegiance to his Majesty King George III., and avow their determination to support him with their lives and fortunes, in the legal exercise of all his just rights and prerogatives. He will remember, that these instructions contain also an expression of their sincere approbation of a connection with Great Britain, and their ardent wishes for a return of that friendly intercourse from which this country had derived so much prosperity and happiness. These sentiments still influenced many of the leading members of the convention of 1775. They could not part with the fond hope that those peaceful days would again return which had shed so much light and warmth over the land; and the report of the king's gracious reception of the petition from Congress tended to cherish and foster that hope, and to render them averse to any means of violence.

But Mr. Henry saw things with a steadier eye and a deeper insight. His judgment was too solid to be duped by appearances; and his heart too firm and manly to be amused by false and flattering hopes. He had long since read the true character of the British court, and saw that no alternative remained for his country but abject submission or heroic resistance. It was not for a soul like Henry's to hesitate between these courses. He had offered upon the altar of liberty no divided heart. The gulf of war which yawned before him was indeed fiery and fearful; but he saw that the awful plunge was inevitable. The body of the convention, however, hesitated. They cast around "a longing, lingering look" on those flowery fields on which peace, and ease, and joy, were still sporting; and it required all the energies of a Mentor like Henry to push them from the precipice, and conduct them over the stormy sea of the revolution, to liberty and glory…

His was a spirit fitted to raise the whirlwind, as well as to ride in and direct it. His was that comprehensive view, that unerring pre-science, that perfect command over the actions of men, which qualified him not merely to guide, but almost to create the destinies of nations.

He rose at this time with a majesty unusual tohim in an exordium, and with all that self-possession by which he was so invariably distin-guished. "No man," he said, "thought more highly than he did of the patriotism, as well as abilities, of the very worthy gentlemen who had just addrest the house. But different men often saw the same subject in different lights; and, therefore, he hoped it would not be thought disre-spectful to those gentlemen, if, entertaining as he did, opinions of a character very opposite to theirs, he should speak forth his sentiments freely, and without reserve. "This," he said, "was no time for ceremony. The question before this house was one of awful moment to the country. For his own part, he considered it as nothing less than a question of freedom or slavery. And in proportion to the magnitude of the subject ought to be the freedom of the debate. It was only in this way that they could hope to arrive at truth, and fulfil the great responsibility which they held to God and their country. Should he keep back his opinions at such a time, through fear of giving offense, he should consider him-self as guilty of treason toward his country, and of an act of disloyalty toward the majesty of heaven, which he revered above all earthly kings."

"Mr. President," said he, "it is natural to man to indulge in the illu-sions of hope. We are apt to shut our eyes against a painful truth—and listen to the song of that siren, till she transforms us into beasts. Is this," he asked, "the part of wise men, engaged in a great and arduous struggle for liberty? Were we disposed to be of a number of those, who having eyes, see not, and having ears, hear not, the things which so nearly con-cern their temporal salvation? For his part, whatever an-guish of spirit it might cost, he was willing to know the whole truth; to know the worst, and to provide for it."

"He had," he said, "but one lamp by which his feet were guided; and that was the lamp of experience. He knew of no way of judging by the past, he wished to know what there had been in the conduct of the British ministry for the last ten years, to justify those hopes with which gentlemen had been pleased to solace themselves and the house? Is it that insidious smile with which our petition has been lately received?

All material contained herein was extracted from the
US Constitution Coach Kit at PowerThink.com
(Over 60,000 Works & Documents of American History)

Trust it not, sir; it will prove a snare to your feet. Suffer not yourselves to be betrayed with a kiss. Ask yourselves how this gracious reception of our petition comports with those warlike preparations which cover our waters and darken our land. Are fleets and armies necessary to a work of love and reconciliation? Have we shown ourselves so unwilling to be reconciled, that force must be called in to win back our love? Let us not deceive ourselves, sir. These are the implements of war and subjugation—the last arguments to which kings resort.

"I ask gentlemen, sir, what means this martial array, if its purpose be not to force us to submission? Can gentlemen assign any other possible motive for it? Has Great Britain any enemy in this quarter of the world, to call for all this accumulation of navies and armies? No, sir, she has none. They are meant for us: they can be meant for no other. They are sent over to bind and rivet upon us those chains which the British ministry have been so long forging. And what have we to oppose to them? Shall we try argument? Sir, we have been trying that for the last ten years. Have we anything new to offer upon the subject? Nothing. We have held the subject up in every light of which it is capable; but it has been all in vain. Shall we resort to entreaty and humble supplication? What terms shall we find, which have not been already exhausted? Let us not, I beseech you, sir, deceive ourselves longer. Sir, we have done everything that could be done to avert the storm which is now coming on. We have petitioned—we have remonstrated—we have supplicated—we have prostrated ourselves before the throne, and have implored its interposition to arrest the tyrannical hands of the ministry and parliament. Our petitions have been slighted; our remonstrances have produced additional violence and insult; our supplications have been disregarded; and we have been spurned, with contempt, from the foot of throne. In vain, after these things, may we indulge the fond hope of peace and reconciliation. There is no longer any room for hope. If we wish to be free—if we mean to preserve inviolate those inestimable privileges for which we have been so long contending—if we mean not basely to abandon the noble struggle in which we have been so long engaged, and which we have pledged ourselves never to abandon, until the glorious object of our contest shall be obtained—we must fight!—I repeat it, sir, we must fight!! An appeal to arms and to the God of hosts, is all that is left us!"

"They tell us, sir," continued Mr. Henry, "that we are weak—unable to cope with so formidable an adversary. But when shall we be stronger. Will it be the next week or the next year? Will it be when we are totally disarmed, and when a British guard shall be stationed in every house?

Shall we gather strength by irresolution and inaction? Shall we acquire the means of effectual resistance by lying supinely on our backs, and hugging the delusive fantom of hope, until our enemies shall have bound us hand and foot? Sir, we are not weak, if we make a proper use of these means which the God of nature hath placed in our power. Three millions of people armed in the holy cause of liberty and in such a country as that which we possess, are invincible by any force which our enemy can send against us. Besides, sir, we shall not fight our battles alone. There is a just God who presides over the destinies of nations, and who will raise up friends to fight our battles for us. The battle, sir, is not to the strong alone; it is to the vigilant, the active, the brave. Besides, sir, we have no election. If we were base enough to desire it, it is now too late to retire from the contest. There is no retreat but in submission and slavery! Our chains are forged. Their clanking may be heard on the plains of Boston! The war is inevitable—and let it come!! I repeat it, sir, let it come!!!

"It is vain, sir, to extenuate the matter. Gentlemen may cry, peace, peace—but there is no peace. The war is actually begun! The next gale that sweeps from the north will bring to our ears the clash of resounding arms! Our brethren are already in the field! Why stand we here idle? What is it that gentlemen wish? What would they have? Is life so dear, or peace so sweet, as to be purchased at the price of chains and slavery? Forbid it, Almighty God—I know not what course others may take; but as for me," cried he, with both his arms extended aloft, his brows knit, every feature marked with the resolute purpose of his soul, and his voice swelled to its boldest note of exclamation—"give me liberty, or give me death!"

He took his seat, No murmur of applause was heard. The effect was too deep. After the trance of a moment, several members started from their seats. The cry, "to arms!" seemed to quiver on every lip, and gleam from every eye. Richard H. Lee arose and supported Mr. Henry, with his usual spirit and elegance. But his melody was lost amid the agitations of that ocean, which the master-spirit of the storm had lifted up on high. That supernatural voice still sounded in their ears, and shivered along their arteries. They heard, in every pause, the cry of liberty or death. They became impatient of speech—their souls were on fire for action.

Lexington, Concord and Bunker Hill

Title: Lexington, Concord and Bunker Hill
Author: William E. H. Lecky
Date: 1775
Source: Great Epochs in American History, Vol.3, pp.110-114

On the night of April 18, 1775, General Gage sent about 800 soldiers to capture an magazine of stores which had been collected for the use of the provincial army in the town of Concord, about eighteen miles from Boston. The road lay through the little village of Lexington, where, about five o'clock on the morning of the 19th, the advance guard of the British found a party of sixty or seventy armed volunteers drawn up to oppose them, on a green beside the road. They refused when summoned to disperse, and the English at once fired a volley, which killed or wounded sixteen of their number. The detachment then proceeded to Concord, where it succeeded in spiking two cannon, casting into the river five hundred pounds of ball and sixty barrels of powder, and destroying a large quantity of flour, and it then prepared to return. The alarm had, however, now been given; the whole country was aroused. Great bodies of yeomen and militia flocked in to the assistance of the provincials. From farm-houses and hedges, and from the shelter of stone walls, bullets poured upon the tired retreating troops, and a complete disaster would probably have occurred had they not been reenforced at Lexington by 900 men and two cannon under Lord Percy. As it was the British lost 65 killed, 180 wounded, and 28 made prisoners, while the American loss was less than 90 men.

The whole province was now in arms. The Massachusetts Congress at once resolved that the New England army should be raised to 30,000 men, and thousands of brave and ardent yeomen were being rapidly drilled into good soldiers. The American camp at Cambridge contained many experienced soldiers who had learnt their profession in the great French war, and very many others who in the ranks of the militia had already acquired the rudiments of military knowledge, and even when they had no previous training, the recruits were widely different from the rude peasants who filled the armies of England. As an American military writer truly said, the middle and lower classes in England, owing to the operation of the game laws, and to the circumstances of their lives, were in general almost as ignorant of the use of a musket as of the use of a catapult. The New England yeomen were accustomed to firearms from their childhood; they were invariably skilful in the use of spade, hatchet, and pickax, so important in military operations; and their great natural quickness and the high level of intelligence which their excellent schools had produced, made it certain that they would not be long in mastering their military duties. The whole country was practically at their disposal. All who were suspected of Toryism were ordered to surrender their weapons. General Gage was blockaded in Boston, and he remained strictly on the defensive, waiting for reenforcements from England, which only arrived at the end of May. Even then, he for some time took no active measures, but contented himself with offering pardon to all insurgents who laid down their arms, except Samuel Adams and John Hancock, and with proclaiming martial law in Massachusetts. He at length, however, determined to extend his lines, so as to include and fortify a very important post, which by a strange negligence had been left hitherto unoccupied.

On a narrow peninsula to the north of Boston, but separated from it by rather less than half a mile of water, lay the little town of Charleston, behind which rose two small connected hills, which commanded a great part both of the town and harbor of Boston. Breed's Hill, which was nearest to Charleston, was about seventy-five feet, Bunker's Hill was about one hundred and ten feet, in height. The peninsula, which was little more than a mile long, was connected with the mainland by a narrow causeway. Cambridge, the headquarters of the American forces, was by road about four miles from Bunker's Hill, but much of the intervening space was occupied by American outposts. The possession, under these circumstances, of Bunker's Hill, was a matter of great military importance, and Gage determined to fortify it. The Americans learnt his intention, and determined to defeat it.

On the night of June 16, an American force under the command of Colonel Prescott, and accompanied by some skilful engineers and by a few field-guns, silently occupied Breed's Hill, and threw up a strong redoubt before daylight revealed their presence to the British. Next day, after much unnecessary delay, a detachment under General Howe was sent from Boston to dislodge them. The Americans had in the meantime received some reenforcements from their camp, but the whole force upon the hill is said not to have exceeded 1,500 men. Most of them were inexperienced volunteers. Many of them were weary with a long night's toil, and they had been exposed for hours to a harassing tho ineffectual fire from the ships in the harbor; but they were now strongly entrenched behind a redoubt and a breastwork. The British engaged on this memorable day consisted in all of between 2,000 and 3,000 regular troops, fresh from the barracks, and supported by artillery.

The town of Charleston, having been occupied by some American riflemen, who poured their fire upon the English from the shelter of the houses, was burnt by order of General Howe, and its flames cast a ghastly splendor upon the scene. The English were foolishly encumbered by heavy knapsacks with three days' provisions. Instead of endeavoring to cut off the Americans by occupying the neck of land to the rear of Breed's Hill, they climbed the steep and difficult ascent in front of the battery, struggling through the long, tangled grass beneath a burning sun, and exposed at every step to the fire of a sheltered enemy. The Americans waited till their assailants were within a few rods of the entrenchment, when they greeted them with a fire so deadly and so sustained that the British line twice recoiled, broken, intimidated, and disordered. The third attack was more successful. The position was carried at the point of the bayonet. The Americans were put to flight, and five out of their six cannon were taken. But the victory was dearly purchased. On the British side 1,054 men, including 89 commissioned officers, fell. The Americans only admitted a loss of 449 men; and they contended that, if they had been properly reenforced, and if their ammunition had not begun to fail, they would have held the position.

The battle of Breed's, or, as it is commonly called, of Bunker's Hill, tho extremely bloody in proportion to the number of men engaged, can hardly be said to present any very remarkable military character, and in a great European war it would have been almost unnoticed. Few battles, however, have had more important consequences. It roused at once the fierce instinct of combat in America, weakened seriously the only British army in New England, and dispelled forever the almost superstitious belief in the impossibility of encountering regular troops with hastily-levied volunteers. The ignoble taunts which had been directed against the Americans were for ever silenced. No one questioned the conspicuous gallantry with which the provincial troops had supported a long fire from the ships and awaited the charge of the enemy, and British soldiers had been twice driven back in disorder before their fire. From this time the best judges predicted the ultimate success of America.

Patrick Henry's "Give Me Liberty Or Give Me Death" Speech, 1775

Title: "Give Me Liberty Or Give Me Death"
Author: Patrick Henry
Date: 1775
Source: America, Vol.3, p.115

Having utterly failed in farming and in trade, Patrick Henry, whose famous speech against British tyranny was made in 1775, studied law for a month in 1760 and had the boldness to ask for license to practice. It was granted to him, at the age of twenty-four, on condition that he would extend his studies before undertaking to practice.

Three years later Henry leapt into prominence by arguing a celebrated case, known as the "Parson's Cause," so brilliantly that the court-room audience bore him in triumph on their shoulders. Thereafter clients were plentiful.

This "liberty or death" exhortation was made shortly after he had served as a delegate to the first Continental Congress. His resolutions to organize the Virginia militia and put the colony in an attitude of defense were adopted unanimously after its delivery. Henry declined a United States Senatorship, declined to be Secretary of State under Washington, nor would he accept the Chief Justiceship of the U. S. Supreme Court.

MR. PRESIDENT: It is natural to man to indulge in the illusions of hope. We are apt to shut our eyes against a painful truth—and listen to the song of that siren, till she transforms us into beasts. Is this the part of wise men, engaged in a great and arduous struggle for liberty? Are we disposed to be of the number of those, who having eyes, see not, and having ears, hear not, the things which so nearly concern their temporal salvation? For my part, whatever anguish of spirit it may cost, I am willing to know the whole truth; to know the worst, and to provide for it.

I have but one lamp by which my feet are guided; and that is the lamp of experience. I know of no way of judging of the future but by the past. And judging by the past, I wish to know what there has been in the conduct of the British ministry for the last ten years, to justify those hopes with which gentlemen have been pleased to solace themselves and the house? Is it that insidious smile with which our petition has been lately received? Trust it not, sir; it will prove a snare to your feet. Suffer not yourselves to be betrayed with a kiss. Ask yourselves how this gracious reception of our petition comports with those warlike

All material contained herein was extracted from the
US Constitution Coach Kit at PowerThink.com
(Over 60,000 Works & Documents of American History)

preparations which cover our waters and darken our land. Are fleets and armies necessary to a work of love and reconciliation? Have we shown ourselves so unwilling to be reconciled that force must be called in to win back our love? Let us not deceive ourselves, sir. These are the implements of war and subjugation—the last arguments to which kings resort. I ask gentlemen, sir, what means this martial array, if its purpose be not to force us to submission? Can gentlemen assign any other possible motive for it? Has Great Britain any enemy in this quarter of the world, to call for all this accumulation of navies and armies? No, sir, she has none. They are meant for us: they can be meant for no other. They are sent over to bind and rivet upon us those chains which the British ministry have been so long forging. And what have we to oppose to them? Shall we try argument? Sir, we have been trying that for the last ten years. Have we anything new to offer upon the subject? Nothing. We have held the subject up in every light of which it is capable; but it has been all in vain. Shall we resort to entreaty and humble supplication? What terms shall we find which have not been already exhausted? Let us not, I beseech you, sir, deceive ourselves longer.

Sir, we have done everything that could be done to avert the storm which is now coming on. We have petitioned—we have remonstrated—we have supplicated—we have prostrated ourselves before the throne, and have implored its interposition to arrest the tyrannical hands of the ministry and parliament. Our petitions have been slighted; our remonstrances have produced additional violence and insult; our supplications have been disregarded; and we have been spurned, with contempt, from the foot of the throne. In vain, after these things, may we indulge the fond hope of peace and reconciliation. There is no longer any room for hope. If we wish to be free—if we mean to preserve inviolate those inestimable privileges for which we have been so long contending—if we mean not basely to abandon the noble struggle in which we have been so long engaged, and which we have pledged ourselves never to abandon until the glorious object of our contest shall be obtained—we must fight!—I repeat it, sir, we must fight!! An appeal to arms and to the God of Hosts, is all that is left us!

They tell us, sir, that we are weak—unable to cope with so formidable an adversary. But when shall we be stronger? Will it be the next week or the next year? Will it be when we are totally disarmed, and when a British guard shall be stationed in every house? Shall we gather strength by irresolution and inaction? Shall we acquire the means of effectual resistance by lying supinely on our backs, and hugging the delusive phantom of hope, until our enemies shall have bound us hand

and foot? Sir, we are not weak, if we make a proper use of those means which the God of nature has placed in our power. Three millions of people, armed in the holy cause of liberty, and in such a country as that which we possess, are invincible by any force which our enemy can send against us. Besides, sir, we shall not fight our battles alone. There is a just God who presides over the destinies of nations; and who will raise up friends to fight our battles for us. The battle, sir, is not to the strong alone; it is to the vigilant, the active, the brave. Besides, sir, we have no election. If we were base enough to desire it, it is now too late to retire from the contest. There is no retreat but in submission and slavery! Our chains are forged. Their clanking may be heard on the plains of Boston! The war is inevitable and let it come!! I repeat it, sir, let it come!!!

It is in vain, sir, to extenuate the matter. Gentlemen may cry, peace, peace—but there is no peace. The war is actually begun! The next gale that sweeps from the north will bring to our ears the clash of resounding arms! Our brethren are already in the field! Why stand we here idle? What is it that gentlemen wish? What would they have? Is life so dear, or peace so sweet, as to be purchased at the price of chains and slavery? Forbid it, Almighty God!—I know not what course others may take; but as for me, give me liberty or give me death!

Washington's Appointment as Commander-in-chief

Title: Washington's Appointment as Commander-in-Chief
Author: Washington Irving
Date: 1775
Source: Great Epochs in American History, Vol.3, pp.118-126

The difficult question was, who should be commander-in-chief? Adams, in his diary, gives us glimpses of the conflict of opinions and interest within doors. There was a Southern party, he said, which could not brook the idea of a New England army commanded by a New England general. "Whether this jealousy was sincere," writes he, "or whether it was mere pride, and a haughty ambition of furnishing a Southern general to command the Northern army, I can not say; but the intention was very visible to me, that Colonel Washington was their object; and so many of our stanchest men were in the plan that we could carry nothing without conceding to it. There was another embarrassment, which was never publicly known, and which carefully concealed by those who knew it: the Massachusetts and other New England delegates were divided. Mr. Hancock and Mr. Cushing hung back; Mr. Paine did not come forward, and even Mr. Samuel Adams was irresolute. Mr. Hancock himself had an ambition to be appointed commander-in-chief. Whether he thought an election a compliment due to him, and intended to have the honor of declining it, or whether he would have accepted it, I know not. To the compliment he had some pretensions; for, at that time, his exertions, sacrifices, and general merits in the cause of his country had been incomparably greater than those of Colonel Washington. But the delicacy of his health, and his entire want of experience in actual service, tho an excellent militia officer, were decisive objections to him in my mind."...

The opinion evidently inclined in favor of Washington; yet it was promoted by no clique of partizans or admirers. More than one of the Virginia delegates, says Adams, were cool on the subject of this appointment; and particularly Mr. Pendleton was clear and full against it. It is scarcely necessary to add that Washington, in this as in every other situation in life, made no step in advance to clutch the impending honor.

Adams, in his diary, claims the credit of bringing the members of Congress to a decision. Rising in his place one day and stating briefly but earnestly the exigencies of the case, he moved that Congress should adopt the army at Cambridge, and appoint a general. Tho this was not the time to nominate the person, "yet," adds he, "as I had reason to believe this was a point of some difficulty, I had no hesitation to declare, that I had but one gentleman in my mind for that important command, and that was a gentleman from Virginia, who was among us and very well known to all of us; a gentleman whose skill and experience as an officer, whose independent fortune, great talents, and excellent universal character would command the approbation of all America, and unitethe cordial exertion of all the colonies better than any other person in the Union. Mr. Washington, who happened to sit near the door, as soon as he heard me allude to him, from his usual modesty, darted into the library-room. Mr. Hancock, who was our president, which gave me an opportunity to observe his countenance, while I was speaking on the state of the colonies, the army at Cambridge and the enemy, heard me with visible pleasure; but when I came to describe Washington for the commander, I never remarked a more sudden and striking change of countenance. Mortification and resentment were exprest as forcibly as his face could exhibit them. When the subject came under debate several delegates opposed the appointment of Washington; not from personal affection, but because the army were all from New England, and had a general of their own, General Artemas Ward, with whom they appeared well satisfied; and under whose command they had proved themselves able to imprison the British army in Boston; which was all that was expected or desired."

The subject was postponed to a future day. In the interim pains were taken out of doors to obtain a unanimity, and the voices were in general so clearly in favor of Washington that the dissentient members were persuaded to withdraw their opposition.

On the 15th of June the army was regularly adopted by Congress, and the pay of the commander-in-chief fixt at five hundred dollars a month. Many still clung to the idea, that in all these proceedings they were merely opposing the measures of the ministry, and not the authority of the crown, and thus the army before Boston wasdesignated as the Continental Army, in contradistinction to that under General Gage, which was called the Ministerial Army.

In this stage of the business Mr. Johnson, of Maryland, rose and nominated Washington for the station of commander-in-chief. The election was by ballot, and was unanimous. It was formally announced to him by the president, on the following day, when he had taken his seat in Congress. Rising in his place, he briefly exprest his high and grateful sense of the honor conferred on him, and his sincere devotion to the cause. "But," added he, "lest some unlucky event should happen unfavorable to my reputation, I beg it may be remembered by every gentleman in the room, that I this day declare, with the utmost sincerity, I do not think myself equal to the command I am honored with. As to pay, I beg leave to assure the Congress that, as no pecuniary consideration could have tempted me to accept this arduous employment, at the expense of my domestic ease and happiness, I do not wish to make any profit of it. I will keep an exact account of my expenses. Those, I doubt not, they will discharge, and that is all I desire."

"There is something charming to me in the conduct of Washington," writes Adams to a friend; "a gentleman of one of the first fortunes upon the continent, leaving his delicious retirement, his family and friends, sacrificing his ease, and hazarding all, in the cause of his country. His views are noble and disinterested. He declared, when he accepted the mighty trust, that he would lay before us an exact account of his expenses, and not accept a shilling of pay."...

In this momentous change in his condition, which suddenly altered all his course of life, and called him immediately to the camp, Washington's thoughts recurred to Mount Vernon, and its rural delights, so dear to his heart, whence he was to be again exiled. His chief concern, however, was on account of the distress it might cause his wife. His letter to her on the subject is written in a tone of manly tenderness. "You may believe me," writes he, "when I assure you, in the most solemn manner, that, so far from seeking this appointment, I have used every endeavor in my power to avoid it, not only from my unwillingness to part with you and the family, but from a consciousness of its being a trust too great for my capacity; and I should enjoy more real happiness in one month with you at home than I have the most distant prospect of finding abroad, if my stay were to be seven times seven years. But as it has been a kind of destiny that has thrown me upon this service, I shall hope that my undertaking it is designed to answer some good purpose. I shall rely confidently on that Providence which has hitherfore preserved, and has been bountiful to me, not doubting but that I shall return safe to you in the fall. I shall feel no pain from the toil or danger of the campaign; my unhappiness will flow from the uneasiness I know you will feel from being left alone. I therefore beg that you will summon your whole fortitude, and pass your time as agreeably as possible. Nothing will give me so much satisfaction as to hear this, and to hear it from your own pen."

And to his favorite brother, John Augustine, he writes: "I am now to bid adieu to you, and to every kind of domestic ease, for a while. I amembarked on a wide ocean, boundless in its prospect, and in which, perhaps, no safe harbor is to be found. I have been called upon by the unanimous voice of the colonies to take the command of the continental army; an honor I neither sought after nor desired, as I am thoroughly convinced that it requires great abilities, and much more experience than I am master of." And, subsequently, referring to his wife: "I shall hope that my friends will visit, and endeavor to keep up the spirits of my wife as much as they can, for my departure will, I know, be a cutting stroke upon her; and on this account alone I have many disagreeable sensations."

On the 20th of June he received his commission from the President of Congress. The following day was fixt upon for his departure for the army. He reviewed previously, at the request of their officers, several militia companies of horse and foot. Every one was anxious to see the new commander, and rarely has the public beau ideal of a commander been so fully answered. He was now in the vigor of his days, forty-three years of age, stately in person, noble in his demeanor, calm and dignified in his deportment; as he sat his horse, with manly grace, his military presence delighted every eye, and wherever he went the air rang with acclamations…

He set out on horseback on the 21st of June, having for military companions of his journey Major-generals Lee and Schuyler, and being accompanied for a distance by several private friends. As an escort he had a "gentleman troop" of Philadelphia, commanded by Captain Markoe; the whole formed a brilliant cavalcade…

Many things concurred to produce perfect harmony of operation between these distinguished men. They were nearly of the same age, Schuyler being one year the youngest. Both were men of agricultural as well as military tastes. Both were men of property, living at their ease in little rural paradises—Washington on the grove-clad heights of Mount Vernon, Schuyler on the pastoral banks of the upper Hudson, where he had a noble estate at Saratoga, inherited from an uncle, and the old family mansion, near the city of Albany, half hid among ancestral trees. Yet both were exiling themselves from these happy abodes, and putting life and fortune at hazard in the service of their country…

They had scarcely proceeded twenty miles from Philadelphia when they were met by a courier, spurring with all speed, bearing dispatches from the army to Congress, communicating tidings of the battle of Bunker's Hill. Washington eagerly inquired particulars; above all, now acted the militia? When told that they stood their ground bravely; sustained the enemy's fire; reserved their own until at close quarters, and then delivered it with deadly effect, it seemed as if a weight of doubt and solicitude were lifted from his heart. "The liberties of the country are safe!" exclaimed he. The news of the battle of Bunker's Hill had startled the whole country; and this clattering cavalcade escorting the commander-in-chief to the army, was the gave and wonder of every town and village…

Escorted by a troop of light horse and a cavalcade of citizens, he proceeded to the headquarters provided for him at Cambridge, three miles distant. As he entered the confines of the camp the shouts of the multitude and the thundering of artillery gave note to the enemy beleaguered in Boston of his arrival. His military reputation had preceded him and excited great expectations. They were not disappointed. His personal appearance, notwithstanding the dust of travel, was calculated to captivate the public eye. As he rode through the camp, amidst a throng of officers, he was the admiration of the soldiery and of a curious throng collected from the surrounding country. Happy was the countryman who could get a full view of him to carry home an account of it to his neighbors. The fair sex were still more enthusiastic in their admiration, if we may judge from the following passage of a letter written by the intelligent and accomplished wife of John Adams to her husband: "Dignity, ease, and complacency, the gentleman and the soldier, look agreeably blended in him. Modesty marks every line and feature of his face."

With Washington, modest at all times, there was no false excitement on the present occasion; nothing to call forth emotions of self-glorification. The honors and congratulations with which he was received, the acclamations of the public, the cheerings of the army, only told him how much was expected from him; and when he looked round upon the raw and rustic levies he was to command, "a mixt multitude of people, under very little discipline, order, or government," scattered in rough encampments about hill and dale, beleaguring a city garrisoned by veteran troops, with ships of war anchored about its harbor, and strong outposts guarding it, he felt the awful responsibilityof his situation, and the complicated and stupendous task before him. He spoke of it, however, not despondingly nor boastfully nd with defiance; but with that solemn and sedate resolution, and that hopeful reliance on Supreme Goodness, which belonged to his magnanimous nature. The cause of his country, he observed, had called him to an active and dangerous duty, but he trusted that Divine Providence, which wisely orders the affairs of men, would enable him to discharge it with fidelity and success.

On the 3d of July, the morning after his arrival at Cambridge, Washington took formal command of the army. It was drawn up on the common about half a mile from headquarters. A multitude had assembled there, for s yet military spectacles were novelties, and the camp was full of visitors, men, women, and children, from all parts of the country, who had relatives among the yeoman soldiery. An ancient elm is still pointed out, under which Washington, as he arrived from headquarters accompanied by General Lee and a numerous suite, wheeled his horse, and drew his sword as commander-in-chief of the armies...

Washington Appointed Commander-in-chief—His Speech of Acceptance

Title: Washington Appointed Commander-in-chief—His Speech of Acceptance
Author: George Washington
Date: June, 1775
Source: America, Vol.3, p.125

Characteristically plainspoken and sparing of words was Washington in accepting command of the Continental Army, tendered him in June, 1775, by the Continental Congress. His nomination was made by Thomas Johnson of Maryland, and was warmly seconded by John Adams.

To fill the post he was beyond question the best qualified man in the colonies. Not only was he competent in military affairs and skilled by precept and experience in the art of war, but his extensive knowledge of the geographical character of the country, and his familiarity with the characteristics and qualifications of the royal army, made him certainly the most dangerous antagonist, as a commanding officer, that the British could have had.

MR. PRESIDENT: Though I am truly sensible of the high honor done me, in this appointment, yet I feel great distress, from a consciousness that my abilities and military experience may not be equal to the extensive and important trust. However, as the Congress desire it, I will enter upon the momentous duty, and exert every power I possess in their service, and for the support of the glorious cause, I beg they will accept my most cordial thanks for this distinguished testimony of their approbation.

But, lest some unlucky event should happen, unfavorable to my reputation, I beg it may be remembered by every gentleman in the room, that I, this day, declare with the utmost sincerity, I do not think myself equal to the command I am honored with.

As to pay, Sir, I beg leave to assure the Congress, that, as no pecuniary consideration could have tempted me to accept this arduous employment, at the expense of my domestic ease and happiness, I do not wish to make any profit from it. I will keep an exact account of my expenses. Those, I doubt not, they will discharge, and that is all I desire.

The Battle of Lexington—
A Contemporary Account

Title: The Battle of Lexington—A Contemporary Account
Author: Salem Gazette
Date: 1775
Source: America, Vol.3, p.119

Six days after the first armed clash of the Revolutionary War occurred at Lexington, Mass., April 19, 1775, the accompanying report appeared in the Salem Gazette. This engagement, together with the contemporaneous one at Concord, was the turning-point between the period of protest and that of resistance in the colonies.

The objective of the British troops was the destruction of military stores at Concord, and also the seizure of John Hancock and Samuel Adams, residing at Lexington. Shortly after sunrise on the day of the battle, and after Paul Revere had spread the alarm, "The regulars are coming," Adams observed prophetically to Hancock, "What a glorious day!"

LAST Wednesday the 19th of April, the troops of His Britannic Majesty commenced hostilities upon the people of this province, attended with circumstances of cruelty, not less brutal than what our venerable ancestors received from the vilest savages of the wilderness. The particulars relative to this interesting event, by which we are involved in all the horrors of a civil war, we have endeavored to collect as well as the present confused state of affairs will admit.

On Tuesday evening a detachment from the army, consisting, it is said, of eight or nine hundred men, commanded by Lieutenant Colonel Smith, embarked at the bottom of the Common in Boston, on board a number of boats, and landed at Phipps's farm, a little way up Charles River, from whence they proceeded with silence and expedition on their way to Concord, about eighteen miles from Boston. The people were soon alarmed, and began to assemble in several towns, before daylight, in order to watch the motion of the troops. At Lexington, six miles below Concord, a company of militia, of about one hundred men, mustered near the Meeting House; the troops came in sight of them just before sunrise; and running within a few rods of them, the commanding officer accosted the militia in words to this effect: "Disperse, you rebels—damn you, throw down your arms and disperse"; upon which the troops huzzaed, and immediately one or two officers discharged their pistols, which were instantaneously followed by the firing of four or five of the soldiers, and then there seemed to be a general discharge from the whole body: eight of our men were killed, and nine wounded. In a few minutes after this action the enemy renewed their march for Concord.

The Battle of Concord

Title: The Battle of Concord
Author: The Reverend William Emerson
Date: 1775
Source: America, Vol.3, p.121

An interesting feature of this account of the Lexington-Concord battle is that it was written by the grandfather of Ralph Waldo Emerson, who wrote the famous hymn sung at the completion of the Concord monument and referring to the "embattl'd farmers" who "fired the shot heard round the world."

At the time of the historic engagement, the Reverend William Emerson had a pastorate at Concord, Massachusetts, which is a short distance from Lexington and some eighteen miles from Boston. He became a chaplain in the Continental Army, and lost his life in the Ethan Allen expedition against Ticonderoga.

This article is printed in Whitney's "Literature of the Nineteenth of April," consisting of contemporaneous accounts of the initial battles of the Revolutionary War.

THIS morning between one and two o'clock we were alarmed by the ringing of the bell—and upon examination found that the troops, to the number of 800, had stolen their march from Boston in boats and barges from the bottom of the Common over to a point in Cambridge near to Inman's farm, and were at Lexington Meeting House, half an hour before sunrise, where they had fired upon a body of our men, and (as we afterward heard) had killed several. This intelligence was brought us at first by Doctor Samuel Prescott, who narrowly escaped the guard that was sent before on horses, purposely to prevent all posts and messengers from giving us timely information. He, by the help of a very Beet horse, crossing several walls and fences, arrived at Concord at the time above mentioned.

When several posts were immediately dispatched, that returning confirmed the account of the Regulars' arrival at Lexington, and that they were on their way to Concord. Upon this a number of our Minute Men belonging to this town and Acton and Lincoln, with several others that were in readiness, marched out to meet them. While the alarm company were preparing to receive them in the town, Captain Minot, who commanded them, thought it proper to take possession of the hill above the Meeting House as the most advantageous situation.

No sooner had we gained it than we were met by the companies that were sent out to meet the troops, who informed us that they were just upon us, and that we must retreat, as their number was more than treble ours. We then retreated from the hill near the Liberty Pole and took a new post back of the town, upon a rising eminence, where we formed into two battalions, and awaited the arrival of the enemy.

Scarcely had we formed, before we saw the British troops, at the distance of a quarter of a mile, glittering in arms, advancing towards us with the greatest celerity. Some were for making a stand, notwithstanding the superiority of their number, but others more prudent thought best to retreat till our strength should be equal to the enemy's by recruits from neighboring towns that were continually coming to our assistance. Accordingly we retreated over the bridge when the troops came into the town, set fire to several carriages for the artillery, destroyed 60 barrels of flour, rifled several houses, took possession of the Town House, destroyed 500 pounds of balls, set a guard of 100 men at the North Bridge and sent up a party to the house of Colonel Barrett, where they were in expectation of finding a quantity of warlike stores; but these were happily secured just before their arrival, by transportation into the woods and other by-places.

In the meantime, the guard set by the enemy to secure the pass at the North Bridge, were alarmed by the approach of our people, who had retreated as mentioned before, and were now advancing, with special orders not to fire upon the troops, unless fired upon. These orders were so punctually observed that we received the fire of the enemy in three several and separate discharges of their pieces, before it was returned by our commanding officer; the firing then soon became general for several minutes, in which skirmish two were killed on each side, and several of the enemy wounded. It may be observed by the way that we were the more cautious to prevent beginning a rupture with the King's troops, as we were then uncertain what had happened at Lexington, and knew [not] that they had begun the quarrel there by first firing upon our people and killing 8 men upon the spot.

The three companies of troops soon quitted their post at the bridge, and retreated in greatest discord and confusion to the main body, who were soon upon the march to meet them. For half an hour the enemy by their marches and counter-marches discovered great fickleness and inconstancy of mind, sometimes advancing, sometimes returning to their former posts, till at length they quitted the town, and retreated by the way they came. In the meantime a party of our men (150) took the back way through the great fields into the east quarter and had placed themselves to advantage, laying in ambush, behind walls, fences and buildings, ready to fire upon the enemy on their retreat.

Farewell to Mrs. Washington

Title: Farewell To Mrs. Washington
Author: George Washington
Date: June, 1775
Source: America, Vol.3, p.127

George Washington met Martha Dandridge, the widow of Daniel Parker Custis, in the Spring of 1758. At their second meeting he made a proposal of marriage which she accepted and on January 6th of the following year they were married.

It is said that after General Washington's death, Martha Washington shut herself up in her room at Mount Vernon and spent her time sitting before the window which looked out on his tomb. Shortly before her death Martha Washington destroyed all of the personal letters from her husband that she had in her possession. The letter given here, dated Philadelphia, June 18, 1775, is one of the few that has come down to us.

MY DEAREST: I am now set down to write to you on a subject, which fills me with inexpressible concern, and this concern is greatly aggravated and increased, when I reflect upon the uneasiness I know it will give you. It has been determined in Congress, that the whole army raised for the defense of the American cause shall be put under my care, and that it is necessary for me to proceed immediately to Boston to take upon me the command of it.

"You may believe me, my dear Patsy, when I assure you, in the most solemn manner, that, so far from seeking this appointment, I have used every endeavor in my power to avoid it, not only from my unwillingness to part with you and the family, but from a consciousness of its being a trust too great for my capacity, and that I should enjoy more real happiness in one month with you at home, than I have the most distant prospect of finding abroad, if my stay were to be seven times seven years. But as it has been a kind of destiny, that has thrown me upon this service, I shall hope that my undertaking it is designed to answer some good purpose. You might, and I suppose did perceive, from the tenor of my letters, that I was apprehensive I could not avoid this appointment, as I did not pretend to intimate when I should return. That was the case. It was utterly out of my power to refuse this appointment, without exposing my character to such censures, as would have reflected dishonor upon myself, and given pain to my friends. This, I am sure, could not, and ought not, to be pleasing to you, and must have lessened me considerably in my own esteem. I shall rely, therefore, confidently on that Providence, which has heretofore preserved and been bountiful to me, not doubting but that I shall return safe to you in the fall. I shall feel no pain from the toil or the danger of the campaign; my unhappiness will flow from the uneasiness I know you will feel from being left alone. I therefore beg, that you will summon your whole fortitude, and pass your time as agreeably as possible. Nothing will give me so much sincere satisfaction as to hear this, and to hear it from your own pen. My earnest and ardent desire is, that you would pursue any plan that is most likely to produce content, and a tolerable degree of tranquillity; as it must add greatly to my uneasy feelings to hear, that you are dissatisfied or complaining at what I really could not avoid.

As life is always uncertain, and common prudence dictates to every man the necessity of settling his temporal concerns, while it is in his power, and while the mind is calm and undisturbed, I have, since I came to this place (for I had not time to do it before I left home) got Colonel Pendleton to draft a will for me, by the directions I gave him, which will I now enclose. The provision made for you in case of my death will, I hope, be agreeable.

I shall add nothing more, as I have several letters to write, but to desire that you will remember me to your friends, and to assure you that I am, with the most unfeigned regard, my dear Patsy, your affectionate, &c."

Washington at Cambridge

Title: Washington at Cambridge
Author: George Washington
Date: July, 1775
Source: America, Vol.3, pp.130-135

Washington's Letter to the President of Congress, on His Arrival at Cambridge to Take Command of the Army

Following his appointment as Commander-in-Chief of the American army, General Washington arrived in Cambridge, Mass., on July 2, 1775, after journeying eleven days from Philadelphia, and on the next day, under the famous elm which marked the spot for nearly a century and a half, he took formal command, succeeding General Artemas Ward. Eight days later he addressed this communication to Congress.

The event took place in Cambridge because it had been decided to press the siege of Boston, and Washington was resolved to drive the British out, as his first task.

Meanwhile the Massachusetts Provincial Congress appointed a Committee of Safety to confer with Washington about a suitable residence for himself and General Lee, who had accompanied him, and a mansion subsequently known as the "Craigie house," belonging to a refugee loyalist, was immediately prepared for their reception.

SIR, I arrived safe at his place on the 3d inst., after a journey attended with a good deal of fatigue, and retarded by necessary attentions to the successive civilities which accompanied me in my whole route. Upon my arrival, I immediately visited the several posts occupied by our troops, and as soon as the weather permitted, reconnoitred those of the enemy. I found the latter strongly entrenched on Bunker's Hill about a mile from Charlestown, and advanced about half a mile from the place of the last action, with their sentries extended about 150 yards on this side of the narrowest part of the neck leading from this place to Charlestown...

The bulk of their army commanded by General Howe, lays on Bunker's Hill, and the remainder on Roxbury Neck, except the Light Horse, and a few men in the town of Boston. On our side we have thrown up entrenchments on Winter and Prospect Hills, the enemy's camp in full view at the distance of little more than a mile. Such intermediate points, as would admit a landing, I have since my arrival taken care to strengthen, down to Sewall's farm, where a strong entrenchment has been thrown up...

My earnest wishes to comply with the instructions of the Congress in making an early and complete return of the state of the army, has led into an involuntary delay in addressing you, which has given me much concern. Having given orders for this purpose immediately on my arrival, and unapprized of the imperfect obedience which had been paid to those of the like nature from General Ward, I was led from day to day to expect they would come in, and therefore detained the messenger. They are not now so complete as I could wish, but much allowance is to be made for inexperience in forms, and a liberty which has been taken (not given) on this subject. These reasons I flatter myself will no longer exist, and of consequence more regularity and exactness in future prevail...

We labor under great disadvantages for want of tents, for though they have been helped out by a collection of now useless sails from the seaport towns, the number is yet far short of our necessities. The colleges and houses of this town are necessarily occupied by the troops, which affords another reason for keeping our present situation. But I most sincerely wish the whole army was properly provided to take the field, as I am well assured, that besides greater expedition and activity in case of alarm, it would highly conduce to health and discipline. As materials are not to be had here, I would beg leave to recommend the procuring a further supply from Philadelphia as soon as possible...

I find myself already much embarrassed for want of a military chest; these embarrassments will increase every day: I must therefore request that money may be forwarded as soon as possible. The want of this most necessary article, will I fear produce great inconveniences if not prevented by an early attention. I find the army in general, and the troops raised in Massachusetts in particular, very deficient in necessary clothing. Upon inquiry there appears no probability of obtaining any supplies in this quarter. And the best consideration of this matter I am able to form, I am of opinion that a number of hunting shirts not less than 10,000, would in a great degree remove this difficulty in the cheapest and quickest manner. I know nothing in a speculative view more trivial, yet if put in practice would have a happier tendency to unite the men, and abolish those provincial distinctions which lead to jealousy and dissatisfaction. In a former part of this letter I mentioned the want of engineers; I can hardly express the disappointment I have experienced on this subject. The skill of those we have, being very imperfect and confined to the mere manual exercise of cannon: Whereas—the war in which we are engaged requires a knowledge comprehending the duties of the field and fortifications. If any persons thus qualified are to be found in the southern colonies, it would be of great public service to forward them with all expedition. Upon the article of ammunition I must reecho the former complaints on this subject: We are so exceedingly destitute, that our artillery will be of little use without a supply both large and seasonable: What we have must be reserved for the small arms, and that managed with the utmost frugality.

I am sorry to observe that the appointments of the general officers in the province of Massachusetts Bay have by no means corresponded with the judgment and wishes of either the civil or military. The great dissatisfaction expressed on this subject and the apparent danger of throwing the army into the utmost disorder, together with the strong representations of the provincial Congress, have induced me to retain the commissions in my hands until the pleasure of the Congress should be farther known, (except General Putnam's which was given the day I came into camp and before I was apprized of these uneasinesses). In such a step I must beg the Congress will do me the justice I believe, that I have been, actuated solely by a regard to the public good. I have not, nor could have any private attachments; every gentleman in appointment, was an entire stranger to me but from character. I must therefore rely upon the candor of the Congress for their favorable construction of my conduct in this particular. General Spencer was so much, disgusted at the preference given to General Putnam that he left the army without visiting me, or making known his intentions in any respect. General Pomroy had also retired before my arrival, occasioned (as is said) by some disappointment from the Provincial Congress. General Thomas is much esteemed and earnestly desired to continue in the service; and as far as my opportunities have enabled me to judge I must join in the general opinion that he is an able good officer and his resignation would be a public loss. The postponing him to Pomroy and Heath whom he has commanded would make his continuance very difficult and probably operate on his mind, as the like circumstance has done on that of Spencer...

The deficiency of numbers, discipline and stores can only lead to this conclusion, that their spirit has exceeded their strength. But at the same time I would humbly submit to the consideration of the Congress, the propriety of making some further provision of men from the other colonies. If these regiments should be completed to their establishment, the dismission of those unfit for duty on account of their age and character would occasion a considerable reduction, and at all events they have been enlisted upon such terms, that they may be disbanded when other troops arrive. But should my apprehensions be realized, and the

regiments here not filled up, the public cause would suffer by an absolute dependence upon so doubtful an event, unless some provision
is made against such a disappointment.

It requires no military skill to judge of the difficulty of introducing
proper discipline and subordination into an army while we have the
enemy in view, and are in daily expectation of an attack, but it is of so
much importance that every effort will be made which time and circumstance will admit. In the meantime I have a sincere pleasure in observing that there are materials for a good army, a great number of
able-bodied men, active zealous in the cause and of unquestionable
courage…

The Battle of Bunker Hill

Title: The Battle of Bunker Hill
Author: A Leader of the Provincial Forces
Date: 1775
Source: America, Vol.3, pp.136-140

This letter, dated June 26, 1775—ten days after the battle—was written
by a colonial participant to a friend in England and was printed a month
or so later in the London Morning Post and Daily Advertiser. It was recently found in the files of that paper, and is included in a volume of
"Letters on the American Revolution," edited by Margaret Wheeler
Willard (Houghton-Mifflin.)

The importance of the Battle of Bunker (or rather, Breed's) Hill in revo-
lutionizing public and private opinion in the colonies is evidenced by
other letters. One written from New York before the news of Bunker Hill
had arrived states, "It is a gross calumny to say that we are aiming at
independency." In the reaction to that battle, however, the feeling
against independence began to break down and in the following year
crystallized into a national desire for freedom. A Quaker writes from
Philadelphia, in 1776, that "the time is not far off when the colonies will
set up an independent standard."

S TRICT orders having been given that no letter shall be received
on board the men-of-war from any of those who have the
courage to appear in arms against the unconstitutional and oppressive
measures of administration, and the late inflated proclamation having
pronounced such severe penalties against those who shall correspond
with men thus acting in defence of all those great and essential privileges which our forefathers ever held so dear, it becomes difficult for

me to convey, or perhaps for you to receive any information from this side of the water, except from men retained in the pay of the administration, who have every inducement which profit and prejudice can inspire to misrepresent the truth. After the windy proclamation of the 12th, our troops became enraged because they were not led on to action. This learned proclamation was burned by the hands of the common hangman at Cambridge, Roxburgh, [Roxbury] and Deutesterwick [Dorchester]. Many went off in disgust that nothing was done; the different parishes sent them back; they stated the case of their desertion. Finding the zeal of the troops so great, and that notwithstanding the threatening of the proclamation, we were not likely to feel the effects of those who bear the sword so soon as was expected, it was resolved to force General Gage to an action. With this in view it was determined to seize possession of the height on the peninsula of Charlestown, which General Gage had occupied before the 19th of April, and erect some batteries on Banhin-hill [Bunker-hill], to batter down the town and General Gage's camp on the Common and his entrenchment on Boston Neck (which is only about three fourths of a mile across). Four thousand men commanded by General Putnam, and led on by Dr. Warren, having prepared every thing for the operation as well as could be contrived or collected were stationed under a half unfinished breastwork and some palisadoes fixed in a hurry. When the enemy were landed, to the number of 2500, as we are since informed, being the light infantry and the grenadiers of the army with a complete train of artillery, howitzers and field pieces, drawn by 200 sailors, and commanded by the most gallant and experienced officers of the last war, they marched to engage 3000 provincials, arrayed in red worsted caps and blue great coats, with guns of different sizes, few of which had bayonets, ill-served artillery, but of invincible courage! The fire from the ships and artillery of the enemy was horrid and amazing; the first onset of the soldiers was bold and fierce, but they were received with equal courage; at length the 38th Regiment gave way, and the rest recoiled. The King's troops were commanded by General Howe, brother to that gallant Lord Howe to whose memory the province of Massachusett's Bay erected a statue. He marched with undaunted spirit at the head of his men; most of his followers were killed round his own person. The King's troops about this time got into much confusion and retreated, but were rallied by the reproaches of General Howe, and the activity of General Clinton who then joined the battle. The King's troops again made their push against Charlestown, which was then set on fire by them. Our right flank being then uncovered, two floating batteries coming in by the mill dam to take us in the rear, more troops coming from Boston, and our ammunition being almost expended, General Putnam ordered the troops on the left to retreat. The confusion was great for twenty minutes, but in less than half an hour we fell into complete order; the regulars were so mauled they durst not pursue us 200 yards, but almost the last shot they fired killed good Dr. Warren, who had dressed himself like Lord Falkland, in his wedding suit, and distinguished himself by unparalleled acts of bravery during the whole action, but particularly in covering the retreat, He was a man of great courage, universal learning and much humanity. It may well be said he is the greatest loss we have sustained. General Putnam, at the age of 60, was as active as the youngest officer in the field. We have lost 104 killed, and 306 wounded; a Lieutenant Colonel and 30 men are prisoners, and we anxiously wait their fate. We lost before the action began 18 men by the fire of the ships and the battery from Boston, burying them before the assault. The number of the King's troops killed and wounded are three times our loss. A sailor belonging to one of the transports, who was busy with many of his companions in rifling the dead, and who has since deserted, assured me the ground was covered with officers. The cannonading was dreadful. The King's troops began firing at a great distance, being scarce of ammunition deferred our fire. It was impossible to send troops from Roxburgh, because we expected an attack there, or at Dorchester neck. I am well informed many of the old English officers are since dead.

When General Gage had the inhabitants of Boston pent up in the town, not less than five hundred marksmen at different times went out in dung carts covered with dirt to join the army, and carried off 10 or 12,000 cartridges of ammunition by the same means, without being discovered. On the 19th two beautiful young men, between 25 and 30 years of age, devoted themselves to death. They marched within General Gage's sentinels on the neck; a sergeant and six men were sent to receive them, thinking they came to lay down their arms; when they approached they told the troops "the King's ministers had treated them as slaves, the King's officers had reported them as cowards, that they came to show the falsity of both reports and the weakness of the proclamation, by sealing with their blood their firm belief in the justice of their cause, upon which they were ready immediately to appear before the presence of God." Here they fired and killed two of the enemy; they were immediately fired at again, and one was instantly killed and the other desperately wounded, but he told the King's troops he did not desire to live, and demanded they should kill him also, which was soon complied with. I do declare as a man of veracity, under all the hardships our people have undergone, I have not heard one complain of his personal suffering. They bewail each others' misfortunes; they complain bitterly of the cruelties of the English administration; they lament the separation of the Empire which is likely to take place, but of their own particular sufferings no man murmurs or complains. Not a soldier dies of his wounds who does not believe he goes directly to heaven, notwithstanding all the anathemas of the general proclamation. If this business continues till November you will have an account of ships and troops. If we could have imagined the Parliament of England could have been so infatuated as appears by their proceedings of last session of Parliament, we should certainly have destroyed the small few then in this province.

Paul Revere Tells of His Midnight Ride—Deposition of 1775

Title: Paul Revere Tells of His Midnight Ride—Deposition of 1775
Author: Paul Revere
Date: 1775
Source: America, Vol.3, pp.141-146

Paul Revere really lived and his midnight ride, celebrated by Longfellow, actually took place. Longfellow obtained the material for his famous poem from a letter which Revere wrote about twenty-two years after the events it describes; and this letter was based on a deposition, reprinted here from the original manuscript, which Revere made shortly after the ride.

Instead of being merely a clever despatch rider, however, Paul Revere was one of the most versatile men of his time—patriot, politician and soldier, goldsmith, artist and engraver, inventor, bell founder, dentist, industrial pioneer. As a goldsmith he was accustomed to deliver his wares, on horseback, to his country customers, thus becoming an expert horseman. In 1774 he had ridden from Boston to Philadelphia scattering the hated Boston Port Act, which provoked the first Continental Congress.

The concluding event described in this deposition is the Battle of Lexington that Revere witnessed.

I, PAUL REVERE, of Boston, in the colony of the Massachusetts Bay in New England; of lawful age, do testify and say; that I was sent for by Dr. Joseph Warren, of said Boston, on the evening of the 18th of April, about 10 o'clock; when he desired me, "to go to Lexington, and inform Mr. Samuel Adams, and the Hon. John Hancock Esq. that there was a number of soldiers, composed of light troops, and grenadiers, marching to the bottom of the common, where was a number of boats to receive them; it was supposed, that they were going to Lexington, by the way of Cambridge River, to take them, or go to Concord, to destroy the colony stores."

I proceeded immediately, and was put across Charles River and landed near Charlestown Battery; went in town, and there got a horse. While in Charlestown, I was informed by Richard Devens Esq. that he met that evening, after sunset, nine officers of the ministerial army [British regulars], mounted on good horses, and armed, going towards Concord.

I set off, it was then about 11 o'clock, the moon shone bright. I had got almost over Charlestown Common, towards Cambridge, when I saw two officers on horse-back, standing under the shade of a tree, in a narrow part of the road. I was near enough to see their holsters and cockades. One of them started his horse towards me, the other up the road, as I supposed, to head me, should I escape the first. I turned my horses short about, and rode upon a full gallop for Mistick Road, he followed me about 300 yards, and finding he could not catch me, returned. I proceeded to Lexington, through Mistick, and alarmed Mr. Adams and Col. Hancock.

After I had been there about half an hour Mr. Daws arrived, who came from Boston, over the Neck.

We set off for Concord, and were overtaken by a young gentleman named Prescot, who belonged to Concord, and was going home. When we had got about half way from Lexington to Concord, the other two stopped at a house to awake the man, I kept along. When I had got about 200 yards ahead of them, I saw two officers as before. I called to my company to come up, saying here was two of them, (for I had told them what Mr. Devens told me, and of my being stopped). In an instant I saw four of them, who rode up to me with their pistols in their bands, said "G—d d—n you, stop. If you go an inch further, you are a dead man." Immediately Mr. Prescot came up. We attempted to get through them, but they kept before us, and swore if we did not turn in to that pasture, they would blow our brains out, (they had placed themselves opposite to a pair of bars, and had taken the bars down). They forced us in. When we had got in, Mr. Prescot said "Put on!" He took to the left, I to the right towards a wood at the bottom of the pasture, intending, when I gained that, to jump my horse and run afoot. Just as I reached it, out started six officers, seized my bridle, put their pistols to my breast, ordered me to dismount, which I did. One of them, who appeared to have the command there, and much of a gentleman, asked me where I came from; I told him. He asked what time I left it. I told him, he seemed surprised, said "Sir, may I crave your name?" I answered "My name is Revere. "What" said he, "Paul Revere"? I answered "Yes." The others abused much; but he told me not to be afraid, no one should hurt me. I told him they would miss their aim. He said they should not, they were only waiting for some deserters they expected down the road. I told him I knew better, I knew what they were after; that I had alarmed the country all the way up, that their boats were caught aground, and I should have 500 men there soon. One of them said they had 1500 coming; he seemed surprised and rode off into the road, and informed them who took me, they came down immediately on a full gallop. One of them (whom I since learned was Major Mitchel of the 5th Reg.) clapped his pistol to my head, and said he was going to ask me some questions, and if I did not tell the truth, he would blow my brains out. I told him I esteemed myself a man of truth, that he had stopped me on the highway, and made me a prisoner, I knew not by what right; I would tell him the truth; I was not afraid. He then asked me the same questions that the other did, and many more, but was more particular; I gave him much the same answers. He then ordered me to mount my horse, they first searched me for pistols. When I was mounted, the Major took the reins out of my hand, and said "By G—d Sir, you are not to ride with reins I assure you"; and gave them to an officer on my right, to lead me. He then ordered 4 men out of the bushes, and to mount their horses; they were country men which they had stopped who were going home; then ordered us to march. He said to me, "We are now going towards your friends, and if you attempt to run, or we are insulted, we will blow your brains out." When we had got into the road they formed a circle, and ordered the prisoners in the center, and to lead me in the front. We rode towards Lexington at a quick pace; they very often insulted me calling me rebel, etc., etc. After we had got about a mile, I was given to the sergeant to lead, he was ordered to take out his pistol, (he rode with a hanger,) and if I ran, to execute the major's sentence.

When we got within about half a mile of the Meeting House we heard a gun fired. The Major asked me what it was for, I told him to alarm the country; he ordered the four prisoners to dismount, they did, then one of the officers dismounted and cut the bridles and saddles off the horses, and drove them away, and told the men they might go about their business. I asked the Major to dismiss me, he said he would carry me, let the consequence be what it will. He then ordered us to march.

When we got within sight of the Meeting House, we heard a volley of guns fired, as I supposed at the tavern, as an alarm; the Major ordered us to halt, he asked me how far it was to Cambridge, and many more questions, which I answered. He then asked the sergeant, if his horse was tired, he said yes; he ordered him to take my horse. I dismounted, and the sergeant mounted my horse; they cut the bridle and saddle of the sergeant's horse, and rode off down the road. I then went to the house were I left Messrs. Adams and Hancock, and told them what had happened; their friends advised them to go out of the way; I went with them, about two miles across road.

After resting myself, I set off with another man to go back to the tavern, to inquire the news; when we got there, we were told the troops were within two miles. We went into the tavern to get a trunk of papers belonging to Col. Hancock. Before we left the house, I saw the ministerial troops from the chamber window. We made haste, and had to pass through our militia, who were on a green behind the Meeting House, to the number as I supposed, about 50 or 60, I went through them; as I passed I heard the commanding officer speak to his men to this purpose; "Let the troops pass by, and don't molest them, without they begin first." I had to go across road; but had not got half gunshot off, when the ministerial troops appeared in sight, behind the Meeting House. They made a short halt, when one gun was fired. I heard the report, turned my head, and saw the smoke in front of the troops. They immediately gave a great shout, ran a few paces, and then the whole fired. I could first distinguish irregular firing, which I supposed was the advance guard, and then platoons; at this time I could not see our militia, for they were covered from me by a house at the bottom of the street. And further saith not.

PAUL REVERE.

The Dramatic Capture of Ticonderoga

Title: The Dramatic Capture of Ticonderoga
Author: Ethan Allen
Date: May, 1775
Source: America, Vol.3, p.147

Coming between the Battles of Lexington and Bunker Hill, the surprise and capture of Fort Ticonderoga, at the head of Lake George, on May 10, 1775, by Colonel Ethan Allen and a band of Green Mountain Boys, was the first complete victory scored by the colonists in the Revolutionary War. This account of it is taken from a "Narrative of Colonel Ethan Allen's Captivity," published in 1779. He was captured near Montreal four months after the Ticonderoga exploit while engaged on a secret mission to Canada.

The ease with which Ticonderoga was taken is partly explained by the fact that it was weakly garrisoned after the cession of Canada to Great Britain. In 1777 Burgoyne invested it and forced its evacuation by the Americans. Later the British were attacked in turn by General Lincoln, who released 100 American prisoners and took 293 of the English, but failed to recover the fort itself.

EVER since I arrived at the state of manhood, and acquainted myself with the general history of mankind, I have felt a sincere passion for liberty. The history of nations doomed to perpetual slavery, in consequence of yielding up to tyrants their natural-born liberties, I read with a sort of philosophical horror; so that the first systematical and bloody attempt, at Lexington, to enslave America, thoroughly electrified my mind, and fully determined me to take part with my country. And, while I was wishing for an opportunity to signalize myself in its behalf, directions were privately sent to me from the then colony (now State) of Connecticut, to raise the Green Mountain Boys, and, if possible, with them to surprise and take the fortress of Ticonderoga. This enterprise I cheerfully undertook; and, after first guarding all the several passes that led thither, to cut off all intelligence between the garrison and the country, made a forced march from Bennington, and arrived at the lake opposite to Ticonderoga, on the evening of the ninth day of May, 1775, with two hundred and thirty valiant Green Mountain Boys; and it was with the utmost difficulty that I procured boats to cross the lake. However, I landed eighty-three men near the garrison, and sent the boats back for the rear guard, commanded by Colonel Seth Warner; but the day began to dawn, and I found myself under necessity to attack the fort before the rear could cross the lake; and, as it was viewed hazardous, I harangued the officers and soldiers in the manner following:

"Friends and fellow-soldiers, You have, for a number of years past been a scourge and terror to arbitrary power. Your valor has been famed abroad, and acknowledged, as appears by the advice and orders to me, from the General Assembly of Connecticut, to surprise and take the garrison now before us. I now propose to advance before you, and, in person, conduct you through the wicket-gate; for we must this morning either quit our pretensions to valor, or possess ourselves of this fortress in a few minutes; and, inasmuch as it is a desperate attempt, which none but the bravest of men dare undertake, I do not urge it on any contrary to his will. You that will undertake voluntarily, poise your firelocks."

The men being, at this time, drawn up in three ranks, each poised his firelock. I ordered them to face to the right, and, at the head of the center-file, marched them immediately to the wicket-gate aforesaid, where I found a sentry posted, who instantly snapped his fusee at me; I ran immediately toward him, and he retreated through the covered way into the parade within the garrison, gave a halloo, and ran under a bomb-proof. My party, who followed me into the fort, I formed on the parade in such a manner as to face the two barracks which faced each other.

The garrison being asleep, except the sentries, we gave three huzzas which greatly surprised them. One of the sentries made a pass at one of my officers with a charged bayonet, and slightly wounded him. My first thought was to kill him with my sword; but, in an instant, I altered the design and fury of the blow to a slight cut on the side of the head, upon which he dropped his gun, and asked quarter, which I readily granted him, and demanded of him the place where the commanding officer kept. He showed me a pair of stairs in the front of a barrack, on the west part of the garrison, which led up to a second story in said barrack, to which I immediately repaired, and ordered the commander, Captain De la Place, to come forth instantly, or I would sacrifice the whole garrison; at which the Captain came immediately to the door, with his breeches in his hand. When I ordered him to deliver me the fort instantly, he asked me by what authority I demanded it. I answered him, "In the name of the great Jehovah, and the Continental Congress."

The authority of the Congress being very little known at that time, he began to speak again; but I interrupted him, and with my drawn sword over his head, again demanded an immediate surrender of the garrison; with which he then complied, and ordered his men to be forthwith paraded without arms, as he had given up the garrison. In the mean time some of my officers had given orders, and in consequence thereof, sundry of the barrack doors were beat down, and about one-third of the garrison imprisoned, which consisted of the said commander, a Lieutenant Feltham, a conductor of artillery, a gunner, two sergeants, and forty-four rank and file; about one hundred pieces of cannon, one thirteen-inch mortar, and a number of swivels. This surprise was carried into execution in the gray of the morning of the tenth of May, 1775. The sun seemed to rise that morning with a superior lustre; and Ticonderoga and its dependencies smiled to its conquerors, who tossed about the flowing bowl, and wished success to Congress, and the liberty and freedom of America.

The Mecklenburg Declaration of Independence

Title: The Mecklenburg Declaration of Independence
Author: Committee of Mecklenburg County
Date: 1775
Source: Harvard Classics, Vol.43, p.166

On April 30, 1819, the Raleigh (North Carolina) Register published the following document, said to have been adopted by the Committee of Mecklenburg county, North Carolina, on May 20, 1775, the day after the receipt of the news of the battle of Lexington. The similarity of some of its phrases to phrases in the Declaration of Independence raised questions as to plagiarism on Jefferson's part, or, on the other hand, as to the authenticity of the Mecklenburg document. It is clear that Jefferson never heard of it before 1819; and the explanation most commonly adopted is, that it is a compilation, based in part on general recollections of certain resolutions, still extant, which were drawn up by the committee-men of Mecklenburg on May 31, 1775

"1. RESOLVED, That whosoever directly or indirectly abetted, or in any way, form, or manner, countenanced the unchartered and dangerous invasion of our rights, as claimed by Great Britain, is an enemy to this Country—to America—and to the inherent and inalienable rights of man.

2. Resolved, That we the citizens of Mecklenburg County, do hereby dissolve the political bands which have connected us to the Mother Country, and hereby absolve ourselves from all allegiance to the British Crown, and abjure all political connection, contract, or association, with that Nation, who have wantonly trampled on our rights

and liberties—and inhumanly shed the innocent blood of American patriots at Lexington.

3. Resolved, That we do hereby declare ourselves a free and independent people, are, and of right ought to be, a sovereign and self-governing Association, under the control of no power other than that of our God and the General Government of the Congress; to the maintenance of which independence, we solemnly pledge to each other, our mutual cooperation, our lives, our fortunes, and our most sacred honor.

4. Resolved, That as we now acknowledge the existence and control of no law or legal officer, civil or military, within this County, we do hereby ordain and adopt, as a rule of life, all, each and every of our former laws—where, nevertheless, the Crown of Great Britain never can be considered as holding rights, privileges, immunities, or authority therein.

5. Resolved, That it is also further decreed, that all, each and every military officer in this County, is hereby reinstated to his former command and authority, he acting conformably to these regulations, and that every member present of this delegation shall henceforth be a civil officer, viz. a Justice of the Peace, in the character of a 'Committeeman,' to issue process, hear and determine all matters of controversy, according to said adopted laws, and to preserve peace, and union, and harmony, in said County, and to use every exertion to spread the love of country and fire of freedom throughout America, until a more general and organized government be established in this province."

Brant to Lord Germaine

Title: Brant to Lord Germaine
Author: Brant
Date: 1776
Source: The World's Famous Orations, Vol.8, pp.5-8

Delivered in London before Lord George Germaine, secretary of state, on March 14, 1776. The originals of this and another speech by Brant are now in London. They have been printed in the "Documents Relating to the Colonial History of New York." Brant had gone to London to secure for the Mohawk Indians redress for lands which they had lost on the Mohawk and Upper Susquehanna Rivers. Redress was promised, but it was understood that the Indians meanwhile, in the war already begun with the Colonies, would give their support to the king. Out of this understanding proceeded the activity of Brant on the New York frontier in aid of the royal cause.

BROTHER GORAH:—We have crossed the great lake and come to this kingdom with our superintendent, Colonel Johnson, from our Confederacy of the Six Nations and their allies, that we might see our father, the great king, and join in informing him, his counselors, and wise men, of the good intentions of the Indians, our brothers, and of their attachment to his majesty and his government.

Brother, the disturbances in America give great trouble to all our nations, and many strange stories have been told to us by the people of that country. The Six Nations, who always loved the king, sent a number of their chiefs and warriors with their superintendent to Canada last summer, where they engaged their allies to join with them in the defense of that country, and when it was invaded by the New England people they alone defeated them.

Brother, in that engagement we had several of our best warriors killed and wounded, and the Indians think it very hard they should have been so deceived by the white people in that country; many returning in great numbers, and no white people supporting the Indians, they were obliged to return to their villages and sit still. We now, brother, hope to see these bad children chastised, and that we may be enabled to tell the Indians who have always been faithful and ready to assist the king what his majesty intends.

Brother, the Mohawks, our particular nation, have on all occasions shown their zeal and loyalty to the great king; yet they have been very badly treated by the people in that country, the city of Albany laying an unjust claim to the lands on which our lower castle is built, as one Klock, and others do those of Canajoharie, our upper village. We have often been assured by our late great friend, Sir William Johnson, who never deceived us, and we know he was told so, that the king and wise men here would do us justice. But this, notwithstanding all our applications, has never been done, and it makes us very uneasy. We also feel for the distress in which our brothers on the Susquehanna are likely to be involved by a mistake made in the boundary we settled in 1768. This also our superintendent has laid before the king. We have only, therefore, to request that his majesty will attend to this matter: it troubles our nation and they can not sleep easy in their beds. Indeed, it is very hard, when we have let the king's subjects have so much land for so little value, they should want to cheat us in this manner of the small spots we have left for our women and children to live on. We are tired out in making complaints and getting no redress. We therefore hope that the assurances now given us by the superintendent may take place and that he may have it in his power to procure us justice.

We shall truly report all that we hear from you to the Six Nations on our return. We are well informed there have been many Indians in this country who came without any authority from their own and gave us much trouble. We desire to tell you, brother, that this is not our case. We are warriors known to all the Nations, and are now here by approbation of many of them, whose sentiments we speak.

Brother, we hope that these things will be considered and that the king or his great men will give us such answer as will make our hearts light and glad before we go, and strengthen our hands, so that we may join our superintendent, Colonel Johnson, in giving satisfaction to all our Nations when we report to them on our return; for which purpose we hope soon to be accommodated with the passage.

Washington's Capture of Boston

Title: Washington's Capture of Boston
Author: George Washington
Date: 1776
Source: Great Epochs in American History, Vol.3, pp.128-132

As some account of the late maneuvers of both armies may not be unacceptable, I shall, hurried as I always am, devote a little time to it. Having received a small supply of powder, very inadequate to our wants, I resolved to take possession of Dorchester Point, lying east of Boston, looking directly into it, and commanding the enemy's lines on Boston Neck. To do this, which I knew would force the enemy to an engagement, or subject them to be enfiladed by our own cannon, it was necessary, in the first instance, to possess two heights (those mentioned in General Burgoyne's letter to Lord Stanley, in his account of the battle of Bunker's Hill), which had the entire command of the point.

Inasmuch as the ground at this point was frozen upward of two feet deep, and as impenetrable as a rock, nothing could be attempted with earth. We were obliged, therefore, to provide an amazing quantity of chandeliers and fascines for the work; and, on the night of the 4th, after a previous severe cannonade and bombardment for three nights together, to divert the enemy's attention from our real design, we removed our material to the spot, under cover of darkness, and took full possession of those heights, without the loss of a single man.

Upon their discovery of the works next morning, great preparations were made for attacking them; but not being ready before afternoon, and the weather getting very tempestuous, much blood was saved, and a very important blow, to one side or the other, was prevented. That this most remarkable interposition of Providence is for some a wise purpose, I have not a doubt. But, as the principal design of the maneuver was to draw the enemy to an engagement under disadvantages to them, as a premeditated plan was laid for this purpose, and seemed to be succeeding to my utmost wish, and as no men seem better disposed to make the appeal than ours did upon that occasion, I can scarcely forbear lamenting the disappointment, unless the dispute is drawing to an accommodation, and the sword going to be sheathed.

The enemy thinking, as we have since learnt, that we had got too securely posted, before the second morning, to be much hurt by them, and apprehending great annoyance from our new works, resolved upon a retreat, and accordingly on the 17th embarked in as much hurry, precipitation, and confusion, as ever troops did, not taking time to fit their transports, but leaving the King's property in Boston, to the amount, as is supposed, of thirty or forty thousand pounds in provisions and stores.

Many pieces of cannon, some mortars, and a number of shot and shells are also left; and bag-gage-wagons and artillery-carts, which they have been eighteen months preparing to take the field with, were found destroyed, thrown into the docks, and drifted upon every shore. In short, Dunbar's destruction of stores after General Braddock's defeat, which made so much noise, affords but a faint idea of what was to be met with here.

The enemy lay from the 17th to the 27th in Nantasket and King's Roads, about nine miles from Boston, to take in water from the islands thereabouts, and to prepare themselves for sea. Whither they are no bound, and where their tents will next be pitched, I know not; but, as New York and Hudson's River are the most important objects they can have in view, as the latter secures the communication with Canada, at the same time that it separates the northern and southern colonies, and the former is thought to abound in disaffected persons, who only wait a favorable opportunity and support to declare themselves openly, it becomes equally important for us to prevent their gaining possession of these advantages; and, therefore, as soon as they embarked, I detached a brigade of six regiments to that government, and, when they sailed, another brigade composed of the same number; and to-morrow another brigade of five regiments will march. In a day or two more, I shall follow myself, and be in New York ready to receive all but the first.

The enemy left all their works standing in Boston and on Bunker's Hill; and formidable they are. The town has shared a much better fate than was expected, the damage done to the houses being nothing equal to report. But the inhabitants have suffered a great deal, in being plundered by thesoldiery at their departure. All those who took upon themselves the style and title of government in Boston, in short, all those who have acted an unfriendly part in the great contest, have shipped themselves off in the same hurry, but under still greater disadvantages than the King's troops, being obliged to man their own vessels, as seamen enough could not be had for the King's transports, and submit to every hardship that can be conceived. One or two have done, what a great number ought to have done long ago, committed suicide.

By all accounts, there never existed a more miserable set of beings, than these wretched creatures now are. Taught to believe that the power of Great Britain was superior to all opposition, and, if not, that foreign aid was at hand, they were even higher and more insulting in their opposition than the regulars. When the order issued, therefore, for embarking the troops in Boston, no electric shock, no sudden explosion of thunder, in a word, not the last trump could have struck them with greater consternation. They were at their wit's end, and, conscious of their black ingratitude, they chose to commit themselves, in the manner I have above described, to the mercy of the waves at a tempestuous season, rather than meet their offended countrymen.

I believe I may with great truth affirm, that no man perhaps since the first institution of armies ever commanded one under more difficult circumstances, than I have done. Many of my difficulties and distresses were of so peculiar a cast, that, in order to conceal them from the enemy, I was obliged to conceal them from myfriends, and indeed from my own army, thereby subjecting my conduct to interpretations unfavorable to my character, especially by those at a distance, who could not in the smallest degree be acquainted with the springs that govern it.

The Drafting of
The Declaration of Independence

Title: The Drafting of "The Declaration of Independence"
Author: James Parton
Date: 1776
Source: Great Epochs in American History, Vol.3, pp.132-138

Mr. Jefferson was naturally urged to prepare the draft. He was chairman of the committee, having received the highest number of votes; he was also its youngest member, and therefore bound to do an ample share of the work; he was noted for his skill with the pen; he was particularly conversant with the points of the controversy; he was a Virginian. The task, indeed, was not very arduous or difficult. Nothing was wanted but a careful and brief recapitulation of wrongs familiar to every patriotic mind, and a clear statement of principles hackneyed from eleven years' iteration. Jefferson made no difficulty about undertaking it, and probably had no anticipation of the vast celebrity that was to follow so slight an exercise of his faculties...

Jefferson then lived in a new brick house out in the fields, near what is now the corner of Market and Seventh Streets, a quarter of a mile from Independence Square. "I rented the second floor," he tells us, "consisting of a parlor and bedroom, ready furnished," rent, thirty-five shillings a week; and he wrote this paper in the parlor, upon a little writing-desk three inches high, which still exists.

He was ready with his draft in time. His colleagues upon the committee suggested a few verbal changes, none of which were important; but, during the three days' discussion of it in the house, it was subjected to a review so critical and sever, that the author sat in his place silently writhing under it, and Dr. Franklin felt called upon to console him with the comic relation of the process by which the sign-board of John Thompson, hatter, makes and sells hats for ready money, was reduced to the name of the hatter and the figure of a hat. Young writers know what he suffered, who, come fresh from the commencement platform to a newspaper office, and have their eloquent editorials (equal to Burke) remorselessly edited, their best passages curtailed, their glowing conclusions and artful openings cut off, their happy epithets and striking similes omitted.

Congress made eighteen suppressions, six additions, and ten alterations; and nearly every one of these changes was an improvement. The author, for example, said that men are endowed with "inherent and inalienable rights." Congress struck out inherent—an obvious improvement. He introduced his catalog of wrongs by these words: "To prove this, let facts be submitted to a candid world, for the truth of which we pledge a faith yet unsullied by falsehood." It was good taste in Congress to strike out the italicized clause. That the passage concerning slavery should have been stricken out by Congress has often been regretted; but would it have been decent in this body to denounce the king for a crime in the guilt of whichthe colonies had shared? Mr. Jefferson wrote in his draft:

"He has waged cruel war against human nature itself, violating its most sacred rights of life and liberty in the persons of a distant people who never offended him, captivating and carrying them into slavery in another hemisphere, or to incur miserable death in their transportation thither. This piratical warfare, the opprobrium of infidel powers, is the warfare of the Christian king of Great Britain. Determined to keep open a market where men should be bought and sold, he has prostituted his negative for suppressing every legislative attempt to prohibit or restrain this execrable commerce. And that this assemblage of horrors might want no fact of distinguished dye, he is now exciting those very people to rise in arms among us, and to purchase that liberty of which he has deprived them, by murdering the people on whom he also obtruded them; thus paying off former crimes committed against the liberties of one people, with crimes which he urges them to commit against the lives of another."

Surely the omission of this passage was not less right than wise. New England towns had been enriched by the commerce in slaves, and the Southern colonies had subsisted on the labor of slaves for a hundred years. The foolish king had committed errors enough; but it was not fair to hold so limited a person responsible for not being a century in advance of his age; nor was it ever in the power of any king to compel his subjects to be slave-owners. It was young Virginia that spoke in this paragraph—Wythe, Jefferson, Madison, and their young friends—not the public mind of America, which was destined to reach it, ninety years after, by the usual way of agony and blood…

The "glittering generality" of the document, "all men are created equal," appears to have been accepted, without objection or remark, as a short and simple reprobation of caste and privilege. Readers are aware that it has not escaped contemptuous comment in recent times. It would have been easy for the author of the Declaration—and I wish he had done so—to put the statement in words which partizan prejudice itself could not have plausibly pretended to misunderstand; for, as the passage stands, its most obvious meaning is not true.

The noblest utterance of the whole composition is the reason given for making the Declaration—"A DECENT RESPECT FOR THE OPINIONS OF MANKIND." This touches the heart. Among the best emotions that human nature knows is the veneration of man for man.

During the 2d, 3d, and 4th of July, Congress was engaged in reviewing the Declaration. Thursday, the fourth, was a hot day; the session lasted many hours; members were tired and impatient. Every one who has watched the sessions of a deliberative body knows how the most important measures are retarded, accelerated, even defeated, by physical causes of the most trifling nature. Mr. Kinglake intimates that Lord Raglan's invasion of the Crimea was due rather to the after-dinner slumbers of the British Cabinet, than to any well-considered purpose. Mr. Jefferson used to relate, with much merriment, that the final signing of the Declaration of Independence washastened by an absurdly trivial cause. Near the hall in which the debates were then held was a livery-stable, from which swarms of flies came into the open windows, and assailed the silk-stockinged legs of honorable members. Handkerchief in hand, they lashed the flies with such vigor as they could command on a July afternoon; but the annoyance became at length so extreme as to render them impatient of delay and they made haste to bring the momentous business to a conclusion.

After such a long and severe strain upon their minds, members seem to have indulged in many a jocular observation as they stood around the table. Tradition has it that when John Hancock had affixt his magnificent signature to the paper, he said, "There, John Bull may read my name without spectacles!" Tradition, also, will never relinquish the pleasure of repeating, that, when Mr. Hancock reminded members of the necessity of hanging together, Dr. Franklin was ready with his, "Yes, we must indeed all hang together, or else, most assuredly, we shall all hang separately." And this may have suggested to the portly Harrison—a "luxurious, heavy gentleman," as John Adams describes him—his remark to slender Elbridge Gerry, that, when the hanging came, he should have the advantage; for Gerry would be kicking in the air long after it was over with himself.

No composition of man was ever received with more rapture than this. It came at a happy time. Boston was delivered, and New York, as yet, but menaced; and in all New England there was not a British soldier who was not a prisoner, nor a king's ship that was not a prize. Between the expulsion of the British troops from Boston, andtheir capture of New York, was the period of the Revolutionary War when the people were most confident and most united. From the newspapers and letters of the times, we should infer that the contest was ending rather than beginning, so exultant is their tone; and the Declaration of Independence, therefore, was received more like a song of triumph than a call to battle.

The paper was signed late on Thursday afternoon, July 4. On the Monday following, at noon, it was publicly read for the first time, in Independence Square, from a platform erected by Rittenhouse for the purpose of observing the transit of Venus. Captain John Hopkins, a young man commanding an armed brig of the navy of the new nation, was the reader; and it required his stentorian voice to carry the words to the distant verge of the multitude who had come to hear it. In the evening, as a journal of the day has it, "our late king's coat-of-arms were brought from the hall of the State House, where the said king's courts were formerly held, and burned amid the acclamation of a crowd of spectators." Similar scenes transpired in every center of population, and at every camp and post. Usually the militia companies, the committee of safety, and other revolutionary bodies, marched in procession to some public place, where they listened decorously to the reading of the Declaration, at the conclusion of which cheers were given and salutes fired; and, in the evening there were illuminations and bonfires. In New York, after the reading, the leaden statue of the late king in Bowling Green was "laid prostate in the dirt," and ordered to be run into bullets. The debtors in prison were also set at liberty. Virginia, before the news of the Declaration had reached her (July 5, 1776), had stricken the king's name out of the prayer-book; and now (July 30), Rhode Island made it a misdemeanor to pray for the king as king, under penalty of a fine of one hundred thousand pounds!

The news of the Declaration was received with sorrow by all that was best in England. Samuel Rogers used to give American guests at his breakfasts an interesting reminiscence of this period. On the morning after the intelligence reached London, his father, at family prayers, added a prayer for the success of the colonies, which he repeated every day until the peace.

The deed was done. A people not formed for empire ceased to be imperial; and a people destined to empire began the political education that will one day give them far more and better than imperial sway.

The Writing of The Declaration of Independence

Title: The Writing of The Declaration of Independence
Author: Thomas Jefferson
Date: 1822
Source: America, Vol.3, pp.166-170

In this illuminating letter to James Madison, written from Monticello during the administration and at the instance of President James Monroe, Thomas Jefferson corrects "a very careless and faulty statement" by John Adams of the circumstances attending the drafting of the Declaration. In so far as Jefferson wrote the Declaration and kept copious notes to refresh his memory, this undoubtedly is the correct and final word upon the subject.

A sensational charge of want of originality, which has been brought against the famous document, may here be noticed. Jefferson declares that while drafting it he consulted "neither book nor pamphlet," but that he did not consider it his business to "invent new ideas altogether."

Richard Henry Lee, one of the signers of the Declaration, who was most vociferous in charging plagiarism, is revealed in Randall's authoritative "Life of Jefferson" as having been responsible himself for the introduction of nearly all the alleged plagarizations.

I RECEIVED the enclosed letters from the President, with a request, that after perusal I would forward them to you, for perusal by yourself also, and to be returned then to him. You have doubtless seen Timothy Pickering's Fourth of July observations on the Declaration of Independence. If his principles and prejudices, personal and political, gave us no reason to doubt whether he had truly quoted the information he alleges to have received from Mr. Adams, I should then say, that in some of the particulars, Mr. Adams' memory has led him into unquestionable error. At the age of eighty-eight, and forty-seven years after the transactions of Independence, this is not wonderful. Nor should I, at the age of eighty, on the small advantage of that difference only, venture to oppose my memory to his, were it not supported by written notes, taken by himself at the moment and on the spot.

He says, "the committee of five, to wit, Dr. Franklin, Sherman, Livingston, and ourselves, met, discussed the subject, and then appointed him and myself to make the draught; that we, as a sub-committee, met, and after the urgencies of each on the other, I consented to undertake the task; that the draught being made, we, the sub-committee, met, and conned the paper over, and he does not remember that he made or suggested a single alteration." Now these details are quite incorrect. The committee of five met; no such thing as a sub-committee was proposed, but they unanimously pressed on myself alone to undertake the draught. I consented; I drew it; but before I reported it to the committee, I communicated it separately to Dr. Franklin and Mr. Adams, requesting their corrections, because they were the two members of whose judgments and amendments I wished most to have the benefit, before presenting it to the committee; and you have seen the original paper now in my hands, with the corrections of Dr. Franklin and Mr. Adams interlined in their own handwritings. Their alterations were two or three only, and merely verbal. I then wrote a fair copy, reported it to the committee, and from them, unaltered, to Congress.

This personal communication and consultation with Mr. Adams, he has misremembered into the actings of a sub-committee. Pickering's observations, and Mr. Adams' in addition, "that it contained no new ideas, that it is a common-place compilation, its sentiments hackneyed in Congress for two years before, and its essence contained in Otis' pamphlet," may all be true. Of that I am not to be the judge. Richard Henry Lee charged it as copied from Locke's treatise on government. Otis' pamphlet I never saw, and whether I had gathered my ideas from reading or reflection I do not know. I know only that I turned to neither book nor pamphlet while writing it. I did not consider it as any part of my charge to invent new ideas altogether, and to offer no sentiment which had ever been expressed before. Had Mr. Adams been so restrained, Congress would have lost the benefit of his bold and impressive advocations of the rights of Revolution. For no man's confident and fervid addresses, more than Mr. Adams', encouraged and supported us through the difficulties surrounding us, which, like the ceaseless action of gravity, weighed on us by night and by day. Yet, on the same ground, we may ask what of these elevated thoughts was new; or can be affirmed never before to have entered the conceptions of man? Whether, also, the sentiments of Independence, and the reasons for declaring it, which make so great a portion of the instrument, had been hackneyed in Congress for two years before the 4th of July, '76, or this dictum also of Mr. Adams be another slip of memory, let history say.

This, however, I will say for Mr. Adams, that he supported the Declaration with zeal and ability, fighting fearlessly for every word of it. As to myself, I thought it a duty to be, on that occasion, a passive auditor of the opinions of others, more impartial judges than I could be, of its merits or demerits. During the debate I was sitting by Doctor

Franklin, and he observed that I was writhing a little under the acrimonious criticisms on some of its parts; and it was on that occasion, that by way of comfort, he told me the story of John Thompson, the hatter, and his new sign. Timothy thinks the instrument the better for having a fourth of it expunged. He would have thought it still better, had the other three-fourths gone out also, all but the single sentiment (the only one he approved), which recommends friendship to his dear England, whenever she is willing to be at peace with us. His insinuations are, that although "the high tone of the instrument was in unison with the warm feelings of the times, this sentiment of habitual friendship to England should never be forgotten, and that the duties it enjoins should especially be borne in mind on every celebration of this anniversary." In other words, that the Declaration, as being a libel on the government of England, composed in times of passion, should now be buried in utter oblivion, to spare the feelings of our English friends and Angloman fellow-citizens. But it is not to wound them that we wish to keep it in mind; but to cherish the principles of the instrument in the bosoms of our own citizens; and it is a heavenly comfort to see that these principles are yet so strongly felt, as to render a circumstance so trifling as this little lapse of memory of Mr. Adams', worthy of being solemnly announced and supported at an anniversary assemblage of the nation on its birthday. In opposition, however, to Mr. Pickering, I pray God that these principles may be eternal, and close the prayer with my affectionate wishes for yourself of long life, health and happiness.

Jefferson's Original Draft of The Declaration

Title: Jefferson's Original Draft of the Declaration
Author: Thomas Jefferson
Date: 1776
Source: America, Vol. 3, pp.171-179

The original copy of the Declaration of Independence, signed at Philadelphia, is preserved at the Patent Office in Washington. It is not divided into paragraphs, but dashes are inserted. The arrangement of paragraphs here followed is that adopted by John Dunlap, who printed the Declaration for the Continental Congress.

The same paragraphs are also made by Jefferson, in the original draft, preserved in the State Department. The names of the Colonies do not appear with those of the signers in the original.

The text which is struck out was removed from the original draft of the Declaration by Congress; additions made by the Congress are indicated with bolded brackets and text. It will be noticed that Congress almost completely rewrote the two concluding paragraphs.

A Declaration by the Representatives of the United States of America, in General Congress Assembled

WHEN, in the course of human events, it becomes necessary for one people to dissolve the political bands which have connected them with another, and to assume among the powers of the earth the separate and equal station to which the laws of nature and of nature's God entitle them, a decent respect to the opinions of mankind requires that they should declare the causes which impel them to the separation.

We hold these truths to be self-evident: that all men are created equal; that they are endowed by their creator with ~~inherent and~~ **[certain]** inalienable rights; that among these are life, liberty, and the pursuit of happiness; that to secure these rights, governments are instituted among men, deriving their just powers from the consent of the governed; that whenever any form of government becomes destructive of these ends, it is the right of the people to alter or to abolish it, and to institute new government laying its foundation on such principles, and organizing its powers in such form, as to them shall seem most likely to effect their safety and happiness. Prudence, indeed, will dictate that governments long established should not be changed for light and transient causes; and accordingly all experience hath shown that mankind are more disposed to suffer while evils are sufferable, than to right themselves by abolishing the forms to which they are accustomed. But when a long train of abuses and usurpations ~~begun at a distinguished period and~~ pursuing invariably the same object, evinces a design to reduce them under absolute despotism, it is their right, it is their duty to throw off such government, and to provide new guards for their future security. Such has been the patient sufferance of these Colonies, and such is now the necessity which constrains them to ~~expunge~~ **[alter]** their former systems of government. The history of the present King of Great Britain is a history of ~~unremitting~~ **[repeated]** injuries and usurpations, ~~among which appears no solitary fact to contradict the uniform tenor of the rest, but all have~~ **[all having]** in direct object the establishment of an absolute tyranny over these States. To prove this, let facts be submitted to a candid world ~~for the truth of which we pledge a faith yet unsullied by falsehood~~.

He has refused his assent to laws the most wholesome and necessary for the public good.

He has forbidden his governors to pass laws of immediate and pressing importance, unless suspended in their operation till his assent should be obtained; and, when so suspended, he has utterly neglected to attend to them.

He has refused to pass other laws for the accommodation of large districts of people, unless those people would relinquish the right of representation in the Legislature, a right inestimable to them, and formidable to tyrants only.

He has called together legislative bodies at places unusual, uncomfortable, and distant from the depository of their public records, for the sole purpose of fatiguing them into compliance with his measures.

He has dissolved representative houses repeatedly ~~and continually~~ for opposing with manly firmness his invasions on the rights of the people.

He has refused for a long time after such dissolutions to cause others to be elected, whereby the legislative powers, incapable of annihilation, have returned to the people at large for their exercise, the State remaining, in the meantime, exposed to all the dangers of invasion from without and convulsions within.

He has endeavored to prevent the population of these States; for that purpose obstructing the laws for naturalization of foreigners, refusing to pass others to encourage their migrations hither, and raising the conditions of new appropriations of lands.

He has ~~suffered~~ [obstructed] the administration of justice ~~totally to cease in some of these States~~ [by] refusing his assent to laws for establishing judiciary powers.

He has made ~~our~~ judges dependent on his will alone for the tenure of their offices, and the amount and payment of their salaries.

He has erected a multitude of new offices, ~~by a self-assumed power~~ and sent hither swarms of new officers to harass our people and eat out their substance.

He has kept among us in times of peace standing armies ~~and ships of war~~ without the consent of our Legislatures.

He has affected to render the military independent of, and superior to, the civil power.

He has combined with others to subject us to a jurisdiction foreign to our constitutions and unacknowledged by our laws, giving his assent to their acts of pretended legislation for quartering large bodies of armed troops among us; for protecting them by a mock trial from punishment for any murders which they should commit on the inhabitants of these States; for cutting off our trade with all parts of the world; for imposing taxes on us without our consent; for depriving us **[in many cases]** of the benefits of trial by jury; for transporting us beyond seas to be tried for pretended offences; for abolishing the free system of English laws in a neighboring province, establishing therein an arbitrary government, and enlarging its boundaries, so as to render it at once an example and fit instrument for introducing the same absolute rule into these ~~States~~ **[Colonies]**; for taking away our charters, abolishing our most valuable laws, and altering fundamentally the forms of our governments; for suspending our own Legislatures, and declaring themselves invested with power to legislate for us in all cases whatsoever.

He has abdicated government here ~~withdrawing his governors, and declaring us out of his allegiance and protection~~ **[by declaring us out of his protection, and waging war against us]**.

He has plundered our seas, ravaged our coasts, burnt our towns, and destroyed the lives of our people.

He is at this time transporting large armies of foreign mercenaries to complete the works of death, desolation, and tyranny already begun with circumstances of cruelty and perfidy **[scarcely paralleled in the most barbarous ages, and totally]** unworthy the head of a civilized nation.

He has constrained our fellow-citizens taken captive on the high seas to bear arms against their country, to become the executioners of their friends and brethren, or to fall themselves by their hands.

He has **[excited domestic insurrection among us, and has]** endeavored to bring on the inhabitants of our frontiers the merciless Indian savages, whose known rule of warfare is an undistinguished destruction of all ages, sexes, and conditions ~~of existence.~~

~~He has incited treasonable insurrections of our fellow-citizens, with the allurements for forfeiture and confiscation of our property.~~

~~He has waged cruel war against human nature itself, violating its most sacred rights of life and liberty in the persons of a distant people who never offended him, captivating and carrying them into slavery in another hemisphere, or to incur miserable death in their transportation thither. This piratical warfare, the opprobrium of infidel powers, is the warfare of the Christian King of Great Britain. Determined to keep open a market where men should be bought and sold, he has prostituted his negative for suppressing every legislative attempt to prohibit or to restrain this execrable commerce. And that this assemblage of horrors might want no fact of distinguished die, he is now exciting those very people to rise in arms among us, and to purchase that liberty of which he has deprived them, by murdering the people on whom he also obtruded them: thus paying off former crimes committed against the liberties of one people with crimes which he urges them to commit against the lives of another.~~

In every stage of these oppressions we have petitioned for redress in the most humble terms: our repeated petitions have been answered only by repeated injuries.

A Prince whose character is thus marked by every act which may define a tyrant is unfit to be the ruler of a **[free]** people ~~who mean to be free. Future ages will scarcely believe that the hardiness of one man adventured, within the short compass of twelve years only, to lay a foundation so broad and so undisguised for tyranny over a people fostered and fixed in principles of freedom.~~

Nor have we been wanting in attentions to our British brethren. We have warned them from time to time of attempts by their legislature to extend ~~a~~ **[an unwarrantable]** jurisdiction over ~~these our States~~ **[us]**. We have reminded them of the circumstances of our emigration and settlement here, ~~no one of which could warrant so strange a pretension: that these were effected at the expense of our own blood and treasure, unassisted by the wealth or the strength of Great Britain: that in constituting indeed our several forms of government, we had adopted one common king, thereby laying a foundation for perpetual league and amity with them: but that submission to their parliament was no part of our Constitution, nor ever in idea, if history may be credited: and,~~ we **[have]** appealed to their native justice and magnanimity ~~as well as to~~ **[and we have conjured them by]** the ties of our common kindred to disavow these usurpations which ~~were likely to~~ **[would inevitably]** interrupt our connection and correspondence. They too have been deaf to the voice of justice and of consanguinity, ~~and when occasions have~~

~~been given them, by the regular course of their laws, of removing from their councils the disturbers of our harmony, they have, by their free election, reestablished them in power. At this very time too, they are permitting their chief magistrate to send over not only soldiers of our common blood, but Scotch and foreign mercenaries to invade and destroy us. These facts have given the last stab to agonizing affection, and manly spirit bids us to renounce forever these unfeeling brethren. We must endeavor to forget our former love for them, and hold them as we hold the rest of mankind, enemies in war, in peace friends. We might have been a free and a great people together; but a communication of grandeur and of freedom, it seems, is below their dignity. Be it so, since they will have it. The road to happiness and to glory is open to us too. We will tread it apart from them, and~~ **[We must therefore]** acquiesce in the necessity ~~eternal~~ separation **[and hold them as we hold the rest of mankind, enemies of war, in peace friends]**!

We therefore the representatives of the United States of America in General Congress assembled, **[appealing to the supreme judge of the world for the rectitude of our intentions,]** do in the name, and by the authority of the good people of these ~~States reject and renounce all allegiance and subjection to the kings of Great Britain and all others who may hereafter claim by, through, or under them; we utterly dissolve all political connection which may heretofore have subsisted between us and the people or parliament of Great Britain: and finally we do assert and declare these Colonies to be free and independent States,~~ **[Colonies, solemnly publish and declare, that these united Colonies are, and of right ought to be, free and independent States; that they are absolved from all allegiance to the British crown, and that all political connection between them and the state of Great Britain is, and ought to be, totally dissolved;]** and that as free and independent States, they have full power to levy war, conclude peace, contract alliances, establish commerce, and to do all other acts and things which independent States may of right do.

And for the support of this declaration, **[with a firm reliance on the protection of divine providence,]** we mutually pledge to each other our lives, our fortunes, and our sacred honor.

Why Jefferson Was Chosen
To Write The Declaration

Title: Why Jefferson Was Chosen To Write The Declaration
Author: John Adams
Date: 1822
Source: America, Vol.3, pp.180-183

In writing this letter to Timothy Pickering forty-six years after the Declaration of Independence was drafted, John Adams did a service not only to its recipient, who had been his Secretary of State, but to posterity. Why, indeed, did the Continental Congress of many graybeards choose Jefferson, a young man of thirty-three, to draft so grave and revolutionary a document? One reason, which Adams neglects to state, was that Jefferson had some time previously written in pamphlet form "A Summary View of the Rights of British America," which provoked the British Government to name its author in a bill to punish sedition. In drafting the famous Declaration, Jefferson simply revised and elaborated the earlier document to suit the greater occasion.

Pickering was successively Postmaster-General of the United States, Secretary of War, as well as of State, and United States Senator.

YOU inquire why so young a man as Mr. Jefferson was placed at the head of the Committee for preparing a Declaration of Independence? I answer: It was the Frankfort advice, to place Virginia at the head of everything. Mr. Richard Henry Lee might be gone to Virginia, to his sick family, for aught I know, but that was not the reason of Mr. Jefferson's appointment. There were three committees appointed at the same time. One for the Declaration of Independence, another for preparing articles of Confederation, and another for preparing a treaty to be proposed to France. Mr. Lee was chosen for the Committee of Confederation, and it was not thought convenient that the same person should be upon both.

Mr. Jefferson came into Congress, in June, 1775, and brought with him a reputation for literature, science, and a happy talent for composition. Writings of his were handed about, remarkable for the peculiar felicity of expression. Though a silent member in Congress, he was so prompt, frank, explicit, and decisive upon committees and in conversation, not even Samuel Adams was more so, that he soon seized upon my heart; and upon this occasion I gave him my vote, and did all in my power to procure the votes of others. I think he had one more vote than any other, and that placed him at the head of the committee. I had the next highest number, and that placed me the second. The committee met, discussed the subject, and then appointed Mr. Jefferson and me to make the draft, I suppose because we were the two first on the list.

The sub-committee met. Jefferson proposed to me to make the draft. I said, "I will not." "You should do it." "Oh! no." "Why will you not? You ought to do it." "I will not." "Why?" "Reasons enough." "What can be your reasons?" "Reason first—You are a Virginian, and a Virginian ought to appear at the head of this business. Reason second—I am obnoxious, suspected and unpopular. You are very much otherwise. Reason third—You can write ten times better than I can." "Well," said Jefferson, "if you are decided, I will do as well as I can." "Very well. When you have drawn it up, we will have a meeting."

A meeting we accordingly had, and conned the paper over. I was delighted with its high tone and the flights of oratory with which it abounded, especially that concerning negro slavery, which, though I knew his Southern brethren would never suffer to pass in Congress, I certainly never would oppose. There were other expressions which I would not have inserted, if I had drawn it up, particularly that which called the King tyrant. I thought this too personal; for I never believed George to be a tyrant in disposition and in nature; I always believed him to be deceived by his courtiers on both sides of the Atlantic, and in his official capacity only, cruel. I thought the expression too passionate, and too much like scolding, for so grave and solemn a document; but as Franklin and Sherman were to inspect it afterwards, I thought it would not become me to strike it out. I consented to report it, and do not now remember that I made or suggested a single alteration.

We reported it to the committee of five. It was read, and I do not remember that Franklin or Sherman criticized anything. We were all in haste. Congress was impatient, and the instrument was reported, as I believed, in Jefferson's handwriting, as he first drew it. Congress cut off about a quarter of it, as I expected they would; but they obliterated some of the best of it, and left all that was exceptionable, if anything in it was. I have long wondered that the original draft has not been published. I suppose the reason is, the vehement philippic against negro slavery.

As you justly observe, there is not an idea in it but what had been hackneyed in Congress for two years before. The substance of it is contained in the declaration of rights and the violation of those rights, in the Journals of Congress, in 1774. Indeed, the essence of it is contained in a pamphlet, voted and printed by the town of Boston, before the first

Congress met, composed by James Otis, as I suppose, in one of his lucid intervals, and pruned and polished by Samuel Adams.

6 August, 1822.

Franklin in France

Title: Franklin in France
Author: Sir George Trevelyan
Date: 1776-1785
Source: Great Epochs in American History, Vol.3, pp.142-148

The early relations between the United States of America, and the monarchies of Europe, may be studied with advantage by those writers who attache little or no importance to the personal factor in history. The prospects of the young republic were seriously, and to all appearance irretrievably, damnified by the mismanagement of Congress; but the position was saved by the ability, the discretion, and the force of one single man. Benjamin Franklin was now past seventy. He had begun to earn his bread as a child of ten; he commenced as an author at sixteen; and he had ever since been working with his hands, and taxing his brain, unintermittently, and to the top of his power. Such exertions were not maintained with impunity. He kept his strength of will unimpaired, his mind clear and lively, and his temper equable, by a lifelong habit of rigid abstemiousness; but he already felt the approach of painful disease that tortured him cruelly before the immense undertaking, which still lay before him, had been half accomplished. In September, 1776, he was elected Commissioner to France, by a unanimous resolution of Congress. Franklin, in the highest sense of the term, was a professional diplomatist; for he had passed sixteen years in England as agent for his colony, and his individual qualities had gained for him a political influence, and a social standing, out of all proportion to the comparatively humble interests which he represented at the British court. The ambassadors of the Great Powers, who were resident in London, treated him as one of themselves. He was old enough to be the father of most among them, and wise enough to be the adviser of all; and, toward the end of his time, they united in regarding him as in some sort the doyen of their body…

From other Americans then resident in Paris Franklin received little help, and a great deal of most unnecessary hindrance. Silas Deane, who had business knowledge and business aptitudes, was of service in arranging contracts and inspecting warlike stores; and Deane, after

Franklin's arrival in Europe, had the good sense to confine himself strictly within his own province. But Arthur Lee was an uneasy, and a most dangerous yoke-fellow. Lee was a sinister personage in the drama of the American revolution;—the assassin of other men's reputation and careers, and the suicide of his own. He now was bent on defaming and destroying Silas Deane, whom he fiercely hated, and on persuading the government at home to transfer Franklin to Vienna, so that he himself might remain behind in France s the single representative of America at the Court of Versailles. The group of politicians in Philadelphia, who were caballing against George Washington, maintained confidential, and not very creditable, relations with Arthur Lee at Paris. His eloquentbrother was his mouthpiece in Congress; and he plied Samuel Adams with a series of venomous libels upon Franklin, which were preserved unrebuked, and too evidently had been read with pleasure.

The best that can be said for Arthur Lee is that, in his personal dealings with colleagues whom he was seeking to ruin, he made no pretense of a friendship which he did not feel; and his attitude toward his brother envoys was, to the last degree, hostile and insulting. He found an ally in Ralph Izard, who lived at Paris, an ambassador in partibus, two hundred leagues away from the capital to which he was accredited; drawing the same salary as Franklin; denouncing him in open letters addrest to the President of Congress, and insisting, with querulous impertinence, on his right to participate in all the secret counsels of the French Court. Franklin for some months maintained an unruffled composure. He had never been quick to mark offenses, and he now had reached that happy period of life when a man values the good-will of his juniors, but troubles himself very little about their disapproval. He ignored the provocation given by his pair of enemies, and extended to them a hospitality which they, on their part, did not refrain from accepting, altho his food and wine might well have choked them. But the moment came when his own self-respect, and a due consideration for the public interest, forbade Franklin any longer to pass over their conduct in silence, and he spoke out in a style which astonished both of them at the time, and has gratified the American leader ever since. He castigated Arthur Lee in as plainand vigorous English as ever was set down on paper, and informed Ralph Izard, calmly but very explicitly, that he would do well to mind his own business.

Franklin, as long as he was on European soil, had no need to stand upon ceremony when dealing with a refractory fellow countryman; for he was in great authority on that side of the Atlantic Ocean. Europe had welcomed and accepted him, not as a mere spokesman and agent of the

government at Philadelphia, but as the living and breathing embodi-
ment of the American republic. No statesman would do business with
anybody but Franklin. No financier would negotiate a loan except with
him, or pay over money into other hands but his. "It was to Franklin
that both the French and English ministries turned, as if he were not
only the sole representative of the United States in Europe, but s if he
were endowed with plenipotentiary power." Nine-tenths of the public
letters addrest to the American Commissioners were brought to his
home; "and" (so his colleague admitted), "they would ever be carried
wherever Doctor Franklin is." He transacted his affairs with Louis the
Sixteenth's ministers on a footing of equality, and (as time went on),
of unostentatious but unquestionable superiority. Thomas Jefferson, an
impartial and most competent observer, had on one occasion been contending that American diplomats were always spoiled for use after they
had been kept seven years abroad. But this (said Jefferson) did not
apply to Franklin, "who was America itself when in France, not subjecting himself to French influence," but imposing American influence
upon France, and upon the whole course and conduct of her national
policy…

His immense and (as he himself was the foremost to acknowledge)
his extravagant popularity was founded on a solid basis of admiration
and esteem. The origin of his fame dated from a time which seemed
fabulously distant to the existing generation. His qualities and accomplishments were genuine and unpretentious; and his services to the
world were appreciated by high and low, rich and poor, in every country
where men learned from books, or profited by the discoveries of science. His Poor Richard—which expounded and elucidated a code of
rules for the every-day conduct of life with sagacity that never failed,
and wit that very seldom missed the mark—had been thrice translated
into French, had gone through many editions, and had been recommended by priests and bishops for common use in their parishes and
diocese. As an investigator, and an experimentalist, he was more widely
known even than as an author; for he had always aimed at making natural philosophy the handmaid of material progress. Those homely and
practical inventions by which he had done so much to promote the comfort and convenience of the average citizen, had caused him to be regarded as a public benefactor in every civilized community throughout
the world. His reputation (so John Adams wrote) was more universal
than that of Leibnitz or Newton. "His name was familiar to government
and people, to foreign countries—to nobility, clergy, and philosophers,
as well as to plebeians—to such a degree that there was scarcely a peas-

ant or a citizen, a valet, coachman, or foot-man, a lady's chambermaid, or scullion in the kitchen, who did not consider him a friend to humankind." If Franklin, at seventy years of age, had visited France as a private tourist, his progress through her cities would have been one long ovation, and her enthusiasm transcended all bounds when, coming as an ambassador from a new world beyond the seas, he appealed to French chivalry on behalf of a young nation struggling for freedom...

When he appeared in public he was drest in good broadcloth of a sober tint; conspicuous with his long straight hair, whitened by age, and not by art; and wearing a pair of spectacles to remedy an old man's dimness of vision, and a cap of fine marten's fur, because he had an old man's susceptibility to cold.

Franklin's costume had not been designed with any idea of pleasing the Parisians, but it obtained an extraordinary success, and has left a mark on history. Fine gentlemen, with their heads full of the new philosophy, regarded his unembroidered coat, and unpowdered locks, as a tacit, but visible, protest against those luxuries and artificialities which they all condemned, but had not the smallest intention of themselves renouncing. He reminded them of everything and everybody that Jean Jacques Rousseau had taught them to admire. The Comte de Segur declared that "Franklin's antique and patriarchal aspect seemed to transport into the midst of an enervated, and servile, civilization a Republican of Rome of the time of Cato and Fabius, or a sage who had consorted with Plato." Some compared him to Diogenes, and some to Phocion—about whom they can haveknown very little; for, if Phocion had been a Pennsylvanian of Anno Domini 1776, he would, beyond all question, have been a strenuous and uncompromising supporter of the British connection. Readers of Emile, who then comprized three-fourths of the fashionable world, delighted to recognize in the American stranger an express and living image of the Savoyard Vicar; and it was believed, with some reason, that his views on religion nearly corresponded to those of Rousseau's famous ecclesiastic, altho Franklin would most certainly have comprest his profession of faith into much shorter compass. The great French ladies were attracted and fascinated by his self-possession, his benign courtesy, and his playful, yet always rational, conversation. The ardor of Franklin's votaries sometimes manifested itself with an exuberance which made it difficult for him to keep his countenance.

A Call For Independence

Title: A Call For Independence
Author: Thomas Paine
Date: 1776
Source: America, Vol.3, p.151

Thomas Paine's "Common Sense" was published anonymously six months before the drafting of the Declaration of Independence, which it advocated and inspired. Indeed, there might never have been any such revolutionary declaration had this pamphlet not been published and read throughout the colonies in the early months of 1776. It converted Washington, who pronounced it, "Sound logic and unanswerable reasoning," and its influence on Jefferson and Franklin was marked. John Adams, who had no love for Paine, once wrote to Jefferson, "History is to ascribe to Paine the Revolution," and Lafayette said repeatedly, "To me America without Paine is unthinkable."

Paine was the son of an English Quaker, a staymaker, and was living somewhat precariously in London in 1774 when Benjamin Franklin, attracted by his genius, persuaded him to emigrate to America, with letters of introduction to his friends.

LEAVING the moral part to private reflection, I shall chiefly confine my further remarks to the following heads:

First, That it is the interest of America to be separated from Britain.

Secondly, Which is the easiest and most practicable plan, reconciliation or independence? with some occasional remarks.

In support of the first, I could, if I judged it proper, produce the opinion of some of the ablest and most experienced men on this continent; and whose sentiments, on that head, are not yet publicly known. It is in reality a self-evident position: For no nation, in a state of foreign dependence, limited in its commerce, and cramped and fettered in its legislative powers, can ever arrive at any material eminence. America does not yet know what opulence is; and although the progress which she has made stands unparalleled in the history of other nations, it is but childhood, compared with what she would be capable of arriving at, had she, as she ought to have, the legislative powers in her own hands. England is, at this time, proudly coveting what would do her no good, were she to accomplish it; and the continent hesitating on a matter, which will be her final ruin if neglected. It is the commerce, and not the conquest of America, by which England is to be benefited, and that would in a great measure continue, were the countries as independent of each other as France and Spain; because in many articles, neither can go to a better market. But it is the independence of this country on Britain or any other, which is now the main and only object worthy of contention, and which, like all other truths discovered by necessity, will appear clearer and stronger every day.

First. Because it will come to that one time or other.

Secondly. Because the longer it is delayed, the harder it will be to accomplish.

I have frequently amused myself both in public and private companies, with silently remarking the specious errors of those who speak without reflecting. And among the many which I have heard, the following seems the most general, viz. that had this rupture happened forty or fifty years hence, instead of now, the Continent would have been more able to have shaken off the dependence. To which I reply, that our military ability at this time, arises from the experience gained in the late war, and which in forty or fifty years time, would have been totally extinct...

Should affairs be patched up with Britain, and she to remain the governing and sovereign power of America, (which as matters are now circumstanced, is giving up the point entirely) we shall deprive ourselves of the very means of sinking the debt we have, or may contract. The value of the back lands, which some of the provinces are clandestinely deprived of, by the unjust extension of the limits of Canada, valued only at five pounds sterling per hundred acres, amount to upwards of twenty-five millions, Pennsylvania currency; and the quit-rents at one penny sterling per acre, to two millions yearly...

I proceed now to the second head, viz. Which is the easiest and most practicable plan, Reconciliation or Independence; with some occasional remarks.

He who takes nature for his guide, is not easily beaten out of his argument, and on that ground, I answer generally, that independence being a single simple line, contained within ourselves; and reconciliation, a matter of exceedingly perplexed and complicated, and in which, a treacherous capricious court is to interfere, gives the answer without a doubt.

The present state of America is truly alarming to every man who is capable of reflection. Without law, without government, without any other mode of power than what is founded on, and granted by courtesy.

Held together by an unexampled concurrence of sentiment, which, is nevertheless subject to change, and which, every secret enemy is endeavoring to dissolve. Our present condition is, legislation without law; wisdom without a plan; a Constitution without a name; and, what is strangely astonishing, perfect independence, contending for dependence. The instance is without a precedent; the case never existed before; and who can tell what may be the event? The property of no man is secure in the present unbraced system of things. The mind of the multitude is left at random, and seeing no fixed object before them, they pursue such as fancy or opinion starts. Nothing is criminal; there is no such thing as treason; wherefore, every one thinks himself at liberty to act as he pleases. The Tories would not have dared to assemble offensively, had they known that their lives, by that act, were forfeited to the laws of the State. A line of distinction should be drawn between English soldiers taken in battle, and inhabitants of America taken in arms. The first are prisoners, but the latter traitors. The one forfeits his liberty, the other his head...

Put us, say some, upon the footing we were on in sixty-three... To be on the footing of sixty-three, it is not sufficient, that the laws only be put on the same state, but that our circumstances, likewise be put on the same state; our burnt and destroyed towns repaired or built up, our private losses made good, our public debts (contracted for defense) discharged; otherwise we shall be millions worse than we were at that enviable period. Such a request, had it been complied with a year ago, would have won the heart and soul of the Continent, but now it is too late. "The Rubicon is passed."

Besides, the taking up arms, merely to enforce the repeal of a pecuniary law, seems as unwarrantable by the divine law, and as repugnant to human feelings, as the taking up arms to enforce the obedience thereto. The object, on either side, does not justify the means; for the lives of men are too valuable, to be cast away on such trifles. It is the violence which is done and threatened to our persons; the destruction of our property by an armed force; the invasion of our country by fire and sword, which conscientiously qualifies the use of arms: And the instant, in which such a mode of defense became necessary, all subjection to Britain ought to have ceased; and the independency of America, should have been considered, as dating its era from, and published, by the first musket that was fired against her. This line is a line of consistency; neither drawn by caprice, nor extended by ambition; but produced by a chain of events, of which the colonies were not the authors.

I shall conclude these remarks, with the following timely and well intended hint. We ought to reflect that there are three different ways, by which an independency may hereafter be effected; and that one of those three, will one day or other, be the fate of America, viz. By the legal voice of the people in Congress; by a military power; or by a mob. It may not always happen that our soldiers are citizens, and the multitude a body of reasonable men; virtue, as I have already remarked, is not hereditary, neither is it perpetual. Should an independency be brought about by the first of those means, we have every opportunity and every encouragement before us, to form the noblest purest constitution on the face of the earth. We have it in our power to begin the world over again. A situation, similar to the present, has not happened since the days of Noah until now. The birthday of a new world is at hand, and a race of men, perhaps as numerous as all Europe contains, are to receive their portion of freedom from the event of a few months. The reflection is awful and in this point of view, how trifling, how ridiculous, do the little paltry cavilings, of a few weak or interested men appear, when weighed against the business of a world...

In short, independence is the only bond that can tie and keep us together. We shall then see our object, and our ears will be legally shut against the schemes of an intriguing, as well as a cruel enemy. We shall then too be on a proper footing to treat with Britain; for there is reason to conclude, that the pride of that court will be less hurt by treating with the American states for terms of peace, than with those she denominates "rebellious subjects," for terms of accommodation. It is our delaying it that encourages her to hope for conquest, and our backwardness tends only to prolong the war. As we have, without any good effect therefrom, withheld our trade to obtain a redress of our grievances, let us now try the alternative, by independently redressing them ourselves, and then offering to open the trade. The mercantile and reasonable part in England will be still with us; because, peace with trade, is preferable to war without it. And if this offer is not accepted, other courts may be applied to. On these grounds I rest the matter. And as no offer hath yet been made to refute the doctrine contained in the former editions of this pamphlet, it is a negative proof, that either the doctrine cannot be refuted, or, that the party in favor of it are too numerous to be opposed. Wherefore instead of gazing at each other with suspicious or doubtful curiosity, let each of us hold out to his neighbor the hearty hand of friendship, and unite in drawing a line, which, like an act of oblivion, shall bury in forgetfulness every former dissension. Let the names of Whig and Tory be extinct; and let none other be heard among us, than those of a good citizen, an open and resolute friend, and a virtuous supporter of the rights of mankind and of the free and independent states of America.

The Siege and Capture of Boston: Washington's Own Reports to the President of Congress

Title: The Siege and Capture of Boston: Washington's Own Reports to the
      President of Congress
Author: George Washington
Date: March, 1776
Source: America, Vol.3, pp.158-165

The evacuation of Boston by the British forces under General Howe was the first military victory Washington achieved after taking command of the Continental Army. The town was besieged for nine months, and while great credit is given Washington for his strategy in fortifying Dorchester Heights, which commanded the town, Howe wrote a friend on March 21, 1776—four days after the evacuation—that he had received no instructions from his Government since the previous October and found his position intolerable.

One of his officers testifies that we were seemingly abandoned by those who had sent us on so nefarious an expedition." Also that "the reason the rebels offered no obstruction to our retreat was for fear of our burning the town, which, had they fired a single shot, would have been done."

The President of Congress, to whom Washington writes during March, 1776, that "your house in Boston has received no damage worth mentioning," was John Hancock.

O N THE 26th ultimo I had the honor of addressing you, and then mentioned that we were making preparations for taking possession of Dorchester Heights. I now beg leave to inform you, that a council of general officers having determined a previous bombardment and cannonade expedient and proper, in order to harass the enemy and divert their attention from that quarter, on Saturday, Sunday, and Monday nights last, we carried them on from our posts at Cobble Hill, Lechmere's Point, and Lamb's Dam. Whether they did the enemy any considerable and what injury, I have not yet heard, but have the pleasure to acquaint you, that they greatly facilitated our schemes, and would have been attended with success equal to our most sanguine expectations, had it not been for the unlucky bursting of two thirteen and three ten inch mortars, among which was the brass one taken in the ordnance brig. To what cause to attribute this misfortune, I know not; whether to any defects in them, or to the inexperience of the bombardiers.

But to return; on Monday evening, as soon as our firing commenced, a considerable detachment of our men, under the command of Brigadier-General Thomas, crossed the neck, and took possession of the two hills, without the least interruption or annoyance from the enemy; and by their great activity and industry, before the morning, advanced the works so far as to be secure against their shot. They are now going on with such expedition, that in a little time I hope they will be complete, and enable our troops stationed there to make a vigorous and obstinate stand. During the whole cannonade, which was incessant the two last nights, we were fortunate enough to lose but two men; one, a lieutenant, by a cannonball taking off his thigh; the other, a private, by the explosion of a shell, which also slightly wounded four or five more.

Our taking possession of Dorchester Heights is only preparatory to taking post on Hook's Hill, and the points opposite to the south end of Boston. It was absolutely necessary, that they should be previously fortified, in order to cover and command them. As soon as the works on the former are finished, measures will be immediately adopted for securing the latter, and making them as strong and defensible as we can. Their contiguity to the enemy will make them of much importance and of great service to us...

In case the ministerial troops have made an attempt to dislodge our men from Dorchester Hills, and the number detached upon the occasion had been so great as to have afforded a probability of a successful attack's being made upon Boston; on a signal given from Roxbury for that purpose, agreeably to a settled and concerted plan, four thousand chosen men, who were held in readiness, were to have embarked at the mouth of Cambridge River, in two divisions, the first under the command of Brigadier-General Sullivan, the second under Brigadier-General Greene; the whole to have been commanded by Major-General Putnam. The first division was to land at the powder-house and gain possession of Beacon Hill and Mount Horam; the second at Barton's Point, or a little south of it, and, after securing that post, to join the other division, and force the enemy's gates and works at the neck, for letting in the Roxbury troops. Three floating batteries were to have preceded, and gone in front of the other boats, and kept up a heavy fire on that part of the town where our men were to land…

YESTERDAY evening a Captain Irvine who escaped from Boston the night before with six of his crew, came to headquarters and gave the following intelligence:

> That our bombardment and cannonade caused a good deal of surprise and alarm in town, as many of the soldiery said they never heard or thought we had mortars or shell; that several of the officers acknowledged they were well and properly directed; that they made much distress and confusion; that the cannon shot for the greatest part went through the houses, and he was told that one took off the legs and arms of six men lying in the barracks on the Neck; that a soldier who came from the lines there on Tuesday morning informed him that 20 men had been wounded the night before. It was reported that others were also hurt, and one of the light horse torn to pieces by the explosion of a shell. This was afterwards contradicted. That early on Tuesday morning Admiral Shuldham discovering the works our people were throwing up on Dorchester Heights, immediately sent an express to General Howe to inform him, and that it was necessary they should be attacked and dislodged from thence, or he would be under the necessity of withdrawing the ships from the harbor, which were under his command; that preparations were directly made for that purpose as it was said, and from twelve to two o'-clock about 3000 men embarked on board the transport which fell down to the Castle with a design of landing on that part of Dorchester next to it, and attacking the works on the Heights at five o'clock next morning; that Lord Percy was appointed to command; that it was generally believed the attempt would have been made, had it not been for the violent storm which happened that night, as I have mentioned before; that he heard several of the privates and one or two sergeants say as they were embarking, that it would be another Bunker Hill affair. He further informs that the army is preparing to leave Boston, and that they will do it in a day or two; that the transports necessary for their embarkation were getting ready with the utmost expedition; that there had been great movements and confusion among the troops night and day preceding his coming out, in hurrying down their cannon, artillery and other stores to the wharves with the utmost precipitation, and were putting 'em on board the ships in such haste that no account or memorandum was taken of them; that most of

the cannon were removed from their works and embarked or embarking; that he heard a woman say, which he took to be an officer's wife, that she had seen men go under the ground at the lines on the Neck without returning; that the ship he commanded was taken up, places fitted and fitting for officers to lodge, and several shot, shells and cannon already on board; that the Tories were to have the liberty of going where they please, if they can get seamen to man the vessels, of which there was a great scarcity; that on that account many vessels could not be carried away and would be burnt; that many of the inhabitants apprehended the town would be destroyed, and that it was generally thought their destination is Halifax…

IN my letter of the 7th and 9th instant, which I had the honor of addressing you, I mentioned the intelligence I had received respecting the embarkation of the troops from Boston; and fully expected, before this, that the town would have been entirely evacuated. Although I have been deceived, and was rather premature in the opinion I had then formed, I have little reason to doubt that the event will take place in a very short time, as other accounts, which have come to hand since, the sailing of a great number of transports from the harbor to Nantasket Road, and many circumstances corresponding therewith, seem to confirm and render it unquestionable. Whether the town will be destroyed is a matter of much uncertainty; but it would seem, from the destruction they are making of sundry pieces of furniture, of many their wagons and carts, which they cannot take wit them as it is said, that it will not; for, if they intended it, the whole might be involved in one general ruin…

IT IS with the greatest pleasure I inform you that on Sunday last, the instant, about nine o'clock in the forenoon, the ministerial army evacuated the town of Boston, and that the forces of the United Colonies are now in actual possession thereof. I beg leave to congratulate you, Sir, and the honorable Congress, on this happy event, and particularly as it was effected without endangering the lives and property of the remaining unhappy inhabitants.

I have great reason to imagine their flight was precipitated by the appearance of a work, which I had ordered to be thrown up last Saturday night on an eminence at Dorchester, which lies nearest to Boston Neck, called Nook's Hill. The town, although it has suffered greatly, is not in so bad a state as I expected to find it; and I have a particular pleasure in being able to inform you, Sir, that your house has received no damage worth mentioning. Your furniture is in tolerable order, and the family pictures are all left entire and untouched. Captain Cazneau takes charge of the whole, until he shall receive further orders from you.

As soon as the ministerial troops had quitted the town, I ordered a thousand men (who had had the smallpox), under command of General Putnam, to take possession of the heights, which I shall endeavor to fortify in such a manner, as to prevent their return, should they attempt it. But, as they are still in the harbor, I thought it not prudent to march off with the main body of the army, until I should be fully satisfied they had quitted the coast. I have, therefore, only detached five regiments, besides the rifle battalion, to New York, and shall keep the remainder here till all suspicion of their return ceases.

The situation in which I found their works evidently discovered, that their retreat was made with the greatest precipitation. They have left their barracks and other works of wood at Bunker's Hill all standing, and have destroyed but a small part of their lines. They have also left a number of fine pieces of cannon, which they first spiked up, also a very large iron mortar; and, (as I am informed,) they have thrown another over the end of your wharf. I have employed proper persons to drill the cannon, and doubt not I shall save the most of them. I am not yet able to procure an exact list of all the stores they have left. As soon as it can be done, I shall take care to transmit it to you. From an estimate of what the quartermaster-general has already discovered, the amount will be twenty-five or thirty thousand pounds.

Part of the powder mentioned in yours of the 6th instant has already arrived. The remainder I have ordered to be stopped on the road, as we shall have no occasion for it here. The letter to General Thomas, I immediately sent to him. He desired leave, for three or four days, to settle some of his private affairs; after which, he will set out for his command in Canada. I am happy that my conduct in intercepting Lord Drummond's letter is approved of by Congress. I have the honor to be, &c.

The Virginia Declaration of Rights

Title: The Virginia Declaration of Rights
Author: George Mason
Date: June 12, 1776
Source: U.S. National Archives and Records Service

Virginia's Declaration of Rights was drawn upon by Thomas Jefferson for the opening paragraphs of the Declaration of Independence. It was widely copied by the other colonies and became the basis of the Bill of Rights. Written by George Mason, it was adopted by the Virginia Constitutional Convention on June 12, 1776.

A DECLARATION OF RIGHTS made by the representatives of the good people of Virginia, assembled in full and free convention which rights do pertain to them and their posterity, as the basis and foundation of government .

Section 1. That all men are by nature equally free and independent and have certain inherent rights, of which, when they enter into a state of society, they cannot, by any compact, deprive or divest their posterity; namely, the enjoyment of life and liberty, with the means of acquiring and possessing property, and pursuing and obtaining happiness and safety.

Section 2. That all power is vested in, and consequently derived from, the people; that magistrates are their trustees and servants and at all times amenable to them.

Section 3. That government is, or ought to be, instituted for the common benefit, protection, and security of the people, nation, or community; of all the various modes and forms of government, that is best which is capable of producing the greatest degree of happiness and safety and is most effectually secured against the danger of maladministration. And that, when any government shall be found inadequate or contrary to these purposes, a majority of the community has an indubitable, inalienable, and indefeasible right to reform, alter, or abolish it, in such manner as shall be judged most conducive to the public weal.

Section 4. That no man, or set of men, is entitled to exclusive or separate emoluments or privileges from the community, but in consideration of public services; which, nor being descendible, neither ought the offices of magistrate, legislator, or judge to be hereditary.

Section 5. That the legislative and executive powers of the state should be separate and distinct from the judiciary; and that the members of the two first may be restrained from oppression, by feeling and participating the burdens of the people, they should, at fixed periods, be reduced to a private station, return into that body from which they were originally taken, and the vacancies be supplied by frequent, certain, and regular elections, in which all, or any part, of the former members, to be again eligible, or ineligible, as the laws shall direct.

Section 6. That elections of members to serve as representatives of the people, in assembly ought to be free; and that all men, having sufficient evidence of permanent common interest with, and attachment to, the community, have the right of suffrage and cannot be taxed or deprived of their property for public uses without their own consent or that of their representatives so elected, nor bound by any law to which they have not, in like manner, assembled for the public good.

Section 7. That all power of suspending laws, or the execution of laws, by any authority, without consent of the representatives of the people, is injurious to their rights and ought not to be exercised.

Section 8. That in all capital or criminal prosecutions a man has a right to demand the cause and nature of his accusation, to be confronted with the accusers and witnesses, to call for evidence in his favor, and to a speedy trial by an impartial jury of twelve men of his vicinage, without whose unanimous consent he cannot be found guilty; nor can he be compelled to give evidence against himself; that no man be deprived of his liberty except by the law of the land or the judgment of his peers.

Section 9. That excessive bail ought not to be required, nor excessive fines imposed, nor cruel and unusual punishments inflicted.

Section 10. That general warrants, whereby an officer or messenger may be commanded to search suspected places without evidence of a fact committed, or to seize any person or persons not named, or whose offense is not particularly described and supported by evidence, are grievous and oppressive and ought not to be granted.

Section 11. That in controversies respecting property, and in suits between man and man, the ancient trial by jury is preferable to any other and ought to be held sacred.

Section 12. That the freedom of the press is one of the great bulwarks of liberty, and can never be restrained but by despotic governments.

Section 13. That a well-regulated militia, composed of the body of the people, trained to arms, is the proper, natural, and safe defense of a free state; that standing armies, in time of peace, should be avoided as dangerous to liberty; and that in all cases the military should be under strict subordination to, and governed by, the civil power.

Section 14. That the people have a right to uniform government; and, therefore, that no government separate from or independent of the government of Virginia ought to be erected or established within the limits thereof.

Section 15. That no free government, or the blessings of liberty, can be preserved to any people but by a firm adherence to justice, moderation, temperance, frugality, and virtue and by frequent recurrence to fundamental principles.

Section 16. That religion, or the duty which we owe to our Creator, and the manner of discharging it, can be directed only by reason and conviction, not by force or violence; and therefore all men are equally entitled to the free exercise of religion, according to the dictates of conscience; and that it is the mutual duty of all to practise Christian forbearance, love, and charity toward each other.

Declaration of Independence

Title: Declaration of Independence
Author: Founders
Date: July 4, 1776

In Congress, July 4, 1776
The Unanimous Declaration
of The Thirteen United States of America

When in the Course of human events, it becomes necessary for one people to dissolve the political bands which have connected them with another, and to assume among the Powers of the earth, the separate and equal station to which the Laws of Nature and of Nature's God entitle them, a decent respect to the opinions of mankind requires that they should declare the causes which impel them to the separation. We hold these truths to be self-evident, that all men are created equal, that they are endowed by their Creator with certain unalienable Rights, that among these are Life, Liberty and the pursuit of Happiness. That to secure these rights, Governments are instituted among Men, deriving their just powers from the consent of the governed, That whenever any Form of Government becomes destructive of these ends, it is the Right of the People to alter or to abolish it, and to institute new Government, laying its foundation on such principles and organizing its powers in such form, as to them shall seem most likely to effect their Safety and Happiness. Prudence, indeed, will dictate that Governments long established should not be changed for light and transient causes; and accordingly all experience hath shown, that mankind are more disposed to suffer, while evils are sufferable, than to right themselves by abolishing the forms to which they are accustomed. But when a long train of abuses and usurpations, pursuing invariably the same Object evinces a design to reduce them under absolute Despotism, it is their right, it is their duty, to throw off such Government, and to provide new Guards for their future security.— Such has been the patient sufferance of these Colonies; and such is now the necessity which constrains them to alter their former Systems of Government. The history of the present King of Great Britain is a history of repeated injuries and usurpations, all having in direct object the establishment of an absolute Tyranny over these States. To prove this, let Facts be submitted to a candid world.

He has refused his Assent to Laws, the most wholesome and necessary for the public good.

He has forbidden his Governors to pass Laws of immediate and pressing importance, unless suspended in their operation till his Assent should be obtained; and when so suspended, he has utterly neglected to attend to them.

He has refused to pass other Laws for the accommodation of large districts of people, unless those people would relinquish the right of Representation in the Legislature, a right inestimable to them and formidable to tyrants only.

He has called together legislative bodies at places unusual, uncomfortable, and distant from the depository or their public Records, for the sole purpose of fatiguing them into compliance with his measures.

He has dissolved Representative Houses repeatedly, for opposing with manly firmness his invasions on the rights of the people.

He has refused for a long time, after such dissolutions, to cause others to be elected; whereby the Legislative powers, incapable of Annihilation, have returned to the People at large for their exercise; the State remaining in the mean time exposed to all the dangers of invasion from without, and convulsions within.

He has endeavoured to prevent the population of these States; for that purpose obstructing the Laws for Naturalization of Foreigners; refusing to pass others to encourage their migration hither, and raising the conditions of new Appropriations of Lands.

He has obstructed the Administration of Justice, by refusing his Assent to Laws for establishing Judiciary powers.

He has made Judges dependent on his Will alone, for the tenure of their offices, and the amount and payment of their salaries.

He has erected a multitude of New Offices, and sent hither swarms of Officers to harass our people, and eat out their substance.

He has kept among us, in times of peace, Standing Armies, without the Consent of our legislatures.

He has affected to render the Military independent of and superior to the Civil power.

He has combined with others to subject us to a jurisdiction foreign to our constitution, and unacknowledged by our laws; giving his Assent to their Acts of pretended Legislation:

For quartering large bodies of armed troops among us:

For protecting them, by a mock Trial, from Punishment for any Murders which they should commit on the Inhabitants of these States:

For cutting off our Trade with all parts of the world:

For imposing Taxes on us without our Consent:

For depriving us in many cases, of the benefits of Trial by Jury:

For transporting us beyond Seas to be tried for pretended offenses:

For abolishing the free System of English Laws in a neighboring Province, establishing therein an Arbitrary government, and enlarging its Boundaries so as to render it at once an example and fit instrument for introducing the same absolute rule into these Colonies:

For taking away our Charters, abolishing our most valuable Laws, and altering fundamentally the Forms of our Governments:

For suspending our own Legislatures, and declaring themselves invested with power to legislate for us in all cases whatsoever.

He has abdicated Government here, by declaring us out of his Protection and waging War against us.

He has plundered our seas, ravaged our Coasts, burnt our towns, and destroyed the lives of our people.

He is at this time transporting large Armies of foreign Mercenaries to compleat the works of death, desolation and tyranny, already begun with circumstances of Cruelty & perfidy scarcely paralleled in the most barbarous ages, and totally unworthy the Head of a civilized nation.

He has constrained our fellow Citizens taken Captive on the high Seas to bear Arms against their Country, to become the executioners of their friends and Brethren, or to fall themselves by their Hands.

He has excited domestic insurrections amongst us, and has endeavoured to bring on the inhabitants of our frontiers, the merciless Indian Savages, whose known rule of warfare, is an undistinguished destruction of all ages, sexes and conditions.

In every state of these Oppressions We have Petitioned for Redress in the most humble terms: Our repeated Petitions have been answered only by repeated injury. A Prince, whose character is thus marked by every act which may define a Tyrant, is unfit to be the ruler of a free people.

Nor have We been wanting in attentions to our Brittish brethren. We have warned them from time to time of attempts by their legislature to extend an unwarrantable jurisdiction over us. We have reminded them of the circumstances of our emigration and settlement here. We have appealed to their native justice and magnanimity, and we have conjured them by the ties of our common kindred to disavow these usurpations, which, would inevitably interrupt our connections and correspondence. They too have been deaf to the voice of justice and of consanguinity. We must, therefore, acquiesce in the necessity, which denounces our Separation, and hold them, as we hold the rest of mankind, Enemies in War, in Peace Friends.

We, Therefore, the Representatives of the United States of America, in General Congress, Assembled, appealing to the Supreme Judge of the world for the rectitude of our intentions, do, in the Name, and by Authority of the good People of these Colonies, solemnly publish and declare, That these United Colonies are, and of Right ought to be Free and Independent States; that they are Absolved from all Allegiance to the British Crown, and that all political connection between them and the State of Great Britain, is and ought to be totally disolved; and that as Free and Independent States, they have full Power to levy War, conclude Peace, contract Alliances, establish Commerce, and to do all other Acts and Things which Independent States may of right do.

And for the support of this Declaration, with a firm reliance on the protection of Divine Providence, we mutually pledge to each other our Lives, our Fortunes and our sacred Honor.

SIGNERS OF THE
DECLARATION OF INDEPENDENCE JULY 4, 1776

John Adams, Samuel Adams, Josiah Bartlett, Carter Braxton, Charles Carroll, Samuel Chase, Abraham Clark, George Clymer, William Ellery, William Floyd, Benjamin Franklin, Elbridge Gerry, Button Gwinnett, Lyman Hall, John Hancock, Benjamin Harrison, John Hart, Richard Henry Lee, Joseph Hewes, Thomas Heyward, Jr., William Hooper, Stephen Hopkins, Fras. Hopkinson, Samuel Huntington, Thomas Jefferson, Frans. Lewis, Francis Lightfoot Lee, Phil. Livingston, Thomas Lynch, Jr., Thomas M'Kean, Arthur Middleton, Lewis Morris, Robert Morris, John Morton, Thomas Nelson, Jr., William Paca, John Penn, George Read, Caesar Rodney, George Ross, Benjamin Rush, Edward Rutledge, Roger Sherman, Jason Smith, Richard Stockton, Thomas Stone, George Taylor, Matthew Thornton, Robert Treat Paine, George Walton, William Whipple, William Williams, James Wilson, Johnothan Witherspoon, Oliver Wolcott, George Wythe.

The Battle of Long Island

Title: The Battle of Long Island
Author: A British Field-Officer
Date: 1776
Source: America, Vol.3, pp.186-188

This letter from a royal field-officer, serving under General Howe at the Battle of Long Island, to his wife at Gloucester, England, is dated from the English camp on Long Island, September 1, 1776, and describes the first serious defeat the American forces suffered during the Revolutionary War. It is one in a collection of newly discovered "Letters on the American Revolution" (Houghton-Mifflin) edited by Margaret Wheeler Willard.

Strongly entrenched on Brooklyn Heights, the Americans numbered some 8,000 men under General Israel Putnam. The British force under General Howe was nearly twice as strong, and succeeded in storming the American position, inflicting an American loss of about 1,000 in killed, wounded and missing, as contrasted to 400 fatalities of their own. General Washington hurried to Long Island from the mainland after the battle, and on the night of August 29-30 he successfully transported the colonial troops.

W E HAVE had a glorious day against the rebels. We landed on this island the 22d, and that day marched toward Brookland Ferry, opposite New York, where this island is separated from the town by the East River, which is about three quarters of a mile over.

We took post within musket shot of their un-finished works. The troops were all on fire to force their lines, but Gen. Howe, in whose conduct the utmost prudence and vigilance have been united, would not permit it.

It was not till eight o'clock at night on the 26th that we received our orders to attack, and at eleven the whole army was in motion. The reserve, commanded by Lord Cornwallis, the first brigade of which our regiment makes a part, and the light infantry of the army, the whole under the command of General Clinton, marched by the right. The road to the right, after a march of about seven miles, brought us to an easy and undefended ascent of the hills, which we possessed at daybreak, and continued our rout, gained the rear of the rebels: and while the Hessians and the rest of the army amused them in front and on the left, the grenadiers and light infantry attacked them in the rear: by this masterly maneuver the rebels were immediately thrown into general confusion, and behaved most shamefully. The numbers killed, wounded, and taken you will see in the Gazette. Some of the Hessians told me they had buried between 400 and 500 in one pit.

Such has been their panic that, on the 30th at night, they evacuated their redoubts and entrenchments, which they had retired to, on Brookland Heights, leaving us in possession of this island, which entirely commands New York. Had the works at Brookland been properly defended our motions must have been retarded at least three weeks. For my part I think matters will soon be brought to an issue.

P.S. I have just heard there has been a most dreadful fray in the town of New York. The New Englanders insisted upon setting the town on fire, and retreating. This was opposed by the New Yorkers, who were joined by the Pennsylvanians, and a battle has been the consequence in which many have lost their lives.

By the steps the General is taking, I imagine he will effectually cut off their retreat at King's Bridge, by which the island of New York is joined to the continent.

The Evacuation of New York

Title: The Evacuation of New York
Author: General George Clinton
Date: 1776
Source: America, Vol.3, pp.189-192

General, later to be for eighteen years Governor, Clinton, here describes a brisk skirmish between the American and British forces on Manhattan Island in 1776, a short time before the town was abandoned to the enemy. It was a dark hour for the struggling colonies, and it is significant that such a slight success as this one reanimated the American troops, recently disheartened by their defeat on Long Island, preceding the defeat at White Plains and the massacre at Fort Washington.

A year later General Clinton was elected first Governor of New York, and from 1805 until his death in 1812 he was Vice-President of the United States. He opposed the ratification of the Federal Constitution as granting too great powers to national officials, and while presiding officer of the Senate he defeated by his deciding vote the re-chartering of the United States Bank.

ABOUT the middle of last week it was determined, for many reasons, to evacuate the City of New York; and accordingly, orders were given for removing the ordnance, military and other stores from thence, which, by Sunday morning was nearly effected. On Saturday, four of the enemy's large ships passed by the city up the North River, and anchored near Grenage, and about as many up the East River, which anchored in Turtle Bay; and from the movements of the enemy on Long Island, and the small Islands in the East River, we had great reason to apprehend they intended to make a landing, and attack our lines somewhere near the city. Our army for some days had been moving upwards this way, and encamping on the heights, southwest of Colonel Morris's, where we intended to form lines, and make our grand stand. On Sunday morning the enemy landed a very considerable body of troops, principally consisting of their Light Infantry and Grenadiers, near Turtle Bay, under cover of a very heavy cannonade from their shipping. Our lines were but thinly manned, as they were then intended only to secure a retreat to the rear of our army, and unfortunately by such troops as were so little disposed to stand in the way of grapeshot that the main body of them almost instantly retreated, nay, fled, without a possibility of rallying them, though General Washington himself, (who rode to the spot on hearing the cannonade) with some other general officers, exerted themselves to effect it.

The enemy, on landing, immediately formed a line across the island. Most of our people were luckily north of it, and joined the army. The few that were in the city crossed the river, chiefly to Paulus-Hook, so that our loss in men, artillery, or stores, is very inconsiderable; I don't believe it exceeds one hundred men, and I fancy most of them, from their conduct, stayed out of choice. Before evening, the enemy landed the main body of their army, took possession of the city, and marched up the island, and encamped on the heights extending from McGowan's and the Black-Horse to the North River.

On Monday morning, about ten o'clock, a party of the enemy, consisting of Highlanders, Hessians, the Light Infantry, Grenadiers, and English troops, (number uncertain,) attacked our advanced party, commanded by Colonel Knowlton, at Martje Davit's Fly. They were opposed with spirit, and soon made to retreat to a clear field, southwest of that about two hundred paces, where they lodged themselves behind a fence covered with bushes. Our people attacked them in front, and caused them to retreat a second time, leaving five dead on the spot. We pursued them to a buckwheat field on the top of a high hill, distant about four hundred paces, where they received a considerable reinforcement, with several field-pieces, and there made a stand. A very brisk action ensued at this place, which continued about two hours. Our people at length worsted them a third time, caused them to fall back into an orchard, from thence across a hollow, and up another hill not far distant from their own lines. A large column of the enemy's army being at this time discovered to be in motion, and the ground we then occupied being rather disadvantageous, a retreat likewise, without bringing on a general action, (which we did not think prudent to risk,) rather insecure, our party was therefore ordered in, and the enemy was well contented to hold the last ground we drove them to.

We lost, on this occasion, Colonel Knowlton, a brave officer, and sixteen privates, killed. Major Leitch, from Virginia, and about eight or ten subaltern officers and privates wounded. The loss of the enemy is uncertain. They carried their dead and wounded off, in and soon after the action; but we have good evidence of their having upwards of sixty killed, and violent presumption of one hundred. The action, in the whole, lasted about four hours.

I consider our success in this small affair, at this time, almost equal to a victory. It has animated our troops, gave them new spirits, and erased every bad impression the retreat from Long Island, &c., had left on their minds. They find they are able, with inferior numbers, to drive [heir enemy, and think of nothing now but conquest.

Since the above affair, nothing material has happened. The enemy keep close to their lines. Our advance parties continue at their former station. We are daily throwing up works to prevent the enemy's advancing. Great attention is paid to Fort Washington, the posts opposite to it on the Jersey shore, and the obstructions in the river, which, I have reason to believe, are already effectual, so as to prevent their shipping passing; however, it is intended still to add to them, as it is of the utmost consequence to keep the enemy below us.

The Battle of White Plains

Title: The Battle of White Plains
Author: General William Heath
Date: 1776
Source: America, Vol.3, pp.193-199

The first of these two letters, which give the best extant eye-witness description of the Battle of White Plains, was written by General Heath, one of the American commanders in that engagement, October 27, 1776; and the second letter, dated from White Plains, N. Y., November 1, 1776, and evidently written by a soldier in the American ranks, was printed in the Pennsylvania Evening Post of November 14, 1776.

Heath, who refers to himself in the third person, had been made a major-general shortly before the White Plains engagement, and subsequently was in command of the Hudson River posts. The position which the Americans first occupied at White Plains was Chatterton Hill, from which General McDougall was forced to withdraw. Lord Howe delayed his attack on the main American army, and on the evening of November 31 Washington took up an unassailable position at North Castle. Clouds were rapidly darkening the American outlook at this time.

IN THE forenoon [October 27, 1776] a heavy cannonade was heard towards Fort Washington. Thirteen Hessians and two or three British soldiers were sent in on this day.

From the American camp to the southwest there appeared to be a very commanding height, worthy of attention. The Commander-in-Chief ordered the general officers who were off duty to attend him, to reconnoitre this ground, on this morning. When arrived at the ground, although very commanding, it did not appear so much so as other grounds to the north, and almost parallel with the left of the army as it was then formed. "Yonder," says Major-General Lee, pointing to the grounds just mentioned, "is the ground we ought to occupy." "Let us, then, go and view it," replied the Commander-in-Chief. When on the way, a Light-Horseman came up in full gallop, his horse almost out of breath, and addressed General Washington, "The British are on the camp, sir." The General observed, "Gentlemen, we have now other business than reconnoitring," putting his horse in full gallop for the camp, and followed by the other officers. When arrived at headquarters, the Adjutant-General, (Reed,) who had remained at camp, informed the Commander-in-Chief that the guards had been all beat in, and the whole American army were now at their respective posts, in order of battle. The Commander-in-Chief turned round to the officers, and only said, "Gentlemen, you will repair to your respective posts, and do the best you can." General Heath, on arriving at his own division, found them all in the lines; and, from the height of his post, found that the first attack was directed against the Americans on Chaderton's hill. The little river Brunx, which ran between the American right and this hill, after running round its north side, turned and ran down on the east and southeast. The British advanced in two columns.

At this instant, the cannonade was brisk on both sides, directed by the British across the hollow and Brunx, against the Americans on the hill, and by them returned. Almost at the same instant, the right column, composed of British troops, preceded by about twenty Light-Horse, in full gallop, and brandishing their swords, appeared on the road leading to the Court-House, and now directly in front of General Heath's division. The Light-Horse leaped the fence of a wheat-field at the foot of the hill, on which Colonel Malcom's regiment was posted, of which the Light-Horse were not aware, until a shot from Lieutenant Fenno's field-piece gave them notice, by striking in the midst of them, and a horseman pitching from his horse. They then wheeled short about, galloped out of the field as fast they came in, rode behind a little hill in the road, and faced about, the tops of their caps only being visible to General Heath where he stood. The column came no further up the road, but wheeled to the left by platoons, as they came up, and, passing through a bar or gateway, directed their head towards the troops on Chaderton's hill, now engaged. When the head of the column had got nearly across the lot, their front got out of sight; nor could the extent of their rear be now discovered.

The sun shone bright, their arms glittered, and perhaps troops never were shown to more advantage than these now appeared. The whole now halted, and, for a few minutes, the men all sat down in the same order in which they stood, no one appearing to move out of his place. The cannonade continued brisk across the Brunx. A part of the left column, composed of British and Hessians, forded the river, and marched along, under the cover of the hill, until they had gained sufficient ground to the left of the Americans, when, by facing to the left, their column became a line parallel with the Americans. When they briskly ascended the hill, the first column resumed a quick march. As the troops which were advancing to the attack ascended the hill, the cannonade on the side of the British ceased, as their own men became exposed to their fire if continued. The fire of small-arms was now very heavy, and without any distinction of sounds. This led some American officers who were looking on to observe that the British were worsted, as their cannon had ceased firing; but a few minutes evinced that the Americans were giving way. They moved off the hill in a great body, neither running nor observing the best order. The British ascended the hill very slowly, and when arrived at its summit, formed and dressed their line, without the least attempt to pursue the Americans. The loss on the side of the Americans was inconsiderable; that of the British was not then known. The British having got possession of this hill, it gave them a vast advantage of the American lines, almost down to the center...

LAST Monday we received intelligence that the enemy, with their whole body, were advancing towards us. The army were immediately alarmed, and part of General Wadsworth's brigade, with some other regiments under the command of General Spencer, consisting in the whole of five or six hundred men, were sent out as an advance party, to skirmish with the enemy, and harass them in their march. We marched on to a hill about one mile and a half from our lines, with an artillery company and two field-pieces, and placed ourselves behind walls and fences, in the best manner we could, to give the enemy trouble. About half after nine o'clock, our advance parties all came in, retreating before the enemy; and the light parties of the enemy, with their advanced guard, consisting of two or three thousand, came in sight, and marched on briskly towards us, keeping the high grounds; and the light horse pranced on a little in the rear, making a very martial appearance.

As our light parties came on to the hills and discovered where we were, the enemy began to cannonade us, and to fling shells from their hobits and small mortars. Their light parties soon came on, and we firing upon them from the walls and fences, broke and scattered them at once; but they would run from our front and get round upon our wings to flank us, and as soon as our fire discovered where we were, the enemy's artillery would at once begin to play upon us in the most furious manner. We kept the walls until the enemy were just ready to surround us, and then we would retreat from one wall and hill to another, and maintain our ground there in the same manner, till numbers were just ready to surround us. Once the Hessian grenadiers came up in front of Colonel Douglass's regiment, and we fired a general volley upon them, at about twenty rods distance, and scattered them like leaves in a whirlwind; and they ran off so far that some of the regiment ran out to the ground where they were when we fired upon them, and brought off their arms and accoutrements, and rum, that the men who fell had with them, which we had time to drink round with before they came on again. They formed at a distance, and waited until their artillery and main body came on, when they advanced in solid columns upon us, and were gathering all around us, ten to our one. Colonel Douglass's and Silliman's regiments fired four or five times on them, as they were advancing and then retreated, but not until the enemy began to fire on their flanks. Colonels Silliman, Douglass, and Arnold behaved nobly, and the men gained much applause. Colonels Webb's, Silliman's, and Douglass's regiments had the principal share in the action. Colonel Webb had four killed, and eight or ten wounded; Colonel Silliman lost six, and had ten or twelve wounded; Colonel Douglass had three killed, and six wounded. Colonels Brooks's, Smallwood's, and Ritzma's regiments, who were drawn up on the hill near the lines, suffered considerably. Our loss in the whole may be seventy or eighty killed or wounded. It is said by all the deserters and captains, who agree in their stories, that the enemy had about three hundred killed and wounded.

The scene was grand and solemn; all the adjacent hills smoked as though on fire, and bellowed and trembled with a perpetual cannonade and fire of fieldpieces, hobits, and mortars. The air groaned with streams of cannon and musket shot; the hills smoked and echoed terribly with the bursting of shells; the fences and walls were knocked down and torn to pieces, and men's legs, arms, and bodies, mangled with cannon and grape-shot all around us. I was in the action, and under as good advantages as any one man, perhaps, to observe all that passed, and write these particulars of the action from my own observation.

No general action was designed on our part, and I believe one thousand men were never, at one time, engaged with the enemy. They came on to the hills opposite our lines, and halted; and after cannonading part of the lines a short time, they became very still and quiet.

Yesterday, (October 31st,) it was observed that they had near finished four or five batteries which they had erected against us; and as our ground, near the center of the town at White Plains, was not good, being overlooked by neighboring hills, the generals, last night, drew off most of the troops from the lines there, and this morning the guards and sentries burned the town and forage all around it, and came off about nine o'clock.

We carried off all our stores, and planted our artillery on the hills about a mile and a half back of the center of the town. The enemy advanced, this forenoon, on to the ground we left, but as soon as they came over the hill, we saluted them with our cannon, and field-pieces, and they advanced no further…

Washington, Discouraged, Appeals to Congress

Title: Washington, Discouraged, Appeals to Congress
Author: George Washington
Date: December, 1776
Source: America, Vol.3, pp.200-205

Of exceptional interest are these two letters, written to Washington's brother, Augustine, and to John Hancock, President of Congress, December 18 and 20, 1776, in that they reveal the desperate plight of the American cause in those dark days and the indomitable spirit of the author. Following the defeats on Long Island and at White Plains, Washington had been hotly pursued through New Jersey by the British, and when he crossed the Delaware into Pennsylvania he had less than 3,000 weary, half-starved, dispirited soldiers.

The tide turned with his capture of 1,000 Hessians at Trenton, and by March, 1777, Washington had not only saved his army but had inspired the despairing colonists with renewed hope and Congress with such confidence in him that almost dictatorial powers were conferred upon Washington. Nothing but his iron resolution prevented the collapse of the Revolution.

O WING to the number of letters, I write, the recollection of any particular one is destroyed, but I think my last to you was by Colonel Woodford, from Hackinsac. Since that time, and a little before, our affairs have taken an adverse turn, but not more than was to be expected from the unfortunate measures, which had been adopted for the establishment of our army. The retreat of the enemy from White Plains led me to think, that they would turn their thoughts to the Jerseys, if no farther, and induced me to cross the North River with some of the troops in order if possible to oppose them. I expected to have met at least five thousand men of the Flying Camp and militia; instead of which I found less than one half of that number, and no disposition in the inhabitants to afford the least aid. This being perfectly well known to the enemy, they threw over a large body of troops, which pushed us from place to place, till we were obliged to cross the Delaware with less than three thousand men fit for duty, owing to the dissolution of our force by short enlistments; the enemy's numbers, from the best accounts, exceeding ten or twelve thousand men…

… We are in a very disaffected part of the province; and, between you and me, I think our affairs are in a very bad situation; not so much from the apprehension of General Howe's army, as from the defection of New York, Jerseys and Pennsylvania…

I have no doubt but General Howe will still make an attempt upon Philadelphia this winter. I see nothing to oppose him a fortnight hence, as the time of all the troops, except those of Virginia reduced (almost to nothing,) and Smallwood's Regiment of Maryland, equally as bad, will expire in less than that time. In a word, my dear Sir, if every nerve is not strained to recruit the new army with all possible expedition, I think the game is pretty near up, owing, in a great measure, to the insidious arts of the enemy, and disaffection of the colonies before mentioned, but principally to the accursed policy of short enlistments, and placing too great a dependence on the militia, the evil consequences of which were foretold fifteen months ago, with a spirit almost prophetic. Before this reaches you, you will no doubt have heard of the captivity of General Lee. This is an additional misfortune, and the more vexatious, as it was by his own folly and imprudence, (and without a view to answer any good,) he was taken, going three miles out of his own camp, and within twenty of the enemy to lodge, a rascally Tory rode in the night to give notice of it to the enemy, who sent a party of Light-Horse that seized and carried him, with every mark of triumph and indignity.

You can form no idea of the perplexity of my situation. No man, I believe, ever had a greater choice of difficulties, and less means to extricate himself from them. However, under a full persuasion of the justice of our cause, I cannot entertain an idea, that it will finally sink, though it may remain for some time under a cloud…

TO THE PRESIDENT OF CONGRESS

THE pay of our artillerists bearing no proportion to that in the English and French service, the murmuring and dissatisfaction thereby occasioned, the absolute impossibility, as I am told, of getting them upon the old terms, and the unavoidable necessity of obtaining them at all events, have induced me, also by advice, to promise officers and men, that their pay shall be augmented twenty-five percent, or that their engagements shall become null and void. This may appear to Congress premature and unwarrant able. But, Sir, if they view our situation in the light it strikes their officers, they will be convinced of the utility of the measure, and that the execution could not be delayed till after their meeting at Baltimore. In short, the present exigency of our affairs will not admit of delay, either in council or the field; for well convinced I am, that, if the enemy go into quarters at all, it will be for a short season. But I rather think the design of General Howe is to possess himself of Philadelphia this winter, if possible; and in truth I do not see what is to prevent him, as ten days more will put an end to the existence of our army. That one great point is to keep us as much harassed as possible, with a view to injure the recruiting service and hinder a collection of stores and other necessaries for the next campaign, I am as clear in, as I am of my existence. If, therefore, we have to provide in the short interval and make these great and arduous prep arations, every matter that in its nature is self-evident is to be referred to Congress, at the distance of a hundred and thirty or forty miles, so much time must necessary elapse, as to defeat the end in view.

It may be said, that this is an application for powers that are too dangerous to be entrusted. I can only add, that desperate diseases require desperate remedies; and I with truth declare, that I have no lust after power, but I wish with as much fervency as any man upon this wide-extended continent for an opportunity of turning the sword into the ploughshare. But my feelings, as an officer and a man, have been such as to force me to say, that no person ever had a greater choice of difficulties to contend with than I have. It is needless to add, that short enlistments, and a mistaken dependence upon militia, have been the origin of all our misfortunes, and the great accumulation of our debt. We find, Sir, that the enemy are daily gathering strength from the disaffected. This strength, like a snow-ball by rolling, will increase unless some means can be devised to check effectually the progress of the enemy's arms. Militia may possibly do it for a little while; but in a little while, also, and the militia of those States, which have been frequently called upon, will not turn out at all; or, if they do, it will be with so much reluctance and sloth, as to amount to the same thing. Instance New Jersey! Witness Pennsylvania! Could anything but the river Delaware have saved Philadelphia? Can any thing (the exigency of the case indeed may justify it) be more destructive to the recruiting service, than giving ten dollars' bounty for six weeks' service of the militia, who come in, you cannot tell how, go, you cannot tell when, and act, you cannot tell where, consume your provisions, exhaust your stores, and leave you at last at a critical moment?

These, Sir, are the men I am to depend upon, ten days hence; this is the basis, on which your cause will and must forever depend, till you get a large standing army sufficient of itself to oppose the enemy. I there fore beg leave to give it as my humble opinion, that eighty-eight battalions are by no means equal to the opposition you are to make, and that a moment's time is not to be lost in raising a greater number, not less, in my opinion and the opinion of my officers, than a hundred and ten. It may be urged that it will be found difficult enough to complete the first number. This may be true, and yet the officers of a hundred and ten battalions will recruit many more men, than those of eighty-eight. In my judgment this is not a time to stand upon expense; our funds are not the only object of consideration. The State of New York have added one battalion (I wish they had made it two) to their quota. If any good officers will offer to raise men upon Continental pay and establishment in this quarter, I shall encourage them to do so, and regiment them when they have done it. If Congress disapprove of this proceeding, they will please to signify it, as I mean it for the best. It may be thought that I am going a good deal out of the line of my duty, to adopt these measures, or to advise thus freely. A character to lose, an estate to forfeit, the inestimable blessing of liberty at stake, and a life devoted, must be my excuse.

The Battles of Trenton and Princeton

Title: The Battles of Trenton and Princeton
Author: General George Washington
Date: December, 1776
Source: America, Vol.3, pp.206-210

It was to fight the battle of Trenton, in New Jersey, December 26, 1776, that Washington at the head of 2,400 men made his famous crossing of the ice-jammed Delaware River. He surprised the Hessians under Colonel Rahl and took more than 1,000 prisoners, paving the way for the equally important victory over the British at Princeton on January third following.

Frederick the Great esteemed this Trenton-Princeton campaign "the most brilliant military performance of the century"; and Cornwallis himself, at a banquet given him and his staff by Washington after the surrender at Yorktown, declared that when history's verdict was made up "the brightest garlands for your Excellency will be gathered, not from the shores of the Chesapeake, but, from the banks of the Delaware."

These are the military reports sent by Washington to John Hancock as President of Congress shortly after the respective battles were fought.

I HAVE the pleasure of congratulating you upon the success of an enterprise, which I had formed against a detachment of the enemy lying at Trenton, and which was executed yesterday morning. The evening of the twenty-fifth I ordered the troops intended for this service to parade back to McKonkey's Ferry, that they might begin to pass as soon as it grew dark, imagining we should be able to throw them all over, with the necessary artillery, by twelve o'clock, and that we might easily arrive at Trenton by five in the morning, the distance being about nine miles. But the quantity of ice, made that night, impeded the passage of the boats so much, that it was three o'clock before the artillery could all be got over; and near four before the troops took up their line of march. This made me despair of surprising the town, as I well knew we could not reach it before the day was fairly broke. But as I was certain there was no making a retreat without being discovered and harassed on repassing the river, I determined to push on at all events. I formed my detachment into two divisions, one to march by the lower or river road, the other by the upper or Pennington road. As the divisions had nearly the same distance to march, I ordered each of them, immediately upon forcing the out-guards, to push directly into the town, that they might charge the enemy before they had time to form.

The upper division arrived at the enemy's advanced posts exactly at eight o'clock; and in three minutes after, I found, from the fire on the lower road, that the divisions had also got up. The out-guards made but small opposition, though, for their numbers, they behaved very well, keeping up a constant retreating fire from behind houses. We presently saw their main body formed; but, from their motions, they seemed undetermined how to act. Being hard pressed by our troops, who had already got possession of their artillery, they attempted to file off by a road on their right, leading to Princeton. But, perceiving their intention, I threw a body of troops in their way, which immediately checked them. Finding from our disposition, that they were surrounded, and that they must inevitably be cut to pieces if they made any further resistance, they agreed to lay down their arms. The number that submitted in this manner was twenty-three officers and eight hundred and eighty six men. Colonel Rahl, the commanding officer, and seven others were found wounded in the town. I do not exactly know how many were killed; but I fancy twenty or thirty, as they never made any regular stand. Our loss is very trifling indeed, only two officers and one or two privates wounded.

In justice to the officers and men, I must add, that their behavior upon this occasion reflects the highest honor upon them. The difficulty of passing the river in a very severe night, and their march through a violent storm of snow and hail, did not in the least abate their ardor; but, when they came to the charge, each seemed to vie with the other in pressing forward; and were I to give a preference to any particular corps, I should do great injustice to the others.

ON TO PRINCETON

I HAVE the honor to inform you, that, since the date of my last from Trenton, I have removed with the army under my command to this place. The difficulty of crossing the Delaware, on account of the ice, made our passage over it tedious, and gave the enemy an opportunity of drawing in their several cantonments, and assembling their whole force at Princeton. Their large pickets advanced towards Trenton, their great preparations, and some intelligence I had received, added to their knowledge, that the 1st of January brought on a dissolution of the best part of our army, gave me the strongest reasons to conclude, that an attack upon us was meditating.

Our situations was most critical, and our force small… On the 2d [of January, 1777], according to my expectation, the enemy began to advance upon us; and, after some skirmishing, the head of their column reached Trenton about four o'clock, whilst their rear was as far back as Maidenhead. They attempted to pass Sanpink Creek, which runs through Trenton, at different places; but, finding the forts guarded, they halted, and kindled their fires. We were drawn up on the other side of the creek. In this situation we remained till dark, cannonading the enemy, and receiving the fire of their field-pieces, which did us but little damage.

Having by this time discovered that the enemy were greatly superior in number, and that their design was to surround us, I ordered all our baggage to be removed silently to Burlington soon after dark; and at twelve o'clock after renewing our fires, and leaving guards at the bridge in Trenton, and other passes on the same stream above, marched by a roundabout road to Princeton, where I knew they could not have much force left, and might have stores. One thing I was certain of, that it would avoid the appearance of a retreat (which was of consequence, or to run the hazard of the whole army being cut off), whilst we might by a fortunate stroke withdraw General Howe from Trenton, and give some reputation to our arms. Happily we succeeded. We found Princeton about sunrise, with only three regiments and three troops of light-horse in it, two of which were on their march to Trenton. These three regiments, especially the two first, made a gallant resistance, and, in killed, wounded, and prisoners, must have lost five hundred men; upwards of one hundred of them were left dead on the field; and, with what I have with me and what were taken in the pursuit and carried across the Delaware, there are near three hundred prisoners, fourteen of whom are officers, all British…

… We took two brass field-pieces; but, for want of horses, could not bring them away. We also took some blankets, shoes, and a few other trifling articles, burned the hay, and destroyed such other things, as the shortness of the time would admit of…

… The militia are taking spirits, and, I am told, are coming in fast from this State [New Jersey]; but I fear those from Philadelphia will scarcely submit to the hardships of a winter campaign much longer, especially as they very unluckily sent their blankets with their baggage to Burlington. I must do them the justice however to add, that they have undergone more fatigue and hardship, than I expected militia, especially citizens, would have done at this inclement season. I am just moving to Morristown, where I shall endeavor to put them under the best cover I can. Hitherto we have been without any; and many of our poor soldiers quite barefoot, and ill clad in other respects…

Samuel Adams on American Independence

Title: Samuel Adams on American Independence
Author: Samuel Adams
Date: 1776
Source: The World's Famous Orations, Vol.8, pp.110-122

From a speech delivered at the State House in Philadelphia, "to a very numerous audience," on August 1, 1776. Abridged.

Born in 1722, died in 1803; Delegate to the First Continental Congress in 1774; Signer of the Declaration of Independence in 1776; Member of the Massachusetts Convention ratifying the Constitution in 1788, Governor of Massachusetts in 1794.

OUR forefathers, 'tis said, consented to be subject to the laws of Great Britain. I will not at the present time dispute it, nor mark out the limits and conditions of their submission; but will it be denied that they contracted to pay obedience and to be under the control of Great Britain because it appeared to them most beneficial in their then present circumstances and situations? We, my countrymen, have the same right to consult and provide for our happiness which they had to promote theirs. If they had a view to posterity in their contracts, it must have been to advance the felicity of their descendants. If they erred in their expectations and prospects, we can never be condemned for a conduct which they would have recommended had they foreseen our present condition.

Ye darkeners of counsel, who would make the property, lives, and religion of millions depend on the evasive interpretations of musty parchments; who would send us to antiquated charters of uncertain and contradictory meaning, to prove that the present generation are not bound to be victims to cruel and unforgiving despotism,—tell us whether our pious and generous ancestors bequeathed to us the miserable privilege of having the rewards of our honesty, industry, the fruits of those fields which they purchased and bled for, wrested from us at the will of men over whom we have no check. Did they contract for us that, with folded arms, we should expect that justice and mercy from brutal and inflamed invaders which have been denied to our supplications at the foot of the throne? Were we to hear our character as a people ridiculed with indifference? Did they promise for us that our meekness and patience should be insulted, our coasts harassed, our towns demolished and plundered, and our wives and offspring exposed to nakedness, hunger, and death, without our feeling the resentment of men, and exerting those powers of self-preservation which God has given us?

No man had once a greater veneration for Englishmen than I entertained. They were dear to me as branches of the same parental trunk, and partakers of the same religion and laws; I still view with respect the remains of the Constitution as I would a lifeless body which had once been animated by a great and heroic soul. But when I am aroused by the din of arms; when I behold legions of foreign assassins paid by Englishmen to imbrue their hands in our blood; when I tread over the uncoffined bodies of my countrymen, neighbors, and friends; when I see the locks of a venerable father torn by savage hands, and a feeble mother, clasping her infants to her bosom, and on her knees imploring their lives from her own slaves, whom Englishmen have allured to treachery and murder; when I behold my country, once the seat of industry, peace, and plenty, changed by Englishmen to a theater of blood and misery, Heaven forgive me if I can not root out those passions which it has implanted in my bosom, and detest submission to a people who have either ceased to be human, or have not virtue enough to feel their own wretchedness and servitude!

Men who content themselves with the semblance of truth, and a display of words talk much of our obligations to Great Britain for protection. Had she a single eye to our advantage? A nation of shopkeepers are very seldom so interested. Let us not be so amused with words! the extension of her commerce was her object. When she defended our coasts, she fought for her customers, and convoyed ourships loaded with wealth, which we had acquired for her by our industry. She has treated us as beasts of burden, whom the lordly masters cherish that they may carry a greater load. Let us inquire also against whom she has protected us? Against her own enemies with whom we had no quarrel, or only on her account, and against whom we always readily exerted our wealth and strength when they were required. Were these Colonies backward in giving assistance to Great Britain, when they were called upon in 1739 to aid the expedition against Cartagena? They at that time sent three thousand men to join the British army, altho the war commenced without their consent.

But the last war, 'tis said, was purely American. This is a vulgar error, which, like many others, has gained credit by being confidently repeated. The dispute between the courts of Great Britain and France related to the limits of Canada and Nova Scotia. The controverted territory was not claimed by any in the Colonies, but by the crown of

Great Britain. It was therefore their own quarrel. The infringement of a right which England had, by the treaty of Utrecht, of trading in the Indian country of Ohio, was another cause of the war. The French seized large quantities of British manufactures and took possession of a fort which a company of British merchants and factors had erected for the security of their commerce. The war was therefore waged in defense of lands claimed by the Crown, and for the protection of British property. The French at that time had no quarrel with America, and, as appears by letters sent from their commander-in-chief to some of the Colonies, wished to remain in peace with us.

The part, therefore, which we then took, and the miseries to which we exposed ourselves ought to be charged to our affection to Britain. These Colonies granted more than their proportion to the support of the war. They raised, clothed, and maintained nearly twenty-five thousand men, and so sensible were the people of England of our great exertions that a message was annually sent to the House of Commons purporting "that his majesty, being highly satisfied with the zeal and vigor with which his faithful subjects in North America had exerted themselves in defense of his majesty's just rights and possessions, recommends it to the House to take the same into consideration and enable him to give them a proper compensation."

But what purpose can arguments of this kind answer? Did the protection we received annul our rights as men, and lay us under an obligation of being miserable?

Who among you, my countrymen, that is a father, would claim authority to make your child a slave because you had nourished him in infancy?

'Tis a strange species of generosity which requires a return infinitely more valuable than anything it could have bestowed; that demands as a reward for a defense of our property a surrender of those inestimable privileges to the arbitrary will of vindictive tyrants, which alone give value to that very property.

Courage, then, my countrymen; our contest is not only whether we ourselves shall be free, but whether there shall be left to mankind an asylum on earth for civil and religious liberty. Dismissing, therefore, the justice of our cause as incontestable, the only question is, What is best for us to pursue in our present circumstances?

The doctrine of dependence on Great Britain is, I believe, generally exploded; but as I would attend to the honest weakness of the simplest of men, you will pardon me if I offer a few words on that subject.

We are now on this continent, to the astonishment of the world, three millions of souls united in one cause. We have large armies, well disciplined and appointed, with commanders inferior to none in military skill, and superior in activity and zeal. We are furnished with arsenals and stores beyond our most sanguine expectations, and foreign nations are waiting to crown our success by their alliances. There are instances of, I would say, an almost astonishing providence in our favor; our success has staggered our enemies, and almost given faith to infidels; so we may truly say it is not our own arm which has saved us.

The hand of Heaven appears to have led us on to be, perhaps, humble instruments and means in the great providential dispensation which is completing. We have fled from the political Sodom; let us not look back lest we perish and become a monument of infamy and derision to the world. For can we ever expect more unanimity and a better preparation for defense; more infatuation of counsel among our enemies, and more valor and zeal among ourselves? The same force and resistance which are sufficient to procure us our liberties will secure us a glorious independence and support us in the dignity of free imperial States. We can not suppose that our opposition has made a corrupt and dissipated nation more friendly to America, or created in them a greater respect for the rights of mankind. We can therefore expect a restoration and establishment of our privileges, and a compensation for the injuries we have received from their want of power, from their fears, and not from their virtues. The unanimity and valor which will effect an honorable peace can render a future contest for our liberties unnecessary. He who has strength to chain down the wolf is a madman if he let him loose without drawing his teeth and paring his nails.

From the day on which an accommodation takes place between England and America, on any other terms than as independent States, I shall date the ruin of this country. a politic minister will study to lull us into security by granting us the full extent of our petitions. The warm sunshine of influence would melt down the virtue which the violence of the storm rendered more firm and unyielding. In a state of tranquillity, wealth, and luxury, our descendants would forget the arts of war and the noble activity and zeal which made their ancestors invincible. Every art of corruption would be employed to loosen the bond of union which renders our resistance formidable. When the spirit of liberty, which now animates our hearts and gives success to our arms, is extinct, our numbers will accelerate our ruin and render us easier victims to tyranny. Ye abandoned minions of an infatuated ministry, if peradventure any should yet remain among us, remember that a Warren and Montgomery are numbered among the dead. Contemplate the mangled bodies of your countrymen, and then say, What should be the reward of such sacrifices? Bid us and our posterity bow the knee, supplicate the friendship, and plow, and sow, and reap, to glut the avarice of the men who have let loose on us the dogs of war to riot in our blood and hunt us from the face of the earth? If ye love wealth better than liberty, the tranquillity of servitude than the animating contest of freedom— go from us in peace. We ask not your counsels or arms. Crouch down and lick the hands which feed you. May your chains sit lightly upon you, and may posterity forget that ye were our countrymen!

To unite the supremacy of Great Britain and the liberty of America is utterly impossible. so vast a continent and of such a distance from the seat of empire will every day grow more unmanageable. The motion of so unwieldy a body can not be directed with any despatch and uniformity without committing to the Parliament of Great Britain powers inconsistent with our freedom. The authority and force which would be absolutely necessary for the preservation of the peace and good order of this continent would put all our valuable rights within the reach of that nation.

As the administration of government requires firmer and more numerous supports in proportion to its extent, the burdens imposed on us would be excessive, and we should have the melancholy prospect of their increasing on our posterity. The scale of officers, from the rapacious and needy commissioner to the haughty governor, and from the governor, with his hungry train, to perhaps a licentious and prodigal viceroy, must be upheld by you and your children. The fleets and armies which will be employed to silence your murmurs and complaints must be supported by the fruits of your industry.

Britain is now, I will suppose, the seat of liberty and virtue, and its legislature consists of a body of able and independent men who govern with wisdom and justice. The time may come when all will be reversed; when its excellent constitution of government will be subverted; when, pressed by debts and taxes, it will be greedy to draw to itself an increase of revenue from every distant province in order to ease its own burdens; when the influence of the crown, strengthened by luxury and a universal profligacy of manners, will have tainted every heart, broken down every fence of liberty and rendered us a nation of tame and contented vassals; when a general election will be nothing but a general auction of boroughs, and when the Parliament, the grand council of the nation, and once the faithful guardian of the State, and a terror to evil ministers, will be degenerated into a body if sycophants, dependent and venal, always ready to confirm any measures, and little more than a public court for registering royal edicts.

Such, it is possible, may some time or other be the state of Great Britain. What will, at that period, be the duty of the Colonies? Will they be still bound to unconditional submission? Must they always continue an appendage to our government and follow it implicitly through every change that can happen to it? Wretched condition, indeed, of millions of freemen as good as ourselves! Will you say that we now govern equitably, and that there is no danger of such revolution? Would to God that this were true! But you will not always say the same. Who shall judge whether we govern equitably or not? Can you give the Colonies any security that such a period will never come? No. The period, countrymen, is already come! The calamities were at our door. The rod of oppression was raised over us. We were roused from our slumbers, and may we never sink into repose until we can convey a clear and undisputed inheritance to our posterity! This day we are called upon to give a glorious example of what the wisest and best of men were rejoiced to view only in speculation. This day presents the world with the most august spectacle that its annals ever unfolded—millions of freemen, deliberately and voluntarily forming themselves into a society for their common defense and common happiness. Immortal spirits of Hampden, Locke, and Sidney, will it not add to your benevolent joys to behold your posterity rising to the dignity of men, and evincing to the world the reality and expediency of your systems, and in the actual enjoyment of that equal liberty, which you were happy when on earth in delineating and recommending to mankind?

Other nations have received their laws from conquerors; some are indebted for a constitution to the suffering of their ancestors through revolving centuries. The people of this country, alone, have formally and deliberately chosen a government for themselves, and with open and uninfluenced consent bound themselves into a social compact. Here no man proclaims his birth or wealth as a title to honorable distinction, or to sanctify ignorance and vice with the name of hereditary authority. He who has most zeal and ability to promote public felicity, let him be the servant of the public. This is the only line of distinction drawn by nature. Leave the bird of night to the obscurity for which nature intended him, and expect only from the eagle to brush the clouds with his wings and look boldly in the face of the sun.

If there is any man so base or so weak as to prefer a dependence on Great Britain to the dignity and happiness of living a member of a free and independent nation, let me tell him that necessity now demands what the generous principle of patriotism should have dictated.

We have no other alternative than independence, or the most ignominious and galling servitude. The legions of our enemies thicken on our plains; desolation and death mark their bloody career, while the mangled corpses of our countrymen seem to cry out to us as a voice from heaven.

Our Union is now complete; our Constitution composed, established, and approved. You are now the guardians of your own liberties. We may justly address you as the decemviri did the Romans, and say: "Nothing that we propose can pass into a law without your consent. Be yourselves, O Americans, the authors of those laws on which your happiness depends."

You have now in the field armies sufficient to repel the whole force of your enemies and their base and mercenary auxiliaries. The hearts of your soldiers beat high with the spirit of freedom; they are animated with the justice of their cause, and while they grasp their swords can look up to Heaven for assistance. Your adversaries are composed of wretches who laugh at the rights of humanity, who turn religion into derision, and would, for higher wages, direct their swords against their leaders or their country. Go on, then, in your generous enterprise with gratitude to Heaven for past success, and confidence of it in the future. For my own part I ask no greater blessing than to share with you the common danger and common glory. If I have a wish dearer to my soul than that my ashes may be mingled with those of a Warren and Montgomery, it is that these American States may never cease to be free and independent.

The Battles of Trenton and Princeton

Title: The Battles of Trenton and Princeton
Author: William E. H. Lecky
Date: 1777
Source: Great Epochs in American History, Vol.3, pp.149-154

Nothing, indeed, could now have saved the American cause but the extraordinary skill and determination of its great leader, combined with the amazing incapacity of his opponents. There is no reason to doubt that Sir William Howe possest in a fair measure the knowledge of the military profession which books could furnish, but not one gleam of energy or originality at this time broke the monotony of his career, and to the blunders of the Jersey campaign the loyalists mainly ascribed the ultimate success of the revolution. The same want of vigilance and enterprise that had allowed them when totally defeated to escape from Long Island, still continued.

When Washington was flying rapidly from an overwhelming force under Lord Cornwallis, Howe ordered the troops to stop at Brunswick, where they remained inactive for nearly a week. In the that delay the destruction of the army of Washington was inevitable. The Americans were enabled to cross the Delaware safely because, owing to a long delay of the British general, the van of the British army only arrived at its bank just as the very last American boat was launched. Even then, had the British accelerated their passage, Philadelphia, the seat and center of the Revolutionary Government, would have certainly fallen. The army of Washington was utterly inadequate to defend it. A great portion of its citizens were thoroughly loyal. The Congress itself, when flying from Philadelphia, declared the impossibility of protecting it, and altho Washington had burnt or removed all the boats for many miles along the Delaware, there were fords higher up which might easily have been forced, and in Trenton itself, which was occupied by the English, there were ample supplies of timber to have constructed rafts for the army.

But Howe preferred to wait till the river was frozen, and in the meantime, tho his army was incomparably superior to that of Washington in numbers, arms, discipline, and experience, he allowed himself to undergo a humiliating defeat. His army was scattered over several widely separated posts, and Trenton, which was one of the most important on the Delaware, was left in the care of a large force of Hessians, whose discipline had been greatly relaxed. Washington perceived that unless he struck some brilliant blow before the close of the year, his cause was hopeless. The whole province was going over to the English. As soon as the river was frozen he expected them to cross in overwhelming numbers, and in a few days he was likely to be almost without an army. At the end of the year the engagement of the greater part of his troops would expire, and on December 24 he wrote to the President of the Congress, "I have not the most distant prospect of retaining them a moment longer than the last of this month, notwithstanding the most pressing solicitations and the obvious necessity for it." Under these desperate circumstances he planned the surprize of Trenton. "Necessity," he wrote, "dire necessity, will, nay, must justify an attack." It was designed with admirable skill and executed with admirable courage. On the night of Christmas, 1776, Washington crossed the Delaware, surprized the German troops in the midst of their Christmas revelries, and with a loss of only two officers and two privates wounded, he succeeded in capturing 1,000 prisoners and in recrossing the river in safety.

The effect of this brilliant enterprise upon the spirits of the American army and upon the desponding, wavering, and hostile sentiments of the population was immediate. Philadelphia for the present was saved, and the Congress speedily returned to it. Immediately after the victory a large force of militia from Pennsylvania joined the camp of Washington, and at the end of December the disbandment of the continental troops, which a week before he had thought inevitable, had been in a great measure averted. "After much persuasion," he wrote, "and the exertions of their officers, half, or a greater proportion of those [the troops] from the eastward have consented to stay six weeks on a bounty of ten dollars. I feel the inconvenience of this advance, and I know the consequences which will result from it, but what could be done? Pennsylvania had allowed the same to her militia; the troops felt their importance and would have their price. Indeed, as their aid is so essential and not to be dispensed with, it is to be wondered at, that they had not estimated it at a higher rate." "This I know is a most extravagant price when compared with the time of service, but… I thought it no time to stand upon trifles when a body of firm troops inured to danger was absolutely necessary to lead on the more raw and undisciplined."

No money was ever better employed. Recrossing the Delaware, Washington again occupied Trenton, and then, evading an overwhelming British force which was sent against him, he fell unexpectedly on Princeton and totally defeated three regiments that were posted there to defend it. The English fell back upon Brunswick, and the greater part of New Jersey was thus recovered by the Americans. A sudden revulsion of sentiments took place in New Jersey. The militia of the province were at last encouraged to take arms for Washington. Recruits began to come in. The manifest superiority of the American generalship and the disgraceful spectacle of a powerful army of European veterans abandoning a large tract of country before a ragged band of raw recruits much less numerous than itself, changed the calculations of the doubters, while a deep and legitimate indignation was created by the shameful outrages that were perpetrated by the British and German troops.

Unfortunately these outrages were no new thing. An ardent American loyalist of New Yorkcomplains that one of the first acts of the soldiers of General Howe when they entered that city was to break open and plunder the College library, the Subscription library, and the Corporation library, and to sell or destroy the books and philosophical apparatus; and he adds, with much bitterness, that during all the months that the rebels were in possession of New York no such outrage was perpetrated, that during a great part of that time the regular law courts had been open, and that they had frequently convicted American soldiers of petty larcenies, and punished them with the full approbation of their officers. In New Jersey the conduct of the English was at least as bad as at New York. A public library was burnt at Trenton. A college and a library were destroyed at Princeton, together with an orrery made by the illustrious Rittenhouse, and believed to be the finest in the world. Whigs and Tories were indiscriminately plundered. Written protections attesting the loyalty of the bearer were utterly disregarded, and men who had exposed themselves for the sake of England to complete ruin at the hands of their own countrymen, found themselves plundered by the troops of the very Power for which they had risked and sacrificed so much. Nor was this all.

A British army had fallen back before an army which was manifestly incomparably inferior to it, and had left the loyalists over a vast district at the mercy of their most implacable enemies. Numbers who had actively assisted the British were obliged to fly to New York, leaving their families and property behind them. Already loyalist risings had been supprest in Maryland, in Dela-ware, and in Carolina, and had been left unsupported by the British army. The abandonment of New Jersey completed the lesson. A fatal damp was thrown upon the cause of the loyalists in America from which it never wholly recovered.

The Defeat of Burgoyne at Saratoga

Title: The Defeat of Burgoyne at Saratoga
Author: Sir Edward Creasy
Date: 1777
Source: Great Epochs in American History, Vol.3, pp.155-164

The war which rent away the North American colonies from England is, of all subjects in history, the most painful for an Englishman to dwell on. It was commenced and carried on by the British ministry in iniquity and folly, and it was concluded in disaster and shame. But the contemplation of it can not be evaded by the historian, however much it may be abhorred. Nor can any military event be said to have exercised more important influence on the future fortunes of mankind than the complete defeat of Burgoyne's expedition in 1777; a defeat which rescued the revolted colonists from certain subjection, and which, by inducing the courts of France and Spain to attack England in their behalf, insured the independence of the United States, and the formation of that transatlantic power which not only America, but both Europe and Asia, now see and feel.

The English had a considerable force in Canada, and in 1776 had completely repulsed an attack which the Americans had made upon that province. The British ministry resolved to avail themselves, in the next year, of the advantage which the occupation of Canada gave them, not merely for the purpose of defense, but for the purpose of striking a vigorous and crushing blow against the revolted colonies. With this view the army in Canada was largely reenforced. Seven thousand veteran troops were sent out from England, with a corps of artillery, abundantly supplied and led by select and experienced officers. Large quantities of military stores were also furnished for the equipment of the Canadian volunteers, who were expected to join the expedition.

It was intended that the force thus collected should march southward by the line of the Lakes, and thence along the banks of the Hudson River. The British army from New York—or a large detachment of it—was to make a simultaneous movement northward, up the line of the Hudson, and the two expeditions were to unite at Albany, a town on that river. By these operations, all communication between the Northern colonies and those of the Center and South would be cut off. An irresistible force would be concentrated, so as to crush all further opposition in New England; and when this was done, it was believed that the other colonies would speedily submit. The Americans had no troops in the field that seemed able to baffle these movements. Their principal army, under Washington, was occupied in watching over Pennsylvania and the South.

Burgoyne had gained celebrity by some bold and dashing exploits in Portugal during the last war; he was personally as brave an officer as ever headed British troops, he had considerable skill as a tactician; and his general intellectual abilities and acquirements were of a high order. He hadseveral very able and experienced officers under him, among whom were Major-General Philips and Brigadier-General Frazer. His regular troops amounted, exclusively of the corps of artillery, to about seven thousand two hundred men, rank and file. Nearly half of these were Germans…

Burgoyne reached the left bank of the Hudson River on July 30th. Hitherto he had overcome every difficulty which the enemy and the nature of the country had placed in his way. His army was in excellent order, and in the highest spirits, and the peril of the expedition seemed over when they were once on the bank of the river which was to be the channel of communication between them and the British army in the South…

The astonishment and alarm which these events produced among the Americans were naturally great; but the colonists showed no disposition to submit. The local governments of the New England States, as well as the Congress, acted with vigor and firmness in their efforts to repel the enemy. General Gates was sent to take the command of the army at Saratoga; and Arnold, a favorite leader of the Americans, was dispatched by Washington to act under him, with reenforcements of troops and guns from the main American army.

Burgoyne's employment of the Indians now produced the worst possible effects. Tho he labored hard to check the atrocities which they were accustomed to commit, he could not prevent the occurrence of many barbarous outrages, repugnant both to the feelings of humanity and to the laws of civilized warfare. The American commanders took care that the reports of theseexcesses should be circulated far and wide, well knowing that they would made the stern New Englanders, not droop, but rage…

While resolute recruits, accustomed to use of firearms, and all partially trained by service in the provincial militias, were thus flocking to the standard of Gates and Arnold at Saratoga, and while Burgoyne was engaged at Fort Edward in providing the means of the further advance of the army through the intricate and hostile country that still lay before him, two events occurred, in each of which the British sustained loss and the Americans obtained advantage, the moral effects of which were even more important than the immediate result of the encounters. When Burgoyne left Canada, General St. Leger was detached from that province with a mixed force of about one thousand men and some light field-pieces across Lake Ontario against Fort Stanwix, which the Americans held. After capturing this, he was to march along the Mohawk River to its confluence with the Hudson, between Saratoga and Albany, where his force and that of Burgoyne's were to unite. But, after some successes, St. Leger was obliged to retreat, and to abandon his tents and large quantities of stores to the garrison.

At the very time that General Burgoyne heard of this disaster he experienced one still more severe in the defeat of Colonel Baum, with a large detachment of German troops, at Bennington, whither Burgoyne had sent them for the purpose of capturing some magazines of provisions, of which the British army stood greatly in need. The Americans, augmented by continual accessions of strength, succeeded, after many attacks, in breaking this corps, which fled into the woods, and left its commander mortally wounded on the field: they then marched against a force of five hundred grenadiers and light infantry, which was advancing to Colonel Baum's assistance under Lieutenant-Colonel Breyman, who, after a gallant resistance, was obliged to retreat on the main army. The British loss in these two actions exceeded six hundred men; and a party of American loyalists, on their way to join the army, having attached themselves to Colonel Baum's corps, were destroyed with it.

Notwithstanding these reverses, which added greatly to the spirit and numbers of the American forces, Burgoyne determined to advance. It was impossible any longer to keep up his communications with Canada by way of the Lakes, so as to supply his army on his southward march; but having, but unremitting exertions, collected provisions for thirty days, he crossed the Hudson by means of a bridge of rafts, and, marching a short distance along its western bank, he encamped on September 14th on the heights of Saratoga, about sixteen miles from Albany. The Americans had fallen back from Saratoga, and were now strongly posted near Stillwater, about half way between Saratoga and Albany, and showed a determination to recede no farther.

Meanwhile Lord Howe, with the bulk of the British army that had lain at New York, had sailed away to the Delaware, and there commenced a campaign against Washington, in which the English general took Philadelphia, and gained other showy but unprofitable successes.

But Sir Henry Clinton, a brave and skilful officer, was left with a considerable force at New York, and he undertook the task of moving up the Hudson to cooperate with Burgoyne. Clinton was obliged for this purpose to wait for reenforcements which had been promised from England, and these did not arrive till September. As soon as he received them, Clinton embarked about three thousand of his men on a flotilla, convoyed by some ships-of-war under Commander Hotham, and proceeded to force his way up the river.

The country between Burgoyne's position at Saratoga and that of the Americans at Stillwater was rugged, and seamed with creeks and watercourses; but, after great labor in making bridges and temporary causeways, the British army moved forward. About four miles from Saratoga, on the afternoon of September 19th, a sharp encounter took place between part of the English right wing, under Burgoyne himself, and a strong body of the enemy, under Gates and Arnold. The conflict lasted till sunset. The British remained masters of the field; but the loss on each side was nearly equal—from five to six hundred men—and the spirits of the Americans were greatly raised by having withstood the best regular troops of the English army.

Burgoyne now halted again, and strengthened his position by fieldworks and redoubts; and the Americans also improved their defenses. The two armies remained nearly within cannon-shot of each other for a considerable time, during which Burgoyne was anxiously looking for intelligence of the promised expedition from New York, which, according to the original plan, ought by this time to have been approaching Albany from the south. At last a messenger from Clinton made his way, with great difficulty, to Burgoyne's camp, and brought the information that Clinton was on his way up the Hudson to attack the American forts which barred the passage up that river to Albany. Burgoyne, in reply, stated his hopes that the promised cooperation would be speedy and decisive, and added that, unless he received assistance before October 10th, he would be obliged to retreat to the Lakes through want of provisions.

The Indians and Canadians now began to desert Burgoyne, while, on the other hand, Gates' army was continually reenforced by fresh bodies of the militia. Burgoyne's force was now reduced to less than six thousand men. The right of his camp was on high ground a little to the west of the river; thence his entrenchments extended along the lower ground to the bank of the Hudson, their line being nearly at a right angle with the course of the stream. The lines were fortified in the center and on the left with redoubts and field-works. The numerical force of the Americans was now greater than the British, even in regular troops, and the numbers of the militia and volunteers which had joined Gate and Arnold were greater still…

It was on October 7th that Burgoyne led his column on the attack; and on the preceding day, the 6th, Clinton had successfully executed a brilliant enterprise against the two American forts which barred his progress up the Hudson. He had captured them both, with severe loss to the American forces opposed to him; he had destroyed the fleet which the Americans had been forming on the Hudson, under the protection of their forts; and the upward river was laid open to his squadron. He was now only a hundred fifty-six miles distant from Burgoyne, and a detachment of one thousand seven hundred men actually advanced within forty miles of Albany. Unfortunately, Burgoyne and Clinton were each ignorant of the other's movements; but if Burgoyne had won his battle on the 7th, he must, on advancing, have soon learned the tidings of Clinton's success, and Clinton would have heard of his.

A junction would soon have been made of the two victorious armies, and the great objects of the campaign might yet have been accomplished. All depended on the fortune of the column with which Burgoyne, on the eventful October 7, 1777, advanced against the American position. There were brave men, both English and German, in its ranks; and, in particular, it comprized one of the best bodies of grenadiers in the British service.

Burgoyne's whole force was soon compelled to retreat toward their camp; the left and center were in complete disorder; but the light infantry and the Twenty-fourth checked the fury of the assailants, and the remains of Burgoyne's column with great difficulty effected their return to their camp, leaving six of their guns in the possession of the enemy, and great numbers of killed and wounded on the field; and especially a large proportion of the artillerymen, who had stood to their guns until shot down or bayoneted beside them by the advancing Americans.

Burgoyne's column had been defeated, but the action was not yet over. The English had scarcely entered the camp, when the Americans, pursuing their success, assaulted it in several places with uncommon fierceness, rushing to the lines through a severe fire of grape-shot and musketry with the utmost fury. Arnold especially, who on this day appeared maddened with the thirst of combat and carnage, urged on the attack against a part of the entrenchments which was occupied by the light infantry under Lord Balcarras. But the English received him with vigor and spirit. The struggle here was obstinate and sanguinary. At length, as it grew toward evening, Arnold having forced all obstacles, entered the works with some of the most fearless of his followers. but in this critical moment of glory and danger, he received a painful wound in the same leg which had already been injured at the assault on Quebec. To his bitter regret, he was obliged to be carried back. His party still continued the attack; but the English also continued their obstinate resistance and at last night fell, and the assailants withdrew from this quarter of the British entrenchments…

Burgoyne now took up his last position on the heights near Saratoga; and hemmed in by the enemy, who refused any encounter, and baffled in all his attempts at finding a path of escape, he there lingered until famine compelled him to capit-ulate. The fortitude of the British army during this melancholy period has been justly eulogized by many native historians…

The articles of capitulation were settled on October 15th, and on that very evening a messenger arrived from Clinton with an account of his successes, and with the tidings that part of his force had penetrated as far as Esopus, within fifty miles of Burgoyne's camp. But it was too late. The public faith was pledged; and the army was indeed too debilitated by fatigue and hunger to resist an attack, if made; and Gates certainly would have made it if the convention had been broken off. Accordingly, on the 17th, the Convention of Saratoga was carried into effect…

When the news of Saratoga reached Paris the whole scene was changed. Franklin and his brother-commissioners found all their difficulties with the French Government vanish. The time seemed to have arrived for the house of Bourbon to take a full revenge for all its humiliations and losses in previous wars. In December a treaty was arranged, and formally signed in the February following, by which France acknowledged the independent United States. This was, of course, tantamount to a declaration of war with England.

Spain soon followed France; and, before long, Holland took the same course. Largely aided by French fleets and troops, the Americans vigorously maintained the war against the armies which England, in spite of her European foes, continued to send across the Atlantic. The treaties of 1783 restored peace to the world; the independence of the United States was reluctantly recognized by their ancient parent and recent enemy.

The Defeat and Surrender of Burgoyne

Title: The Defeat and Surrender of Burgoyne
Author: Frederika Charlotte Louise, Baroness von Riedesel
Date: 1777
Source: America, Vol.3, p.21

This article is from the "Letters and Journals" of Baroness von Riedesel, whose husband commanded the German troops in Burgoyne's army at the Battle of Saratoga, October 9, 1777. After the surrender to General Gates, both General Riedesel and his wife were prisoners for nearly three years. They were exchanged in 1780 and Riedesel was given command of the British forces on Long Island, his wife accompanying him.

Burgoyne with 11,000 men was marching south from Canada to join forces with General Howe. A dispatch directing General Howe to proceed up the Hudson had been written, but Lord North in his haste to leave London for a holiday did not sign it. It was pigeon-holed and not found until it turned up years later in the British army archives. But for this inadvertence, the battle of Saratoga might have been a British victory.

W E were halted at six o'clock in the morning [October 9, 1777], to our general amazement. General Burgoyne ordered the artillery to be drawn up in a line, and to have it counted. This gave much dissatisfaction, as a few marches more would have ensured our safety. My husband was exhausted by fatigue, and took a seat in the calash, where my maids made room for him; and he slept for three hours upon my shoulder. In the meantime, Captain Willoe brought me his pocket-book, containing bank-notes, and Captain Geismar, a beautiful watch, a ring, and a well provided purse, requesting me to keep them, which I promised to do to the last. At length we recommenced our march; but scarcely an hour had elapsed, before the army was again halted, because the enemy was in sight. They were but two hundred in number, who came to reconnoitre, and who might easily have been taken, had not General Burgoyne lost all his presence of mind. The rain fell in torrents… On the 9th, it rained terribly the whole day; nevertheless we kept ourselves ready to march. The savages had lost their courage, and they walked off in all directions. The least untoward event made them dispirited, especially when there was no opportunity for plunder. My chamber-maid exclaimed the whole day against her fate, and seemed mad with despair. I begged her to be quiet, unless she wished to be taken for a savage. Upon this she became still more extravagant, and asked me, "If I should be sorry for it?"—"Surely,"

All material contained herein was extracted from the
US Constitution Coach Kit at PowerThink.com
(Over 60,000 Works & Documents of American History)

replied I.—She then tore her cap from her head, and let her hair fall upon her face. "You take it quite easily," said she, "for you have your husband; but we have nothing but the prospect of being killed, or of losing the little we possess...

We reached Saratoga about dark, which was but half an hour's march from the place where we had spent the day. I was quite wet, and was obliged to remain in that condition, for want of a place to change my apparel. I seated myself near the fire, and undressed the children, and we then laid ourselves upon some straw.—I asked General Phillips, who came to see how I was, why we did not continue our retreat, my husband having pledged himself to cover the movement, and to bring off the army in safety. "My poor lady," said he, "you astonish me. Though quite wet, you have so much courage as to wish to go farther in this weather. What a pity it is that you are not our commanding general! He complains of fatigue, and has determined upon spending the night here, and giving us a supper.

It is very true, that General Burgoyne liked to make himself easy, and that he spent half his nights in singing and drinking, and diverting himself... I refreshed myself at 7 o'clock, the next morning, (the 10th of October,) with a cup of tea, and we all expected that we should soon continue our march... About 2 o'clock, we heard again a report of muskets and cannon, and there was much alarm and bustle among our troops. My husband sent me word, that I should immediately retire into a house which was not far off. I got into my calash with my children, and when we were near the house, I saw, on the opposite bank of the Hudson, five or six men, who aimed at us with their guns. Without knowing what I did, I threw my children into the back part of the vehicle, and laid myself upon them. At the same moment the fellow fired, and broke the arm of a poor English soldier, who stood behind us, and who being already wounded sought a shelter. Soon after our arrival, a terrible cannonade began, and the fire was principally directed against the house, where we had hoped to find a refuge, probably because the enemy inferred, from the great number of people who went towards it, that this was the headquarters of the generals, while, in reality, none were there except women and crippled soldiers. We were at last obliged to descend into the cellar, where I laid myself in a corner near the door. My children put their heads upon my knees. An abominable smell, the cries of the children, and my own anguish of mind, did not permit me to close my eyes, during the whole night. On the next morning, the cannonade begun anew, but in a different direction... Eleven cannon-balls passed through the house, and made a tremendous noise. A poor soldier, who was about to have a leg amputated, lost the other by one of these balls. All his comrades ran away at that moment, and when they returned, they found him in one corner of the room, in the agonies of death. I was myself in the deepest distress, not so much on account of my own dangers, as of those to which my husband was exposed, who, however, frequently sent me messages, inquiring after my health…

The want of water continuing to distress us, we could not but be extremely glad to find a soldier's wife so spirited as to fetch some from the river, an occupation from which the boldest might have shrunk, as the Americans shot every one who approached it. They told us afterwards that they spared her on account of her sex…

On the 17th of October, the capitulation was carried into effect. The generals waited upon the American General Gates, and the troops surrendered themselves prisoners of war and laid down their arms. The time had now come for the good woman who had risked her life to supply us with water, to receive the reward of her services. Each of us threw a handful of money into her apron; and she thus received more than twenty guineas. At such a moment at least, if at no other, the heart easily overflows with gratitude.

At last, my husband's groom brought me a message to join him with the children. I once more seated myself in my dear calash, and, while riding through the American camp, was gratified to observe that no body looked at us with disrespect, but, on the contrary, greeted us, and seemed touched at the sight of a captive mother with three children. I must candidly confess that I did not present myself, though so situated, with much courage to the enemy, for the thing was entirely new to me. When I drew near the tents, a good looking man advanced towards me, and helped the children from the calash, and kissed and caressed them: he then offered me his arms, and tears trembled in his eyes. "You tremble," said he; "do not be alarmed, I pray you." "Sir," cried I, "a countenance so expressive of benevolence, and the kindness which you have evinced towards my children, are sufficient to dispel all apprehension." He then ushered me into the tent of General Gates…

… The gentleman who had received me with so much kindness, came and said to me, "You may find it embarrassing to be the only lady in such a large company of gentlemen; will you come with your children to my tent, and partake of a frugal dinner, offered with the best will?" "By the kindness you show to me," returned I, "you induce me to believe that you have a wife and children." He informed me that he was General Schuyler. He regaled me with smoked tongues, which

All material contained herein was extracted from the
US Constitution Coach Kit at PowerThink.com
(Over 60,000 Works & Documents of American History)

were excellent, with beef steaks, potatoes, fresh butter, and bread. Never did a dinner give me so much pleasure as this. I was easy, after many months of anxiety, and I read the same happy change in the countenances of those around me…

Lafayette Arrives in America

Title: Lafayette Arrives in America
Author: Marie Paul Joseph, Marquis de Lafayette
Date: 1777
Source: America, Vol.3, pp.217-221

He Records His Early Impressions

General Marie Paul Joseph, Marquis de Lafayette, to give the distinguished French patriot and friend of Washington his full name, was less than twenty years of age when he landed at Georgetown, South Carolina, en route to Philadelphia to offer his military services to Congress. In view of his youth, it may surprise the reader of the accompanying letter to his wife, dated Charleston, June 19, 1777, to find him sending love to their children. However, Lafayette had married at the age of seventeen.

Seized with enthusiasm for the cause of the American colonists, along with admiration for Washington, he fitted out a ship in disobedience to the French Government, and, sailing from Pasages, in Spain, arrived in America with eleven companions, among them Baron de Kalb. His presence did much to give new hope to supporters of the Revolutionary cause at a time when they were most discouraged.

MY last letter to you, my dear love, has informed you, that I arrived safely in this country, after having suffered a little from seasickness during the first weeks of the voyage; that I was then, the morning after I landed, at the house of a very kind officer; that I had been nearly two months on the passage, and that I wished to set off immediately. It spoke of everything most interesting to my heart; of my sorrow at parting from you, and of our dear children; and it said, besides, that I was in excellent health. I give you this abstract of it, because the English may possibly amuse themselves by seizing it on its way. I have such confidence in my lucky star, however, that I hope it will reach you. This same star has befriended me, to the astonishment of everybody here. Trust to it yourself, and be assured that it ought to calm all your fears. I landed after having sailed several days along a coast, which swarmed with hostile vessels. When I arrived, everybody said that my vessel must inevitably be taken, since two British frigates blockaded the harbor. I even went so far as to send orders to the captain, both by land and sea, to put the men on shore and set fire to the ship, if not yet too late. By a most wonderful good fortune, a gale obliged the frigates to stand out to sea for a short time. My vessel came in at noon-day, without meeting friend or foe.

At Charleston I have met General Howe, an American officer now in the service. The Governor of the State is expected this evening from the country. All with whom I wished to become acquainted here, have shown me the greatest politeness and attention. I feel entirely satisfied with my reception, although I have not thought it best to go into any detail respecting my arrangements and plans. I wish first to see Congress. I hope to set out for Philadelphia in two days. Our route is more than two hundred and fifty leagues by land. We shall divide ourselves into small parties. I have already purchased horses and light carriages for the journey. Some French and American vessels are here, and are to sail together to-morrow morning, taking advantage of a moment when the frigates are out of sight. They are armed, and have promised me to defend themselves stoutly against the small privateers, which they will certainly meet. I shall distribute my letters among the different ships.

I will now tell you about the country and its inhabitants. They are as agreeable as my enthusiasm had painted them. Simplicity of manners, kindness, love of country and of liberty, and a delightful equality everywhere prevail. The wealthiest man and the poorest are on a level; and, although there are some large fortunes, I challenge any one to discover the slightest difference between the manners of these two classes respectively towards each other. I first saw the country life at the house of Major Huger. I am now in the city, where everything is very much after the English fashion, except that there is more simplicity, equality, cordiality, and courtesy here than in England. The city of Charleston is one of the handsomest and best built, and its inhabitants among the most agreeable, that I have ever seen. The American women are very pretty, simple in their manners, and exhibit a neatness, which is everywhere cultivated even more studiously than in England. What most charms me is, that all the citizens are brethren. In America, there are no poor, nor even what we call peasantry. Each individual has his own honest property, and the same rights as the most wealthy landed proprietor. The inns are very different from those of Europe; the host and hostess sit at table with you, and do the honors of a comfortable meal;

and, on going away, you pay your bill without higgling. When one does not wish to go to an inn, there are country-houses where the title of a good American is a sufficient passport to all those civilities paid in Europe to one's friend.

As to my own reception, it has been most agreeable in every quarter; and to have come with me secures the most flattering welcome. I have just passed five hours at a grand dinner, given in honor of me by an individual of this city. Generals Howe and Moultrie, and several officers of my suite, were present. We drank healths and tried to talk English. I begin to speak it a little. To-morrow I shall go with these gentlemen to call on the Governor of the State, and make arrangements for my departure. The next day the commanding officers here will show me the city and its environs, and then I shall set out for the army.

Considering the pleasant life I lead in this country, my sympathy with the people, which makes me feel as much at ease in their society as if I had known them for twenty years, the similarity between their mode of thinking and my own, and my love of liberty and of glory, one might suppose that I am very happy. But you are not with me; my friends are not with me; and there is no happiness for me far from you and them. I ask you, if you still love me; but I put the same question much oftener to myself, and my heart always responds, Yes. I am impatient beyond measure to hear from you. I hope to find letters at Philadelphia. My only fear is, that the privateer, which is to bring them, may be captured on her passage. Although I suppose I have drawn upon me the special displeasure of the English, by taking the liberty to depart in spite of them, and by landing in their very face, yet I confess they will not be in arrears with me, should they capture this vessel, my cherished hope, on which I so fondly depend for letters from you. Write frequent and long letters. You do not know the full extent of the joy with which I shall receive them. Embrace Henrietta tenderly. May I say embrace tenderly our children? The father of these poor children is a rover, but a good and honest man at heart; a good father, who loves his family dearly, and a good husband, who loves his wife with all his heart.

Remember me to your friends and my own, to the dear society, once the society of the court, but which by the lapse of time has become the society of the Wooden Sword. We republicans think it all the better. I must leave off for want of paper and time; and if I do not repeat to you ten thousand times that I love you, it is not from any want of feeling, but from modesty; since I have the presumption to hope, that I have already convinced you of it. The night is far advanced, and the heat dreadful. I am devoured by insects; so, you see, the best countries have their disadvantages. Adieu.

Lafayette in the American Revolution

Title: Lafayette in the American Revolution
Author: Marie Paul Joseph, Marquis de Lafayette
Date: 1777-1784
Source: America, Vol.3, pp.222-234

This account of his first visit to America and of his military service on Washington's staff is much the fullest and most important part of the "Memoirs, Correspondence and Manuscripts of General Lafayette," published by his family. Under the head of the American Revolution are comprised eight years of his life, from the beginning of 1777 until the end of 1784, the latter being his twenty-eighth year of age.

On the breaking out of the war between France and England, Lafayette returned home (January, 1779) and it was largely through his exertions that the French government dispatched a land force as well as a fleet to the aid of the Americans.

Returning to his command in 1781, Lafayette was hotly engaged by Cornwallis in Virginia. Once Cornwallis exulted, "The boy cannot escape me." Not many weeks later he surrendered, and Lafayette was publicly thanked by Washington. In the middle of the article Lafayette changes from the first to the third person in this account.

YOU ask me at what period I first experienced my ardent love of liberty and glory? I recollect no time of my life anterior to my enthusiasm for anecdotes of glorious deeds, and to my projects of travelling over the world to acquire fame. At eight years of age, my heart beat when I heard of an hyaena that had done some injury, and caused still more alarm, in our neighborhood, and the hope of meeting it was the object of all my walks. When I arrived at college, nothing ever interrupted my studies, except my ardent wish of studying without restraint. I never deserved to be chastised, but, in spite of my usual gentleness, it would have been dangerous to have attempted to do so; and I recollect with pleasure that, when I was to describe in rhetoric a perfect courser, I sacrificed the hope of obtaining a premium, and described the one who, on perceiving the whip, threw down his rider. Republican anecdotes always delighted me; and, when my new connections wished to obtain for me a place at court, I did not hesitate dis-

All material contained herein was extracted from the
US Constitution Coach Kit at PowerThink.com
(Over 60,000 Works & Documents of American History)

pleasing them to preserve my independence. I was in that frame of mind
when I first learnt the troubles in America: they only be came thoroughly known in Europe in 1776, and the memorable declaration of
the 4th of July reached France at the close of that same year.

After having crowned herself with laurels and enriched herself with
conquests, after having become mistress of all seas, and after having
insulted all nations, England had turned her pride against her own
colonies. North America had long been displeasing to her: she wished
to add new vexations to former injuries, and to destroy the most sacred
privileges...

(1776.) When I first learnt the subject of this quarrel, my heart es-
poused warmly the cause of liberty, and I thought of nothing but of
adding also the aid of my banner. Some circumstances, which it would
be needless to relate, had taught me to expect only obstacles in this
case from my own family: I depended, therefore, solely upon myself;
and I ventured to adopt for a device on my arms these words,—"Cur
non?"—that they might equally serve as an encouragement to myself,
and as a reply to others. Silas Deane was then at Paris; but the ministers
feared to receive him, and his voice was overpowered by the louder ac-
cents of Lord Stormont. He despatched privately to America some old
arms, which were of little use, and some young officers, who did but
little good, the whole directed by M. de Beaumarchais; and, when the
English ambassador spoke to our court, it denied having sent any car-
goes, ordered those that were preparing to be discharged, and dismissed
from our ports all American privateers. While wishing to address myself in a direct manner to Mr. Deane, I became the friend of Kalb, a
German in our employ, who was applying for service with the insurgents (the expression in use at that time), and who became my interpreter. He was the person sent by M. de Choiseul to examine the
English colonies; and on his return he received some money, but never
succeeded in obtaining an audience, so little did that minister in reality
think of the revolution whose retrograde movements some persons have
inscribed to him! When I presented to Mr. Deane my boyish face (for
I was scarcely nineteen years of age), I spoke more of my ardor in the
cause than of my experience; but I dwelt much upon the effect my departure would excite in France, and he signed our mutual agreement...

Preparations were making to send a vessel to America, when very
bad tidings arrived from thence. New York, Long Island, White Plains,
Fort Washington, and the Jerseys had seen the American forces successively destroyed by thirty-three thousand Englishmen or Germans.

Three thousand Americans alone remained in arms, and these were closely pursued by General Howe. From that moment all the credit of the insurgents vanished: to obtain a vessel for them was impossible. The envoys themselves thought it right to express to me their own discouragement, and persuade me to abandon my project. I called upon Mr. Deane, and I thanked him for his frankness. "Until now, sir," said I, "you have only seen my ardor in your cause, and that may not prove at present wholly useless. I shall purchase a ship to carry out your officers. We must feel confidence in the future, and it is especially in the hour of danger that I wish to share your fortune." My project was received with approbation; but it was necessary afterwards to find money, and to purchase and arm a vessel secretly: all this was accomplished with the greatest despatch.

The period was, however, approaching, which had been long fixed, for my taking a journey to England. I could not refuse to go without risking the discovery of my secret, and by consenting to take this journey I knew I could better conceal my preparations for a greater one. This last measure was also thought most expedient by MM. Franklin and Deane, for the doctor himself was then in France; and, although I did not venture to go to his home, for fear of being seen, I corresponded with him through M. Carmichael, an American less generally known. I arrived in London with M. de Poix; and I first paid my respects to Bancroft, the American, and afterwards to his British Majesty…

After having suffered dreadfully in the Channel, and being reminded, as a consolation, how very short the voyage would be, I arrived at M. de Kalb's house in Paris, concealed myself three days at Chaillot, saw a few of my friends and some Americans, and set out for Bordeaux, where I was for some time unexpectedly delayed. I took advantage of that delay to send to Paris, from whence the intelligence I received was by no means encouraging; but, as my messenger was followed on his road by one from the government, I lost not a moment in setting sail, and the orders of my sovereign were only able to overtake me at Pasage, a Spanish port, at which we stopped on our way. The letters from my own family were extremely violent, and those from the government were peremptory. I was forbidden to proceed to the American continent under the penalty of disobedience; I was enjoined to repair instantly to Marseilles, and await there further orders. A sufficient number of commentaries were not wanting upon the consequences of such an anathema, the laws of the state, and the power and displeasure of the government; but the grief of his wife, who was pregnant, and the thoughts of his family and friends, had far more effect upon M. de

Lafayette. As his vessel could no longer be stopped, he returned to Bordeaux to enter into a justification of his own conduct; and, in a declaration to M. de Fumel, he took upon himself all the consequences of his present evasion. As the court did not deign to relax in its determination, he wrote to M. de Maurepas that that silence was a tacit consent, and his own departure took place soon after that joking despatch. After having set out on the road to Marseilles, he retraced his steps, and, disguised as a courier, he had almost escaped all danger, when, at Saint Jean de Luz, a young girl recognized him; but a sign from him silenced her, and her adroit fidelity turned away all suspicion. It was then that M. de Lafayette rejoined his ship, the 26th of April, 1777; and on that same day, after six months' anxiety and labor, he set sail for the American continent.

(1777.) As soon as M. de Lafayette had recovered from the effects of sea-sickness, he studied the language and trade he was adopting. A heavy ship, two bad cannons, and some guns could not have escaped from the smallest privateer. In his present situation, he resolved rather to blow up the vessel than to surrender. He concerted measures to achieve this end with a brave Dutchman named Bedaulx, whose sole alternative, if taken, would have been the gibbet. The captain insisted upon stopping at the islands; but government orders would have been found there, and he followed a direct course, less from choice than from compulsion. At forty leagues from shore, they were met by a small vessel. The captain turned pale, but the crew were attached to M. de Lafayette, and the officers were numerous: they made a show of resistance. It turned out, fortunately, to be an American ship, whom they vainly endeavored to keep up with; but scarcely had the former lost sight of M. de Lafayette's vessel, when it fell in with two English frigates,—and this is not the only time when the elements seemed bent on opposing M. de Lafayette, as if with the intention of saving him. After having encountered for seven weeks various perils and chances, he arrived at Georgetown, in Carolina. Ascending the river in a canoe, his foot touched at length the American soil; and he swore that he would conquer or perish in that cause. Landing at midnight at Major Huger's house, he found a vessel sailing for France, which appeared only waiting for his letters. Several of the officers landed, others remained on board, and all hastened to proceed to Charlestown. .

To repair to the Congress of the United States, M. de Lafayette rode nearly nine hundred miles on horseback. Before reaching the capital of Pennsylvania, he was obliged to travel through the two Carolinas, Virginia, Maryland, and Delaware. While studying the language and customs of the inhabit ants, he observed also new productions of nature and new methods of cultivation. Vast forests and immense rivers combine to give to that country an appearance of youth and majesty. After a fatiguing journey of one month he beheld at length that Philadelphia, so well known in the present day, and whose future grandeur Penn appeared to designate when he laid the first stone of its foundation.

After having accomplished his noble manoeuvres at Trenton and Princeton, General Washington had remained in his camp at Middlebrook. The English, finding themselves frustrated in their first hopes, combined to make a decisive campaign. Burgoyne was already advancing with ten thousand men, preceded by his proclamation and his savages. Ticonderoga, a famous stand of arms, was abandoned by Saint-Clair. He drew upon himself much public odium by this deed, but he saved the only corps whom the militia could rally around. Whilst the generals were busied assembling that militia, the Congress recalled them, sent Gates in their place, and used all possible means to support him. At that same time the great English army, of about eighteen thousand men, had sailed from New York, and the two Howes were uniting their forces for a secret enterprise. Rhode Island was occupied by an hostile corps; and General Clinton, who had remained at New York, was there preparing for an expedition. To be able to withstand so many various blows, General Washington, leaving Putnam on the North river, crossed over the Delaware, and encamped, with eleven thousand men, within reach of Philadelphia.

It was under these circumstances that M. de Lafayette first arrived in America; but the moment, although important to the common cause, was peculiarly unfavorable to strangers. The Americans were displeased with the pretensions, and disgusted with the conduct, of many Frenchmen. The imprudent selections they had in some cases made, the extreme boldness of some foreign adventurers, the jealousy of the army, and strong national prejudices, all contributed to confound disinterested zeal with private ambition, and talents with quackery. Supported by the promises which had been given by Mr. Deane, a numerous band of foreigners besieged the Congress. Their chief was a clever but very imprudent man; and, although a good officer, his excessive vanity amounted almost to madness. With M. de Lafayette, Mr. Deane had sent out a fresh detachment; and every day such crowds arrived that the Congress had finally adopted the plan of not listening to any stranger. The coldness with which M. de Lafayette was received might have been taken as a dismissal; but, without appearing disconcerted by the manner in which the deputies addressed him, he entreated them to return to Congress, and read the following note:—

"After the sacrifices I have made, I have the right to exact two favors: one is, to serve at my own expense; the other is, to serve at first as volunteer."

This style, to which they were so little accustomed, awakened their attention: the despatches from the envoys were read over; and, in a very flattering resolution, the rank of major-general was granted to M. de Lafayette...

The two Howes having appeared before the capes of the Delaware, General Washington came to Philadelphia, and M. de Lafayette beheld for the first time that great man. Although he was surrounded by officers and citizens, it was impossible to mistake for a moment his majestic figure and deportment; nor was he less distinguished by the noble affability of his manner. M. de Lafayette accompanied him in his examination of the fortifications. Invited by the General to establish himself in his house, he looked upon it from that moment as his own: with this perfect ease and simplicity was formed the tie that united two friends, whose confidence and attachment were to be cemented by the strongest interests of humanity...

After having menaced the Delaware, the English fleet again disappeared, and during some days the Americans amused themselves by making jokes at its expense. These jokes, however, ceased when it reappeared in the Chesapeake; and, in order to approach it more closely during the disembarkation, the patriot army crossed through the town. Their heads covered with green branches, and marching to the sound of drums and fifes, these soldiers, in spite of their state of nudity, offered an agreeable spectacle to the eyes of all the citizens. General Washington was marching at their head, and M. de Lafayette was by his side. The army stationed itself upon the heights of Wilmington, and that of the enemy landed in the Elk River, at the bottom of Chesapeake bay...

After having advanced as far as Wilmington, the General had detached a thousand men under Maxwell, the most ancient brigadier in the army. At the first march of the English, he was beaten by their advance-guard near Christiana Bridge. During that time the army took but an indifferent station at Newport. They then removed a little south, waited two days for the enemy, and, at the moment when these were marching upon their right wing, a nocturnal council of war decided that the army was to proceed to the Brandywine. The stream bearing that name covered its front. The ford called Chad's Ford, placed nearly in the center, was defended by batteries. It was in that hardly examined station that, in obedience to a letter from Congress, the Americans awaited the battle... M. de Lafayette, as volunteer, had always accompanied the General. The left wing remaining in a state of tranquillity, and the right appearing fated to receive all the heavy blows, he obtained permission to join Sullivan. At his arrival, which seemed to inspirit the troops, he found that, the enemy having crossed the ford, the corps of Sullivan had scarcely had time to form itself on a line in front of a thinly wooded forest. A few moments after, Lord Cornwallis formed in the finest order. Advancing across the plain, his first line opened a brisk fire of musketry and artillery. The Americans returned the fire, and did much injury to the enemy; but, their right and left wings having given way, the generals and several officers joined the central division, in which were M. de Lafayette and Stirling, and of which eight hundred men were commanded in a most brilliant manner by Conway, an Irishman, in the service of France. By separating that division from its two wings, and advancing through an open plain, in which they lost many men, the enemy united all his fire upon the center: the confusion became extreme; and it was while M. de Lafayette was rallying the troops that a ball passed through his leg. At that moment all those remaining on the field gave way. M. de Lafayette was indebted to Gimat, his aide-de-camp, for the happiness of getting upon his horse. General Washington arrived from a distance with fresh troops. M. de Lafayette was preparing to join him, when loss of blood obliged him to stop and have his wound bandaged: he was even very near being taken. Fugitives, cannon, and baggage now crowded without order into the road leading to Chester. The General employed the remaining daylight in checking the enemy: some regiments behaved extremely well, but the disorder was complete. During that time the ford of Chad was forced, the cannon taken, and the Chester road became the common retreat of the whole army. In the midst of that dreadful confusion, and during the darkness of the night, it was impossible to recover; but at Chester, twelve miles from the field of battle, they met with a bridge which it was necessary to cross. M. de Lafayette occupied himself in arresting the fugitives. Some degree of order was re-established; the generals and the Commander-in-Chief arrived; and he had leisure to have his wound dressed.

It was thus, at twenty-six miles from Philadelphia, that the fate of that town was decided (11th September, 1777). The inhabitants had heard every cannon that was fired there. The two parties, assembled in two distinct bands in all the squares and public places, had awaited the event in silence. The last courier at length arrived, and the friends of liberty were thrown into consternation. The Americans had lost from 1,000 to 1,200 men. Howe's army was composed of about 12,000 men. Their losses had been so considerable that their surgeons, and those in the country, were found insufficient; and they requested the American army to supply them with some for their prisoners. If the enemy had marched to Derby, the army would have been cut up and destroyed. They lost an all-important night; and this was perhaps their greatest fault during a war in which they committed so many errors...

In spite of the Declaration of Independence of the New States, everything there bore the appearance of a civil war. The names of Whig and Tory distinguished the republicans and royalists; the English army was still called the regular troops; the British sovereign was always designated by the name of the king. Provinces, towns, and families were divided by the violence of party spirit: brothers, officers in the two opposing armies, meeting by chance in their father's house, have seized their arms to fight with each other. While in all the rancor of their pride, the English committed horrible acts of license and cruelty, while discipline dragged in her train those venal Germans who knew only how to kill, burn and pillage, in that same army were seen regiments of Americans, who, trampling under foot their brethren, assisted in enslaving their wasted country...

Washington at Valley Forge

Title: Washington at Valley Forge—Conditions Described by Doctor Albigence
        Waldo
Author: Doctor Albigence Waldo
Date: [Not given]
Source: America, Vol.3, pp.235-243

Dr. Waldo was a surgeon from Connecticut, of Puritan ancestry, who had volunteered his services to General Washington in the Fall of 1777 and remained throughout that memorable winter with the army at Valley Forge. This is perhaps the best account of the heroism displayed in the darkest period of American affairs, before the French alliance assured money, ships and troops in aid of the Revolution. It is part of a daily diary kept by Dr. Waldo during his military service, beginning on December 12, 1777.

Washington chose Valley Forge as winter quarters for his army partly for its defensibility and partly to protect Congress, then in session at

York, Pa., from a sudden British attack. It was here that Baron Steuben trained, disciplined and reorganized the American army, enabling it to fight with greater efficiency in subsequent campaigns, and it was here (May 1, 1778) that news reached Washington of the French alliance.

A BRIDGE of wagons made across the Schuylkill last night consisting of 36 wagons, with a bridge of rails be tween each. Some skirmishing over the river. Militia and dragoons brought into camp several prisoners. Sunset. We are ordered to march over the river. It snows. I'm sick; eat nothing—no whiskey—no baggage—Lord—Lord—Lord! The army was until sun rise crossing the river—some at the wagon bridge, and some at the raft bridge below. Cold and uncomfortable.

Dec. 13th.—The army marched three miles from the west side of the river and encamped hear a place called the Gulf, and not an improper name either; for this Gulf seems well adapted by its situation to keep us from the pleasure and enjoyments of this world, or being conversant with anybody in it. It is an excellent place to raise the ideas of a philosopher beyond the glutted thoughts and reflections of an Epicurean. His reflections will be as different from the common reflections of mankind as if he were unconnected with the world, and only conversant with material beings. It cannot be that our superiors are about to hold consultation with Spirits infinitely be neath their Order—by bringing us into these utmost regions of the terraqueous sphere. No—it is, upon consideration, for many good purposes since we are to winter here—1st. There is plenty of wood and water. 2dly. There are but few families for the soldiery to steal from—though far be it from a soldier to steal—3rdly. There are warm sides of hills to erect huts on. 4thly. They will be heavenly minded like Jonah when in the belly of a great fish. 6thly. They will not become homesick as is sometimes the case when men live in the open world—since the reflections which must naturally arise from their present habitation, will lead them to the more noble thoughts of employing their leisure hours in filling their knapsacks with such materials as may be necessary on the journey to another home.

Dec. 14th.—Prisoners and deserters are continually coming in. The army who have been surprisingly healthy hitherto—now begin to grow sickly from the continued fatigues they have suffered this campaign. Yet they still show spirit of alacrity and contentment not to be expected from so young troops. I am sick—discontented—and out of humor. Poor food—hard lodging—cold weather—fatigue—nasty clothes—

nasty cookery—vomit half my time—smoked out of my senses—the Devil's in't—I can't endure it—Why are we sent here to starve and freeze—What sweet felicities have I left at home;—A charming wife— pretty children—good beds—good food—good cookery—all agreeable—all harmonious. Here, all confusion—smoke cold—hunger and filthiness. A pox on my bad luck! Here comes a bowl of beef soup— full of burnt leaves and dirt, sickish enough to make a Hector spew. Away with it, boys—I'll live like the chameleon upon air. Poh! Poh! cries patience within me—you talk like a fool. Your being sick covers your mind with a melancholic gloom, which makes everything about you appear gloomy. See the poor soldier, when in health—with what cheerfulness he meets his foes and encounters every hardship—if barefoot—he labors through the mud and cold with a song in his mouth extolling War and Washington—if his food be bad—he eats it notwithstanding with seeming content—blesses God for a good stomach—and whistles it into digestion. But harkee patience—a moment— There comes a soldier—his bare feet are seen through his worn out shoes—his legs nearly naked from the tattered remains of an only pair of stockings—his breeches not sufficient to cover his nakedness—his shirt hanging in strings—his hair disheveled—his face meager—his whole appearance pictures a person forsaken and discouraged. He comes, and cries with an air of wretchedness and despair, "I am sick, my feet lame, my legs are sore, my body covered with this tormenting itch, my clothes are worn out, my constitution is broken, my former activity is exhausted by fatigue, hunger and cold. I fail fast, I shall soon be no more! and all the reward I shall get will be, "Poor Will is dead."...

Dec. 18th.—Universal Thanksgiving—a roasted pig at night. God be thanked for my health which I have pretty well recovered. How much better should I feel, were I assured my family were in health. But the same good Being who graciously preserves me is able to preserve them—and bring me to the ardently wished for enjoyment of them again.

Rank and precedence make a good deal of disturbance and confusion in the American army. The army are poorly supplied with provision, occasioned, it is said, by the neglect of the Commissary of Purchases. Much talk among officers about discharges. Money has become of too little consequence...

Dec. 21st.—Preparations made for huts. Provision scarce. Mr. Ellis went homeward—sent a letter to my wife. Heartily wish myself at home—my skin and eyes are almost spoiled with continual smoke.

A general cry through the camp this evening among the soldiers—
"No Meat!—No Meat!"—the distant vales echoed back the melancholy
sound—"No Meat! No Meat!" Imitating the noise of crows and owls,
also, made a part of the confused music.

What have you for our dinners, boys? "Nothing but fire cake and
water, Sir." At night—"Gentle men, the supper is ready." What is your
supper, Lads? "Fire cake and water, Sir."

Dec. 22d.—Lay excessive cold and uncomfortable last night—my
eyes are started out from their orbits like a rabbit's eyes, occasioned by
a great cold—and smoke.

What have you got for breakfast, lads? "Fire cake and water, Sir."
The Lord send that our Commissary of Purchases may live on fire cake
and water…

Our Division is under marching orders this morning. I am ashamed
to say it, but I am tempted to steal fowls if I could find them—or even
a whole hog—for I feel as if I could eat one. But the impoverished
country about us, affords but little matter to employ a thief—or keep a
clever fellow in good humor. But why do I talk of hunger and hard
usage, when so many in the world have not even fire cake and water to
eat…

23d.—The party that went out last evening has not returned to-day.
This evening an excellent player on the violin in that soft kind of music
which is so finely adapted to stir up the tender passions, while he was
playing in the next tent to mine these kind soft airs it immediately called
up in remembrance all the endearing expressions—the tender sentiments—the sympathetic friendship that has given so much satisfaction
and sensible pleasure to me from the first time I gained the heart and
affections of the tenderest of the fair…

Dec. 24th.—Party of the 22d returned. Huts go on slowly—cold
and smoke make us fret. But man kind are always fretting, even if they
have more than their proportion of the blessings of life. We are never
easy—always repining at the Providence of an All wise and Benevolent
Being—blaming our country—or faulting our friends. But I don't know
of anything that vexes a man's soul more than hot smoke continually
blowing into his eyes, and when he attempts to avoid it, is met by a
cold and piercing wind…

Dec. 25th, Christmas.—We are still in tents—when we ought to be
in huts—the poor sick suffer much in tents this cold weather—But we

now treat them differently from what they used to be at home, under the inspection of old women and Dr. Bolus Linctus. We give them mutton and grog—and a capital medicine once in a while—to start the disease from its foundation at once. We avoid—piddling pills, powders, bolus's linctus's, cordials, and all such in significant matters whose powers are only rendered important by causing the patient to vomit up his money instead of his disease. But very few of the sick men die.

Dec. 26th.—Party of the 22d not returned. The enemy have been some days the west Schuylkill from opposite the city to Derby—Their intentions are not yet known. The city is at present pretty clear of them. Why don't his Excellency rush in and retake the city, in which he will doubtless find much plunder?—Because he knows better than to leave his post and be caught like a… fool cooped up in the city. He has always acted wisely hitherto. His conduct when closely scrutinized is uncensurable. Were his inferior Generals as skillful as himself, we should have the grandest choir of officers ever God made…

Dec. 28th.—Yesterday upwards of fifty officers in Gen. Greene's Division resigned their commissions; six or seven of our regiment are doing the like to-day. All this is occasioned by officers' families being so much neglected at home on account of provisions. Their wages will not buy considerable, purchase a few trifling comfortables here in camp, and maintain their families at home, while such extravagant prices are demanded for the common necessaries of life, what then have they to purchase clothes and other necessaries with? It is a melancholy reflection that what is of the most universal importance, is most universally neglected—I mean keeping up the credit of money.

The present circumstances of the soldier is better by far than the officer, for the family of the soldier is provided for at the public expense if the articles they want are above the common price; but the officer's family are obliged not only to beg in the most humble manner for the necessaries of life but also to pay for them afterwards at the most exorbitant rates—and even in this manner, many of them who depend entirely on their money, cannot procure half the material comforts that are wanted in a family. This produces continual letters of complaint from home…

Dec. 31st.—Adjutant Selden learned me how to darn stockings—to make them look like knit work—first work the thread in a parallel manner, then catch these over and over as above…

1778. January 1st.—New Year. I am alive. I am well.

Huts go on briskly and our camp begins to appear like a spacious city…

Bought an embroidered jacket.

How much we affect to appear of consequence by a superfluous dress,—and yet custom—(that law which none may fight against) has rendered this absolutely necessary and commendable. An officer frequently fails of being duly noticed, merely from the want of a genteel dress…

Sunday, Jan. 4th.—Properly accoutered I went to work at masonry.—None of my Mess were to dictate me, and before night (being found with mortar and stone) I almost completed a genteel chimney to my magnificent hut—however, as we had short allowance of food and no grog—my back ached before night.

I was called to relieve a soldier thought to be dying—he expired before I reached the hut. He was an Indian—an excellent soldier—and an obedient good natured fellow…

8th.—Unexpectedly got a furlough. Set out for home. The very worst of riding—mud and mire.

We had gone through inoculation before this furlough.

Lodged at—Porters	£0	12	0
Breakfasted at Weaver Jan. 9th just by Bartholomews	0	5	
Grog	0	4	
Hyelyars Tavern 3 1/2 from Caryls, dined Shocking riding!	0	5	10
Lodged at a private house three miles this side Delaware in Jersey and Breakfasted	0	6	0
Treat Serj. Palmer with Baggage…	0	5	2
Mattersons Tavern 13 m De War…	0	4	0
Mattersons	0	2	0
Conarts Tavern 10 M	0	5	0
Sharps or McCurdys, 4 M	13	0	
Capt. Porter's Cross Road 2 M. from McCurdy's Lodged—5 Dol. 1 Sixth . .	1	10	
Breakfasted at the pretty Cottagers Jan. 11th	0	5	6
1 M. from Porters—Horses…	0	0	
Lodgings &c	0	11	0
Bullions Tavern (Vealtown)…	0	5	0
Morristown Dined	0	5	0
Poquonnack 10 M. from N. Y. at Jennings Tavern and a narrow bed—Lodged here. Landlady with toothache— Children keep a squalling	0	19	

Roome's or Romer's Tavern—Good tavern—11 Mile from Jennings…	0	20	0
For 2 bowls Grog and Rum Vaulk's house—	£0	10	0
Honey and Bread and Oats	0	12	
Good old squeaking Widow Ann Hopper, 26 M. from Jenning's, fine living, for horse, Supper, Lodged, Breakfasted.	0	12	0
Satyr Tavern—Lodged and Supped…	0	9	6
Judge Coe's, 9 M. from King's Ferry Dinner, Oats	0	6	0
	£8	19	6

Letters of Lafayette and Washington

Title: Letters of Lafayette and Washington
Author: Lafayette and Washington
Date: 1777
Source: America, Vol.3, pp.245-250

To an American nothing relating to Lafayette is of more interest than his friendship with Washington. More than a hundred of the letters that passed between the two men are given in Lafayette's Memoirs, and they constitute by far the most interesting and important portion of the correspondence there preserved. The first letters, including the two here printed, belong to the trying time of Conway's Cabal, and show the complete confidence which Washington and Lafayette reposed in each other, despite their wide difference in age.

The story of their enduring friendship, as warm on one side as on the other, written in these letters, is a part of the great history which Washington and Lafayette helped to make in America and in France. The Lafayette letter was dated from his camp December 30, 1777. Washington's reply was dated from his headquarters the following day.

MY DEAR GENERAL:—I went yesterday morning to headquarters, with an in tention of speaking to your Excellency, but you were too busy, and I shall state in this letter what I wished to say. I need not tell you how sorry I am at what has lately happened; it is a necessary result of my tender and respectful friendship for you, which is as true and candid as the other sentiments of my heart, and much stronger than so new an acquaintance might seem to admit. But another reason for my concern is my ardent and perhaps enthusiastic wish for the happiness and liberty of this country. I see plainly that

America can defend herself, if proper measures are taken; but I begin to fear that she may be lost by herself and her own sons.

"When I was in Europe, I thought that here almost every man was a lover of liberty, and would rather die free than live a slave. You can conceive my astonishment when I saw that Toryism was as apparently professed as Whigism itself. There are open dissensions in Congress; parties who hate one another as much as the common enemy; men who, without knowing anything about war, undertake to judge you, and to make ridiculous comparisons. They are infatuated with Gates, without thinking of the difference of circumstances, and believe that attacking is the only thing necessary to conquer. These ideas are entertained by some jealous men, and perhaps secret friends of the British government, who want to push you, in a moment of ill humor, to some rash enterprise upon the lines, or against a much stronger army.

"I should not take the liberty of mentioning these particulars to you, if I had not received a letter from a young, good-natured gentleman at Yorktown, whom Conway has ruined by his cunning and bad advice, but who entertains the greatest respect for you. I have been surprised to see the poor establishment of the Board of War, the difference made between northern and southern departments, and the orders from Congress about military operations. But the promotion of Conway is beyond all my expectations. I should be glad to have new major-generals, because, as I know that you take some interest in my happiness and reputation, it will perhaps afford an occasion for your Excellency to give me more agreeable commands in some instances. On the other hand, General Conway says he is entirely a man to be disposed of by me, he calls himself my soldier, and the reason of such behavior towards me is, that he wishes to be well spoken of at the French Court; and his protector, the Marquis de Castries, is an intimate acquaintance of mine.

"But since the letter of Lord Stirling, I have inquired into his character, and found that he is an ambitious and dangerous man. He has done all in his power to draw off my confidence and affection from you. His desire was to engage me to leave this country. I now see all the general officers of the army against Congress. Such disputes, if known to the enemy, may be attended with the worst consequences. I am very sorry whenever I perceive troubles raised among defenders of the same cause; but my concern is much greater, when I find officers coming from France, officers of some character in my country, to whom a fault of that kind may be imputed. The reason for my fondness for

Conway was his being a very brave and very good officer. However, that talent for manoeuvering, which seems so extraordinary to Congress, is not so very difficult a matter for any man of common sense, who applies himself to it. I must render to General Duportail and some other French officers, who have spoken to me, the justice to say, that I found them as I could wish upon this occasion, although it has made a great noise among many in the army. I wish your Excellency could let them know how necessary you are to them, and engage them at the same time to keep peace and reinstate love among themselves, till the moment when these little disputes shall not be attended with such inconveniences. It would be too great a pity, that slavery, dishonor, ruin, and the unhappiness of a whole nation, should issue from trifling differences betwixt a few men.

"You will perhaps find this letter very unimportant; but I was desirous of explaining to you some of my ideas, because it will contribute to my satisfaction to be convinced, that you, my dear General, who have been so indulgent as to permit me to look on you as a friend, should know my sentiments. I have the warmest love for my country, and for all good Frenchmen. Their success fills my heart with joy; but, Sir, besides that Conway is an Irishman, I want countrymen, who in every point do honor to their country. That gentle man had engaged me, by entertaining my imagination with ideas of glory and shining projects, and I must confess this was a too certain way of deceiving me. I wish to join to the few theories about war, which I possess, and to the few dispositions which nature has given me, the experience of thirty campaigns, in the hope that I should be able to be more useful in my present sphere. My desire of deserving your approbation is strong; and, whenever you shall employ me, you can be certain of my trying every exertion in my power to succeed. I am now bound to your fate, and I shall follow it and sustain it, as well by my sword as by all the means in my power. You will pardon my importunity. Youth and friendship perhaps make me too warm, but I feel the greatest concern at recent events. With the most tender and profound respect, I have the honor to be, &c."

MY DEAR MARQUIS:—Your favor of yesterday conveyed to me fresh proof of that friendship and attachment, which I have happily experienced since the first of our acquaintance, and for which I entertain sentiments of the purest affection. It will ever constitute part of my happiness to know that I stand well in your opinion; because I am satisfied that you can have no views to answer by throwing out false colors, and that you possess a mind too exalted to condescend to low arts and intrigues to acquire a reputation. Happy, thrice happy, would it have been for this army, and the cause we are embarked in, if the same generous spirit had pervaded all the actors in it. But one gentleman, whose name you have mentioned, had, I am confident, far different views. His ambition and great desire of being puffed off, as one of the first officers of the age, could only be equalled by the means which he used to obtain them; but, finding that I was determined not to go beyond the line of my duty to indulge him in the first, nor to exceed the strictest rules of propriety to gratify him in the second, he became my inveterate enemy; and he has, I am persuaded, practised every art to do me an injury, even at the expense of reprobating a measure, which did not succeed, that he himself advised to. How far he may have accomplished his ends, I know not; and, except for considerations of a public nature, I care not; for it is well known, that neither ambitious nor lucrative motives led me to accept my present appointments; in the discharge of which, I have endeavored to observe one steady and uniform system of conduct, which I shall invariably pursue, while I have the honor to command, regard less of the tongue of slander or the powers of detraction. The fatal tendency of disunion is so obvious, that I have in earnest terms exhorted such officers as have expressed their dissatisfaction at General Conway's promotion, to be cool and dispassionate in their decision upon the matter; and I have hopes that they will not suffer any hasty determination to injure the service. At the same time, it must be acknowledged that officers' feelings upon these occasions are not to be restrained, although you may control their actions.

"The other observations contained in your letter have too much truth in them; and it is much to be lamented that things are not now as they formerly were; but we must not, in so great a contest, expect to meet with nothing but sunshine. I have no doubt that everything happens for the best, that we shall triumph over all our misfortunes, and in the end be happy; when, my dear Marquis, if you will give me your company in Virginia, we will laugh at our past difficulties and the folly of others; and I will endeavor, by every civility in my power, to show you how much and how sincerely I am your affectionate and obedient servant."

France Recognizes American Independence

Title: France Recognizes American Independence
Author: Benjamin Franklin
Date: 1778
Source: America, Vol.3, pp.251-253

This letter, written by Franklin in 1778, while serving as the American Commissioner in Paris, to Thomas Cushing, the Colonial statesman whom Dr. Samuel Johnson accused of aiming at an American crown, announces the conclusion of negotiations with the French Government that began with the sending of Silas Deane to Paris in 1775. Before he was superseded by Franklin, Deane acted as the official United States delegate to the French Court, and, besides securing and transmitting supplies, induced many French officers—by lavish promises—to take service in the American army.

While in France Franklin was of great aid in founding the American navy, and especially in furthering the operations of John Paul Jones. He negotiated loans to the United States amounting to many millions of francs. In 1782 he signed the preliminary articles of peace, and the next year (September 3,) he was a signer of the Treaty of Paris.

I RECEIVED your favor by Mr. Austin, with your most agreeable congratulations on the success of the American arms in the Northern Department. In return, give me leave to congratulate you on the success of our negotiations here, in the completion of the two treaties with his most Christian Majesty: the one of amity and commerce, on the plan of that proposed by Congress, with some good additions; the other of alliance for mutual defence, in which the most Christian king agrees to make a common cause with the United States, if England attempts to obstruct the commerce of his subjects with them; and guarantees to the United States their liberty, sovereignty, and independence, absolute and unlimited, with all the possessions they now have, or may have, at the conclusion of the war; and the States in return guarantee to him his possessions in the West Indies. The great principle in both treaties is a perfect equality and reciprocity; no advantage to be demanded by France, or privileges in commerce, which the States may not grant to any and every other nation.

In short, the king has treated with us generously and magnanimously; taken no advantage of our present difficulties, to exact terms which we would not willingly grant, when established in prosperity and power. I may add that he has acted wisely, in wishing the friendship contracted by these treaties may be durable, which probably might not be if a contrary conduct had taken place.

Several of the American ships, with stores for the Congress, are now about sailing under the convoy of a French squadron. England is in great consternation, and the minister, on the 17th instant, confessing that all his measures had been wrong and that peace was necessary, proposed two bills for quieting America; but they are full of artifice and deceit, and will, I am confident, be treated accordingly by our country.

I think you must have much satisfaction in so valuable a son, whom I wish safe back to you, and am, with great esteem, etc.,

B. FRANKLIN.

P.S.—The treaties were signed by the plenipotentiaries on both sides February 6th, but are still for some reasons kept secret, though soon to be published. It is understood that Spain will soon accede to the same. The treaties are forwarded to Congress by this conveyance.

A Warning Against Conciliation

Title: A Warning Against Conciliation
Author: Patrick Henry
Date: June, 1778
Source: America, Vol.3, pp.254-257

Inseparable from the American Revolution is the name of Patrick Henry, the Virginia counterpart of Samuel Adams of Massachusetts, Continental congressman, governor and leader of the patriots. Unfortunately there is no text preserved of a single one of his glowing speeches. The extract below, from a letter, dated Williamsburg, June 18, 1778, to a fellow Virginian, Richard Henry Lee, at that time serving as a member of Congress in Philadelphia, shows his spirit; the issue was a plan of conciliation proposed by Great Britain after the French alliance with the United States. Patrick Henry was then Governor of Virginia.

As a member of the second Continental Congress, Lee was recognized as one of the really influential leaders of the revolutionary movement, and he became famous through his motion of June 7, 1776, that the colonies should be free and independent States, a motion followed by the Declaration of Independence.

BOTH your last letters came to hand to-day. I felt for you, on seeing the order in which the balloting placed the delegates in Congress. It is an effect of that rancorous malice, that has so long followed you, through that arduous path of duty which you have invariably travelled, since America resolved to resist her oppressors. Is it any pleasure to you, to remark, that at the same era in which these men figure against you, public spirit seems to have taken its flight from Virginia? It is too much the case; for the quota of our troops is not half made up, and no chance seems to remain or completing it. The Assembly voted three hundred and fifty horse, and two thousand men, to be forth with raised, and to join the grand army. Great bounties are offered, but I fear, the only effect will be, to expose our State to contempt, for I believe no soldiers will enlist, especially in the infantry.

Can you credit it; no effort was made for supporting, or restoring public credit! I pressed it warmly on some, but in vain. This is the reason we get no soldiers. We shall issue fifty or sixty thousand dollars in cash, to equip the cavalry, and their time is to expire at Christmas. I believe they will not be in the field before that time. Let not Congress rely on Virginia for soldiers. I tell you my opinion, they will not be got here until a different spirit prevails. I look at the past condition of America, as at a dreadful precipice, from which we have escaped, by means of the generous French, to whom I will be everlastingly bound by the most heartfelt gratitude. But I must mistake matters, if some of those men who traduce you, do not prefer the offers of Britain. You will have a different game to play now with the commissioners. How comes Governor Johnstone there? I do not see how it comports with his past life. Surely Congress will never recede from our French friends. Salvation to America depends upon our holding fast our attachment to them. I shall date our ruin from the moment that it is exchanged for anything Great Britain can say or do. She can never be cordial with us. Baffled, defeated, disgraced by her colonies, she will ever meditate revenge.

We can find no safety but in her ruin, or at least in her extreme humiliation, which has not happened, and cannot happen until she is deluged with blood, or thoroughly purged by a revolution, which shall wipe from existence the present King with his connections, and the present system, with those who aid and abet it. For God's sake, my dear sir, quit not the councils of your country, until you see us forever disjoined from Great Britain. The old leaven still works. The flesh pots of Egypt are still savoury to degenerate palates. Again, we are undone if the French alliance is not religiously observed. Excuse my freedom. I know your love to our country, and this is my motive. May heaven give you health and prosperity.

The Capture of Vincennes

Title: The Capture of Vincennes
Author: George Rogers Clark
Date: 1778
Source: America, Vol.3, pp.257-266

The conquest of the great territory north of the Ohio River by General Clark in 1778-9 was one of the most heroic episodes of the Revolutionary period, and one of the most important in its consequences. By reason of it, the Treaty of Paris denominated the Mississippi instead of the Ohio as our western boundary.

Clark, whose Memoirs were written at the special request of Jefferson and Madison, and from which this article was taken, was sent by Governor Patrick Henry to subjugate the North-west with a force of less than 200 men. Suffering almost incredible hardships, they placed the country under control of Virginia.

Clark died in poverty near Louisville, Kentucky. Late in life, when his native State sent him a sword, he exclaimed: "When Virginia needed a sword, I gave her one. She now sends me a toy. I want bread!"—thrust the sword in the ground and broke it with his crutch.

EVERYTHING being ready, on the 5th of February, after receiving a lecture and absolution from the priest, we crossed the Kaskaskia River with one hundred and seventy men, marched about three miles and encamped, where we lay until the 7th, and set out. The weather wet (but fortunately not cold for the season) and a great part of the plains under water several inches deep. It was difficult and very fatiguing marching. My object was now to keep the men in spirits. I suffered them to shoot game on all occasions, and feast on it like Indian war-dancers, each company by turns inviting the others to their feasts, which was the case every night, as the company that was to give the feast was always supplied with horses to lay up a sufficient store of wild meat in the course of the day, myself and principal officers putting on the woodsmen, shouting now and then, and running as much through the mud and water as any of them... Crossing a narrow deep lake in the canoes, and marching some distance, we came to a copse of timber called the Warrior's Island. We were now in full view of the fort and town, not a shrub between us, at about two miles' distance. Every man now feasted his eyes, and forgot that he had suffered anything, saying that all that had passed was owing to good policy and nothing but what a man could bear; and that a soldier had no right to think, etc.,—passing from one extreme to another, which is common in such cases. It was now we had to display our abilities. The plain between us and the town was not a perfect level. The sunken grounds were covered with water full of ducks. We observed several men out on horseback, shooting them, within a half mile of us, and sent out as many of our active young Frenchmen to decoy and take one of these men prisoner in such a manner as not to alarm the others, which they did. The information we got from this person was similar to that which we got from those we took on the river, except that of the British having that evening completed the wall of the fort, and that there was a good many Indians in town.

Our situation was now truly critical,—no possibility of retreating in case of defeat, and in full view of a town that had, at this time, upward of six hundred men in it,—troops, inhabitants and Indians. The crew of the galley, though not fifty men, would have been now a reenforcement of immense magnitude to our little army (if I may so call it), but we would not think of them. We were now in the situation that I had labored to get ourselves in. The idea of being made prisoner was foreign to almost every man, as they expected nothing but torture from the savages, if they fell into their hands. Our fate was now to be determined, probably in a few hours. We knew that nothing but the most daring conduct would insure success. I knew that a number of the inhabitants wished us well, that many were lukewarm to the interest of either, and I also learned that the grand chief, the Tobacco's son, had but a few days before openly declared, in council with the British, that he was a brother and friend to the Big Knives. These were favorable circumstances; and, as there was but little probability of our remaining until dark undiscovered, I determined to begin the career immediately, and wrote the following placard to the inhabitants:—

TO THE INHABITANTS OF VINCENNES:

Gentlemen,—Being now within two miles of your village, with my army, determined to take your fort this night, and not being willing to surprise you, I take this method to request such of you as are true citizens and willing to enjoy the liberty I bring you to remain still in your houses; and those, if any there be, that are friends to the King will instantly repair to the fort, and join the hair-buyer general, and fight like men. And, if any such as do not go to the fort shall be discovered afterward, they may depend on severe punishment. On the contrary, those who are true friends to liberty may depend on being well treated; and I once more request them to keep out of the streets. For every one I find in arms on my arrival I shall treat him as an enemy.

(Signed) G. R. CLARK.

… We anxiously viewed this messenger until he entered the town, and in a few minutes could discover by our glasses some stir in every street that we could penetrate into, and great numbers running or riding out into the commons, we supposed, to view us, which was the case. But what surprised us was that nothing had yet happened that had the appearance of the garrison being alarmed,—no drum nor gun. We began to suppose that the information we got from our prisoners was false, and that the enemy already knew of us, and were prepared… A little before sunset we moved, and displayed ourselves in full view of the town, crowds gazing at us. .

We moved on slowly in full view of the town; but, as it was a point of some consequence to us to make ourselves appear formidable, we, in leaving the covert that we were in, marched and countermarched in such a manner that we appeared numerous…

The firing now commenced on the fort, but they did not believe it was an enemy until one of their men was shot down through a port, as drunken Indians frequently saluted the fort after night. The drums now sounded, and the business fairly commenced on both sides. Reenforcements were sent to the attack of the garrison, while other arrangements were making in town… We now found that the garrison had known nothing of us; that, having finished the fort that evening, they had amused themselves at different games, and had just retired before my letter arrived, as it was near roll-call. The placard being made public, many of the inhabitants were afraid to show themselves out of the houses for fear of giving offense, and not one dare give information…

The garrison was soon completely surrounded, and the firing continued without intermission (except about fifteen minutes a little before day) until about nine o'clock the following morning. It was kept up by the whole of the troops, joined by a few of the young men of the town, who got permission, except fifty men kept as a reserve… I had made myself fully acquainted with the situation of the fort and town and the parts relative to each. The cannon of the garrison was on the upper floors of strong blockhouses at each angle of the fort, eleven feet above the surface, and the ports so badly cut that many of our troops lay under the fire of them within twenty or thirty yards of the walls. They did no damage, except to the buildings of the town, some of which they much shattered; and their musketry, in the dark, employed against woodsmen covered by houses, palings, ditches, the banks of the river, etc., was but of little avail, and did no injury to us except wounding a man or two. As we could not afford to lose men, great care was taken to preserve them sufficiently covered, and to keep up a hot fire in order to intimidate the enemy as well as to destroy them... A little before day the troops were withdrawn from their positions about the fort, except a few parties of observation, and the firing totally ceased. Orders were given, in case of Lamotte's approach, not to alarm or fire on him without a certainty of killing or taking the whole. In less than a quarter of an hour, he passed within ten feet of an officer and a party that lay concealed. Ladders were flung over to them; and, as they mounted them, our party shouted. Many of them fell from the top of the walls,—some within, and others back; but, as they were not fired on, they all got over, much to the joy of their friends. But, on considering the matter, they must have been convinced that it was a scheme of ours to let them in, and that we were so strong as to care but little about them or the manner of their getting into the garrison...

The firing immediately commenced on both sides with double vigor; and I believe that more noise could not have been made by the same number of men. Their shouts could not be heard for the firearms; but a continual blaze was kept around the garrison, without much being done, until about daybreak, when our troops were drawn off to posts prepared for them, about sixty or seventy yards from the fort. A loophole then could scarcely be darkened but a rifle-ball would pass through it. To have stood to their cannon would have destroyed their men, without a probability of doing much service. Our situation was nearly similar. It would have been imprudent in either party to have wasted their men, without some decisive stroke required it.

Thus the attack continued until about nine o'clock on the morning of the 24th. Learning that the two prisoners they had brought in the day before had a considerable number of letters with them, I supposed it an express that we expected about this time, which I knew to be of the greatest moment to us, as we had not received one since our arrival in the country; and, not being fully acquainted with the character of our enemy, we were doubtful that those papers might be destroyed, to prevent which I sent a flag [with a letter] demanding the garrison...

We met at the church, about eighty yards from the fort, Lieutenant-governor Hamilton, Major Hay, superintendent of Indian affairs, Captain Helm, their prisoner, Major Bowman, and myself. The conference began. Hamilton produced terms of capitulation, signed, that contained various articles, one of which was that the garrison should be surrendered on their being permitted to go to Pensacola on parole. After deliberating on every article, I rejected the whole. He then wished that I would make some proposition. I told him that I had no other to make than what I had already made,—that of his surrendering as prisoners at discretion. I said that his troops had behaved with spirit; that they could not suppose that they would be worse treated in consequence of it; that, if he chose to comply with the demand, though hard, perhaps the sooner the better; that it was in vain to make any proposition to me; that he, by this time, must be sensible that the garrison would fall; that both of us must [view?] all blood spilt for the future by the garrison as murder; that my troops were already impatient, and called aloud for permission to tear down and storm the fort...

We took our leave, and parted but a few steps, when Hamilton stopped, and politely asked me if I would be so kind as to give him my reasons for refusing the garrison any other terms than those I had offered. I told him I had no objections in giving him my real reasons, which were simply these: that I knew the greater part of the principal Indian partisans of Detroit were with him; that I wanted an excuse to put them to death or otherwise treat them as I thought proper; that the cries of the widows and the fatherless on the frontiers, which they had occasioned, now required their blood from my hand; and that I did not choose to be so timorous as to disobey the absolute commands of their authority, which I looked upon to be next to divine; that I would rather lose fifty men than not to empower myself to execute this piece of business with propriety; that, if he chose to risk the massacre of his garrison for their sakes, it was his own pleasure; and that I might, perhaps, take it into my head to send for some of those widows to see it executed.

Major Hay paying great attention, I had observed a kind of distrust in his countenance, which in a great measure influenced my conversation during this time. On my concluding, "Pray, sir," said he, "who is it that you call Indian partisans?" "Sir," I replied, "I take Major Hay to be one of the principal." I never saw a man in the moment of execution so struck as he appeared to be,—pale and trembling, scarcely able to stand. Hamilton blushed, and, I observed, was much affected at his behavior. Major Bowman's countenance sufficiently explained his disdain for the one and his sorrow for the other... Some moments elapsed without a word passing on either side. From that moment my resolutions changed respecting Hamilton's situation. I told him that we would return to our respective posts; that I would reconsider the matter, and let him know the result. No offensive measures should be taken in the meantime. Agreed to; and we parted. What had passed being made known to our officers, it was agreed that we should moderate our resolutions.

In the course of the afternoon of the 24th the following articles were signed:

I. Lieutenant-governor Hamilton engages to deliver up to Colonel Clark Fort Sackville, as it is at present, with all the stores, etc.

II. The garrison are to deliver themselves as prisoners of war, and march out with their arms and accouterments, etc.

III. The garrison to be delivered up at ten o'clock to-morrow.

IV. Three days time to be allowed the garrison to settle their accounts with the inhabitants and traders of this place.

V. The officers of the garrison to be allowed their necessary baggage, etc.

Signed at Post St. Vincent [Vincennes] 24th of February, 1779.

Agreed for the following reasons: the remoteness from succor; the state and quantity of provisions, etc.; unanimity of officers and men in its expediency; the honorable terms allowed; and, lastly, the confidence in a generous enemy.

The business being now nearly at an end, troops were posted in several strong houses around the garrison and patroled during the night to prevent any deception that might be attempted. The remainder on duty lay on their arms, and for the first time for many days past got some rest... During the siege, I got only one man wounded. Not being able to lose many, I made them secure themselves well. Seven were badly wounded in the fort through ports... Almost every man had conceived a favorable opinion of Lieutenant-governor Hamilton,—I believe what affected myself made some impression on the whole; and I was happy to find that he never deviated, while he stayed with us, from that dignity of conduct that became an officer in his situation. The morning of the 25th approaching, arrangements were made for receiving the garrison [which consisted of seventy-nine men], and about ten o'clock it was delivered in form; and everything was immediately arranged to the best advantage.

Wayne Surprises and Storms Stony Point

Title: Wayne Surprises and Storms Stony Point
Author: George Washington
Date: July, 1779
Source: America, Vol.3, pp.267-272

This communication, dated from his headquarters at New Windsor, July 21, 1779, from Washington to John Jay, President of Congress, together with the accompanying report of General Anthony Wayne to Washington of his recapture of Stony Point from the British on July 16, 1779, was first published in the Pennsylvania Gazette and General Advertiser twelve days after the event. It followed an earlier report from Wayne to Washington, dated at Stony Point, July 16, 2 A.M., stating briefly, "The fort and garrison with Colonel Johnston are officers. Our officers and men behaved like men who are determined to be free." These reports were published by order of Congress and kindled widespread enthusiasm in the colonies.

With 1,200 men Wayne took 543 prisoners, the American loss being 15 killed and 83 wounded. Following the victory the fortifications were dismantled and the place abandoned, the British reoccupying it soon afterwards.

WASHINGTON TO CONGRESS

ON THE 16th instant I had the honor to inform Congress of a successful attack upon the enemy's post at Stony Point, on the preceding night, by Brigadier-General Wayne, and the corps of light infantry under his command. The ulterior operations in which we have been engaged, have hitherto put it out of my power to transmit the particulars of this interesting event. They will now be found in the inclosed report, which I have received from General Wayne. To the encomiums he has deservedly bestowed on the officers and men under his command, it gives me pleasure to add that his own conduct throughout the whole of this arduous enterprise, merits the warmest approbation of Congress. He improved upon the plan recommended by me, and executed it in a manner that does signal honor to his judgment and to his bravery. In a critical moment of the assault, he received a flesh wound in the head with a musket ball, but continued leading on his men with unshaken firmness.

I now beg leave, for the private satisfaction of Congress, to explain the motives which induced me to direct the attempt.

It has been the unanimous sentiment to evacuate the captured post at Stony Point, remove the cannon and stores, and destroy the works, which was accomplished on the night of the 18th, one piece of heavy cannon only excepted. For want of proper tackling within reach to transport the cannon by land, we were obliged to send them to the fort by water. The movements of the enemy's vessels created some uneasiness on their account, and induced me to keep one of the pieces for their protection, which finally could not be brought off, without risking more for its preservation than it was worth. We also lost a galley which was ordered down to cover the boats. She got under way, on her return the afternoon of the 18th. The enemy began a severe and continued cannonade upon her, from which having received some injury, which disabled her from proceeding, she was run ashore. Not being able to get her afloat till late in the floodtide, and one or two of the enemy's vessels under favor of the night, having passed above her, she was set on fire and blown up.

It is probable Congress will be pleased to bestow some marks of consideration upon those officers who distinguished themselves upon this occasion. Every officer and man of the corps deserves great credit, but there were particular ones whose situation placed them foremost in danger, and made their conduct most conspicuous... I forgot to mention, that two flags and two standards were taken, the former belonging to the garrison, and the latter to the 17th regiment. These shall be sent to Congress by the first convenient opportunity.

WAYNE TO WASHINGTON

I HAVE the honor to give you a full and particular relation of the reduction of this point, by the light-infantry under my command.

On the 15th instant at 12 o'clock we took up our line of march from Sandy-beach, distant 14 miles from this place; the roads being exceedingly bad and narrow, and having to pass over high mountains, through deep morasses, and difficult defiles, we were obliged to move in single files the greatest part of the way. At eight o'clock in the evening, the van arrived at Mr. Springsteel's, within one and a half miles of the enemy, and formed into columns as fast as they came up, agreeable to the order of battle annexed; viz. Colonels Febiger's and Meig's regiments, with Major Hull's detachment, formed the right column; Colonel Butler's regiment and Major Murfree's two companies, the left. The troops remained in this position until several of the principal officers, with myself, had returned from reconnoitering the works. Half after eleven o'clock, being the hour fixed on, the whole moved forward, the van of the right consisted of one hundred and fifty volunteers, properly officered, who advanced with unloaded muskets and fixed bayonets, under the command of Lieutenant Colonel Fleury; these were preceded by twenty picked men, and a vigilant and brave officer, to remove the abatis and other obstructions. The van of the left consisted of one hundred volunteers, under the command of Major Steward, with unloaded muskets and fixed bayonets, also preceded by a brave and determined officer, with twenty men, for the same purpose as the other.

At 12 o'clock the assault was to begin on the right and left flanks of the enemy's works, while Major Murfree amused them in front; but a deep morass covering their whole front, and at this time overflowed by the tide, together with other obstructions, rendered the approaches more difficult than were at first apprehended, so that it was about twenty minutes after twelve before the assault began, previous to which I placed myself at the head of Febiger's regiment or right column, and gave the troops the most pointed orders not to fire on any account, but place their whole dependence on the bayonet, which order was literally and faithfully obeyed. Neither the deep morass, the formidable and double rows of abatis, or the strong works in front and flank, could damp the ardor of the troops, who in the face of a most tremendous and incessant fire of musketry, and from cannon loaded with grape-shot, forced their way at the point of the bayonet, through every obstacle, both columns meeting in the center of the enemy's works nearly at the same instant. Too much praise cannot be given to Lieutenant Colonel Fleury, (who struck the enemy's standard with his own hand) and to Major Steward, who commanded the advanced parties, for their brave and prudent conduct.

Colonels Butler, Meigs, and Febiger conducted themselves with that coolness, bravery, and perseverance, that will ever insure success. Lieutenant Colonel Hays was wounded in the thigh, bravely fighting at the head of his battalion. I should take up too much of your Excellency's time, was I to particularize every individual who deserves it, for his bravery on this occasion. I cannot, however, omit Major Lee, to whom I am indebted for frequent and very useful intelligence, which contributed much to the success of the enterprise, and it is with the greatest pleasure I acknowledge to you, I was supported in the attack by all the officers and soldiers under my command, to the utmost of my wishes. The officers and privates of the artillery exerted themselves in turning the cannon against Verplanck's Point, and forced them to cut the cables of their shipping, and run down the river.

I should be wanting in gratitude was I to omit mentioning Captain Fishbourn and Mr. Archer, my two aids-de-camp, who on every occasion showed the greatest intrepidity, and supported me into the works after I received my wound in passing the last abatis.

Inclosed are the returns of the killed and wounded of the light infantry, as also of the enemy, together with the number of prisoners taken, likewise of the ordnance and stores found in the garrison.

I forgot to mention to your Excellency, that previous to my marching, I had drawn General Muhlenberg into my rear, who with three hundred men of his brigade took post on the opposite side of the marsh so as to be in readiness either to support me, or to cover a retreat in case of accident, and I have no doubt of his faithfully and effectually executing either, had there been any occasion for him.

The humanity of our brave soldiery, who scorned to take the lives of a vanquished foe calling for mercy, reflects the highest honor on them, and accounts for the few of the enemy killed on the occasion.

I am not satisfied with the manner in which I have mentioned the conduct of Lieutenants Gibbons and Knox, the two gentlemen who led the advanced parties of twenty men each—their distinguished bravery deserves the highest commendation—the first belongs to the sixth Pennsylvania regiment, and lost 17 men killed and wounded in the attack; the last belongs to the ninth ditto, who was more fortunate in saving his men though not less exposed.

The Capture of the Serapis by the Bon Homme Richard

Title: The Capture of the Serapis By the Bon Homme Richard
Author: Commodore John Paul Jones
Date: 1779
Source: America, Vol.3, pp.273-281

This report of the naval battle between the Bon Homme Richard, one of four vessels furnished the United States by France, and the British ship Serapis, was sent by John Paul Jones to Benjamin Franklin, then our commissioner in Paris, and by Franklin was forwarded to Congress. It was written October 3, 1779, on board the Serapis, which Jones and his men had boarded before the Bon Homme Richard sank.

Jones, who was the first man to hoist the American flag on a man-of-war, had engaged the vastly superior Serapis, convoying 40 British merchantmen, off the coast of Scotland.

In an account of the battle by Lieutenant Richard Dale, of the Bon Homme Richard, we are told that at a certain desperate stage of the fight Jones was hailed by Captain Pearson, of the Serapis, who asked, "Has your ship struck?"—to which Jones answered, "I have not yet begun to fight."

WHEN I had the honor of writing to you on the 11th of August [1779], previous to my departure from the Road of Groaix, I had before me the most flattering prospect of rendering essential service to the common cause of France and America. I had a full confidence in the voluntary inclination and ability of every captain under my command to assist and support me in my duty with cheerful emulation; and I was persuaded that every one of them would pursue glory in preference to interest...

On the morning of the 23d, the brig from Holland not being in sight, we chased a brigantine that appeared laying to windward. About noon we saw and chased a large ship that appeared coming round Flamborough Head from the northward, and at the same time I manned and armed one of the pilot boats to sail in pursuit of the brigantine, which now appeared to be the vessel that I had forced ashore. Soon after this a fleet of 41 sail appeared off Flamborough Head, bearing N.N.E. This induced me to abandon the single ship which had been anchored in Burlington Bay. I also called back the pilot boat, and hoisted a signal for a general chase. When the fleet discovered us bearing down, all the merchant ships crowded sail towards the shore. The two ships of war that protected the fleet at the same time steered from the land, and made the disposition for the battle. In approaching the enemy, I crowded every possible sail, and made the signal for the line of battle, to which the Alliance showed no attention. Earnest as I was for the action, I could not reach the commodore's ship until seven in the evening. Being then within pistol shot, when he hailed the Bon Homme Richard, we answered him by firing a whole broadside.

The battle, being thus begun, was continued with unremitting fury. Every method was practiced on both sides to gain an advantage, and rake each other; and I must confess that the enemy's ship, being much more manageable than the Bon Homme Richard, gained thereby several times an advantageous situation, in spite of my best endeavors to prevent it. As I had to deal with an enemy of greatly superior force, I was under the necessity of closing with him, to prevent the advantage which he had over me in point of maneuver. It was my intention to lay the Bon Homme Richard athwart the enemy's bow, but, as that operation required great dexterity in the management of both sails and helm, and some of our braces being shot away, it did not exactly succeed to my wishes. The enemy's bowsprit, however, came over the Bon Homme Richard's poop by the mizzen mast, and I made both ships fast together in that situation, which by the action of the wind on the enemy's sails forced her stern close to the Bon Homme Richard's bow, so that the ships lay square alongside of each other, the yards being all entangled, and the cannon of each ship touching the opponent's side.

When this position took place, it was 8 o'clock, previous to which the Bon Homme Richard had received sundry eighteen-pounds shot below the water, and leaked very much. My battery of 12-pounders, on which I had placed my chief dependence, being commanded by Lieutenant Dale and Colonel Weibert, and manned principally with American seamen and French volunteers, were entirely silenced and abandoned. As to the six old eighteen-pounders that formed the battery of the lower gun-deck, they did no service whatever. Two out of three of them burst at the first fire, and killed almost all the men who were stationed to manage them. Before this time, too, Colonel de Chamillard, who commanded a party of 20 soldiers on the poop, had abandoned that station after having lost some of his men. These men deserted their quarters.

I had now only two pieces of cannon, nine-pounders, on the quarter deck, that were not silenced; and not one of the heavier cannon was fired during the rest of the action. The purser, Mr. Mease, who commanded the guns on the quarter deck, being dangerously wounded in the head, I was obliged to fill his place, and with great difficulty rallied a few men, and shifted over one of the lee quarter-deck guns, so that we afterward played three pieces of 9-pounders upon the enemy. The tops alone seconded the fire of this little battery, and held out bravely during the whole of the action, especially the main top, where Lieutenant Stack commanded. I directed the fire of one of the three cannon against the main-mast, with double-headed shot, while the other two were exceedingly well served with grape and canister shot to silence the enemy's musketry, and clear her decks, which was at last effected.

The enemy were, as I have since understood, on the instant of calling for quarters when the cowardice or treachery of three of my under officers induced them to call to the enemy. The English commodore asked me if I demanded quarters; and, I having answered him in the most determined negative, they renewed the battle with double fury. They were unable to stand the deck; but the fire of their cannon, especially the lower battery, which was entirely formed of 18-pounders, was incessant. Both ships were set on fire in various places, and the scene was dreadful beyond the reach of language. To account for the timidity of my three under officers,—I mean the gunner, the carpenter, and the master-at-arms,—I must observe that the two first were slightly wounded; and, as the ship had received various shots under water, and one of the pumps being shot away, the carpenter expressed his fear that she would sink, and the other two concluded that she was sinking, which occasioned the gunner to run aft on the poop without my knowledge to strike the colors. Fortunately for me, a cannon ball had done that before by carrying away the ensign staff, He was therefore reduced to the necessity of sinking, as he supposed, or of calling for quarter; and he preferred the latter.

All this time the Bon Homme Richard had sustained the action alone, and the enemy, though much superior in force, would have been very glad to have got clear, as appears by their own acknowledgments, and by their having let go an anchor the instant that I laid them on board, by which means they would have escaped, had I not made them well fast to the Bon Homme Richard.

At last, at half-past 9 o'clock, the Alliance appeared, and I now thought the battle at an end; but, to my utter astonishment, he discharged a broadside full into the stern of the Bon Homme Richard. We called to him for God's sake to forbear firing into the Bon Homme Richard; yet he passed along the off side of the ship, and continued firing. There was no possibility of his mistaking the enemy's ship for the Bon Homme Richard, there being the most essential difference in their appearance and construction; besides, it was then full moonlight, and the side of the Bon Homme Richard were all black, while the sides of the prizes were yellow; yet, for the greater security, I showed the signal of our reconnoissance by putting out three lanterns, one at the head (bow), another at the stern, (quarter), and the third in the middle in a horizontal line.

Every tongue cried that he was firing into the wrong ship, but nothing availed. He passed round, firing into the Bon Homme Richard's head, stern, and broadside; and by one of his volleys killed several of my best men, and mortally wounded a good officer on the forecastle.

My situation was really deplorable. The Bon Homme Richard received various shot under water from the Alliance, the leak gained on the pumps, and the fire increased much on board both ships. Some officers persuaded me to strike, of whose courage and good sense I entertain a high opinion. My treacherous master-at-arms let loose all my prisoners without my knowledge, and my prospect became gloomy indeed. I would not, however, give up the point. The enemy's main-mast began to shake, their firing decreased, ours rather increased, and the British colors were struck at half an hour past 10 o'clock.

This prize proved to be the British ship of war the Serapis, a new ship of 44 guns, built on their most approved construction, with two complete batteries, one of them of 18-pounders, and commanded by the brave Commodore Richard Pearson. I had yet two enemies to encounter far more formidable than the Britons,—I mean fire and water. The Serapis was attacked only by the first, but the Bon Homme Richard was assailed by both. There were five feet of water in the hold, and, though it was moderate from the explosion of so much gunpowder, the three pumps that remained could with difficulty only keep the water from gaining. Fire broke out in various parts of the ship, in spite of all the water that could be thrown to quench it, and at length broke out as low as the powder magazine, and within a few inches of the powder.

In that dilemma I took out the powder upon deck, ready to be thrown overboard at the last extremity; and it was ten o'clock the next day, the 24th, before the fire was entirely extinguished. With respect to the situation of the Bon Homme Richard, the rudder was cut entirely off the stern frame, and the transoms were almost entirely cut away; the timbers, by the lower deck especially, from the main-mast to the stern, being greatly decayed with age, were mangled beyond my power of description; and a person must have been an eye-witness to form a just idea of the tremendous scene of carnage, wreck, and ruin that everywhere appeared. Humanity cannot but recoil from the prospect of such finished horror, and lament that war should produce such fatal consequences.

After the carpenters, as well as Captain de Cottineau, and other men of sense, had well examined and surveyed the ship (which was not finished before five in the evening), I found every person to be convinced that it was impossible to keep the Bon Homme Richard afloat so as to reach a port if the wind should increase, it being then only a very moderate breeze. I had but little time to remove my wounded, which now became unavoidable, and which was effected in the course of the night and next morning. I was determined to keep the Bon Homme Richard afloat, and, if possible, to bring her into port. For that purpose the first lieutenant of the Pallas continued on board with a party of men to attend the pumps, with boats in waiting ready to take them on board in case the water should gain on them too fast. The wind augmented in the night and the next day, on the 25th, so that it was impossible to prevent the good old ship from sinking. They did not abandon her till after 9 o'clock. The water was then up to the lower deck, and a little after ten I saw with inexpressible grief the last glimpse of the Bon Homme Richard. No lives were lost with the ship, but it was impossible to save the stores of any sort whatever. I lost even the best part of my clothes, books, and papers; and several of my officers lost all their clothes and effects...

We this day anchored here [off the Texel, Holland], having since the action been tossed to and fro by contrary winds. I wished to have gained the Road of Dunkirk on account of our prisoners, but was over-ruled by the majority of my colleagues. I shall hasten up to Amsterdam; and there, if I meet with no orders for my government, I will take the advice of the French ambassador. It is my present intention to have the Countess of Scarborough ready to transport the prisoners from hence to Dunkirk, unless it should be found more expedient to deliver them to the English ambassador, taking his obligation to send to Dunkirk, &c., immediately an equal number of American prisoners. I am under strong apprehensions that our object here will fail, and that through the imprudence of M. de Chaumont, who has communicated everything he knew or thought on the matter to persons who cannot help talking of it at a full table. This is the way he keeps state secrets, though he never mentioned the affair to me.

Arnold's Treason (Lecky)

Title: Arnold's Treason
Author: William E. H. Lecky
Date: 1780
Source: Great Epochs in American History, Vol.3, pp.172-181

In September, 1780, a terrible shock was given to the confidence of their army by the discovery of the treachery of Benedict Arnold. To anyone who attentively follows the letters of Washington, it will appear evident that there was no officer in the American army of whom for a long period he wrote in terms of higher, warmer, and more frequent eulogy. Arnold was in truth an eminently brave and skil-ful soldier, and in the early stages of the struggle his services had been of the most distinguished kind. In conjunction with Colonel Allen, he had obtained the first great success of the war by capturing Ticonderoga and Crown Point in the summer of 1775. He had fallen wounded leading the forlorn hope against Quebec on the memorable day on which Montgomery was killed. In the gallant stand that was made at Ticonderoga in October, 1776, he had been placed at the head of the American fleet, and his defense of Lake Champlain against overwhelming odds had been one of the most brilliant episodes of the whole American war. He took a leading part in the campaign which ended with the capitulation of Saratoga, led in person that fierce attack on the British lines on October 7, 1777, which made the position of Burgoyne a hopeless one, was himself one of the first men to enter the British lines, and fell severely wounded at the head of his troops. No American soldier had shown a more reckless courage. Hardly any had displayed greater military skill or possest to a higher degree the confidence of the army; and if the wound he received near Saratoga had proved fatal, Benedict Arnold would have now ranked among the very foremost in the hagiology of American patriotism.

There were men, however, in Congress who greatly disliked him, and seemed to feel a peculiar pleasure in humiliating him; and in February, 1777, when Congress appointed five major-generals, Arnold was not on the list, tho every one of the officers was his junior in standing. Washington was extremely displeased at this marked slight shown to one who, as he truly said, had "always distinguished himself as a judicious, brave officer, of great activity, enterprise, and perseverance." The letters of Arnold show how keenly he felt the wrong, and he spoke seriously of throwing up his commission, but was dissuaded by Washington. A few months later he displayed the most splendid daring in a skirmish with the English near Danbury, and his horse fell pierced by no less than nine bullets. Congress then granted him the promotion that had been hitherto withheld, and presented him with a horse as a token of his conspicuous gallantry, but he never regained his seniority. The wound which he had received near Sara-toga was painful and disabling, and he for a long time could only move about with assistance. Being incapable of taking an active part in the war, Washington placed him in command at Philadelphia after that city had been evacuated by the English, and he there fell under new and powerful influences. His first wife had died in the summer of 1775, when he was in the midst of his Northern campaign, and, in April, 1779, after a long courtship, he married Miss Shippen, a young lady of great beauty and attraction, who belonged to one of the leading families in Philadelphia, and to a family of Tory sympathies. He loved her deeply and faithfully and there is something inexpressibly touching in the tender affection and the undeviating admiration for her husband, which she retained through all the vicissitudes of his dark and troubled life.

He mixt much in the best society at Philadelphia, and altho the more decided loyalists had been driven into exile, the social atmosphere was still very Tory, and many of the best and most respected citizens were secretly sighing for the overthrow of what they regarded as the revolutionary tyranny, and for a return to the settled condition of the past. He kept open house, plunged into expenses far greater than he could meet, and, like many other American officers, entered into several enterprises which were not military. He speculated largely. He took part in various commercial undertakings. He had shares in privateering expeditions, but his speculations do not appear to have been successful, and he was sinking rapidly into debt. Party spirit ran furiously at Philadelphia, and Arnold, who had nothing of the tact and self-control of Washington, soon made many enemies.

A long series of charges against him were laid before Congress, some of them deeply affecting his honor, and amounting to little short of an imputation of swindling, while others were of the most trivial description. Congress referred the matter to a committee, which reported in favor of Arnold; but, in spite of this report, Congress insisted on sending Arnold, on some of the charges, before a court-martial. The proceedings were greatly delayed, and nearly a year passed between the promulgation of the charges and the final decision, and during all this time the commander of the chief town in the States, and one of the most distinguished generals in the American service, was kept in a condition of the most painful and humiliating suspense. He resented it fiercely, and was little mollified by the result of the court-martial. On all the graver charges he was acquitted, and he was condemned only on two counts of the most petty character. He had exceeded his powers in giving a passport to a vessel containing American property which was in Philadelphia while that town was occupied by the English, and he had, on one occasion, employed public wagons to convey some of his private property. This, the court-martial said, ought not to have been done," tho Arnold had no design of employing the wagons otherwise than at his own private expense, nor of defrauding the public, nor of injuring or impeding the public service." For these two offenses he was condemned to the great humiliation of a formal and a public reprimand.

Washington, who was obliged to execute the sentence of the court-martial, did the utmost in his power to mitigate the blow, and nothing could be more skilful than the language with which he made his reprimand the vehicle of a high eulogy on the services and the character of Arnold. While the sentence of the court-martial was in suspense, another stroke had fallen which affected both his fortune and his reputation. During his command in Canada, he had often acted as commissary and quartermaster. Much public money had passed through his hands, and he had large claims upon Congress. His accounts were examined at great length, and after great delay, by the Board of Treasury and by the committee of Congress, they were found to be in much confusion, which was possibly due to the hurry and turmoil of an active campaign, and a large part of the claims of Arnold were disallowed. How far the sentence was just, it is now impossible to say…

Early in 1779 he had sent some letters to Clinton under the name of Gustavus, in which, without revealing his name or his rank, and without making any positive overtures, he had exprest his dislike to the French alliance, and had from time to time given the British commander pieces of authentic intelligence. On the English side the correspondence was chiefly conducted under a false name by Major Andre, the Adjutant General of the British army, a young officer of singular promise and popularity. After the sentence of the court-martial, Arnold appears at last to have fully determined to go over to the English, and he was equally determined not to go over as a mere insignificant and isolated individual. Ambition, cupidity, and revenge must all be gratified. At Saratoga he had done much to ruin the British cause. He would now undo, and more than undo, his work, annihilate by an act of skilful treachery the only considerable army in the North, restore America to peace and to British rule, and make himself the Monk of the Revolution.

Few great plots have more nearly succeeded. Tho there had been murmurs about the leniency of Arnold to Tories and about the admission of Tories into his society, his fidelity to the American cause seems to have been quite unsuspected, and Washington especially looked upon him with the most perfect confidence. On the plea that his wound was not yet sufficiently cured, Arnold excused himself from serving actively with Washington in the field, but he asked for and easily obtained the command of West Point, which included all the American forts in the highlands, and was the essential key of the whole American position. he arrived at West Point in the first week of August, and lost very little time in concerting with Clinton for a surrender of the post to the British.

Clinton has been absurdly blamed for listening to these overtures, but he only acted as any general of any nation would have acted, and he would have deserved the gravest censure if he had neglected such an opportunity of bringing to an end the desolation and the bloodshed of the war. It was necessary to send a confidential agent to arrange the details of the surrender and the terms of the bargain, and this task was committed to Andre. Arnold invited him to come within the American lines, but both Clinton and Andre himself positively declined the proposal, and Clinton was determined that nothing should be done that could bring Andre under the category of a spy. A British sloop called the Vulture, with Andre on board, sailed up the Hudson River to within a few miles of the American camp; and Washington having just left the camp on a visit to the French commander at Hartford, a boat, with muffled oars, was sent by Arnold a little before midnight to the Vulture to bring Andre to shore. The boatmen were wholly ignorant of the nature of their mission. They were furnished with a passport authorizing them to pass freely with a flag of truce, but they were told that it was of public interest that the expedition should be secret.

Arnold and Andre met at a lonely spot on the bank of the river. The meeting was on the night of September 21. Andre wore his uniform, covered by a blue great-coat, and the spot where the interview took place was outside the American lines, so that if they had been arrested there, Andre could not have been treated otherwise than as a prisoner of war. The nights, however, were still short, and the daylight having dawned before the affair was fully arranged, it became necessary either to leave it unfinished and risk the dangers of a second interview, or else to seek some place of concealment. Arnold then induced Andre to enter the American lines and take shelter in the house of a man named Smith, who was devoted to the American General, and who had already been employed to bring Andre to shore. He remained there during the day, and in the evening, all being arranged, Andre prepared to return.

In the meantime, however, the Vulture had been noticed with suspicion by the American soldiers, and had been compelled to change her position in consequence of a cannon which was brought to bear on her. The risk of carrying Andre back by water was so great that Smith refused to incur it, and the only chance of safety was to return by land to New York, a distance of about thirty miles. To accomplish this object Andre exchanged his British uniform for a civilian's dress; he obtained from Arnold a pass enabling him under the name of John Anderson to traverse the American lines, and he concealed in his boots unsigned papers written by Arnold containing such full and detailed information as would enable Clinton without difficulty to seize the fortifications of West Point. On the evening of the 22d he passed the American lines in safety under the guidance of Smith, and slept in a house beyond them, and the next day he set out alone to complete his journey. It is strange to thinkhow largely the course of modern history depended upon that solitary traveler, for had Andre reached New York, the plot would almost certainly have succeeded, and the American Revolution been crusht. He had not, however, proceeded far, when he was stopt by three young men, who were playing cards near the road. They have been called militiamen, but appear, according to better accounts, to have been members of a party who were engaged in cattle stealing for their own benefit. Had Andre produced at once his pass, he would probably have been allowed to proceed in safety, but in the confusion of the moment he believed that the men were British, and he proclaimed himself a British officer. Finding his mistake, he then produced his pass, but his captors at once proceeded to search him, and tho they found little or no money, they discovered the papers in his boots, and altho Andre promised that they would obtain a large reward if they released him, or took him to New York, they determined to carry him to the nearest American outpost. Colonel Jamieson, who commanded there, recognized the handwriting of Arnold, but he did not realize the treachery of his chief, and he sent a letter to Arnold, informing him that papers of a very compromising character had been found on a person just arrested, who carried a pass signed by the General. The papers were sent on to Washington, who was now returning from Hartford.

Arnold was expecting the arrival of Washington, and his house was filled with company when the letter, announcing the arrest of Andre, arrived. For a moment he is said to have changed countenance, but he quickly recovered himself, rose from the table, and telling his guests that he had an immediate call to visit one of the forts at the opposite side of the river, he ordered a horse to be at once brought to the door. He called his wife upstairs, and, after a short interview, left her in a fainting condition, mounted his horse, galloped at full speed down the steep descent to the river, and, springing into a barge, ordered the boatmen to row him to the middle of the stream. They obeyed his command, and he then told them to row swiftly to the Vulture. He was going there, he said, with a flag of truce, and as he must be back in time to receive Washington, there was not a moment to be lost. As he passed the American batteries he waved a white handkerchief as a sign of truce, and in a short time, and before any rumors of his treason were abroad, he stood on the deck under the British flag.

Arnold's Treason (Washington and Greene)

Title: Arnold's Treason
Author: George Washington and Nathaniel Greene
Date: 1780
Source: America, Vol.3, pp.282-285

Goaded as by what he regarded as the injustice of Congress in ordering Washington to publicly rebuke him for having abused his military authority and for favoring Tories, although a court-martial had acquitted him of intentional wrongdoing, Benedict Arnold, one of the bravest and most capable officers in the American army, conspired to surrender the important fortress of West Point to the British. On September 23, 1780, three days before Washington wrote the first of the accompanying documents to Colonel Nathaniel Wade, the plot was frustrated by the capture of the British go-between, Major Andre. On the following day Washington sent the second communication, from his Headquarters at the Robinson house, across the Hudson from West Point, to Congress.

"The gentlemen of Arnold's [staff] family" were Colonels Varick and Franck, who, with the Joshua Smith mentioned by Washington, were acquitted of conspiring with Arnold.

G ENERAL ARNOLD is gone to the enemy. I have just received a line from him, in-closing one to Mrs. Arnold, dated on board the Vulture. From this circumstance, and Colonel Lamb's being detached on some business, the command of the garrison for the present devolves upon you. I request you will be as vigilant as possible, and as the enemy may have it in contemplation to attempt some enterprise, even to-night, against these posts, I wish you to make, immediately after receipt of this, the best disposition you can of your force, so as to have a proportion of men in each work on the west side of the river. You will see or hear from me further to-morrow.

I HAVE the honor to inform Congress that I arrived here [his headquarters in the New York Highlands] at about twelve o'clock on my return from Hartford. Some hours previous to my arrival General Arnold went from his quarters, which were this place, and, as it was supposed, over the river to the garrison at West Point, whither I proceeded myself, in order to visit the post.

I found General Arnold had not been there during the day, and on my return to his quarters he was still absent. In the meantime a packet had arrived from Lieutenant Colonel Jameson, announcing the capture of a John Anderson who was endeavoring to go to New York with several interesting and important papers, all in the handwriting of General

Arnold. This was also accompanied with a letter from the prisoner, avowing himself to be Major John Andre, Adjutant to the British army, relating the manner of his capture, and endeavoring to show that he did not come under the description of a spy. From these several circumstances, and information that the general seemed to be thrown into some degree of agitation, on receiving a letter a little time before he went from his quarters, I was led to conclude immediately that he had heard of Major Andre's captivity, and that he would, if possible, escape to the enemy, and accordingly took such measures as appeared the most probable to apprehend him. But he had embarked in a barge and proceeded down the river, under a flag, to the Vulture ship of war, which lay at some miles below Stony and Verplank's Points.

He wrote me a letter after he got on board. Major Andre is not arrived yet, but I hope he is secure, and that he will be here to-day.

I have been and am taking precaution which I trust will prove effectual, to prevent the important consequences which this conduct on the part of General Arnold was intended to produce. I do not know the party that took Major Andre, but it is said that it consisted of only a few militia, who acted in such a manner upon the occasion, as does them the highest honor, and proves them to be men of great virtue. As soon as I know their names, I shall take pleasure in transmitting them to Congress. I have taken such measures with respect to the gentlemen of General Arnold's family, as prudence dictated; but from everything that has hitherto come to my knowledge, I have the greatest reason to believe they are perfectly innocent. I early secured Joshua H. Smith, the person mentioned in the close of General Arnold's letter, and find him to have had considerable share in this business.

GENERAL NATHANIEL GREENE'S
ADDRESS TO THE ARMY

TREASON of the blackest dye was yesterday discovered. General Arnold, who commanded at West Point, lost to every sense of honor, of private and public obligation, was about to deliver up that important post into the hands of the enemy. Such an event must have given the American cause a dangerous, if not a fatal wound; but the treason has been timely discovered, to prevent the fatal misfortune. The providential train of circumstances which led to it affords the most convincing proof that the liberties of America are the object of Divine protection. At the same time that the treason is to be regretted, the general cannot help congratulating the army on the happy discovery.

Our enemies, despairing of carrying their point by force, are prac-
ticing every base art to effect by bribery and corruption what they cannot accomplish in a manly way. Great honor is due to the American
army that this is the first instance of treason of the kind, where many
were to be expected from the nature of the dispute. The brightest orna-
ment in the character of the American soldiers is their having been
proof against all the arts and seductions of an insidious enemy. Arnold
has made his escape to the enemy, but Major Andre, the Adjutant General in the British army, who came out as a spy, is our prisoner.

His Excellency the Commander-in-Chief, has arrived at West Point
from Hartford, and is no doubt taking proper measures to unravel fully
so hellish a plot.

Andre, Facing Execution, Writes to Washington

Title: Andre, Facing Execution, Writes to Washington
Author: John Andre
Date: 1780
Source: America, Vol.3, pp.286-290

The Andre episode is one of the most painful in Revolutionary history.
Major John Andre, a British officer of high character and standing, representing the British General, Sir Henry Clinton, met General Benedict
Arnold, in secret, to arrange the betrayal of West Point, with its stores
and magazines, including nearly the whole stock of powder of the American army. After the meeting near West Point Andre was on his way
down the Hudson to New York when captured at Tarrytown. Incriminat-
ing documents found on his person brought about his trial, conviction
and military execution as a spy, on October 2, 1780.

The first of these letters was written by Major Andre to General Washington on September 24th, the day after his capture. As an appendix to
the letter is a paper drawn up by Andre recounting the facts of the case.
The concluding letter was written by Andre to Washington on the eve of
his execution.

WHAT I have as yet said concerning myself was in the justifiable attempt to be extricated; I am too little accustomed to
duplicity to have succeeded.

I beg your Excellency will be persuaded that no alteration in the
temper of my mind, or apprehension for my safety, induces me to take

the step of addressing you, but that it is to rescue myself from an imputation of having assumed a mean character for treacherous purposes or self-interest; a conduct incompatible with the principles that actuate me, as well as with my condition in life.

It is to vindicate my fame that I speak, and not to solicit security.

The person in your possession is Major John Andre, adjutant-general to the British army.

The influence of one commander in the army of his adversary is an advantage taken in war. A correspondence for this purpose I held; as confidential (in the present instance) with his Excellency Sir Henry Clinton.

To favor it, I agreed to meet upon ground not within the posts of either army, a person who was to give me intelligence; I came up in the Vulture man-of-war for this effect, and was fetched by a boat from the ship to the beach. Being there, I was told that the approach of day would prevent my return, and that I must be concealed until the next night. I was in my regimentals and had fairly risked my person.

Against my stipulation, my intention, and without my knowledge beforehand, I was conducted within one of your posts. Your Excellency may conceive my sensation on this occasion, and will imagine how much more must I have been affected by a refusal to reconduct me back the next night as I had been brought. Thus become a prisoner, I had to concert my escape. I quitted my uniform, and was passed another way in the night, without the American posts, to neutral ground, and informed I was beyond all armed parties and left to press for New York. I was taken at Tarrytown by some volunteers.

Thus, as I have had the honor to relate, was I betrayed (being adjutant-general of the British army) into the vile condition of an enemy in disguise within your posts.

Having avowed myself a British officer, I have nothing to reveal but what relates to myself, which is true on the honor of an officer and a gentleman.

The request I have to make to your Excellency, and I am conscious I address myself well, is, that in any rigor policy may dictate, a decency of conduct towards me may mark, that though unfortunate I am branded with nothing dishonorable, as no motive could be mine but the service of my King, and as I was involuntarily an impostor.

Another request is, that I may be permitted to write an open letter to Sir Henry Clinton, and another to a friend for clothes and linen.

I take the liberty to mention the condition of some gentlemen at Charleston, who, being either on parole or under protection, were engaged in a conspiracy against us. Though their situation is not similar, they are objects who may be set in exchange for me, or are persons whom the treatment I receive might affect.

It is no less, Sir, in a confidence of the generosity of your mind, than on account of your superior station, that I have chosen to importune you with this letter. I have the honor to be, with great respect, Sir, your Excellency's most obedient humble servant.

* * * * *

ON the 20th of September, I left New York to get on board the Vulture, in order (as I thought) to meet General Arnold there in the night. No boat, however, came off, and I waited on board until the night of the 21st. During the day, a flag of truce was sent from the Vulture to complain of the violation of a military rule in the instance of a boat having been decoyed on shore by a flag, and fired upon. The letter was addressed to General Arnold, signed by Captain Sutherland, but written in my hand and countersigned "J. Anderson, secretary." Its intent was to indicate my presence on board the Vulture. In the night of the 21st a boat with Mr. Smith and two hands came on board, in order to fetch Mr. Anderson on shore, and, if too late to bring me back, to lodge me until the next night in a place of safety. I went into the boat, landed, and spoke with Arnold. I got on horseback with him to proceed to Smith's house, and in the way passed a guard I did not expect to see, having Sir Henry Clinton's directions not to go within an enemy's post, or to quit my own dress.

In the morning A. quitted me, having himself made me put the papers I bore between my stockings and feet. Whilst he did it, he expressed a wish in case of any accident befalling me, that they should be destroyed, which I said, of course would be the case, as when I went into the boat I should have them tied about with a string and a stone. Before we parted, some mention had been made of my crossing the river, and going by another route; but, I objected much against it, and thought it was settled that in the way I came I was also to return.

Mr. Smith to my great mortification persisted in his determination of carrying me by the other route; and, at the decline of the sun, I set out on horseback, passed King's Ferry, and came to Crompond, where a party of militia stopped us and advised we should remain. In the morning I came with Smith as far as within two miles and a half of Pine's Bridge, where he said he must part with me, as the Cowboys infested the road thenceforward. I was now near thirty miles from Kingsbridge, and left to the chance of passing that space undiscovered. I got to the neighborhood of Tarrytown, which was far beyond the points described as dangerous, when I was taken by three volunteers, who, not satisfied with my pass, rifled me, and, finding papers, made me a prisoner.

I have omitted mentioning, that, when I found myself within an enemy's posts, I changed my dress.

* * * * *

BUOYED above the terror of death, by the consciousness of a life devoted to honorable pursuits, and stained with no action that can give me remorse, I trust that the request I make to your Excellency at this serious period, and which is to soften my last moments, will not be rejected.

Sympathy towards a soldier will surely induce your Excellency and a military tribunal to adapt the mode of my death to the feelings of a man of honor.

Let me hope, Sir, that if aught in my character impresses you with esteem towards me, if aught in my misfortunes marks me as the victim of policy and not of resentment, I shall experience the operation of these feelings in your breast, by being informed that I am not to die on a gibbet.

I have the honor to be your Excellency's most obedient and most humble servant.

The Execution of Andre

Title: The Execution of Andre
Author: General William Heath
Date: 1780
Source: America, Vol.3, pp.291-294

General Heath, a witness of the hanging of Andre, had been assigned to the command of the Hudson River posts in 1779, and except for a short interval remained there until the close of the war. His memoirs, from which this account, dated October 2, 1780, was taken, were published in 1798 by authority of Congress.

The hanging of Andre took place at Tappan, a hamlet in Rockland County, south of Nyack, New York. A monument, erected there by Cyrus W. Field, has several times been partly destroyed and then restored. A tablet to Andre's memory was placed in Westminster Abbey early in the nineteenth century, and in 1821 his body was disinterred at Tappan and conveyed to Westminster Abbey.

MAJOR ANDRE is no more among the living. I have just witnessed his exit. It was a tragical scene of the deepest interest. During his confinement and trial, he exhibited those proud and elevated sensibilities which designate greatness and dignity of mind. Not a murmur or a sigh ever escaped him, and the civilities and attentions bestowed on him were politely acknowledged.

Having left a mother and two sisters in England, he was heard to mention them in terms of the tenderest affection, and in his letter to Sir Henry Clinton, he recommends them to his particular attention.

The principal guard officer who was constantly in the room with the prisoner, relates that when the hour of his execution was announced to him in the morning, he received it without emotion, and while all present were affected with silent gloom, he retained a firm countenance, with calmness and composure of mind. Observing his servant enter the room in tears, he exclaimed, "Leave me till you can show yourself more manly."

His breakfast being sent to him from the table of General Washington, which had been done every day of his confinement, he partook of it as usual, and having shaved and dressed himself, he placed his hat on the table, and cheerfully said to the guard officers, "I am ready at any moment, gentlemen, to wait on you."

The fatal hour having arrived, a large detachment of troops was paraded, and an immense concourse of people assembled; almost all our general and field officers, excepting his Excellency and his staff, were present on horseback; melancholy and gloom pervaded all ranks, and the scene was affectingly awful. I was so near during the solemn march to the fatal spot, as to observe every movement, and share in every emotion which the sad scene was calculated to produce.

Major Andre walked from the stone house, in which he had been confined, between two of our subaltern officers, arm in arm; the eyes of the immense multitude were fixed on him, who, rising superior to the fears of death, appeared as if conscious of the dignity which he displayed.

He betrayed no want of fortitude, but retained a complacent smile on his countenance, and politely bowed to several gentlemen whom he knew, which was respectfully returned. It was his earnest desire to be shot, as being the mode of death most fitting to the feelings of a military man, and he had indulged the hope that his request would be granted.

At the moment, therefore, when suddenly he came in view of the gallows, he involuntarily started backwards, and made a pause. "Why this emotion, sir?" said an officer by his side. Instantly recovering his composure, he said, "I am reconciled to my death, but I detest the mode." While waiting and standing near the gallows, I observed some degree of trepidation; placing his foot on a stone, and rolling it over and choking in his throat, as if attempting to swallow.

So soon, however, as he perceived that things were in readiness, he stepped quickly into the wagon, and at this moment he appeared to shrink, but instantly elevating his head with firmness, he said, "It will be but a momentary pang," and he took from his pocket two white handkerchiefs; the provost marshal with one loosely pinioned his arms, and with the other, the victim, after taking off his hat and stock, bandaged his own eyes with perfect firmness, which melted the hearts, and moistened the cheeks, not only of his servant, but of the throng of spectators.

When the rope was appended to the gallows, he slipped the noose over his head and adjusted it to his neck, without the assistance of the awkward executioner. Colonel Scammel now informed him that he had an opportunity to speak, if he desired it; he raised the handkerchief from his eyes and said, "I pray you to bear me witness that I meet my fate like a brave man.

The wagon being now removed from under him, he was suspended and instantly expired; it proved indeed "but a momentary pang." He was dressed in his royal regimentals and boots, and his remains, in the same dress, were placed in an ordinary coffin, and interred at the foot of the gallows; and the spot was consecrated by the tears of thousands. Thus died in the bloom of life, the accomplished Major Andre, the pride of the royal army.

The Last Days of the Revolution

Title: The Last Days of the Revolution
Author: James Madison
Date: 1780
Source: America, Vol.3, pp.295-300

Madison was at this time a young Virginia lawyer who had graduated, nine years earlier, from Princeton College. Already he had been a delegate, in 1770, to the Revolutionary convention of Virginia and was a member of the first Legislature elected under the Virginia Constitution.

This review of the final events and battles of the war, which was rapidly approaching its end at Yorktown, was written while Madison was a member of the Continental Congress sitting in Philadelphia. Later he cooperated with Alexander Hamilton and John Jay in producing the famous publication known as the Federalist, which powerfully influenced popular opinion in favor of the Constitution. About thirty of the eighty odd papers of that work are attributed to him.

THE insuperable difficulties which opposed a general conquest of America seemed as early as the year 1779 to have been felt by the enemy, and to have led them into the scheme of directing their operations and views against the Southern States only. Clinton accordingly removed with the principal part of his force from New York to South Carolina, and laid siege to Charleston, which, after an honorable resistance, was compelled to surrender to a superiority of force. Our loss in men, besides the inhabitants of the town, was not less than two thousand. Clinton returned to New York. Cornwallis was left with about five thousand troops to pursue his conquests. General Gates was appointed to the command of the Southern department, in place of Lincoln, who commanded in Charleston at the time of its capitulation. He met Cornwallis on the 16th of August, 1780, near Camden, in the upper part of South Carolina and on the border of North Carolina. A general action ensued, in which the American troops were defeated with considerable loss, though not without making the enemy pay a good price for their victory. Cornwallis continued his progress into North Carolina, but afterwards retreated to Camden.

The defeat of Gates was followed by so general a clamor against him, that it was judged expedient to recall him. Greene was sent to succeed in the command. About the time of his arrival at the army, Cornwallis, having been reinforced from New York, resumed his enterprise into North Carolina. A detachment of his best troops was totally defeated by Morgan with an inferior number, and consisting of a major

All material contained herein was extracted from the
US Constitution Coach Kit at PowerThink.com
(Over 60,000 Works & Documents of American History)

part of militia detached from Greene's army. Five hundred were made prisoners, between two and three hundred killed and wounded, and about the like number escaped. This disaster, instead of checking the ardor of Cornwallis, afforded a new incentive to a rapid advance, in the hope of recovering his prisoners. The vigilance and activity, however, of Morgan, secured them. Cornwallis continued his pursuit as far as the Dan river, which divides North Carolina from Virginia. Greene, whose inferior force obliged him to recede this far before the enemy, received such succors of militia on his entering Virginia that the chase was reversed. Cornwallis, in his turn, retreated precipitately. Greene overtook him on his way to Wilmington, and attacked him. Although the ground was lost on our side, the British army was so much weakened by the loss of five or six hundred of their best troops, that their retreat towards Wilmington suffered little interruption.

Greene pursued as long as any chance of reaching his prey remained, and then, leaving Cornwallis on his left, took an oblique direction towards Camden, which, with all the other posts in South Carolina except Charleston and Ninety-Six, have, in consequence, fallen again into our possession. His army lay before the latter when we last heard from him. It contained seven or eight hundred men and large quantities of stores. It is nearly two hundred miles from Charleston, and, without some untoward accident, cannot fail of being taken. Greene has detachments all over South Carolina, some of them within a little distance of Charleston; and the resentments of the people against their late insolent masters ensure him all the aids they can give in reestablishing the American Government there. Great progress is also making in the redemption of Georgia.

As soon as Cornwallis had refreshed his troops at Wilmington, abandoning his Southern conquests to their fate, he pushed forward into Virginia. The parricide Arnold had a detachment at Portsmouth when he lay on the Dan; Philips had reinforced him so powerfully from New York, that the junction of the two armies at Petersburg could not be prevented. The whole force amounted to about six thousand men. The force under the Marquis de Lafayette, who commanded in Virginia, being greatly inferior, did not oppose them, but retreated into Orange and Culpeper in order to meet General Wayne, who was on his way from Pennsylvania to join him. Cornwallis advanced northward as far as Chesterfield, in the county of Caroline, having parties at the same time at Page's warehouse and other places in its vicinity. A party of horse, commanded by Tarleton, was sent with all the secrecy and celerity possible to surprise and take the General Assembly and Executive who had retreated from Richmond to Charlottesville. The vigilance of a young gentleman who discovered the design and rode express to Charlottesville prevented a complete surprise. As it was, several delegates were caught, and the rest were within an hour of sharing the same fate. Among the captives was Colonel Lyon of Hanover. Mr. Kinlock, a member of Congress from South Carolina, was also caught at Mr. John Walker's, whose daughter he had married some time before. Governor Jefferson had a very narrow escape. The members of the Government rendezvoused at Stanton, where they soon made a House.

Mr. Jefferson's year having expired, he declined a reelection, and General Nelson has taken his place. Tarleton's party retreated with as much celerity as it had advanced. On the junction of Wayne with the Marquis and the arrival of militia, the latter faced about and advanced rapidly on Cornwallis, who retreated to Richmond, and thence precipitately to Williamsburg, where he lay on the 27th ultimo. The Marquis pursued, and was at the same time within twenty miles of that place. One of his advanced parties had had a successful skirmish within six miles of Williamsburg. Bellini has, I understand, abided patiently in the college the dangers and inconveniences of such a situation. I do not hear that the consequences have condemned the experiment. Such is the present state of the war in the Southern Department.

In the Northern, the operations have been for a considerable time in a manner suspended. At present, a vigorous siege of New York by General Washington's army, aided by five or six thousand French troops under Count de Rochambeau, is in contemplation, and will soon commence. As the English have the command of the water, the result of such an enterprise must be very uncertain. It is supposed, however, that it will certainly oblige the enemy to withdraw their force from the Southern States, which may be a more convenient mode of relieving them than by marching the troops from New York at this season of the year to the southward. On the whole, the probable conclusion of this campaign is, at this juncture, very flattering, the enemy being on the defensive in every quarter...

The great advantage the enemy have over us lies in the superiority of their navy, which enables them continually to shift the war into defenseless places, and to weary out our troops by long marches. The squadron sent by our ally to our support did not arrive till a reinforcement on the part of the enemy had counteracted their views. They have been almost constantly blocked up at Rhode Island by the British fleet. The effects of a hurricane in the last spring on the latter gave a temporary advantage to the former, but circumstances delayed the improvement of it till the critical season was past. Mr. Destouches, who commanded the French fleet, nevertheless hazarded an expedition into Chesapeake Bay. The object of it was to cooperate with the Marquis de Lafayette in an attack against Arnold, who lay at Portsmouth with about fifteen hundred British troops. Had he got into the bay, and taken a favorable station, the event would certainly have been adequate to our hopes. Unfortunately, the British fleet, which followed the French immediately from Rhode Island, reached the capes of Virginia first. On the arrival of the latter, a regular and fair combat took place. It lasted for several hours, and ended rather in favor of our allies. As the enemy, however, were nearest the capes, and one of the French ships had lost her rudder, and was otherwise much damaged, the commander thought it best to relinquish his object, and return to his former station. The damage sustained by the enemy, according to their own representation, exceeded that of the French; and as their number of ships and weight of metal were both superior, it does great honor to the gallantry and good conduct of Mr. Destouches. Congress, and indeed the public at large, were so sensible of this, that their particular thanks were given him on the occasion.

Washington's Services in the War

Title: Washington's Services in the War
Author: William E. H. Lecky
Source: Great Epochs in American History, Vol.3, pp.200-203

To the appointment of Washington, far more than to any other single circumstance, is due the ultimate success of the American Revolution, tho in purely intellectual powers, Washington was certainly inferior to Franklin, and perhaps to two or three other of his colleagues. There is a theory which once received the countenance of some considerable physiologists, tho it is now, I believe, completely discarded, that one of the great lines of division among man may be traced to the comparative development of the cerebrum and the cerebellum. To the first organ it was supposed belong those special gifts or powers which make men poets, orators, thinkers, artists, conquerors, or wits. To the second belong the superintending, restraining, discerning, and directing faculties which enable men to employ their several talents with sanity and wisdom, which maintain the balance and the proportion of intellect and character, and make sound judgments and well-regulated lives. The theory, however untrue in its physiological aspect, corresponds to a real distinction in human minds and characters, and it was especially in the second order of faculties that Washington excelled. His mind was not quick or remarkably original. His conversation had no brilliancy or wit. He was entirely without the gift of eloquence, and he had very few accomplishments. He knew no language but his own, and except for a rather strong turn for mathematics, he had no taste which can be called purely intellectual. There was nothing in him of the meteor or the cataract, nothing that either dazzled or overpowered. A courteous and hospitable country gentleman, a skilful farmer, a very keen sportsman, he probably differed little in tastes and habits from the better members of the class to which he belonged; and it was in a great degree in the administration of a large estate and in assiduous attention to county and provincial business that he acquired his rare skill in reading and managing men.

As a soldier the circumstances of his career brought him into the blaze, not only of domestic, but of foreign criticism, and it was only very gradually that his superiority was fully recognized. Lee, who of all American soldiers had seen most service in the English army, and Conway, who had risen to great repute in the French army, were both accustomed to speak of his military talents with extreme disparagement; but personal jealousy and animosity undoubtedly colored their judgments. Kalb, who had been trained in the best military schools of the Continent, at first pronounced him to be very deficient in the strength, decision, and promptitude of a general; and, altho he soon learned to form the highest estimate of his military capacity, he continued to lament that anexcessive modesty led him too frequently to act upon the opinion of inferior men, rather than upon his own most excellent judgment. In the army and the Congress more than one rival was opposed to him. He had his full share of disaster; the operations which he conducted, if compared with great European wars, were on a very small scale; and he had the immense advantage of encountering in most cases generals of singular incapacity.

It may, however, be truly said of him that his military reputation steadily rose through many successive campaigns, and before the end of the struggle he had outlived all rivalry, and almost all envy. He had a thorough knowledge of the technical part of his profession, a good eye for military combinations, an extraordinary gift of military administration. Punctual, methodical, and exact in the highest degree, he excelled in managing those minute details which are so essential to the efficiency of an army, and he possest to an eminent degree not only the common courage of a soldier, but also that much rarer form of courage which can endure long-continued suspense, bear the weight of great responsibility, and encounter the risks of misrepresentation and unpopularity. For several years, and usually in the neighborhood of superior forces, he commanded a perpetually fluctuating army, almost wholly destitute of discipline and respect for authority, torn by the most violent personal and provincial jealousies, wretchedly armed, wretchedly clothed, and sometimes in imminent danger of starvation.

In civil as in military life, he was preeminent among his contemporaries for the clearness andsoundness of his judgment, for his perfect moderation and self-control, for the quiet dignity and the indomitable firmness with which he pursued every path which he had deliberately chosen. Of all the great men in history he was the most invariably judicious, and there is scarcely a rash word or action or judgment recorded of him. Those who knew him well, noticed that he had keen sensibilities and strong passions; but his power of self-command never failed him, and no act of his public life can be traced to personal caprice, ambition, or resentment. In the despondency of long-continued failure, in the elation of sudden success, at times when his soldiers were deserting by hundreds and when malignant plots were formed against his reputation, amid the constant quarrels, rivalries, and jealousies of his subordinates, in the dark hour of national ingratitude, and in the midst of the most universal and intoxicating flattery, he was always the same calm, wise, just, and single-minded man, pursuing the course which he believed to be right, without fear or favor or fanaticism; equally free from the passions that spring from interest, and from the passions that spring from imagination. He never acted on the impulse of an absorbing or uncalculating enthusiasm, and he valued very highly fortune, position, and reputation; but at the command of duty he was ready to risk and sacrifice them all. He was in the highest sense of the words a gentleman and a man of honor, and he carried into public life the severest standard of private morals.

The Battle of Yorktown

Title: The Battle of Yorktown
Author: General Charles Cornwallis
Date: 1781
Source: America, Vol.3, pp.301-306

Out of the many journals and letters written by participants in the Virginia campaign, this account of the battle and capitulation of York town, addressed by Cornwallis to the British Commander-in-Chief in America, Sir Henry Clinton, is given as the official statement of the defeated general. It was dated from York town, October 20, 1781.

Cornwallis had served under Clinton at the reduction of Charleston, S. C., the year before, and subsequently had defeated Gates at Camden, S. C., and Greene at Guilford Court House, N. C., before sweeping against Lafayette in Virginia. The trap laid by Lafayette in conjunction with Washington and Rochambeau on land, aided by a French fleet under De Grasse, was sprung, and Cornwallis, to escape annihilation, surrendered on October 19—virtually ending the Revolutionary War.

I HAVE the mortification to inform your Excellency that I have been forced to give up the Posts of York and Gloucester, and to surrender the troops under my command, by capitulation, on the 19th instant, as prisoners of war to the combined forces of America and France.

I never saw this post in a very favorable light, but when I found I was to be attacked in it in so unprepared a state, by so powerful an army and artillery, nothing but the hopes of relief would have induced me to attempt its defense, for I would either have endeavored to escape to New York by rapid marches from the Gloucester side, immediately on the arrival of General Washington's troops at Williamsburg, or I would, notwithstanding the disparity of numbers, have at tacked them in the open field, where it might have been just possible that fortune would have favored the gallantry of the handful of troops under my command, but being assured by your Excellency's letters that every possible means would be tried by the navy and army to relieve us, I could not think myself at liberty to venture upon either of those desperate attempts; therefore, after remaining for two days in a strong position in front of this place in hopes of being attacked, upon observing that the enemy were taking measures which could not fail of turning my left flank in a short time, and receiving on the second evening your letter of the 24th of September, informing me that the relief would sail about the 5th of October, I withdrew within the works on the night of the 29th of September, hoping by the labor and firmness of the soldiers to protract the defense until you could arrive. Everything was to be expected from the spirit of the troops, but every disadvantage attended their labor, as the works were to be continued under the enemy's fire, and our stock of intrenching tools, which did not much exceed 400 when we began to work in the latter end of August, was now much diminished.

The enemy broke ground on the night of the 30th, and constructed on that night, and the two following days and nights, two redoubts, which, with some works that had belonged to our outward position, occupied a gorge between two creeks or ravines, which come from the river on each side of the town. On the night of the 6th of October they made their first parallel, extending from its right on the river, to a deep ravine on the left, nearly opposite to the center of this place, and embracing our whole left at a distance of 600 yards. Having perfected this parallel, their batteries opened on the evening of the 9th against our left, and other batteries fired at the same time against a redoubt advanced over the creek upon our right, and defended by about 120 men of the 23rd regiment and marines, who maintained that post with uncommon gallantry. The fire continued incessant from heavy cannon, and from mortars and howitzers throwing shells from 8 to 16 inches, until all our guns on the left were silenced, our work much damaged, and our loss of men considerable. On the night of the 11th they began their second parallel, about 300 yards nearer to us. The troops being much weakened by sickness, as well as by the fire of the besiegers, and observing that the enemy had not only secured their flanks, but proceeded in every respect with the utmost regularity and caution, I could not venture so large sorties as to hope from them any considerable effect, but otherwise, I did everything in my power to interrupt this work by opening new embrasures for guns and keeping up a constant fire from all the howitzers and small mortars that we could man.

On the evening of the 14th they assaulted and carried two redoubts that had been advanced about 300 yards for the purpose of delaying their approaches, and covering our left flank, and during the night included them in their second parallel, on which they continued to work with the utmost exertion. Being perfectly sensible that our works could not stand many hours after the opening of the batteries of that parallel, we not only continued a constant fire with all our mortars and every gun that could be brought to bear upon it, but a little before daybreak on the morning of the 16th, I ordered a sortie of about 350 men, under the direction of Lieut.-Colonel Abercrombie, to attack two batteries which appeared to be in the greatest forwardness, and to spike the guns. A detachment of Guards with the 80th company of Grenadiers, under the command of Lieut.-Colonel Lake, attacked the one, and one of light infantry, under the command of Major Armstrong, attacked the other, and both succeeded in forcing the redoubts that covered them, spiking 11 guns, and killing or wounding about 100 of the French troops, who had the guard of that part of the trenches, and with little loss on our side.

This action, though extremely honorable to the officers and soldiers who executed it, proved of little public advantage, for the cannon having been spiked in a hurry, were soon rendered fit for service again, and before dark the whole parallel and batteries appeared to be nearly complete. At this time we knew that there was no part of the whole front attacked on which we could show a single gun, and our shells were nearly expended. I, therefore, had only to choose between preparing to surrender next day, or endeavoring to get off with the greatest part of the troops, and I determined to attempt the latter...

In this situation, with my little force divided, the enemy's batteries opened at daybreak. The passage between this place and Gloucester was much exposed, but the boats having now returned, they were ordered to bring back the troops that had passed during the night, and they joined us in the forenoon without much loss. Our works, in the meantime, were going to ruin, and not having been able to strengthen them by an abattis, nor in any other manner but by a slight fraizing, which the enemy's artillery were demolishing wherever they fired, my opinion entirely coincided with that of the engineer and principal officers of the army, that they were in many places assailable in the forenoon, and that by the continuance of the same fire for a few hours longer, they would be in such a state as to render it desperate, with our numbers, to attempt to maintain them. We at that time could not fire a single gun; only one 8-inch and little more than 100 Cohorn shells remained. A diversion by the French ships of war that lay in the mouth of York River was to be expected.

Our numbers had been diminished by the enemy's fire, but particularly by sickness, and the strength and spirits of those in the works were much exhausted, by the fatigue of constant watching and unremitting duty. Under all these circumstances, I thought it would have been wanton and inhuman to the last degree to sacrifice the lives of this small body of gallant soldiers, who had ever behaved with so much fidelity and courage, by exposing them to an assault which, from the numbers and precautions of the enemy, could not fail to succeed. I therefore proposed to capitulate; and I have the honor to enclose to your Excellency the copy of the correspondence between General Washington and me on that subject, and the terms of capitulation agreed upon. I sincerely lament that better could not be obtained, but I have neglected nothing in my power to alleviate the misfortune and distress of both officers and soldiers. The men are well clothed and provided with necessaries, and I trust will be regularly supplied by the means of the officers that are permitted to remain with them.

The treatment, in general, that we have received from the enemy since our surrender has been perfectly good and proper, but the kindness and attention that has been shown to us by the French officers in particular—their delicate sensibility of our situation—their generous and pressing offer of money, both public and private, to any amount— has really gone beyond what I can possibly describe, and will, I hope, make an impression on the breast of every British officer, whenever the fortune of war should put any of them into our power.

Washington Reports the Yorktown Surrender

Title: Washington Reports the Yorktown Surrender
Author: George Washington
Date: 1781
Source: America, Vol.3, pp.307-309

This report to Congress of the surrender of Cornwallis was written by Washington in the Moore house near Yorktown, Va., October 19, 1781, where the terms of surrender had been dictated earlier in the day. Curiously enough, General Benjamin Lincoln, who the year before had surrendered Charleston, S. C., to Cornwallis, was chosen by Washington to receive Cornwallis's sword at Yorktown. The terms at Yorktown were the same as those at Charleston.

Cornwallis, whom ill health confined to his headquarters in York town, was represented on the momentous occasion by General O'Hara, of his staff. The courtesy and generosity of the victorious allies have been warmly attested by the British commander, who was tendered an elaborate dinner by General Washington, at which all the staff officers of the French, British and American military and naval forces were present.

IHAVE the honor to inform Congress that a reduction of the British army, under the command of Lord Cornwallis, is most happily effected. The unremitted ardor, which actuated every officer and soldier in the combined army on this occasion, has principally led to this important event at an earlier period than my most sanguine hopes had induced me to expect.

The singular spirit of emulation, which animated the whole army from the first commencement of our operations, has filled my mind with the highest pleasure and satisfaction, and had given me the happiest presages of success.

On the 17th instant, a letter was received from Lord Cornwallis, proposing a meeting of commissioners to consult on terms for the surrender of the posts of York and Gloucester. This letter (the first which had passed between us) opened a correspondence, a copy of which I do myself the honor to enclose; that correspondence was followed by the definitive capitulation, which was agreed to and signed on the 19th, a copy of which is also herewith transmitted and which, I hope, will meet the approbation of Congress.

I should be wanting in the feelings of gratitude, did I not mention on this occasion, with the warmest sense of acknowledgment, the very cheerful and able assistance which I have received in the course of our operation from his Excellency the Count de Rochambeau and all his officers of every rank in their respective capacities. Nothing could equal the zeal of our allies, but the emulating spirit of the American officers, whose ardor would not suffer their exertions to be exceeded.

The very uncommon degree of duty and fatigue, which the nature of the service required from the officers and engineers and artillery of both armies, obliges me particularly to mention the obligations I am under to the commanding and other officers of those corps.

I wish it was in my power to express to Congress how much I feel myself indebted to the Count de Grasse and the officers of the fleet under his command, for the distinguished aid and support which has been afforded by them, between whom and the army the most happy concurrence of sentiments and views has subsisted, and from whom every possible cooperation has been experienced, which the most harmonious intercourse could afford.

Articles of Capitulation, Yorktown

Title: Articles of Capitulation, Yorktown
Author: The U.S. and British Governments
Date: 1781
Source: Harvard Classics, Vol.43, p.180

The surrender of Cornwallis, arranged in these articles, virtually brought to a close the hostilities in the war between Great Britain and her American colonies, and assured the independence of the United States.

Settled between his Excellency General Washington, Commander-in-Chief of the combined Forces of America and France; his Excellency the Count de Rochambeau, Lieutenant-General of the Armies of the King of France, Great Cross of the royal and military Order of St. Louis, commanding the auxiliary Troops of his Most Christian Majesty in America; and his Excellency the Count de Grasse, Lieutenant-General of the Naval Armies of his Most Christian Majesty, Commander of the Order of St. Louis, Commander-in-Chief of the Naval Army of France in the Chesapeake, on the one Part; and the Right Honorable Earl Cornwallis, Lieutenant-General of his Britannic Majesty's Forces, commanding the Garrisons of York and Gloucester; and Thomas Symonds, Esquire, commanding his Britannic Majesty's Naval Forces in York River in Virginia, on the other Part.

ARTICLE I. The garrisons of York and Gloucester, including the officers and seamen of his Britannic Majesty's ships, as well as other mariners, to surrender themselves prisoners of war to the combined forces of America and France. The land troops to remain prisoners to the United States, the navy to the naval army of his Most Christian Majesty.

Granted.

ARTICLE II. The artillery, arms, accoutrements, military chest, and public stores of every denomination, shall be delivered unimpaired to the heads of departments appointed to receive them.

Granted.

ARTICLE III. At twelve o'clock this day the two redoubts on the left flank of York to be delivered, the one to a detachment of American infantry, the other to a detachment of French grenadiers.

Granted.

The garrison of York will march out to a place to be appointed in front of the posts, at two o'clock precisely, with shouldered arms, colors cased, and drums beating a British or German march. They are then to ground their arms, and return to their encampments, where they will remain until they are despatched to the places of their destination. Two works on the Gloucester side will be delivered at one o'clock to a detachment of French and American troops appointed to possess them. The garrison will march out at three o'clock in the afternoon; the cavalry with their swords drawn, trumpets sounding, and the infantry in the manner prescribed for the garrison of York. They are likewise to return to their encampments until they can be finally marched off.

ARTICLE IV. Officers are to retain their side-arms. Both officers and soldiers to keep their private property of every kind; and no part of their baggage or papers to be at any time subject to search or inspection. The baggage and papers of officers and soldiers taken during the siege to be likewise preserved for them.

Granted.

It is understood that any property obviously belonging to the inhabitants of these States, in the possession of the garrison, shall be subject to be reclaimed.

ARTICLE V. The soldiers to be kept in Virginia, Maryland, or Pennsylvania, and as much by regiments as possible, and supplied with the same rations of provisions as are allowed to soldiers in the service of America. A field-officer from each nation, to wit, British, Anspach, and Hessian, and other officers on parole, in the proportion of one to fifty men to be allowed to reside near their respective regiments, to visit them frequently, and be witnesses of their treatment; and that their officers may receive and deliver clothing and other necessaries for them, for which passports are to be granted when applied for.

Granted.

ARTICLE VI. The general, staff, and other officers not employed as mentioned in the above articles, and who choose it, to be permitted to go on parole to Europe, to New York, or to any other American maritime posts at present in the possession of the British forces, at their own option; and proper vessels to be granted by the Count de Grasse to carry them under flags of truce to New York within ten days from this date, if possible, and they to reside in a district to be agreed upon hereafter, until they embark. The officers of the civil department of the army and navy to be included in this article. Passports to go by land to be granted to those to whom vessels cannot be furnished.

Granted.

ARTICLE VII. Officers to be allowed to keep soldiers as servants, according to the common practice of the service. Servants not soldiers are not to be considered as prisoners, and are to be allowed to attend their masters.

Granted.

ARTICLE VIII. The Bonetta sloop-of-war to be equipped, and navigated by its present captain and crew, and left entirely at the disposal of Lord Cornwallis from the hour that the capitulation is signed, to receive an aid-de-camp to carry despatches to Sir Henry Clinton; and such soldiers as he may think proper to send to New York, to be permitted to sail without examination. When his despatches are ready, his Lordship engages on his part, that the ship shall be delivered to the order of the Count de Grasse, if she escapes the dangers of the sea. That she shall not carry off any public stores. Any part of the crew that may be deficient on her return, and the soldiers passengers, to be accounted for on her delivery.

ARTICLE IX. The traders are to preserve their property, and to be allowed three months to dispose of or remove them; and those traders are not to be considered as prisoners of war.

The traders will be allowed to dispose of their effects, the allied army having the right of preemption. The traders to be considered as prisoners of war upon parole:

ARTICLE X. Natives or inhabitants of different parts of this country, at present in York or Gloucester, are not to be punished on account of having joined the British army.

This article cannot be assented to, being altogether of civil resort.

ARTICLE XI. Proper hospitals to be furnished for the sick and wounded. They are to be attended by their own surgeons on parole; and they are to be furnished with medicines and stores from the American hospitals.

The hospital stores now at York and Gloucester shall be delivered for the use of the British sick and wounded. Passports will be granted for procuring them further supplies from New York, as occasion may require; and proper hospitals will be furnished for the reception of the sick and wounded of the two garrisons.

ARTICLE XII. Wagons to be furnished to carry the baggage of the officers attending the soldiers, and to surgeons when travelling on account of the sick, attending the hospitals at public expense.

They are to be furnished if possible.

ARTICLE XIII. The shipping and boats in the two harbours, with all their stores, guns, tackling, and apparel, shall be delivered up in their present State to an officer of the navy appointed to take possession of them, previously unloading the private property, part of which had been on board for security during the siege.

Granted.

ARTICLE XIV. No article of capitulation to be infringed on pretence of reprisals; and if there be any doubtful expressions in it, they are to be interpreted according to the common meaning and acceptation of the words.

Granted.

Done at Yorktown, in Virginia, October 19th, 1781.

CORNWALLIS,

THOMAS SYMONDS.

Done in the Trenches before Yorktown, in Virginia, October 19th, 1781.

GEORGE WASHINGTON,

LE COMTE DE ROCHAMBEAU,

LE COMTE DE BARRAS,

En mon nom & celui du

COMTE DE GRASSE.

Explaining the Treaty of Paris

Title: Explaining the Treaty of Paris
Author: Adams, Franklin, Jay and Laurens
Date: 1782
Source: America, Vol.4, pp.42-47

This is the official statement made by the four American ministers plenipotentiary to Robert R. Livingston, then superintendent of foreign affairs, of the conditions of the preliminary treaty. This document is dated Paris, December 14, 1782. The treaty it describes was made definitive on September 3, 1783, and thus ended the Revolutionary War. Simultaneously Great Britain made peace with France and Spain at Versailles.

As finally concluded the treaty recognized the Mississippi as the western boundary of the United States, and the Great Lakes and the St. Lawrence as the northern boundary to the forty-fifth parallel. Americans were to enjoy practically the same fishing rights as the colonists had. Collection of debts was to be facilitated by both governments, and confiscations were to cease. The navigation of the Mississippi was declared free to both Britons and Americans. Featuring the negotiations leading to the recognition of American independence was the skill, talent and patience of the American commissioners.

WE have the honor to congratulate Congress on the signature of the preliminaries of a peace between the Crown of Great Britain and the United States of America, to be inserted in a definitive treaty so soon as the terms between the Crowns of France and Great Britain shall be agreed on. A copy of the articles is here inclosed, and we cannot but flatter ourselves that they will appear to Congress, as they do to all of us, to be consistent with the honor and interest of the United States, and we are persuaded Congress would be more fully of that opinion, if they were apprised of all the circumstances and reasons which have influenced the negotiation. Although it is impossible for us to go into that detail, we think it necessary, nevertheless, to make a few remarks on such of the articles as appear most to require elucidation.

REMARKS ON ARTICLE 2ND,
RELATIVE TO BOUNDARIES.

The Court of Great Britain insisted on retaining all the territories comprehended within the Province of Quebec, by the act of Parliament respecting it. They contended that Nova Scotia should extend to the River Kennebec; and they claimed not only all the lands in the western country and on the Mississippi, which were not expressly included in our charters and governments, but also such lands within them as remained ungranted by the King of Great Britain. It would be endless to enumerate all the discussions and arguments on the subject.

We knew this Court and Spain to be against our claims to the western country, and having no reason to think that lines more favorable could ever have been obtained, we finally agreed to those described in this article; indeed, they appear to leave us little to complain of, and not much to desire. Congress will observe, that although our northern line is in a certain part below the latitude of forty-five, yet in others it extends above it, divides the Lake Superior, and gives us access to its western and southern waters, from which a line in that latitude would have excluded us.

REMARKS ON ARTICLE 4TH, RESPECTING CREDITORS.

We had been informed that some of the States had confiscated British debts; but although each State has a right to bind its own citizens, yet, in our opinion, it appertains solely to Congress, in whom exclusively are vested the rights of making war and peace, to pass acts against the subjects of a power with which the confederacy may be at war. It therefore only remained for us to consider whether this article is founded in justice and good policy.

In our opinion, no acts of government could dissolve the obligations of good faith resulting from lawful contracts between individuals of the two countries prior to the war. We knew that some of the British creditors were making common cause with the refugees and other adversaries of our independence; besides, sacrificing private justice to reasons of state and political convenience is always an odious measure; and the purity of our reputation in this respect, in all foreign commercial countries, is of infinitely more importance to us than all the sums in question. It may also be remarked that American and British creditors are placed on an equal footing.

REMARKS ON ARTICLE 5TH AND 6TH, RESPECTING REFUGEES.

These articles were among the first discussed and the last agreed to. And had not the conclusion of this business at the time of its date been particularly important to the British administration, the respect which both in London and Versailles is supposed to be due to the honor, dignity and interest of royalty, would probably have forever prevented our bringing this article so near to the views of Congress and the sovereign rights of the States as it now stands. When it is considered that it was utterly impossible to render this article perfectly consistent, both with American and British ideas of honor, we presume that the middle line adopted by this article, is as little unfavorable to the former as any that could in reason be expected.

As to the separate article, we beg leave to observe, that it was our policy to render the navigation of the River Mississippi so important to Britain as that their views might correspond with ours on that subject. Their possessing the country on the river north of the line from the Lake of the Woods affords a foundation for their claiming such navigation. And as the importance of West Florida to Britain was for the same reason rather to be strengthened than otherwise, we thought it advisable to allow them the extent contained in the separate article, especially as before the war it had been annexed by Britain to West Florida, and would operate as an additional inducement to their joining with us in agreeing that the navigation of the river should forever remain open to both. The map used in the course of our negotiations was Mitchell's.

As we had reason to imagine that the articles respecting the boundaries, the refugees and fisheries did not correspond with the policy of this Court, we did not communicate the preliminaries to the minister until after they were signed; (and not even then the separate article). We hope that these considerations will excuse our having so far deviated from the spirit of our instructions. The Count de Vergennes, on perusing the articles appeared surprised, (but not displeased), at their being so favorable to us.

We beg leave to add our advice, that copies be sent us of the accounts directed to be taken by the different States, of the unnecessary devastations and sufferings sustained by them from the enemy in the course of the war. Should they arrive before the signature of the definitive treaty, they might possibly answer very good purposes.

The Meaning of American Democracy

Title: The Meaning of American Democracy
Author: Francois Jean, Marquis de Chastellux
Date: 1782
Source: America, Vol.4, pp.61-76

In his "Travels in America During the Years 1780-81-82," Chastellux, who was a major-general in the French army under Rochambeau and was present at the surrender of Cornwallis at Yorktown, recounts his interesting experiences and observations in this country. He wrote voluminously about America during and directly after the Revolution, and his writings all display the intelligent sympathy apparent in this extract from a letter addressed to Professor Madison, father of President Madison.

Chastellux draws what is regarded as a remarkably accurate picture of the United States in its formative critical period. Other of his written work was highly praised by Voltaire, who is said to have ranked it above that of Montesquieu.

IF...we form an idea of the American Republic we must be careful not to confound the Virginians, whom warlike as well as mercantile, an ambitious as well as speculative genius brought upon the continent, with the New Englanders who owe their origin to enthusiasm; we must not expect to find precisely the same men in Pennsylvania, where the first colonists thought only of keeping and cultivating the deserts, and in South Carolina where the production of some exclusive articles fixes the general attention on external commerce, and establishes unavoidable connections with the old world. Let it be observed, too, that agriculture which was the occupation of the first settlers, was not an adequate means of assimilating the one with the other, since there are certain species of culture which tend to maintain the equality of fortune, and others to destroy it.

These are sufficient reasons to prove that the same principles, the same opinions, the same habits do not occur in all the thirteen United States, although they are subject nearly to the same force [sort?] of government. For, notwithstanding that all their constitutions are not similar, there is through the whole a democracy, and a government of representation, in which the people give their suffrage by their delegates. But if we choose to overlook those shades which distinguish this confederated people from each other; if we regard the thirteen States only as one nation, we shall even then observe that she must long retain the impression of those circumstances, which have conducted her to liberty. Every philosopher acquainted with mankind, and who has studied the springs of human action, must be convinced that, in the present revolution, the Americans have been guided by two principles, while they imagined they were following the impulse of only one. He will distinguish, a positive and a negative principle, in their legislation, and in their opinions.

I call that principle positive which in so enlightened a moment as the present reason alone could dictate to a people making choice of that government which suited them the best; I call that a negative principle which they oppose to the laws and usages of a powerful enemy for whom they had contracted a well founded aversion. Struck with the example of the inconveniences offered by the English government, they had recourse to the opposite extreme, convinced that it was impossible to deviate from it too much...

In England, a septennial Parliament invites the King to purchase a majority on which he may reckon for a long period; the American assemblies therefore must be annual; on the other side of the water, the executive power, too uncontrolled in its action, frequently escapes the vigilance of the legislative authority; on this continent, each officer, each minister of the people must be under the immediate dependence of the assemblies, so that his first care on attaining office, will be to court the popular favor for a new election. Among the English, employments confer, and procure rank and riches, and frequently elevate their possessors to too great a height: among the Americans, offices neither conferring wealth, nor consideration, will not, it is true, become objects of intrigue or purchase, but they will be held in so little estimation as to make them avoided, rather than sought after, by the most enlightened citizens, by which means every employment will fall into the hands of new and untried men, the only persons who can expect to hold them to advantage.

In continuing to consider the thirteen United States under one general point of view, we shall observe still other circumstances which have influenced as well the principles of the government, as the national spirit. These thirteen States were at first colonies; now the first necessity felt in all rising colonies is population; I say in rising colonies, for I doubt much whether that necessity exists at present, so much as is generally imagined. Of this however I am very sure, that there will still be a complaint of want of population, long after the necessity has ceased; Americans will long continue to reason as follows: we must endeavor to draw foreigners among us, for which purpose it is indispensably necessary to afford them every possible advantage; every person once within the State, shall be considered therefore as a member of that State, as a real citizen. Thus one year's residence in the same place shall suffice to establish him an inhabitant, and every inhabitant shall have the right of voting, and shall constitute a part of the sovereign power; from whence it will result that this sovereignty will communicate and divide itself without requiring any pledge, any security from the person who is invested with it. This has arisen from not considering the possibility of other emigrants than those from Europe, who are supposed to fix themselves in the first spot where they may form a settlement; we shall one day, however, see frequent emigrations from State to State; workmen will frequently transplant themselves, many of them will be obliged even to change situations from the nature of their employments, in which case it will not be singular to see the elections for a district of Connecticut, decided by inhabitants of Rhode Island or New York.

Some political writers, especially the more modern, have advanced, that property alone should constitute the citizen. They are of opinion that he alone whose fortune is necessarily connected with its welfare has a right to become a member of the State. In America, a specious answer is given to this reasoning; among us, say they, landed property is so easily acquired, that every workman who can use his hands, may be looked upon as likely soon to become a man of property. But can America remain long in her present situation? And can the regimen of her infant state agree with her, now she has assumed the virile robe?

The following, Sir, is a delicate question which I can only propose to a philosopher like you. In establishing among themselves a purely democratic government, had the Americans a real affection for a democracy, And if they have wished all men to be equal, is it not solely, because, from the very nature of things, they were themselves nearly in that situation? For to preserve a popular government in all its integrity, it is not sufficient, not to admit either rank or nobility, riches alone never fail to produce marked differences, by so much the greater, as there exist no others. Now such is the present happiness of America that she has no poor, that every man in it enjoys a certain ease and independence, and that if some have been able to obtain a smaller portion of them than others, they are so surrounded by resources, that the future is more looked to, than their present situation. Such is the general tendency to a state of equality; that the same enjoyments which would be deemed superfluous in every other part of the world, are here considered as necessaries... Now, Sir, let us suppose that the increase of population may one day reduce your artisans to the situation in which they are found in France and England. Do you in that case really believe that your principles are so truly democratic, as that the landholders and the opulent, will still continue to regard them as their equals?... I shall ask you then, whether under the belief of possessing the most perfect democracy, you may not find that you have insensibly attained a point more remote from it, than every other Republic... Now observe, Sir, that in your present form of government, you have not attached either sufficient grandeur, or dignity to any place, to render its possessor illustrious, still less the whole class from which he may be chosen. You have thrown far from you all hereditary honors, but have you bestowed sufficient personal distinctions? Have you reflected that these distinctions, far from being less considerable than those which took place among the Greeks and Romans, ought rather to surpass them? The reason of this is very obvious: the effect of honors and distinctions is by so much the more marked, as it operates on the greater number of men assembled together... Men must be moved by some fixed principle; is it not better that this should be by vanity than interest? I have no doubt that love of country will always prove a powerful motive, but do not flatter yourself that this will long exist with the same spirit. The greatest efforts of the mind, like those of the body, are in resistance; and the same may happen with respect to the State, as in matters of opinion, to which we cease to be attached, when they cease to be contested.

The Cost of the War

Title: The Cost of the War
Author: Richard Hildreth
Date: 1775-1783
Source: Great Epochs in American History, Vol.3, p.204-208

The independence of the United States had not been achieved except at very heavy cost. Not to dwell on the manifold calamities of the war—towns burned, the country ravaged, the frontiers attacked by the Indians, property plundered by the enemy or imprest for the public service, citizens called out to serve in the militia or drafted into the regular army, nakedness, disease, and sometimes hunger in the camp, the miseries of the hospitals, the horrors of the British prison ships—worse than all, the remorseless fury and rancorous vindictiveness of civil hatred; besides all this, the mere pecuniary cost of the war had imposed a very heavy burden, amounting to not much less than a hundred and seventy millions of dollars—a greater outlay, in proportion to the wealth of the country, than ten times as much would be at the present moment. Of this sum two-thirds had been expended by Congress, and the balance by the individual States. It had been raised in four ways: by taxes under the disguise of a depreciating currency; by taxes directly imposed; by borrowing; and by running in debt.

Of the two hundred millions issued by Congress in Continental bills of credit, eighty-eight millions, received into the State treasuries in payment of taxes at the rate of forty for one, had been replaced by bills of the "new tenor," to the amount of four millions four hundred thousand dollars, bearing interest at six per cent. Massachusetts, New Hampshire, and Rhode Island had thus taken up and redeemed their entire quota of the old paper. Connecticut, Delaware, the Carolinas, and Georgia had taken up none; the remaining States but a part of their quota. Besides the bills thus redeemed, near forty millions were in the Federal treasury. As to the outstanding seventy millions, there was no thought of redeeming or funding them at any higher rate than seventy-five or a hundred for one. Many of these bills were in the State treasuries, into which they had come in payment of taxes; but a large amount remained also in the hands of individuals.

The depreciation and subsequent repudiation of this paper had imposed a tax upon the country to the amount of perhaps seventy millions of specie dollars—a tax very unequal and unfair in its distribution, falling heaviest on the ignorant and helpless; the source in private business of numberless frauds, sanctioned, in fact, by the laws of the States, which had continued to make the bills a legal tender after they had fallen to a tenth, a twentieth, and even a fortieth part of their nominal value. But in what other way could Congress have realized anything like the same sum of money? How else could the war have been carried on at all?

Besides the Continental paper issued by Congress, all the States had put out bills of their own. In some States, as Massachusetts and Pennsylvania, these bills had been called in and fundedat their nominal value. In others, especially at the South, they had been partially redeemed by the issue of land warrants. The remainder had shared the fate of the Continental money, being either suffered to fall dead in the hands of the holders, or being funded at an immense depreciation. No State had made such profuse issues as Virginia, and such of her bills as were not paid in for land warrants were finally funded at the rate of a thousand for one.

Besides the taxes thus indirectly imposed, very heavy direct taxes had been levied, especially toward the conclusion of the war. The amount raised by the States, whether through the medium of repudiated paper or taxes, it is impossible to ascertain with precision, but it probably did not exceed thirty millions of dollars. The remaining seventy millions of the expense of the war still hung over the Confederacy in the shape of debt.

Congress had begun to borrow while the issue of paper was still going on; and after that issue stopt, to borrow and to run in debt became the chief Federal resources. A Federal debt had been thus contracted to the amount of some forty-four millions of dollars, of which about ten millions were due in Europe, principally to the French court. Franklin had signed contracts for the repayment of moneys advanced by France to the amount of thirty-four million livres, about seven million dollars. All the back interest was remitted; the reimbursement of the principal was to be made by instalments, to commence three years after peace. To this sum was to be added the small loan from Spain, the larger one from the French farmers-general, and so much of the Dutchloan as Adams had succeeded in getting subscribed. It was the produce of the subscription to this loan, amounting to about $700,000, which formed the resource of Morris for meeting the treasury notes in which the three months' pay had been advanced to the furloughed soldiers. That fund, however, was soon exhausted, and a considerable number of the bills drawn upon it were likely to come back protested; but, by paying an enormous premium, Adams succeeded in borrowing an additional amount of about $800,000, out of which the bills of Morris were met. The loan in Holland, formerly yielded to the solicitations of Laurens, formed a part of the French debt. It had been lent, in fact, to France for the benefit of the United States. The Federal debt, besides this amount due abroad, included eleven millions and a half, specie value, borrowed on loan-office certificates at home; six millions due to the army for deficiencies and depreciation of pay; five millions due to the officers for the commutation of their half pay for life; and about twelve millions more on unliquidated accounts, including, also, arrears of interest on the loan-office debt, of which but little had been paid since 1781, at which period the French Government had refused to advance any more money for that purpose. These unliquidated accounts included, also, certificates for supplies imprest for the army, and a mass of unsettled claims in the old currency, in all the departments, civil and military, which the officers appointed for that purpose were busy in reducing to specie value. Besides this Federal debt, each State was burdened with a particular debt of its own; the whole together amounting to some twen-ty-five or six millions of dollars, thus raising the total indebtedness of the country, State and Federal, to the beforementioned sum of seventy millions.

One large portion of the wealthy men of colonial times had been expatriated, and another part had been impoverished by the Revolution. In their place a new moneyed class had sprung up, especially in the Eastern States, men who had grown rich in the course of the war s sutlers, by privateering, by speculations in the fluctuating paper money, and by other operations not always of the most honorable kind. Large claims against their less fortunate neighbors had accumulated in the hands of these men, many of whom were disposed to press their legal rights to the utmost.

The fisheries, formerly a chief resource of New England, broken up by the war, had not yet been reestablished. The farmers no longer found that market for their produce which the French, American, and British armies had furnished. There was an abundance of discontented persons more or less connected with the late army, deprived by the peace of their accustomed means of support, and without opportunity to engage in productive industry. The community, from these various causes, was fast becoming divided into two embittered factions of creditors and debtors.

Washington Resigns His Commission To Congress

Title: Washington Resigns His Commission To Congress
Author: Rev. William Gordon, D.D.
Date: 1783
Source: America, Vol.3, pp.310-313

Dr. Gordon was an English minister, who came to America in 1770 and occupied a pulpit at Roxbury, Mass., until 1786, when he returned to England. During the Revolutionary War he sided with the colonists, making careful researches while the war was in progress, and in 1788 published his "History of the Rise and Independence of the United States, Including the Late War," from which this account is derived. It has been considered one of the most valuable sources for the history of the Revolution.

It is probable that during the year preceding the resignation of his commission to Congress on December 23, 1783, Washington, had he so desired, could have founded a monarchy, sustained by his army. He took the course, on the contrary, of quelling this disposition on the part of his soldiers whenever it showed itself.

GENERAL WASHINGTON, after delivering in his accounts, hastened to Annapolis, where he arrived on the evening of the 19th of December. The next day he informed Congress of his arrival in that city, with the intention of asking leave to resign the commission he had the honor of holding in their service, and desired to know their pleasure in what manner it would be most proper to offer his resignation—whether in writing or at an audience. They resolved that it should be at a public audience, the following Tuesday at twelve o'clock. The general had been so reserved with regard to the time of his intended resignation, that Congress had not the least apprehension of its being either so soon or so sudden.

When the day was arrived, and the hour approached for fixing the patriotic character of the American Chief, the gallery was filled with a beautiful group of elegant ladies, and some graced the floor of Congress. On this were likewise the governor, council and legislature of Maryland, several general officers, the consul general of France, and the respectable citizens of Annapolis. Congress were seated and covered, as representatives of the sovereignty of the Union, the spectators were uncovered and standing. The general was introduced to a chair by the secretary, who, after a decent interval, ordered silence. A short pause ensued, when the Honorable Thomas Mifflin, the president, informed the general, that "the United States in Congress assembled were prepared to receive his communications": on which he rose with great dignity, and delivered this address:

"Mr. President, The great events on which my resignation depended having at length taken place, I have now the honor of offering my sincere congratulations to Congress, and of presenting myself before them to surrender into their hands the trust committed to me, and to claim the indulgence of retiring from the service of my country.

"Happy in the confirmation of our independence and sovereignty, and pleased with the opportunity afforded the United States, of becoming a respectable nation, I resign with satisfaction the appointment I accepted with diffidence—a diffidence in my abilities to accomplish so arduous a task; which however was superseded by a confidence in the rectitude of our cause, the support of the supreme power of the Union, and the patronage of Heaven.

"The successful termination of the war has verified the most sanguine expectations; and my gratitude for the interposition of providence, and the assistance I have received from my countrymen, increases with every review of the momentous contest.

"While I repeat my obligations to the army in general, I should do injustice to my own feelings not to acknowledge, in this place, the peculiar services and distinguished merits of the gentlemen who have been attached to my person during the war. It was impossible the choice of confidential officers to compose my family should have been more fortunate. Permit me, sir, to recommend in particular, those who have continued in the service to the present moment, as worthy of the favorable notice and patronage of Congress.

"I consider it as an indispensable duty to close this last act of my official life by commending the interests of our dearest country to the protection of Almighty God, and those who have the superintendence of them to His holy keeping.

"Having now finished the work assigned me, I retire from the great theater of action, and bidding an affectionate farewell to this august body, under whose orders I have so long acted, I here offer my commission, and take my leave of all the employments of public life."

The general was so powerfully impressed, with the great and interesting scenes that crowded in upon his imagination while speaking, that he would have been scarce able to have uttered more than the closing period. He advanced and delivered to the President his commission, with a copy of his address. Having resumed his place, he received in a standing posture the... answer of Congress; which the President delivered with elegance; but not without such a sensibility as changed, and spread a degree of paleness over, his countenance...

Washington Bids His Army Farewell

Title: Washington Bids His Army Farewell
Author: George Washington
Date: November, 1783
Source: America, Vol.3, pp.314-320

The scene which attended Washington's farewell to the rank and file of his army at Rocky Hill, near Princeton, New Jersey, on Sunday, November 2, 1783, was only less affecting than his formal leave-taking with his leading officers at Fraunce's Tavern in New York a month later when

Washington said: "With a heart full of love and gratitude I must now take my leave of you. I most devoutly wish that your latter days may be as prosperous and happy as your former ones have been glorious and honorable... I shall be obliged to you if each will come and take me by the hand." Many of the officers, including Washington, wept audibly.

His much more elaborate address at Princeton, written in the third person, is said to have been prepared by Alexander Hamilton. In tone it is very similar to Washington's splendid letter of June 8, 1783, to the Governors of the States with regard to the necessity of establishing a firm and dignified Federal Government.

THE United States in Congress assembled, after giving the most honorable testimony to the Federal armies, and presenting them with the thanks of their country for their long, eminent and faithful services, having thought proper, by their proclamation bearing date the 18th day of October last, to discharge such part of the troops as were engaged for the war, and to permit the officers on furlough to retire from services from and after to-morrow; which proclamation having been communicated in the public papers for the information and government of all concerned, it only remains for the Commander-in-Chief to address himself once more, and that for the last time, to the armies of the United States (however widely dispersed the in dividuals who compose them may be), and to bid them an affectionate, a long farewell.

But before the Commander-in-Chief takes final leave of those he holds most dear, he wishes to indulge himself a few moments in calling to mind a slight review of the past. He will then take the liberty of exploring with his military friends their future prospects, of advising the general line of conduct, which, in his opinion, ought to be pursued; and he will conclude the address by expressing the obligations he feels himself under for the spirited and able assistance he has experienced from them, in the performance of an arduous office.

A contemplation of the complete attainment (at a period earlier than could have been expected) of the object, for which we contended against so formidable a power, cannot but inspire us with astonishment and gratitude. The disadvantageous circumstances on our part, under which the war was undertaken, can never be forgotten. The singular interpositions of Providence in our feeble condition were such, as could scarcely escape the attention of the most unobserving; while the unparalleled perseverance of the armies of the United States, through almost every possible suffering and discouragement for the space of eight long years, was little short of a standing miracle.

It is not the meaning nor within the compass of this address, to detail the hardship peculiarly incident to our service, or to describe the distresses, which in several instances have resulted from the extremes of hunger and nakedness, combined with the rigors of an inclement season; nor is it necessary to dwell on the dark side of our past affairs. Every American officer and soldier must now console himself for any unpleasant circumstances, which may have occurred, by a recollection of the uncommon scenes in which he has been called to act no inglorious part, and the astonishing events of which he has been a witness; events which have seldom, if ever before, taken place on the stage of human action; nor can they probably ever happen again. For who has before seen a disciplined army formed at once from such raw materials? Who, that was not a witness, could imagine that the most violent local prejudices would cease so soon; and that men, who came from the different parts of the continent, strongly disposed by the habits of education to despise and quarrel with each other, would instantly become but one patriotic band of brothers? Or who, that was not on the spot, can trace the steps by which such a wonderful revolution has been effected, and such a glorious period put to all our warlike toils?

It is universally acknowledged that the enlarged prospects of happiness, opened by the confirmation of our independence and sovereignty, almost exceeds the power of description. And shall not the brave men, who have contributed so essentially to these inestimable acquisitions, retiring victorious from the field of war to the field of agriculture, participate in all the blessings, which have been obtained? In such a republic, who will exclude them from the rights of citizens, and the fruits of their labors? In such a country, so happily circumstanced, the pursuits of commerce and the cultivation of the soil will unfold to industry the certain road to competence. To those hardy soldiers, who are actuated by the spirit of adventure, the fisheries will afford ample and profitable employment; and the extensive and fertile regions of the West will yield a most happy asylum to those, who, fond of domestic enjoyment, are seeking for personal independence. Nor is it possible to conceive that any one of the United States will prefer a national bankruptcy, and a dissolution of the Union, to a compliance with the requisition of Congress, and the payment of its just debts; so that the officers and soldiers may expect considerable assistance, in recomencing their civil occupations, from the public, which must and will most inevitably be paid.

In order to effect this desirable purpose, and to remove the prejudices, which may have taken possession of the minds of any of the good people of the States, it is earnestly recommended to all the troops, that, with strong attachments of the Union, they should carry with them into civil society the most conciliating dispositions, and that they should prove themselves not less virtuous and useful as citizens than they have been persevering and victorious as soldiers. What though there should be some envious individuals who are unwilling to pay the debt the public has contracted, or to yield the tribute due to merit; yet let such unworthy treatment produce no invective, or any instance of intemperate conduct. Let it be remembered that the unbiased voice of the free citizens of the United States has promised the just reward and given the merited applause. Let it be known and remembered that the reputation of the Federal armies is established beyond the reach of malevolence; and let a consciousness of their achievements and fame still incite the men who composed them to honorable actions; under the persuasion that the private virtues of economy, prudence and industry, will not be less amiable in civil life, than more splendid qualities of valor, perseverance, and enterprise were in the field. Every one may rest assured that much, very much, of the future happiness of the officers and men, will depend upon the wise and manly conduct which shall be adopted by them when they are mingled with the great body of the community. And, although the General has so frequently given it as his opinion in the most public and explicit manner, that, unless the principles of the Federal government were properly supported, and the powers of the Union increased, the honor, dignity, and justice of the nation would be lost forever; yet he cannot help repeating, on this occasion, so interesting a sentiment, and leaving it as his last injunction to every officer and soldier, who may view the subject in the same serious point of light, to add his best endeavors to those of his worthy fellow citizens towards effecting these great and valuable purposes, on which our very existence as a nation so materially depends.

The Commander-in-Chief conceives little is now wanting to enable the soldier to change the military character into that of the citizen, but that steady and decent tenor of behavior which has generally distinguished, not only the army under his immediate command, but the different detachments and separate armies, through the course of the war. From their good sense and prudence he anticipates the happiest consequences; and, while he congratulates them on the glorious occasion which renders their services in the field no longer necessary, he wishes to express the strong obligations he feels himself under for the assistance he has received from every class and in every instance. He presents his thanks in the most serious and affectionate manner to the general officers, as well for their counsel, on many interesting occasions, as for their ardor in promoting the success of the plans he had adopted; to the commandants of regiments and corps, and to the other officers for their great zeal and attention in carrying his orders promptly into execution; to the staff for their alacrity and exactness in performing the duties of their several departments; and to the non-commissioned officers and private soldiers for their extraordinary patience and suffering, as well as their invincible fortitude in action. To the various branches of the army, the general takes this last and solemn opportunity of professing his inviolable attachment and friendship. He wishes more than bare professions were in his power; that he were really able to be useful to them all in future life. He flatters himself, however, they will do him the justice to believe, that whatever could with propriety be attempted by him has been done.

And being now to conclude these his last public orders, to take his ultimate leave in a short time of the military character, and to bid a final adieu to the armies he has so long had the honor to command, he can only again offer in their behalf his recommendations to their grateful country, and his prayers to the God of armies. May ample justice be done them here, and may the choicest of Heaven's favors, both here and hereafter, attend those, who, under the Divine auspices, have secured innumerable blessings for others. With these wishes and this benediction, the Commander-in-Chief is about to retire from service. The curtain of separation will soon be drawn, and the military scene to him will be closed forever.

A New World Power

Title: A New World Power
Author: Thomas Pownall
Date: c.1800
Source: America, Vol.4, pp.11-17

At the time Pownall wrote this article, at the beginning of the nineteenth century, he was a Member of Parliament and introduced a bill for making peace with the United States, which he previously had declared were lost forever as English colonies. The bill was defeated, largely because Pownall, although he had attended the Albany Congress in 1754, and had been governor of Massachusetts from 1757 to 1760, was regarded as a visionary. This is the first published prophecy of the future greatness of the United States as a sovereign nation.

Posterity credits Pownall with possessing deep insight in foreseeing, among other things, the future preponderance of the English race in America. He had an instinctive grasp of American political tendencies, and was a supporter of the rights of the colonies.

NORTH AMERICA is become a new primary planet in the system of the world, which while it takes its own course, in its own orbit, must have effect on the orbit of every other planet, and shift the common center of gravity of the whole system of the European world.

North America is de facto an independent power which has taken its equal station with other powers, and must be so de jure. The politicians of the Governments of Europe may reason or negotiate upon this idea, as a matter sub lite. The powers of those Governments may fight about it as a new power coming into establishment; such negotiations, and such wars, are of no consequence either to the right or the fact. It would be just as wise, and just as effectual, if they were to go to war to decide, or set on foot negotiations to settle, to whom for the future the sovereignty of the moon should belong. The moon has been long common to them all, and they may all in their turns profit of her reflected light. The independence of America is fixed as fate; she is mistress of her own fortune; knows that she is so, and will actuate that power which she feels she has, so as to establish her own system, and to change the system of Europe...

If the powers of Europe will view the state of things as they do really exist, and will treat them as being what they are, the lives of thousands may be spared; the happiness of millions may be secured; and the peace of the whole world preserved. If they will not, they will be plunged into a sea of troubles, a sea of blood, fathomless and boundless. The war that has begun to rage betwixt Britain, France and Spain, which is almost gorged betwixt Britain and America, will extend itself to all the maritime, and most likely, afterwards, to all the inland powers of Europe; and like the Thirty Years' War of the sixteenth and seventeenth centuries, will not end, but as that did, by a new and general resettlement of powers and interests, according to the new spirit of the new system which has taken place...

There is nowhere in the European part of the old world such a greatness of interwoven and combined interest, communicating through such largeness of territory, as that in North America, possessed and actuated by the English nation. The northern and southern parts of Europe, are possessed by different a nations, actuated by different spirits, and conducted under very different systems...

On the contrary, when the site and circumstances of the large extended territories of North America are examined, one finds everything united in it which forms greatness of dominions, amplitude and growth of state.

The nature of the coast and of the winds upon that coast, is such as renders marine navigation, from one end of its extent to the other, a perpetually moving intercourse of communion: and the nature of the rivers which open (where marine navigation ends) an inland navigation which, with short interruptions, carries on a circulation throughout the whole, renders such inland navigation but a further process of that communion; all which becomes, as it were, a one vital principle of life, extended through a one organized being...

Whether the islands, in those parts called the West Indies, are naturally parts of this North American communion, is a question, in the detail of it, of curious speculation, but of no doubt as to the fact...

The civilizing activity of the human race, is what forms the growth of state...

In this new world we see all the inhabitants not only free, but allowing an universal naturalization to all who wish to be so; and an uncontrolled liberty of using any mode of life they choose, or any means of getting a livelihood that their talents lead them to. Free of all restraints, which take the property of themselves out of their own hands, their souls are their own, and their reason; they are their own masters, and they act; their labor is employed on their own property, and what they produce is their own. In a country like this, where every man has the full and free exertion of his powers, where every man may acquire any share of the good things thereof, or of interest and power which his spirit can work him up to; there, an unabated application of the powers of individuals, and a perpetual struggle of their spirits, sharpens their wits, and gives constant training to the mind. The acquirement of information in things and business, which becomes necessary to this mode of life, gives the mind, thus sharpened, and thus exercised, a turn of inquiry and investigation which forms a character peculiar to these people, which is not to be met with, nor ever did exist in any other to the same degree, unless in some of the ancient republics, where the people were under the same predicament. This turn of character, which, in the ordinary occurrences of life, is called inquisitiveness, and which, when exerted about trifles, goes even to a degree of ridicule in many instances, is yet, in matters of business and commerce, a most useful and efficient talent...

... In America, the wisdom and not the man is attended to; and America is peculiarly a poor man's country... They find themselves at liberty to follow what mode they like; they feel that they can venture to try experiments, and that the advantages of their discoveries are their own. They, therefore, try what the soil claims, what the climate permits, and what both will produce and sustain to the greatest advantage...

Although the civilizing activity of America does not, by artificial and false helps, contrary to the natural course of things, inconsistent with, and checking the first applications of, its natural labor, and before the community is ripe for such endeavor, attempt to force the establishment of manufactures; yet following, as use and experience lead, the natural progress of improvement, it is every year producing a surplus profit; which surplus, as it enters again into the circulation of productive employment, creates an accumulating accelerated progressive series of surpluses. With these accumulated surpluses of the produce of the earth and seas, and not with manufactures, the Americans carry on their commercial exertions. Their fish, wheat, flour, rice, tobacco, indigo, live stock, barrel pork and beef (some of these articles being peculiar to the country and staple commodities) form the exports of their commerce. This has given them a direct trade to Europe; and, with some additional articles, a circuitous trade to Africa and the West Indies.

The same ingenuity of mechanic handicraft, which arises concomitant with agriculture, does here also rise concomitant with commerce, and is exerted in shipbuilding: it is carried on, not only to serve all the purposes of their own carriage, and that of the West Indies in part, but to an extent of sale, so as to supply great part of the shipping of Britain; and further, if it continues to advance with the same progress, it will supply great part of the trade of Europe also with shipping, at cheaper rates than they can anywhere, or by any means, supply themselves.

Thus their commerce, although subsisting (while they were subordinate provinces) under various restrictions, by its advancing progress in ship-building, has been striking deep root, and is now shot forth an active commerce, growing into amplitude of state and great power...

I will here, therefore, from this comparison of the spirit of civilizing activity in the old and in the new world, as one sees it in its application to agriculture, handicrafts, and mechanics, and finally in an active commerce, spatiating on an amplitude of base, the natural communion of a great country, and rising in a natural progression, venture to assert, that in this point, North America has advanced, and is every day advancing, to growth of state, with a steady and continually accelerating motion, of which there has never yet been any example in Europe.

But farther; when one looks to the progressive population which this fostering happiness does, of course, produce, one cannot but see, in North America, that God's first blessing, "Be fruitful and multiply; replenish the earth and subdue it," has operated in full manifestation of His will…

This might have been, indeed, the spirit of the British Empire, America being a part of it: This is the spirit of the Government of the new Empire of America, Great Britain being no part of it. It is a vitality, liable, indeed, to many disorders, many dangerous diseases; but it is young and strong, and will struggle, by the vigor of internal healing principles of life, against those evils, and surmount them; like the infant Hercules, it will strangle these serpents in its cradle. Its strength will grow with its years, and it will establish its constitution, and perfect adultness in growth of state.

To this greatness of empire it will certainly arise. That it is removed three thousand miles distant from its enemy; that it lies on another side of the globe where it has no enemy; that it is earth-born, and like a giant ready to run its course, are not alone the grounds and reasons on which a speculatist may pronounce this. The fostering care with which the rival powers of Europe will nurse it, ensures its establishment beyond all doubt or danger.

Facing Bankruptcy and Mutiny

Title: Facing Bankruptcy and Mutiny
Author: John Fiske
Date: 1783
Source: America, Vol.4, pp.27-35

The fate of the Republic has never been more precarious than during the period that immediately followed the surrender of Cornwallis at York town. There was no money to pay off the army, and the soldiers were daily becoming more restive and irritated.

Newburgh, New York, was the headquarters of the army from March, 1782, until the latter part of 1783, and it was there that the Newburgh Addresses were circulated, that the army was disbanded, and that Washington received the famous Nicola letter proposing that he become King. There is no doubt, as the historian, Fiske, indicates, but that Washington could have formed a monarchy at this time and been al-most unanimously supported by the army. Its mutinous temper is man-ifested in this review, taken from John Fiske's "Critical Period of American History" and is reprinted here by special arrangement with the publishers, Houghton, Mifflin and Company.

IMPOSSIBLE as Congress found it to fill the quotas of the army, the task of raising a revenue by requisitions upon the States was even more discouraging. Every State had its own war debt, and several were applicants for foreign loans not easy to obtain, so that none could without the greatest difficulty raise a surplus to hand over to Congress. The Continental rag money had ceased to circulate by the end of 1780, and our foreign credit was nearly ruined. The French Government began to complain of the heavy demands which the Americans made upon its exchequer, and Vergennes, in sending over a new loan in the fall of 1782, warned Franklin that no more must be expected. To save American credit from destruction it was at least necessary that the in-terest on the public debt should be paid. For this purpose Congress in 1781 asked permission to levy a five per cent. duty on imports. The modest request was the signal for a year of angry discussion. Again and again it was asked, If taxes could thus be levied by any power outside the State, why had we ever opposed the Stamp Act or the tea duties? The question was indeed a serious one, and as an instance of reasoning from analogy seemed plausible enough. After more than a year Mas-sachusetts consented, by a bare majority of two in the House and one in the Senate, reserving to herself the right of appointing the collectors. The bill was then vetoed by Governor Hancock, though one day too late, and so it was saved. But Rhode Island flatly refused her consent, and so did Virginia, though Madison earnestly pleaded the cause of the public credit. For the current expenses of the government in that same year $9,000,000 were needed. It was calculated that $4,000,000 might be raised by a loan, and the other $5,000,000 were demanded of the States. At the end of the year $422,000 had been collected, not a cent of which came from Georgia, the Carolinas, or Delaware. Rhode Island, which paid $38,000, did the best of all according to its resources. Of the Continental taxes assessed in 1783, only one-fifth part had been paid by the middle of 1785. And the worst of it was that no one could point to a remedy for this state of things, or assign any probable end to it.

Under such circumstances the public credit sank at home as well as abroad. Foreign creditors—even France, who had been nothing if not generous with her loans—might be made to wait; but there were creditors at home who, should they prove ugly, could not be so easily put off. The disbandment of the army in the summer of 1783, before the British troops had evacuated New York, was hastened by the impossibility of paying the soldiers and the dread of what they might do under such provocation. Though peace had been officially announced, Hamilton and Livingston urged that, for the sake of appearances if for no other reason, the army should be kept together so long as the British remained in New York, if not until they should have surrendered the western frontier posts. But Congress could not pay the army, and was afraid of it,—and not without some reason. Discouraged at the length of time which had passed since they had received any money, the soldiers had begun to fear lest, now that their services were no longer needed, their honest claims would be set aside... At this critical moment Washington had earnestly appealed to Congress, and against the strenuous opposition of Samuel Adams had at length extorted the promise of half-pay for life. In the spring of 1782, seeing the utter inability of Congress to discharge its pecuniary obligations, many officers began to doubt whether the promise would ever be kept. It had been made before the Articles of Confederation, which required the assent of nine States to any such measure, had been finally ratified. It was well known that nine States had never been found to favor the measure, and it was now feared that it might be repealed or repudiated, so loud was the popular clamor against it.

All this comes of republican government, said some of the officers; too many cooks spoil the broth; a dozen heads are as bad as no head; you do not know whose promises to trust; a monarchy, with a good king whom all men can trust, would extricate us from these difficulties.

In this mood, Colonel Louis Nicola, of the Pennsylvania line, a foreigner by birth, addressed a long and well-argued letter to Washington, setting forth the troubles of the time, and urging him to come forward as a savior of society, and accept the crown at the hands of his faithful soldiers. Nicola was an aged man, of excellent character, and in making this suggestion he seemed to be acting as spokesman of a certain clique or party among the officers—how numerous is not known. Washington instantly replied that Nicola could not have found a person to whom such a scheme could be more odious, and he was at a loss to conceive what he had ever done to have it supposed that he could for one moment listen to a suggestion so fraught with mischief to his country. Lest the affair, becoming known, should enhance the popular distrust of the army, Washington said nothing about it. But as the year went by, and the outcry against half-pay continued, and Congress showed symptoms of a willingness to compromise the matter, the discontent of the army increased. Officers and soldiers brooded alike over their wrongs. "The Army," said General Macdougall, "is verging to that state which, we are told, will make a wise man mad." The peril of the situation was increased by the well-meant but injudicious whisperings of other public creditors, who believed that if the army would only take a firm stand and insist upon a grant of permanent funds to Congress for liquidating all public debts, the States could probably be prevailed upon to make such a grant. Robert Morris, the able Secretary of Finance, held this opinion, and did not believe that the States could be brought to terms in any other way. His namesake and assistant, Gouverneur Morris, held similar views, and gave expression to them in February, 1783, in a letter to General Greene, who was still commanding in South Carolina. When Greene received the letter, he urged upon the legislature of that State, in most guarded and moderate language, the paramount need of granting a revenue to Congress, and hinted that the army would not be satisfied with anything less. The assembly straightway flew into a rage, and shouted, "No dictation by a Cromwell!" South Carolina had consented to the five percent. impost, but now she revoked it, to show her independence; and Greene's eyes were opened at once to the danger of the slightest appearance of military intervention in civil affairs.

At the same time a violent outbreak in the army at Newburgh was barely prevented by the unfailing tact of Washington. A rumor went about the camp that it was generally expected the army would not disband until the question of pay should be settled, and that the public creditors looked to them to make some such demonstration as would overawe the delinquent States. General Gates had lately emerged from the retirement in which, he had been fain to hide himself after Camden, and had rejoined the army, where there was now such a field for intrigue. An odious aroma of impotent malice clings about his memory on this last occasion on which the historian needs to notice him. He plotted in secret with officers of the staff and others. One of his staff, Major Armstrong, wrote an anonymous appeal to the troops, and another, Colonel Barber, caused it to be circulated about the camp. It named the next day for a meeting to consider grievances. Its language was inflammatory. "My friends!" it said, "after seven long years your suffering courage has conducted the United States of America through a doubtful and bloody war; and peace returns to bless—whom? A country willing to redress your wrongs, cherish your worth, and reward your services? Or is it rather a country that tramples upon your rights, disdains your cries, and insults your distresses?… If such be your treatment while the swords you wear are necessary for the defence of America, what have you to expect when those very swords, the instruments and companions of your glory, shall be taken from your sides, and no mark of military distinction left but your wants, infirmities and scars? If you have sense enough to discover and spirit to oppose tyranny, whatever garb it may assume, awake to your situation. If the present moment be lost, your threats hereafter will be as empty as your entreaties now. Appeal from the justice to the fears of government, and suspect the man who would advise to longer forbearance."

Better English has seldom been wasted in a worse cause. Washington, the man who was aimed at in the last sentence, got hold of the paper next day, just in time, as he said, "to arrest the feet that stood wavering on a precipice." The memory of the revolt of the Pennsylvania line, which had so alarmed the people in 1781, was still fresh in men's minds; and here was an invitation to more wholesale mutiny, which could hardly fail to end in bloodshed, and might precipitate the perplexed and embarrassed country into civil war.

Washington issued a general order, recognizing the existence of the manifesto, but overruling it so far as to appoint the meeting for a later day, with the senior major-general who happened to be Gates, to preside. This order, which neither discipline nor courtesy could disregard, in a measure tied Gates's hands, while it gave Washington time to ascertain the extent of the disaffection. On the appointed day he suddenly came into the meeting, and amid profoundest silence broke forth in a most eloquent and touching speech. Sympathizing keenly with the sufferings of his hearers, and fully admitting their claims, he appealed to their better feelings, and reminded them of the terrible difficulties under which Congress labored, and of the folly of putting themselves in the wrong. He still counselled forbearance as the greatest of victories, and with consummate skill he characterized the anonymous appeal as undoubtedly the work of some crafty emissary of the British, eager to disgrace the army which they had not been able to vanquish. All were hushed by that majestic presence and those solemn tones. The knowledge that he had refused all pay, while enduring more than any other man in the room, gave added weight to every word. In proof of the good faith of Congress, he began reading a letter from one of the members, when, finding his sight dim, he paused and took from his pocket the new pair of spectacles which the astronomer David Rittenhouse had just sent him. He had never worn spectacles in public, and as he put them on he said, in his simple manner and with his pleasant smile, "I have grown gray in your service, and now find myself growing blind." While all hearts were softened he went on reading the letter, and then withdrew, leaving the meeting to its deliberations.

There was a sudden and mighty revulsion of feeling. A motion was reported declaring "unshaken confidence in the justice of Congress"; and it was added that "the officers of the American army view with abhorrence and reject with disdain the infamous proposals contained in a late anonymous address to them." The crestfallen Gates, as chairman, had nothing to do but put the question and report it carried unanimously; for if any still remained obdurate they no longer dared to show it. Washington immediately set forth the urgency of the case in an earnest letter to Congress and one week later the matter was settled by an act commuting half-pay for life into a gross sum equal to five years' full pay, to be discharged at once by certificates bearing interest at six percent. Such poor paper was all that Congress had to pay with, but it was all ultimately redeemed; and while the commutation was advantageous to the government, it was at the same time greatly for the interest of the officers, while they were looking out for new means of livelihood, to have their claims adjusted at once, and to receive something which could do duty as a respectable sum of money...

Mutinous Troops Threaten Congress

Title: Mutinous Troops Threaten Congress
Author: Elias Boudinot
Date: 1783
Source: America, Vol.4, pp.36-42

This letter, dated Princeton, New Jersey, July 15, 1783, was written by the president of the Continental Congress to our ministers plenipotentiary, Adams, Franklin and Jay, who were in Paris negotiating the treaty of peace with Great Britain, which concluded the Revolutionary War. It was Boudinot who signed its ratification.

A few days before this letter was written, Congress, being openly defied and menaced by a considerable number of Pennsylvania recruits, who objected to being discharged from the army without pay, had hurriedly adjourned from Philadelphia to Princeton. Never before or since has the Congress of the United States undergone such a humiliating ordeal; and the episode clearly illustrates the general demoralization of the country in those trying days.

Boudinot was a member of the first three Congresses, was director of the Mint from 1795 to 1805, and was the first president of the American Bible Society.

A S CONGRESS has yet elected any minister for foreign affairs, and knowing the importance of your being fully informed of every public transaction relative to these States, I have concluded that you would not think it amiss to hear from me on the subject of the removal of Congress to this place, though I can not consider this communication as official, but merely for your information in my individual capacity.

The state of our finances making it indispensably necessary to abridge the public expenses in every instance that would not endanger the Union, we concluded to reduce the army by discharging all the soldiers enlisted for the war, with a proportionate number of officers, on condition that the discharge should operate no otherwise than as a furlough, until the ratification of the definitive treaty.

This not only eased us of a heavy disbursement of ready cash for subsistence money and rations, but gratified many of the army who wished to be at home in the early part of the summer, to provide for the following winter. Three months' pay was ordered which could not otherwise be complied with, but by a paper anticipation of the taxes, payable in six months.

By an inevitable accident, the notes did not arrive at the army till six days after the soldiers were discharged and had left the camp. This, together with some difficulty in settling their accounts, created an uneasiness among the troops, but by the General's address and the good conduct of the officers, they all retired peaceably to their different States, though without a single farthing of cash to buy themselves a meal of victuals.

In the barracks in Philadelphia and at Lancaster, in the State of Pennsylvania, there were a number of new recruits, who had been enlisted since the months of December and January last, and who had not yet taken the field; these soldiers having not been brought under any regular discipline, made many objections against accepting their discharges, and gave their officers reasons to fear some difficulty in getting rid of them; but the Secretary of War thought he had satisfied them by assuring them of the like pay with the rest of the army. On the 15th of June a petition was received from the sergeants, requiring a redress of their grievances, in a very turbulent and indecent style, of which no notice was taken… A committee was immediately appointed to confer with the executive council of Pennsylvania, and to endeavor to get them to call out the militia to stop the mutineers; but to no purpose; the council thinking that the citizens would not choose to risk themselves when fair means might do… On the 19th the troops arrived and joined those at the barracks in the city, who had been increased in number by a few companies of old soldiers arrived the day before from Charles Town.

The whole being very orderly and quiet, Congress adjourned on Friday the 20th, as usual, till Monday morning. On the 21st one of the committee called on me and informed that the soldiers at the barracks were very disorderly and had cast off the authority of their officers; that it was suspected they had a design, the following night, against the bank, and advised me to call Congress without delay. This I did, to meet in half an hour. The soldiers by accident hearing of it, very fortunately hastened their designs a day or two sooner than was intended. The Members of Congress had just got together, except one, when the State House (in which also the President and Supreme Executive Council were then sitting) was surrounded by about three hundred armed men with fixed bayonets under the command of seven sergeants. Congress immediately sent for General St. Clair and demanded the reason of this hostile appearance, who informed of his having just arrived in town from his seat in the country in obedience to the orders of Congress of the day preceding; that he had received information from the commanding officer of the mutinous disposition of the troops, who had marched from the barracks contrary to the orders of their officers, and that the veteran troops from Charles Town had been unwillingly forced into the measure. The president of the State then appeared, and produced the insolent paper which had been sent into him by the sergeants.

Congress determined they would enter on no deliberations while thus surrounded, but ordered General St. Clair immediately to endeavor to march the mutineers back to the barracks by such means as were in his power.

After several prudent and wise measures the General prevailed on the sergeants to return to their barracks, convincing them that if they were aggrieved they had a right to make it known in a decent manner through any persons they might think proper to appoint. But previous to this, after waiting, surrounded by this armed force for near three hours, Congress broke up and we passed through the files of the mutineers without the least opposition, though at times before our adjournment the soldiers, many of whom were very drunk, threatened Congress by name.

The mutineers had taken possession of the powder house and several public arsenals in this city, with some field pieces from the public yard…

The committee, not being able to meet the council till Sunday morning, were then prevailed on to wait for an answer till Monday morning. However, hoping that the council would change their sentiments, the committee did not think proper to give me their advice till Tuesday at two o'clock in the afternoon. In the mean time the mutineers kept in arms, refusing all obedience to their officers, and in possession of the powder house and magazines of military stores. On Tuesday morning the officers reported to me that the preceding evening the sergeants, notwithstanding some talk of submission and return to their duty, had presented six officers with a commission each; and one refusing to accept it, they threatened him with immediate death; and that, at the time of the report, they were getting very drunk and in a very riotous state. By the second report of the committee you will be acquainted with the particulars of the transaction, with the addition that the behavior of the six officers was very mysterious and unaccountable. At two o'clock, agreeably to the advice of the committee, I summoned Congress to meet at this place on Thursday the 26th of June, issued a proclamation and left the city.

As soon as it was known that Congress was going, the council were informed that there was great reason to expect a serious attack on the Bank the night following, on which the president of the State collected about one hundred soldiers and kept guard all night. On Wednesday it was reported that Congress had sent for the Commander-in-Chief with the whole northern army and the militia of New Jersey, who were to be joined by the Pennsylvania militia, in order to quell the mutiny, which was no otherwise true than ordering a detachment of a few hundred men from the North River. The sergeants, being alarmed, soon proposed a submission, and the whole came in a body to the president of the State, making a most submissive acknowledgment of their misconduct, and charging the whole on two of the officers whom they had commissioned to represent their grievances (a Captain Carbery and Lieutenant Sullivan), who were to have headed them as soon as they should have proceeded to violence. These officers immediately escaped to Chester and then got on board a vessel bound to London.

The sergeants describe the plan laid by these officers as of the most irrational and diabolical nature, not only against Congress and the council, but also against the city and bank. They were to be joined by straggling parties from different parts of the country, and after executing their horrid purposes were to have gone off with their plunder to the East Indies. However incredible this may appear, the letters from Sullivan to Colonel Moyland, his commanding officer, from Chester and the capes, clearly show that it was a deep-laid scheme. It appears clearly to me that next to the continued care of Divine Providence, the miscarriage of this plan is owing to the unexpected meeting of Congress on Saturday, and their decided conduct in leaving the city until they could support the Federal government with dignity.

It is also said that two of the citizens have been concerned in this wicked plot, but they are not yet ascertained. They were certainly encouraged by some of the lower class as well as by the general supineness in not quelling the first movement. Some very suspicious circumstances attending the conduct of the other four officers, who were commissioned by the sergeants, have caused them to be arrested. The whole matter has so far subsided. The detachment under General Howe, from the northern army, has arrived in the vicinity of the city, and a court of enquiry is endeavoring to develop the whole affair.

The citizens are greatly chagrined at the predicament in which they stand, and endeavor to lay the blame on the council for not calling on them and proving them, while the council justify themselves by the ad-

vice of the militia officers, whom they called together for that purpose.
The citizens are universally petitioning Congress to return to the city,
assuring us of their constant protection…

The Treaty of Paris Negotiations

Title: The Treaty of Paris Negotiations
Author: John Fiske
Date: 1783
Source: America, Vol.4, pp.48-60

This account of the negotiations of the most important treaty (September 3, 1783) ever made by the United States is taken from John Fiske's
"Critical Period of American History," the most popular and valuable of
his contributions to American history. More than any other writer of his
time (1842-1901) Fiske brought home to the national consciousness a
philosophic view of American history, by his remarkable power of expression and his balanced judgments.

This article does much to confirm the evidence that the treaty of 1783
between Great Britain and the United States, which marked the close
of the Revolution, was, on the part of the American commissioners,
Adams, Franklin, Jay and Laurens, "one of the most brilliant triumphs
in the whole history of modern diplomacy."

FROM the policy which George III pursued with regard to Lord
Shelburne at this time, one would suppose that in his secret
heart the king wished, by foul means since all others had failed, to defeat the negotiations for peace and to prolong the war. Seldom has there
been a more oddly complicated situation. Peace was to be made with
America, France, Spain and Holland. Of these powers, America and
France were leagued together by one treaty of alliance, and France and
Spain by another, and these treaties in some respects conflicted with
one another in the duties which they entailed upon the combatants.
Spain, though at war with England for purposes of her own, was bitterly
hostile to the United States; and France, thus leagued with two allies
which pulled in opposite directions, felt bound to satisfy both, while
pursuing her own ends against England. To deal with such a chaotic
state of things, an orderly and harmonious government in England
should have seemed indispensably necessary. Yet on the part of England the negotiations of a treaty of peace was to be the work of two
secretaries of state who were both politically and personally hostile to
each other. Fox, as secretary of state for foreign affairs, had to super-

All material contained herein was extracted from the
US Constitution Coach Kit at PowerThink.com
(Over 60,000 Works & Documents of American History)

intend the negotiations with France, Spain, and Holland. Shelburne was secretary of state for home and colonial affairs; and as the United States were still officially regarded as colonies, the American negotiations belonged to his department. With such a complication of conflicting interests, George III might well hope that no treaty could be made.

The views of Fox and Shelburne as to the best method of conceding American independence were very different. Fox understood that France was really in need of peace, and he believed that she would not make further demands upon England if American independence should once be recognized. Accordingly, Fox would have made this concession at once as a preliminary to the negotiation. On the other hand, Shelburne felt sure that France would insist upon further concessions, and he thought it best to hold in reserve the recognition of independence as a consideration to be bargained for. Informal negotiations began between Shelburne and Franklin, who for many years had been warm friends. In view of the impending change of government, Franklin had in March sent a letter to Shelburne, expressing a hope that peace might soon be restored. When the letter reached London the new ministry had already been formed, and Shelburne, with the consent of the cabinet, answered it by sending over to Paris an agent, to talk with Franklin informally, and ascertain the terms upon which the Americans would make peace.

The person chosen for this purpose was Richard Oswald, a Scotch merchant, who owned large estates in America,—a man of very frank disposition and liberal views, and a friend of Adam Smith. In April, Oswald had several conversations with Franklin. In one of these conversations Franklin suggested that, in order to make a durable peace, it was desirable to remove all occasion for future quarrel; that the line of frontier between New York and Canada was inhabited by a lawless set of men, who in time of peace would be likely to breed trouble between their respective governments; and that therefore it would be well for England to cede Canada to the United States. A similar reasoning would apply to Nova Scotia. By ceding these countries to the United States it would be possible, from the sale of unappropriated lands, to indemnify the Americans for all losses of private property during the war, and also to make reparation to the Tories, whose estates had been confiscated. By pursuing such a policy, England, which had made war on America unjustly, and had wantonly done it great injuries, would achieve not merely peace, but reconciliation, with America; and reconciliation, said Franklin, is "a sweet word." No doubt this was a bold tone for Franklin to take, and perhaps it was rather cool in him to ask for Canada and

Nova Scotia; but he knew that almost every member of the Whig ministry had publicly expressed the opinion that the war against America was an unjust and wanton war; and being, moreover, a shrewd hand at a bargain, he began by setting his terms high.

Oswald doubtless looked at the matter very much from Franklin's point of view, for on the suggestion of the cession of Canada he expressed neither surprise nor reluctance. Franklin had written on a sheet of paper the main points of his conversation, and, at Oswald's request, he allowed him to take the paper to London to show to Lord Shelburne, first writing upon it a note expressly declaring its informal character. Franklin also sent a letter to Shelburne, describing Oswald as a gentleman with whom he found it very pleasant to deal. On Oswald's arrival in London, Shelburne did not show the notes of the conversation to any of his colleagues, except Lord Ashburton. He kept the paper over one night, and then returned it to Franklin without any formal answer. But the letter he showed to the cabinet, and on the 23d of April it was decided to send Oswald back to Paris, to represent to Franklin that, on being restored to the same situation in which she was left by the treaty of 1763, Great Britain would be willing to recognize the independence of the United States. Fox was authorized to make a similar representation to the French government, and the person whom he sent to Paris for this purpose was Thomas Grenville, son of the author of the Stamp Act.

As all British subjects were prohibited from entering into negotiations with the revolted colonies, it was impossible for Oswald to take any decisive step until an enabling act should be carried through Parliament. But while waiting for this he might still talk informally with Franklin. Fox thought that Oswald's presence in Paris indicated a desire on Shelburne's part to interfere with the negotiations with the French government; and indeed, the king, out of his hatred of Fox and his inborn love of intrigue, suggested to Shelburne that Oswald "might be a useful check on that part of the negotiations which was in other hands." But Shelburne paid no heed to this crooked advice, and there is nothing to show that he had the least desire to intrigue against Fox. If he had, he would certainly have selected some other agent than Oswald, who was the most straightforward of mend and scarcely close-mouthed enough for a diplomatist. He told Oswald to impress it upon Franklin that if America was to be independent at all she must be independent of the whole world, and must not enter into any secret arrangement with France which might limit her entire freedom of action in the future. To the private memorandum which desired the cession of Canada for three reasons, his answers were as follows: "1. By way of repara-tion.—Answer. No reparation can be heard of. 2. To prevent future wars.—Answer. It is to be hoped that some more friendly method will be found. 3. As a fund of indemnification to loyalists.—Answer. No independence to be acknowledged without their being taken care of." Besides, added Shelburne, the Americans would be expected to make some compensation for the surrender of Charleston, Savannah, and the city of New York, still held by British troops. From this it appears that Shelburne, as well as Franklin, knew how to begin by asking more than he was likely to get...

The task of making a treaty of peace was simplified both by a change of the British ministry and by the total defeat of the Spaniards and French at Gibraltar in September. Six months before, England had seemed worsted in every quarter. Now England, though defeated in America, was victorious as regarded France and Spain. The avowed object for which France had entered into alliance with the Americans was to secure the independence of the United States, and this point was now substantially gained. The chief object for which Spain had entered into alliance with France was to drive the English from Gibraltar, and this point was now decidedly lost. France had bound herself not to de-sist from the war until Spain should recover Gibraltar; but now there was little hope of accomplishing this, except by some fortunate bargain in the treaty, and Vergennes tried to persuade England to cede the great stronghold in exchange for West Florida, which Spain had lately con-quered, or for Oran or Guadaloupe. Failing in this, he adopted a plan for satisfying Spain at the expense of the United States; and he did this the more willingly as he had no love for the Americans, and did not wish to see them become too powerful. France had strictly kept her pledges; she had given us valuable and timely aid in gaining our inde-pendence; and the sympathies of the French people were entirely with the American cause. But the object of the French government had been simply to humiliate England, and this end was sufficiently accom-plished by depriving her of her thirteen colonies...

Upon another important point the views of the French government were directly opposed to American interests. The right to catch fish on the banks of Newfoundland had been shared by treaty between France and England; and the New England fishermen, as subjects of the king of Great Britain, had participated in this privilege. The matter was of very great importance, not only to New England, but to the United States in general. Not only were the fisheries a source of lucrative trade to the New England people, but they were the training school of a splendid race of seamen, the nursery of naval heroes whose exploits were by and by to astonish the world. To deprive the Americans of their share in these fisheries was to strike a serious blow at the strength and resources of the new nation. The British government was not inclined to grant the privilege, and on this point Vergennes took sides with England, in order to establish a claim upon her for concessions advantageous to France in some other quarter. With these views, Vergennes secretly aimed at delaying the negotiations; for as long as hostilities were kept up, he might hope to extort from his American allies a recognition of the Spanish claims and a renouncement of the fisheries, simply by threatening to send them no further assistance in men or money. In order to retard the proceedings, he refused to take any steps whatever until the independence of the United States should first be irrevocably acknowledged by Great Britain, without reference to the final settlement of the rest of the treaty. In this Vergennes was supported by Franklin, as well as by Jay, who had lately arrived in Paris to take part in the negotiations. But the reasons of the American commissioners were very different from those of Vergennes. They feared that, if they began to treat before independence was acknowledged, they would be unfairly dealt with by France and Spain, and unable to gain from England the concessions upon which they were determined.

Jay soon began to suspect the designs of the French minister. He found that he was sending M. de Rayneval as a secret emissary to Lord Shelburne under an assumed name; he ascertained that the right of the United States to the Mississippi valley was to be denied; and he got hold of a dispatch from Marbois, the French secretary of legation at Philadelphia, to Vergennes, opposing the American claim to the Newfoundland fisheries. As soon as Jay learned these facts, he sent his friend Dr. Benjamin Vaughan to Lord Shelburne to put him on his guard, and while reminding him that it was greatly for the interest of England to dissolve the alliance between America and France, he declared himself ready to begin the negotiations without waiting for the recognition of independence, provided that Oswald's commission should speak of the thirteen United States of America, instead of calling them colonies and naming them separately. This decisive step was taken by Jay on his own responsibility, and without the knowledge of Franklin, who had been averse to anything like a separate negotiation with England. It served to set the ball rolling at once. After meeting the messengers from Jay and Vergennes, Lord Shelburne at once perceived the antagonism that had arisen between the allies, and promptly took advantage of it. A new commission was made out for Oswald, in which the British government first described our country as the United States; and early in October negotiations were begun and proceeded rapidly. On the part of England, the affair was conducted by Oswald, assisted by Strachey and Fitzherbert, who had succeeded Grenville. In the course of the month John Adams arrived in Paris, and a few weeks later Henry Laurens, who had been exchanged for Lord Cornwallis and released from the Tower, was added to the company. Adams had a holy horror of Frenchmen in general, and of Count Vergennes in particular. He shared that common but grossly mistaken view of Frenchmen which regards them as shallow, frivolous and insincere; and he was indignant at the position taken by Vergennes on the question of the fisheries. In this, John Adams felt as all New Englanders felt, and he realized the Importance of the question from a national point of view, as became the man who in later years was to earn lasting renown as one of the chief founders of the American navy. His behavior on reaching Paris was characteristic. It is said that he left Count Vergennes to learn of his arrival through the newspapers. It was certainly some time before he called upon him, and he took occasion, besides, to express his opinions about republics and monarchies in terms which courtly Frenchmen thought very rude.

The arrival of Adams fully decided the matter as to a separate negotiation with England. He agreed with Jay that Vergennes should be kept as far as possible in the dark until everything was cut and dried, and Franklin was reluctantly obliged to yield. The treaty of alliance between France and the United States had expressly stipulated that neither power should ever make peace without the consent of the other, and in view of this Franklin was loath to do anything which might seem like abandoning the ally whose timely interposition had alone enabled Washington to achieve the crowning triumph of Yorktown. In justice to Vergennes, it should be borne in mind that he had kept strict faith with us in regard to every point that had been expressly stipulated; and Franklin, who felt that he understood Frenchmen better than his colleagues, was naturally unwilling to seem behindhand in this respect. At the same time, in regard to matters not expressly stipulated, Vergennes was clearly playing a sharp game against us; and it is undeniable that, without departing technically from the obligations of the alliance, Jay and Adams—two men as honorable as ever lived—played a very sharp defensive game against him. The traditional French subtlety was no match for Yankee shrewdness. The treaty with England was not concluded until the consent of France had been obtained, and thus the express stipulation was respected; but a thorough and detailed agreement was reached as to what the purport of the treaty should be, while our not too friendly ally was kept in the dark. The annals of modern diplomacy have afforded few stranger spectacles. With the indispensable aid of France we had just got the better of England in fight, and now we proceeded amicably to divide territory and commercial privileges with the enemy, and to make arrangements in which the ally was virtually ignored. It ceases to be a paradox, however, when we remember that with the change of government in England some essential conditions of the case were changed. The England against which we had fought was the hostile England of Lord North; the England with which we were now dealing was the friendly England of Shelburne and Pitt. For the moment, the English race, on both sides of the Atlantic, was united in its main purpose and divided only questions of detail, while the rival colonizing power, which sought to work in a direction contrary to the general interests of English-speaking people, was in great measure disregarded...

The articles were signed on the 30th of November, six days before the meeting of Parliament. Hostilities in America were to cease at once, and upon the completion of the treaty the British fleets and armies were to be immediately withdrawn from every place which the held within the limits of the United States. A supplementary and secret article provided that if England, on making peace with Spain, should recover West Florida, the northern boundary of that province should be a line running due east from the mouth of the Yazoo River to the Chattahoochee.

Thus by skilful diplomacy the Americans had gained all that could reasonably be asked, while the work of making a general peace was greatly simplified. It was declared in the preamble that the articles here signed were provisional, and that the treaty was not to take effect until terms of peace should be agreed on between England and France. Without delay, Franklin laid the whole matter, except the secret article, before Vergennes, who forthwith accused the Americans of ingratitude and bad faith...

On the part of the Americans the treaty of Paris was one of the most brilliant triumphs in the whole history of modern diplomacy. Had the affair been managed by men of ordinary ability, some of the greatest results of the Revolutionary War would probably have been lost; the new republic would have been cooped up between the Atlantic Ocean and the Alleghany Mountains; our westward expansion would have been impossible without further warfare in which European powers would have been involved; and the formation of our Federal Union would doubtless have been effectively hindered, if not, indeed, altogether prevented. To the grand triumph the varied talents of Franklin, Adams and Jay alike contributed.

Treaty with Great Britain, 1783 (The Treaty of Paris)

Title: Treaty with Great Britain
Author: The U.S. and British Governments
Date: 1783
Source: Harvard Classics, Vol.43, pp.185-191

Less than five months after the surrender of Cornwallis, the British Parliament passed an act to enable the king to make peace till July 1783. In the end of November, 1782, a provisional treaty was signed, the negotiations on behalf of Congress having been conducted by Benjamin Franklin, John Adams, John Jay, and Henry Laurens. On September 3, 1783, this treaty was made definitive in the form here printed, and the complete independence of the American States acknowledged by Great Britain.

DEFINITIVE TREATY OF PEACE BETWEEN THE UNITED STATES OF AMERICA AND HIS BRITANNIC MAJESTY, CONCLUDED AT PARIS, SEPTEMBER 3, 1783; RATIFIED BY CONGRESS, JANUARY 14, 1784; PROCLAIMED, JANUARY 14, 1784.

IN the name of the Most Holy and Undivided Trinity.

It having pleased the Divine Providence to dispose the hearts—of the most serene and most potent Prince George the Third, by the Grace of God King of Great Britain, France, and Ireland, Defender of the Faith, Duke of Brunswick and Luneburg, Arch Treasurer and Prince Elector of the Holy Roman Empire, &c., and of the United States of America, to forget all past misunderstandings and differences that have unhappily interrupted the good correspondence and friendship which they mutually wish to restore; and to establish such a beneficial and satisfactory intercourse between the two countries, upon the ground of reciprocal advantages and mutual convenience, as may promote and secure to both perpetual peace and harmony: And having for this desirable end already laid the foundation of peace and reconciliation, by the provisional articles, signed at Paris, on the 30th of Nov., 1782, by the commissioners empowered on each part, which articles were agreed to be inserted in and to constitute the treaty of peace proposed to be concluded between the Crown of Great Britain and the said United States, but which treaty was not to be concluded until terms of peace should be agreed upon between Great Britain and France, and His Britannic Majesty should be ready to conclude such treaty accordingly; and the treaty between Great Britain and France having since been concluded, His Britannic Majesty and the United States of America, in order to carry into full effect the provisional articles above mentioned, according to the tenor thereof, have constituted and appointed, that is to Say, His Britannic Majesty on his part, David Hartley, esqr., member of the Parliament of Great Britain; and the said United States on their part, John Adams, esqr., late a commissioner of the United States of America at the Court of Versailles, late Delegate in Congress from the State of Massachusetts, and chief justice of the said State, and Minister Plenipotentiary of the said United States to their High Mightinesses the States General of the United Netherlands; Benjamin Franklin, esq're, late Delegate in Congress from the State of Pennsylvania, president of the convention of the said State, and Minister Plenipotentiary from the United States of America at the Court of Versailles; John Jay, esq're, late President of Congress, and Chief Justice of the State of New York, and Minister Plenipotentiary from the said United States at the Court of Madrid, to be the Plenipotentiaries for the concluding and signing the present definitive treaty; who, after having reciprocally communicated their respective full powers, have agreed upon and confirmed the following articles:

ARTICLE I

His Britannic Majesty acknowledges the said United States, viz. New Hampshire, Massachusetts Bay, Rhode Island, and Providence Plantations, Connecticut, New York, New Jersey, Pennsylvania, Delaware, Maryland, Virginia, North Carolina, South Carolina, and Georgia, to be free, sovereign and independent States; that he treats with them as such, and for himself, his heirs and successors, relinquishes all claims to the Government, proprietory and territorial rights of the same, and every part thereof.

ARTICLE II

And that all disputes which might arise in future, on the subject of the boundaries of the said United States may be prevented, it is hereby agreed and declared, that the following are, and shall be their boundaries, viz.: From the northwest angle of Nova Scotia, viz. that angle which is formed by a line drawn due north from the source of Saint

Croix River to the Highlands; along the said Highlands which divide those rivers that empty themselves into the river St. Lawrence, from those which fall into the Atlantic Ocean, to the northwesternmost head of Connecticut River; thence down along the middle of that river, to the forth-fifth degree of north latitude; from thence, by a line due west on said latitude, until it strikes the river Iroquois or Cataraquy; thence along the middle of said river into Lake Ontario, through the middle of said lake until it strikes the communication by water between that lake and Lake Erie; thence along the middle of said communication into Lake Erie, through the middle of said lake until it arrives at the water communication between that lake and Lake Huron; thence along the middle of said water communication into the Lake Huron; thence through the middle of said lake to the water communication between that Lake and Lake Superior; thence through Lake Superior northward of the Isles Royal and Phelipeaux, to the Long Lake; thence through the middle of said Long Lake, and the water communication between it and the Lake of the Woods, to the said Lake of the Woods; thence through the said lake to the most northwestern point thereof, and from thence on a due west course to the river Mississippi; thence by a line to be drawn along the middle of the said river Mississippi until it shall intersect the northernmost part of the thirty-first degree of north latitude. South, by a line to be drawn due east from the determination of the line last mentioned, in the latitude of thirty-one degrees north of the Equator, to the middle of the river Apalachicola or Catahouche; thence along the middle thereof to its junction with the Flint River; thence, straight to the head of St. Mary's River; and thence down along the middle of St. Mary's River to the Atlantic Ocean. East, by a line to be drawn along the middle of the river St. Croix, from its mouth in the Bay of Fundy to its source, and from its source directly north to the aforesaid Highlands, which divide the rivers that fall into the Atlantic Ocean from those which fall into the river St. Lawrence; comprehending all islands within twenty leagues of any part of the shores of the United States, and lying between lines to be drawn due east from the points where the aforesaid boundaries between Nova Scotia on the one part, and East Florida on the other, shall respectively touch the Bay of Fundy and the Atlantic Ocean; excepting such islands as now are, or heretofore have been, within the limits of the said province of Nova Scotia.

ARTICLE III

It is agreed that the people of the United States shall continue to enjoy unmolested the right to take fish of every kind on the Grand

Bank, and on all the other banks of Newfoundland; also in the Gulph of Saint Lawrence, and at all other places in the sea where the inhabitants of both countries used at any time heretofore to fish. And also that the inhabitants of the United States shall have liberty to take fish of every kind on such part of the coast of Newfoundland as British fishermen shall use (but not to dry or cure the same on that island) and also on the coasts, bays, and creeks of all other of His Britannic Majesty's dominions in America; and that the American fishermen shall have liberty to dry and cure fish in any of the unsettled bays, harbours, and creeks of Nova Scotia, Magdalen Islands, and Labrador, so long as the same shall remain unsettled; but so soon as the same or either of them shall be settled, it shall not be lawful for the said fishermen to dry or cure fish at such settlement, without a previous agreement for that purpose with the inhabitants, proprietors, or possessors of the ground.

ARTICLE IV

It is agreed that creditors on either side shall meet with no lawful impediment to the recovery of the full value in sterling money, of all bona fide debts heretofore contracted.

ARTICLE V

It is agreed that the Congress shall earnestly recommend it to the legislatures of the respective States, to provide for the restitution of all estates, rights, and properties which have been confiscated, belonging to real British subjects, and also of the estates, rights and properties of persons resident in districts in the possession of His Majesty's arms, and who have not borne arms against the said United States. And that persons of any other description shall have free liberty to go to any part or parts of any of the thirteen United States, and therein to remain twelve months, unmolested in their endeavours to obtain the restitution of such of their estates, rights, and properties as may have been confiscated; and that Congress shall also earnestly recommend to the several States a reconsideration and revision of all acts or laws regarding the premises, so as to render the said laws or acts perfectly consistent, not only with justice and equity, but with that spirit of conciliation which, on the return of the blessings of peace, should universally prevail. And that Congress shall also earnestly recommend to the several States, that the estates, rights, and properties of such last mentioned persons, shall be restored to them, they refunding to any persons who may be now in possession, the bona fide price (where any has been given) which such persons may have paid on purchasing any of the said lands, rights, or properties, since the confiscation. And it is agreed, that all persons who

All material contained herein was extracted from the
US Constitution Coach Kit at PowerThink.com
(Over 60,000 Works & Documents of American History)

have any interest in confiscated lands, either by debts, marriage settlements, or otherwise, shall meet with no lawful impediment in the prosecution of their just rights.

ARTICLE VI

That there shall be no future confiscations made, nor any prosecutions commenced against any person or persons for, or by reason of the part which he or they may have taken in the present war; and that no person shall, on that account, suffer any future loss or damage, either in his person, liberty, or property; and that those who may be in confinement on such charges, at the time of the ratification of the treaty in America, shall be immediately set at liberty, and the prosecutions so commenced be discontinued.

ARTICLE VII

There shall be a firm and perpetual peace between His Britannic Majesty and the said States, and between the subjects of the one and the citizens of the other, wherefore all hostilities, both by sea and land, shall from henceforth cease: All prisoners on both sides shall be set at liberty, and His Britannic Majesty shall, with all convenient speed, and without causing any destruction, or carrying away any negroes or other property of the American inhabitants, withdraw all his armies, garrisons, and fleets from the said United States, and from every port, place, and harbour within the same; leaving in all fortifications the American artillery that may be therein: And shall also order and cause all archives, records, deeds, and papers, belonging to any of the said States, or their citizens, which, in the course of the war, may have fallen into the hands of his officers, to be forthwith restored and deliver'd to the proper States and persons to whom they belong.

ARTICLE VIII

The navigation of the river Mississippi, from its source to the ocean, shall forever remain free and open to the subjects of Great Britain, and the citizens of the United States.

ARTICLE IX

In case it should so happen that any place or territory belonging to Great Britain or to the United States, should have been conquer'd by the arms of either from the other, before the arrival of the said provisional articles in America, it is agreed, that the same shall be restored without difficulty, and without requiring any compensation.

ARTICLE X

The solemn ratifications of the present treaty, expedited in good and due form, shall be exchanged between the contracting parties, in the space of six months, or sooner if possible, to be computed from the day of the signature of the present treaty. In witness whereof, we the undersigned, their Ministers Plenipotentiary, have in their name and in virtue of our full powers, signed with our hands the present definitive treaty, and caused the seals of our arms to be affix'd thereto.

Done at Paris, this third day of September, in the year of our Lord one thousand seven hundred and eighty-three.

D. HARTLEY [L. S.]; JOHN ADAMS [L. S.]
B. FRANKLIN [L. S.]; JOHN JAY [L. S.]

The Public Land Problem

Title: The Public Land Problem
Author: Thomas Paine
Date: 1784
Source: America, Vol.4, pp.18-26

This attack by Thomas Paine on Virginia's unlimited claims to western territory followed closely upon an appeal to Congress from the settlers of Kentucky, denying the rights of Virginia to govern what was known as the Illinois country, or Northwest Territory, as a dependency, and asking to be taken into the Union as a State. The aforesaid territory, including Kentucky proper, had been acquired by conquest of Colonel George Rogers Clark the year before Paine wrote this remonstrance.

Following the British defeat at Yorktown, the conflicting claims of other colonies and land companies, and the refusal of Maryland otherwise to join the Union, led Virginia, in 1784, to cede the disputed territory to the Confederation—largely as a result of public opinion growing out of this article—reserving only a small portion for her war veterans.

THE condition of the vacant western territory of America makes a very different case to that of the circumstances of trade in any of the States. Those very lands, formed, in contemplation, the fund by which the debt of America would in a course of years be redeemed. They were considered as the common right of all; and it is only till lately that any pretension of claims has been made to the contrary...

... in the year 1609, the South-Virginia company applied for new powers from the Crown of England, which were granted them in a new patent, and the boundaries of the grant enlarged; and this is the charter or patent on which some of the present Virginians ground their pretension to boundless territory...

But whether the charter, as it is called, ought to be extinct or not, cannot make a question with us. All the parties concerned in it are deceased, and no successors, in any regular line of succession, appear to claim. Neither the London company of adventurers, their heirs or assigns, were in possession of the exercise of this charter at the commencement of the Revolution; and therefore the State of Virginia does not, in point of fact, succeed to and inherit from the company...

But if, as I before mentioned, there was a charter, which bore such an explanation, and that Virginia stood in succession to it, what would that be to us any more than the will of Alexander, had he taken it in his head to have bequeathed away the world? Such a charter or grant must have been obtained by imposition and a false representation of the country, or granted in error, or both; and in any of, or all, these cases, the United States must reject the matter as something they can know nothing of, for the merits will not bear an argument, and the pretention of right stands upon no better ground...

The claim being unreasonable in itself and standing on no ground of right, but such as, if true, must from the quarter it is drawn be offensive, has a tendency to create disgust and sour the minds of the rest of the states. Those lands are capable, under the management of the United States, of repaying the charges of the war, and some of which, as I shall here after show, might, I presume, be made an immediate advantage of.

I distinguish three different descriptions of lands in America at the commencement of the Revolution. Proprietary or chartered lands, as was the case in Pennsylvania. Crown lands, within the described limits of any of the crown governments; and crown residuary lands that were without or beyond the limits of any province; and those last were held in reserve whereon to erect new governments and lay out new provinces; as appears to have been the design by Lord Hillsborough's letter and the president's answer, wherein he says "with respect to the establishment of a new colony on the back of Virginia, it is a subject of too great political importance for me to presume to give an opinion upon; however permit me, my lord, to observe, that when that part of the country shall become populated it may be a wise and prudent measure."

The expression is a "new colony on the back of Virginia;" and referred to lands between the heads of the rivers and the Ohio. This is a proof that those lands were not considered within but beyond the limits of Virginia as a colony; and the other expression in the letter is equally descriptive, namely, "We do not presume to say to whom our gracious sovereign shall grant his vacant lands." Certainly then, the same right, which, at that time, rested in the crown rests now in the more supreme authority of the United States...

It must occur to every person on reflection that those lands are too distant to be within the government of any of the present States...

It is only the United States, and not any single State, that can lay off new States and incorporate them in the union by representation; therefore the situation which the settlers on those lands will be in, under the assumed right of Virginia, will be hazardous and distressing, and they will feel themselves at last like aliens to the commonwealth of Israel, their habitations unsafe and their title precarious...

It seldom happens that the romantic schemes of extensive dominion are of any service to a government, and never to a people. They assuredly end at last in loss, trouble, division and disappointment. And was even the title of Virginia good, and the claim admissible, she would derive more lasting and real benefit by participating it than by attempting the management of an object so infinitely beyond her reach. Her share with the rest, under the supremacy of the United States, which is the only authority adequate to the purpose, would be worth more to her, than what the whole would produce under the management of herself alone, and that for several reasons.

First, because her claim not being admissible nor yet manageable, she cannot make a good title to the purchasers, and consequently can get but little for the lands.

Secondly, because the distance the settlers will be at from her, will immediately put them out of all government and protection, so far, at least, as relate to Virginia; and by this means she will render her frontiers a refuge to desperadoes, and a hiding place from justice; and the consequence will be perpetual unsafety to her own peace and that of the neighboring States...

Lastly, because she must sooner or later relinquish them, and therefore to see her own interest wisely at first, is preferable to the alternative of finding it out by misfortune at last...

I have already remarked that only the United States and not any particular State can lay off new States and incorporate them in the union by representation; keeping, therefore, this idea in view, I ask, might not a substantial fund be quickly created by laying off a new State, so as to contain between twenty and thirty million of acres, and opening a land office in all the countries in Europe for hard money, and in this country for supplies in kind at a certain price...

If twenty millions of acres of this new State be patented and sold at twenty pounds sterling per hundred acres they will produce four million pounds sterling, which, if applied to continental expenses only will support the war for three years should Britain be so unwise to herself to prosecute it against her own direct interest and against the interest and policy of all Europe. The several States will then have to raise taxes for their internal government only, and the continental taxes as soon as the fund begins to operate will lessen, and if sufficiently productive will cease...

I shall now enquire into the effects which the laying out of a new State, under the authority of the United States, will have upon Virginia.

It is the very circumstance she ought to and must wish for when she examines the matter through all its cases and consequences.

The present settlers being beyond her reach, and her supposed authority over them remaining in herself, they will appear to her as revolters, and she to them as oppressors; and this will produce such a spirit of mutual dislike that in a little time a total disagreement will take place, to the disadvantage of both.

But under the authority of the United States the matter is manageable, and Virginia will be eased of a disagreeable consequence.

Besides this, a sale of the lands, continentally, for the purpose of supporting the expense of the war, will save her a greater share of taxes than what the small sale she could make herself, and the small price she could get for them, would produce.

She would likewise have two advantages which no other State in the Union enjoys, first, a frontier State for her defense against the incursions of the Indians; and the second is, that the laying out and peopling a new State on the back of an old one, situated as she is, is doubling the quantity of its trade.

The new State, which is here proposed to be laid out, may send its exports down the Mississippi, but its imports must come through

Chesapeake Bay, and consequently Virginia will become the market for the new State; because, though there is a navigation from it, there is none into it, on account of the rapidity of the Mississippi.

There are certain circumstances that will produce certain events whether men think of them or not. The events do not depend upon thinking, but are the natural consequence of acting; and according to the system which Virginia has gone upon, the issue will be that she will get involved with the back settlers in a contention about rights till they dispute with her her own claims, and, soured by the contention, will go to any other State for their commerce; both of which may be prevented, a perfect harmony established, the strength of the States increased, and the expenses of the war defrayed, by settling the matter now on the plan of a general right; and every day it is delayed the difficulty will be increased and the advantages lessened…

As the laying out new States will some time or other be the business of the country, and as it is yet a new business to us; and as the influence of the war has scarcely afforded leisure for reflecting on distant circumstances, I shall throw together a few hints for facilitating that measure, whenever it may be proper for adopting it.

The United States now standing on the line of sovereignty, the vacant territory is their property collectively, but the persons by whom it may hereafter be peopled will have an equal right with ourselves; and therefore, as new States shall be laid off and incorporated with the present, they will become partakers of the remaining territory with us who are already in possession. And this consideration ought to heighten the value of lands to new emigrants; because, in making purchases, they not only gain an immediate property, but become initiated into the right and heirship of the States to a property in reserve, which is an additional advantage to what any purchasers under the late government of England enjoyed.

The setting off the boundary of any new State will naturally be the first step, and as it must be supposed not to be peopled at the time it is laid off, a constitution must be formed, by the United States, as the rule of government in any new State, for a certain term of years, (perhaps ten) or until the State become peopled to a certain number of inhabitants; after which, the whole and sole right of modeling their government to rest with themselves.

A question may arise, whether a new State should immediately possess an equal right with the present ones in all cases which may come before Congress.

This, experience will best determine; but at first view of the matter it appears thus: That it ought to be immediately incorporated into the Union on the ground of a family right, such a State standing in the line of a younger child of the same stock; but as new emigrants will have something to learn when they first come to America, and a new State requiring aid rather than capable of giving it, it might be most convenient to admit its immediate representation into Congress, there to sit, hear, and debate, on all questions and matters, but not to vote on any till after the expiration of seven years.

I shall in this place take the opportunity of renewing a hint which I formerly threw out in the pamphlet "Common Sense," and which the several States will, sooner or later, see the convenience, if not the necessity, of adopting; which is, that of electing a Continental Convention, for the purpose of forming a Continental Constitution, defining and describing the powers and authority of Congress.

American Characteristics

Title: American Characteristics
Author: Benjamin Franklin
Date: 1784
Source: America, Vol.4, pp.68-76

Franklin was justly considered in Europe as a preeminent authority on all matters relating to social conditions in America. His writings enjoyed almost as large a circulation abroad as they did in this country, and his reputation grew with his success. "It was," wrote John Adams, "more universal than that of Leibnitz or Newton, Frederick the Great or Voltaire, and his character more beloved and esteemed than all of them."

Franklin was besieged by European publishers for pamphlets and for contributions of a literary character. This article was published in both London and Paris in 1784, the year after Franklin, then in France, had signed the definitive Treaty of Paris and asked to be relieved of his mission. His request was not granted until 1785 when Congress adopted a resolution permitting "the Honorable Benjamin Franklin to return to America as soon as convenient."

MANY persons in Europe having directly or by letters, expressed to the writer of this, who is well acquainted with North America, their desire of transporting and establishing themselves in that country; but who appear to him to have formed through ignorance, mistaken ideas and expectations of what is to be obtained there; he thinks it may be useful, and prevent inconvenient, expensive and fruitless removals and voyages of improper persons, if he gives some clearer and truer notions of that part of the world than appear to have hitherto prevailed...

The truth is, that though there are in that country few people so miserable as the poor of Europe, there are also very few that in Europe would be called rich. It is rather a general happy mediocrity that prevails. There are few great proprietors of the soil, and few tenants; most people cultivate their own lands, or follow some handicraft or merchandise; very few are rich enough to live idly upon their rents or incomes; or to pay the high prices given in Europe, for painting, statues, architecture and the other works of art that are more curious than useful. Hence the natural geniuses that have arisen in America, with such talents, have uniformly quitted that country for Europe, where they can be more suitably rewarded. It is true that letters and mathematical knowledge are in esteem there, but they are at the same time more common than is apprehended; there being already existing nine colleges, or universities, viz. four in New England, and one in each of the provinces of New York, New Jersey, Pennsylvania, Maryland, and Virginia, all furnished with learned professors; besides a number of smaller academies. These educate many of their youth in the languages and those sciences that qualify men for the professions of divinity, law, or physic. Strangers indeed are by no means excluded from exercising those professions; and the quick increase of inhabitants everywhere gives them a chance of employ, which they have in common with the natives. Of civil offices or employments, there are few; no superfluous ones as in Europe; and it is a rule established in some of the States, that no office should be so profitable as to make it desirable...

These ideas prevailing more or less in all the United States, it cannot be worth any man's while, who has a means of living at home, to expatriate himself in hopes of obtaining a profitable civil office in America, and as to military offices, they are at an end with the war, the armies being disbanded. Much less is it advisable for a person to go thither who has no other quality to recommend him but his birth. In Europe it has indeed its value; but it is a commodity that cannot be carried to a worse market than to that of America, where people do not enquire concerning a stranger, "What is he?" but "What can he do?" If he has any useful art, he is welcome; and if he exercises it, and behaves well, he will be respected by all that know him; but a mere man of quality, who on that account wants to live upon the public, by some office or salary, will be despised and disregarded...

With regard to encouragements for strangers from Government, they are really only what are derived from good laws and liberty. Strangers are welcome because there is room enough for them all, and therefore the old inhabitants are not jealous of them; the laws protect them sufficiently, so that they have no need of the patronage of great men; and every one will enjoy securely the profits of his industry. But if he does not bring a fortune with him, he must work and be industrious to live. One or two years' residence give him all the rights of a citizen; but the Government does not at present, whatever it may have done in former times, hire people to become settlers, by paying their passages, giving land, negroes, utensils, stock, or any other kind of emolument whatsoever. In short, America is the land of labor, and by no means what the English call Lubberland, and the French Pays de Cocagne, where the streets are said to be paved with half-peck loaves, the houses tiled with pancakes, and where the fowls fly about ready roasted, crying, "Come eat me!"...

Land being cheap in that country, from the vast forests still void of inhabitants, and not likely to be occupied in an age to come, insomuch that the propriety of a hundred acres of fertile soil full of wood may be obtained near the frontiers in many places, for eight or ten guineas, hearty young laboring men, who understand the husbandry of corn and cattle, which is nearly the same in that country as in Europe, may easily establish themselves there. A little money saved of the good wages they receive there while they work for others, enables them to buy the land and begin their plantation, in which they are assisted by the good will of their neighbors, and some credit. Multitudes of poor people from England, Ireland, Scotland and Germany, have by this means in a few years become wealthy farmers, who in their own countries, where all the lands are fully occupied, and the wages of labor low, could never have emerged from the mean condition wherein they were born.

From the salubrity of the air, the healthiness of the climate, the plenty of good provisions, and the encouragement to early marriages by the certainty of subsistence in cultivating the earth, the increase of inhabitants by natural generation is very rapid in America, and becomes still more so by the accession of strangers; hence there is a continual demand for more artisans of all the necessary and useful kinds, to supply those cultivators of the earth with houses, and with furniture and utensils of the grosser sorts, which cannot so well be brought from Europe. Tolerably good workmen in any of those mechanic arts, are sure to find employ, and to be well paid for their work, there being no restraints preventing strangers from exercising any art they understand, nor any permission necessary. If they are poor, they begin first as servants or journeymen; and if they are sober, industrious, and frugal, they soon become masters, establish themselves in business, marry, raise families, and become respectable citizens.

Also, persons of moderate fortunes and capitals, who having a number of children to provide for, are desirous of bringing them up to industry, and to secure estates for their posterity, have opportunities of doing it in America, which Europe does not afford. There they may be taught and practice profitable mechanic arts, without incurring disgrace on that account; but on the contrary acquiring respect by such abilities. There small capitals laid out in lands, which daily become more valuable by the increase of people, afford a solid prospect of ample fortunes thereafter for those children. The writer of this has known several instances of large tracts of land, bought on what was then the frontier of Pennsylvania, for ten pounds per hundred acres, which, after twenty years, when the settlements had been extended far beyond them, sold readily, without any improvements made upon them, for three pounds per acre. The acre in America is the same with the English acre, or the acre of Normandy...

Several of the Princes of Europe having of late, from [formed?] an opinion of advantage to arise by producing all commodities and manufactures within their own dominions, so as to diminish or render useless their importations, have endeavored to entice workmen from other countries, by high salaries, privileges, &c... This, however, has rarely been done in America; and when it has been done, it has rarely succeeded, so as to establish a manufacture, which the country was not yet so ripe for as to encourage private persons to set it up; labor being generally too dear there, and hands difficult to be kept together, every one desiring to be a master, and the cheapness of land inclining many to leave trades for agriculture. Some indeed have met with success, and are carried on to advantage; but they are generally such as require only a few hands, or wherein great part of the work is performed by machines...

Great establishments of manufacture require great numbers of poor to do the work for small wages; these poor are to be found in Europe, but will not be found in America, till the lands are all taken up and cultivated, and the excess of people who cannot get land, want employment... Therefore the Governments in America do nothing to encourage such projects. The people, by this means, are not imposed on, either by the merchant or mechanic; if the merchant demands too much profit on imported shoes, they buy of the shoemaker; and if he asks too high a price, they take them of the merchant. Thus the two professions are checks on each other. The shoemaker, however, has, on the whole, a considerable profit upon his labor in America, beyond what he had in Europe, as he can add to his price a sum nearly equal to all the expenses of freight and commission, risk or insurance, &c., necessarily charged by the merchant. And the case is the same with the workmen in every other mechanic art. Hence it is, that artisans generally live better and more easily in America than in Europe; and such as are good economists, make a comfortable provision for age, and for their children. Such may, therefore, remove with advantage to America.

In the old long-settled countries of Europe... artisans, who fear creating future rivals in business, refuse to take apprentices, but upon conditions of money, maintenance, or the like, which the parents are unable to comply with... In America, the rapid increase of inhabitants takes away that fear of rivalship, and artisans willingly receive apprentices from the hope of profit by their labor, during the remainder of the time stipulated, after they shall be instructed. Hence it is easy for poor families to get their children instructed; for the artisans are so desirous of apprentices, that many of them will even give money to the parents, to have boys from ten to fifteen years of age bound apprentices to them, till the age of twenty-one; and many poor parents have, by that means, on their arrival in the country, raised money enough to buy land sufficient to establish themselves, and to subsist the rest of their family by agriculture. These contracts for apprentices are made before a magistrate, who regulates the agreement according to reason and justice; and having in view the formation of a future useful citizen, obliges the master to engage by a written indenture, not only that during the time of service stipulated, the apprentice shall be duly provided with meat, drink, apparel, washing and lodging, and at its expiration with a complete new suit of clothes, but also that he shall be taught to read, write and cast accounts; and that he shall be well instructed in the art or profession of his master, or some other, by which he may afterwards gain a livelihood, and be able in his turn to raise a family. . This desire among the masters to have more hands employed in working for them, induces them to pay the passages of young persons, of both sexes, who on their arrival agree to serve them one, two, three, or four years; those who have already learned a trade agreeing for a shorter term, in proportion to their skill, and the consequent immediate value of their service; and those who have none, agreeing for a longer term, in consideration of being taught an art their poverty would not permit them to acquire in their own country.

The almost general mediocrity of fortune that prevails in America, obliging its people to follow some business for subsistence, those vices that arise usually from idleness are in a great measure prevented. Industry and constant employment are great preservatives of the morals and virtue of a nation. Hence bad examples to youth are more rare in America, which must be a comfortable consideration to parents. To this may be truly added, that serious religion, under its various denominations, is not only tolerated, but respected and practised. Atheism is unknown there; infidelity rare and secret; so that persons may live to a great age in that country without having their piety shocked by meeting with either an atheist or an infidel. And the Divine Being seems to have manifested His approbation of the mutual forbearance and kindness with which the different sects treat each other, by the remarkable prosperity with which He has been pleased to favor the whole country.

PowerThink Publishing is pleased to present

US CONSTITUTION COACH KIT
Reagan Leadership Edition

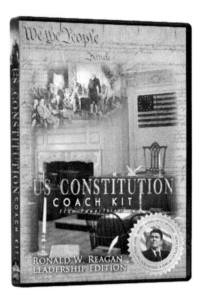

Includes The 5000 Year Leap, The Making of America, and over 60,000 original source documents & works of American History

- ▶The Founding Fathers: Delegates to the Constitutional Convention
- ▶Autobiography of Benjamin Franklin
- ▶Writings of Thomas Jefferson
- ▶Writings of James Madison
- ▶Dictionary of American History
- ▶Common Sense
- ▶The Wealth of Nations
- ▶1,100 Key Firsthand & Source Documents
- ▶1,000 Landmark Supreme Court Decisions
- ▶US Congress Collection
- ▶12,000+ Famous Quotes
- ▶The First Written Constitution

- ▶Constitution of the United States
- ▶Journal of the Federal Convention
- ▶The Federalist Papers
- ▶Elliot's Debates
- ▶A Plea for the Constitution
- ▶Democracy in America
- ▶History of the United States
- ▶History of the American People
- ▶History of the American Nation
- ▶Public Papers of the President
- ▶Magna Carta
- ▶The Mayflower Compact
- ▶Declaration of Independence

Plus 1,000s More!

All at your finger tips

Use your computer for what it was invented for!

Never before have so many works been so easily accessible. Feel the pulse of history through some of the greatest works of American history.

- ▶ Each title is indexed for easy search and navigation

- ▶ Customize your library with personal notes, high-lighters and bookmarks

- ▶ Export, save, and print for use in school, speeches and more

Bonus Content

- ▶ **Ultimate Handheld US History Library**
  Over 50,000 works for your mobile device

- ▶ **Complete Christian Collection - Basic Edition**
  109 works with over 2 million links

- ▶ **The American Values Collection**
  100+ works for your PC and mobile device

- ▶ **Reagan Speaks**
  Key speeches in video, audio and PDF

- ▶ **A More Perfect Union**
  DVD video of the making of the Constitution

Available at **www.powerthink.com**
Save 20% with the coupon code 'reagan'

A More Perfect Union
America Becomes A Nation

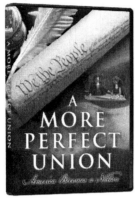

An enactment of the birth of the US Constitution shot on location at Independence Hall and other historic locations.

No other representation of the making of the Constitution is as captivating or moving as this award-winning full-length movie dramatizing the events of the summer of 1787.

Filmed on location at Independence Hall and other historic locations in Virginia, you will witness Washington, Madison, Franklin, Jefferson, Adams, Randolph, and others play their parts during this period and be in the room with the actual delegates who decide the fate of a new nation and create a new Constitution.

The US Constitution
Pocket Reference

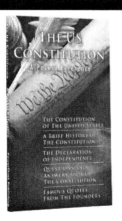

Includes:

- The Complete US Constitution
- A Brief History of the US Constitution
- The Declaration of Independence
- Q & A Pertaining to the Constitution
- Famous Quotes from the Founder
- 101 Questions to Ask Candidates.

This 96 page booklet gives you everything you need and more to gain a knowledge of the US Constitution and other key documents.